FRITS NOSKE

THE SIGNIFIER AND THE SIGNIFIED

STUDIES IN THE OPERAS OF MOZART AND VERDI

CLARENDON PRESS · OXFORD
1990

Oxford University Press, Walton Street, Oxford OX2 6DP
Oxford New York Toronto
Delhi Bombay Calcutta Madras Karachi
Petaling Jaya Singapore Hong Kong Tokyo
Nairobi Dar es Salaam Cape Town
Melbourne Auckland
and associated companies in
Berlin Ibadan

Oxford is a trade mark of Oxford University Press

Published in the United States
by Oxford Univerity Press, New York

British Library Cataloguing in Publication Data
Noske, Frits, 1920–
The signifier and the signified: studies in the operas
of Mozart and Verdi.
1. Opera in German & opera in Italian. Mozart, Wolfgang Amadeus, 1756–1791
2. Opera in Italian. Verdi, Giuseppe, 1813–1901
I. Title
782.1'092'4
ISBN 0–19–816201–4

Library of Congress Cataloging in Publication Data
Noske, Frits, 1920–
The signifier and the signified: studies in the operas
of Mozart and Verdi/Frits Noske.
p. cm.
Includes the Boccanegra correspondence between G. Verdi and A. Boito in Italian
with an English translation.
Reprint. Originally published: The Hague: Nijhoff, 1977.
Includes bibliographical references.
1. Opera. 2. Mozart, Wolfgang Amadeus, 1756–1791. Operas.
3. Verdi, Giuseppe, 1813–1901. Operas.
I. Title.
ML1700.1.N67 1990
782.1'092'2—dc20 89-27902 CIP MN
ISBN 0–19–816201–4: £12.95

Printed in Hong Kong

PREFACE TO THE PAPERBACK EDITION

No study is ever finished, and this is particularly true of the present work dealing with aspects of musico-dramatic structure in opera. Yet for technical reasons it was impossible to present this paperback edition with a revised text. I do not consider this a serious disadvantage. Because of the ambiguity inherent in every work of art, any new approach to problems of structure in opera will inevitably be controversial. I entertain the hope that controversy resulting from my arguments will eventually lead to deeper insight.

A few titles should be added to the list of my articles dealing with the subject matter of these studies but not included in the book itself, namely: 'Verdi's Macbeth: Romanticism or Realism?' in *Ars Musica—Musica Scientia, Festschrift Heinrich Hüschen* (Cologne, 1980), pp. 359–63; and 'Verbal to Musical Drama: Adaptation or Creation?' in *Drama, Dance and Music*, ed. J. Redmond (Cambridge, 1981), pp. 143–52. A paper read at the 1985 International Symposium in Nieborów (Poland), 'From Idea to Sound: Philip's Monologue in Verdi's Don Carlos', will be published shortly in the Report of this conference. As for the article on Wagner's use of the musical figure of death, announced on page 214, footnote 23, this has appeared in *Die Musikforschung*, vol. 31 (1978), pp. 285–302, and in Italian translation in *La drammaturgia musicale*, ed. L. Bianconi (Bologna, 1986), pp. 255–75.

Airiolo (Ticino)   F. N.
May 1989

PREFACE

The studies collected in this volume deal with the interpretation of opera. In most cases the results are based on structural analysis, a concept which may require some clarification in this context. During the past decade 'structure' and 'structural' have become particularly fashionable terms lacking exact denotation and used for the most divergent purposes. As employed here, structural analysis is concerned with such concepts as 'relationship', 'coherence' and 'continuity', more or less in contrast to formal analysis which deals with measurable material. In other words, I have analysed the structure of an opera by seeking and examining *factors* in the musico-dramatic *process*, whereas analysts of form are generally preoccupied with the study of *elements* contained in the musical *object*.

Though admittedly artificial, the dichotomy of form and structure may elucidate the present situation with regard to the study of opera. Today, nearly one hundred years after the death of Wagner, the proclaimed antithesis of *Oper und Drama* is generally taken for what it really was: a means to propagate the philosophy of its inventor. The conception of opera (whether 'continuous' or composed of 'numbers') as a special form of drama is no longer contested. Nevertheless musical scholarship has failed to draw the consequences from this view and few scholars realize the need to study general theory of drama and more specifically the dramatic experience. Instead musicologists have treated opera as a musical object, analysing its component elements as if they were consecutive movements of a symphony or a string quartet. Questions concerning both verbal and musical drama, as, for example, manipulation of time, point of attack, monologue and dialogue, dramatic rhythm or audience participation are almost always ignored in scholarly writings on opera. Even specific operatic problems (e.g. what is the exact function of a libretto?) are evaded or overlooked. It seems as if musicology is overpreoccupied with opera history, to the neglect of its phenomenology.

There are of course exceptions, only two of which I shall mention here. Although Oscar Bie's *Die Oper* (Berlin 1913) is outdated, its initial section dealing with the genre's dialectic *(Die Paradoxie der Oper)* still provides fascinating reading. A more recent publication, *Opera as Drama* by Joseph Kerman (New York 1956), may be considered a landmark in twentieth-century operatic literature. In the introductory chapter the author clearly states his basic view: "Like poetry, music can reveal the quality of action, and thus determine dramatic form in the most serious sense". Kerman may not have been the first to say this; what is refreshing, however, is his faithful adherence to this idea, with the result that his shrewd observations throw a new light on famous operas from Monteverdi to Strawinsky. The fact that I have occasionally expressed disagreement with certain of Kerman's points should not be misinterpreted. I find the core of his argument entirely convincing and every reader familiar with it may easily trace its influence on the development of my thinking.

My approach to the topics discussed in this book is essentially based on the study of the theory of drama. Although, in general, dramatic criticism through the ages has been concerned with music only marginally, the reading of various treatises and essays ranging from Aristotle to Artaud and Brecht has nevertheless helped me to gain insight into musical drama as a cultural phenomenon of Western civilization. Among twentieth-century theorists whose writings have provided considerable stimulus are George Pierce Baker, T. S. Eliot, Northrop Frye, Una Ellis-Fermor, Francis Fergusson and Eric Bentley.

Another factor that figured strongly in the preparation of these studies is the dramatic experience. However useful attentive reading of operatic scores may be, it is the theatre which ultimately reveals the truth. This was proven to me when in January 1973 I had the opportunity to follow in detail the staging of Verdi's *Attila* at the Teatro Regio in Parma, attending all rehearsals either in the wings or in a box. Watching the second-act finale on the stage, I realized that my original interpretation of this particular ensemble, based entirely on study of the score, had been faulty.

Lastly, my study of semiotics has influenced this book. Like structuralism, the theory of signs has recently become a dangerously fashionable subject in scholarly and even in less learned circles. Still its usefulness cannot be denied. Drama is essentially a matter of communication, and since on our planet communication is effected by means of signs, the study of the sign process is of vital importance for the student of opera. As in the case of dramatic theory I have tried to avoid burdening the reader with a surfeit of technical details and terminology. This does not alter the fact that most of these studies are concerned with the musico-dramatic sign, and of course Appendix I deals explicitly with opera and semiotics.

Little further need be said here about the two musical dramatists whose works form the subject matter of this book. To speak of their greatness could only result in clichés or truisms. Many lines have been written about their unrivalled insight into human nature, and it is perhaps that quality which induced me to choose the opera scores of Mozart and Verdi over those of other masters. For in the last resort the study of art is nothing but the study of man.

*   *
*

The essays grew out of lectures and graduate seminars for the Universities of Leyden, Amsterdam, Illinois (Urbana), Iowa (Iowa City), the Eastman School of Music (Rochester, N.Y.), the *Institut für Theaterwissenschaft* (University of Vienna), the Salzburg *Mozarteum*, the Dutch Mozart Society, and the Third and Fourth International Verdi Conferences (Milan 1972, Chicago 1974). Appendix I is a revision of a paper read at the First International Conference of Semiotic Studies (Milan 1974) and in a more extended form at the International Colloquium on "The Function of Tragedy" (Ghent 1975). To the editors of *The Musical Quarterly*, *Music and Letters*, *Studia Musicologica*, *Theatre Research* and the *Atti del 3° congresso internazionale di studi verdiani* I am grateful for permission to print revised versions of previously published material. It should also be mentioned here that two further articles on Verdi are not included in this book, i.e. *Verdi und die Belagerung von Haarlem*, published in *Convivium Musicorum, Festschrift Wolfgang Boetticher* (Berlin 1974), and *Schiller e la genesi del "Macbeth" verdiano* (Nuova Rivista Musicale Italiana, vol. X, 1976, pp. 196–203).

The number of persons and institutions to whom I am indebted for help and advice is considerable. First of all I want to thank Rita Benton (University of Iowa) who graciously took the time to correct my English and to offer critical observations. The insights I gained from extensive talks and correspondence with my friend and colleague Pierluigi Petrobelli (King's College, University of London) are truly invaluable; I am also grateful to him for his guidance in the labyrinth of Verdian source material. Both Julian Budden (BBC, London) and Philip Gossett (University of Chicago) have cordially shared with me their vast knowledge of nineteenth-century Italian opera. As for the *Istituto di studi verdiani* in Parma, without the unwearying help of its Director, Maestro Mario

Medici, and staff (Lina Re, Marisa Di Gregorio Casati, Marcello Conati and Marcello Pavarani) the second half of this book could hardly have been written. I also remember with pleasure the lively conversations held with Luigia and Gian Paolo Minardi during my frequent sojourns in Parma. Furthermore I am indebted to Signorina Gabriella Carrara Verdi for permission to examine at Sant'Agata the Boito-Verdi correspondence on the revision of *Simon Boccanegra*, and to Signora Luciana Pestalozza and Maestro Fausto Broussard who gave me ample opportunity to study autograph scores of Donizetti, Mercadante and Verdi in the Ricordi Archives at Milan.

Last, a word of thanks to my students, whose contributions are far from negligible. If some of the critical remarks they offered during seminar sessions on both sides of the Atlantic have anonymously found their way into this volume, it is only fitting that they should be duly acknowledged here. From my students I have also learned that research and teaching are of equal scholarly importance and that each benefits from the simultaneous practice of both.

University of Amsterdam   FRITS NOSKE
December 1976

TABLE OF CONTENTS

ACKNOWLEDGMENTS

Several chapters of this book are revised versions of articles previously published in various periodicals. It concerns:

Musical Quotation as a Dramatic Device: The Fourth Act of 'Le Nozze di Figaro', The Musical Quarterly, vol. 54 (1968), pp. 185–198 (Ch. 1).

Social Tensions in 'Le Nozze di Figaro', Music and Letters, vol. 50 (1969), pp. 45–62 (Ch. 2).

'Don Giovanni': Musical Affinities and Dramatic Structure, Studia Musicologica, vol. 12 (1970), pp. 167–203 (Ch. 3).

'Don Giovanni': An Interpretation, Theatre Research/Recherches Théâtrales, vol. 13 (1973), pp. 60–74 (Ch. 4).

Verdi and The Musical Figure of Death, Atti del III° congresso internazionale di studi verdiani, Parma 1974, pp. 349–386 (Ch. 8).

Ritual Scenes in Verdi's Operas, Music & Letters, vol. 54 (1973), pp. 415–439 (Ch. 10).

PART ONE

MOZART

CHAPTER I

'LE NOZZE DI FIGARO':
MUSICAL QUOTATION AS
A DRAMATIC DEVICE

Mozart's practice of borrowing from his own works as well as from the works of others is a matter of record, but it has never been systematically investigated.[1] Yet such a study methodically undertaken would surely give us some insight into the composer's creative process. This holds true especially for opera, governed as it is by rationally perceptible elements – characters, words, situations – whose meaningful interpretation is essential to our knowledge of the function of music in the dramatic structure.

The present chapter deals with a special kind of musical relationship: the quotation, as exemplified by six previously undiscussed instances in the fourth act of *Le Nozze di Figaro*. Quotation, as intended here, is to be distinguished from other types of musical affinity. For example, each of the characters in the opera expresses himself in a personal idiom, either directly by his voice or indirectly by the orchestra. This implies that certain melodic or rhythmic elements pervade the whole score (e.g. Count Almaviva's hot-tempered anapaestic motifs and dotted rhythms, Figaro's march-like outbursts, Susanna's descending leaps of large intervals and her coquettish triplets). It is obvious that musical characteristics of this kind cannot be taken as quotations. They belong to the musical physiognomy of the *dramatis personae*.

Another category lying outside the scope of this study is formed by musical relationships that defy dramatic interpretation. The following rhythmic motif plays an important part in the opera (ex. 1).

---

[1] Jean Chantavoine's *Mozart dans Mozart* (Paris, 1948) cannot really be called a serious study. It contains more than 250 examples of thematic interrelation, many of which are imaginary. The commentaries are extremely superficial and sometimes even nonsensical. For instance, the alleged relationship between the first-act chorus of *Le nozze di Figaro* and the theme of the piano variations on *La belle Françoise* (K. 353) is explained by the fact that the opera is based on a French play (pp. 60–61).

EXAMPLE I

It occurs (mostly in a descending line) in various situations, such as Bartolo's aria,[2] the first terzetto (chair scene),[3] the finale of the second act,[4] the Count's aria,[5] and the last finale.[6] In the ensembles it expresses astonishment and confusion, elsewhere it underlines anger and indignation. Susanna, Figaro,[7] and Cherubino[8] use it in quite a different way. There can be no doubt that we are dealing here with a purely musical formula, one of the score's materials. The motif reminds us of opera's ambiguous nature. Essentially opera is not only a dramatic structure but also a musical one, and each structure has its special exigencies.

Unlike these types of musical interrelation, the quotation is always rationally interpretable. In many cases the explanation will be found in the text, but in some instances true understanding derives necessarily from the dramatic implications rather than the words themselves.

*   *
*

I. Figaro's cavatina "Se vuol ballare" (Act I, No. 3) is a typical example of logical divergency between musical and dramatic structure. The piece consists of a theme with three variations, followed by a literal repeat of the theme and a short coda. Although the variation technique is rather freely handled, the formal scheme guarantees a certain stability. From a dramatic point of view, however, the cavatina is anything but homogeneous. Figaro feels unsure of himself and, in spite of his bravery, there is an unmistakable undercurrent of uneasiness and frustration. Mozart expresses this by musical contrasts (sudden changes of dynamics, tempo and time) which are, strictly speaking, incompatible with the 18th-century conception of the operatic cavatina.[9] The reason for Figaro's instability is discretely indicated in the orchestration. By adding two horns to the theme's string accompaniment, Mozart anticipates his well-known joke in

---

[2] No. 4, b. 20–21.
[3] No. 7, *passim.*
[4] No. 15, b. 57–58, 181–183, 200ff., 218ff., 234ff., 271ff., 496–498, etc.
[5] No. 17, *passim.*
[6] No. 28, b. 352ff.
[7] No. 2, b. 84ff.
[8] No. 6, b. 91ff.
[9] See MGG, article *Cavatine* (W. Kahl).

EXAMPLE 2

Figaro's fourth-act aria "Aprite un po' quegli occhi" (Act IV, No. 26, b. 102–106). But the affinity between aria and cavatina appears more clearly if the following fragments are compared (ex. 2).

A detailed analysis of these two passages shows that they are closely related. Both start on a pedal point, above which the voice and orchestra, ascending stepwise, are carried toward a climax (in the cavatina the scale covers a seventh, in the aria a sixth). The cavatina's alternation of forte and piano is actually a dynamic stretto, the distance gradually becoming smaller. Notwithstanding the 'terrace dynamics' this suggests a crescendo, corresponding with the one explicitly prescribed in the aria. On the culmination point, the bass is chromatically augmented and produces a chord of the diminished seventh (cavatina, b. 51–53; aria, b. 66 and b. 94). The break of the tension is rendered by a sudden transition to piano (a musical translation of the cavatina's text). The voice, violins, and woodwinds then descend stepwise, while the bass proceeds in contrary movement with an additional chromatic note.

The aria's affinities with the cavatina are easily explained: what Figaro feared is now going to happen. Right after the climax of the aria he sings for the first time the words "il resto nol dico" ("*I won't say the rest*") which, in the coda, will be replaced by the mocking horn call.

The differences between the two fragments do not contradict this interpretation. On the contrary, they clearly underline the distinction between two phases of Figaro's attitude during the day of the opera's action. In the cavatina he is tense and nervous. The scale over the dominant pedal point is interrupted by rests. The tonic chord is systematically avoided. Even the final bars do not bring a solution, since they turn toward the dominant of the relative minor key (b. 55). Moreover the tension is considerably augmented by the prolongation of the most striking dissonance found in this passage (the diminished seventh chord). In the aria, Figaro's mood is different. Self-pity, expressed with buffo pathos, predominates. Tension is replaced by bitterness, and it seems as if Figaro is ready to accept his fate. With a single exception, the tonic chord returns on the first beat of each bar of the pedal point, and this stability is confirmed by the perfect cadence at the end of the fragment (b. 68–70). Unlike the cavatina, the chord of the diminished seventh in the aria occupies only half a bar.

Can the passage rightly be called a conscious quotation? The point may be argued, but here the question is only of secondary importance, since dramatic relationship of the aria and the cavatina is beyond doubt. On the evening of the *giorno di follia* Figaro involuntarily alludes to the morning when his torments first announced themselves. And this 'reprise' throws light on a special aspect of his complex character: the pessimism behind his mask of exuberance.

II. In the finale of the fourth act, the mutually contradictory observations of Marcellina's aria "Il capro e la capretta" (No. 24) and Figaro's aria "Aprite un po' quegli occhi" (No. 26) are put to the test. A musical quotation illustrates this in a striking way. It is to be found in the G major section *(più moto)*, where the Count courts his wife (dressed as Susanna). The Countess' first rejoinder is practically identical to a motif of Figaro's aria. Shortly afterwards it is quoted again, in the relative minor key, this time by the Count. Originally the motif did not belong to Figaro, but to Marcellina (ex. 3).[10]

EXAMPLE 3

The motif occurs thirteen times, twice in Marcellina's aria,[11] eight times in Figaro's,[12] and three in the finale.[13] If one compares the corresponding text fragments, Mozart's intention becomes clear: woman's virtue is the subject of contrasting opinions and ambiguous situations. For Marcellina

---

[10] Cf. Chantavoine, *op. cit.*, p. 67–68. He mentions the interrelation between the arias of Marcellina and Figaro, but overlooks the quotations in the finale.

[11] No. 24, b. 65–68.

[12] No. 26, b. 57–61 and 85–89.

[13] No. 28, b. 55–56 and 81–83.

this virtue is beyond all doubt. Inconstancy and cruelty are only to be found in men:

> Sol noi povere femmine,
> Che tanto amiam quest' uomini,
> Trattate siam dai perfidi
> Ognor con crudeltà.

> *But we poor women who cherish*
> *these men so much, we are always*
> *treated with cruelty by the*
> *faithless creatures.*

This is radically opposed by Figaro:

> Son rose spinose,
> Son volpi vezzose,
> Son orse benigne,
> Colombe maligne,
> Maestre d'inganni,
> Amiche d'affanni,
> Che fingono, mentono,
> Amore non senton,
> Non senton pietà.

> *They are thorny roses,*
> *charming foxes,*
> *sweet bears,*
> *malicious doves,*
> *masters of deceit,*
> *friends of terror,*
> *who feign, lie,*
> *feeling neither love*
> *nor pity.*

In the finale, theory is replaced by practice. Misled by the travesti, Figaro cannot but think that his words are confirmed by Susanna's conduct:

> Giacchè così vi piace,
> eccomi quì, signor.

> *Because it pleased you, here I am, sir.*

and the Count pours oil on the flame:

> Ricevi anco un brillante,
> Che a te porge un'amante
> In pegno del suo amor.

> *Accept also a jewel which a lover*
> *offers you as a pledge of his love.*

Thus, in the use of the motif various characters and situations are reflected. Actually the characters do not quote each other; it is Mozart, who winks at his audience.

III. We find the next quotation in the finale's central section, the E♭ duet. Its dramatic structure is conditioned by Susanna's lapse. After only twenty bars she forgets to alter her voice and is recognized by Figaro. The tables are turned; Susanna's playful mood gives way to serious indignation, while Figaro, relieved from a heavy burden, takes the comedian's part. By placing Susanna's 'unmasking' at the beginning of the duet, Mozart offers his hero ample opportunity to exploit the new misunderstanding and to risk, for the third time in one day, a box on the ear. Figaro starts with a few traditional *sospiri* (b. 170–171: the rests separating the syllables of "Ah Madama!"), but soon he confines himself to an imitation of Susanna's personal idiom. The tender appoggiaturas of the garden aria "Deh vieni, non tardar" (No. 27, b. 34, 39, 53 and 58) are (unintentionally?) parodied (b. 184, 188). Finally Figaro quotes the principal theme, depriving it however of its rhythmical subtleties, which are beyond his grasp (ex. 4).

EXAMPLE 4

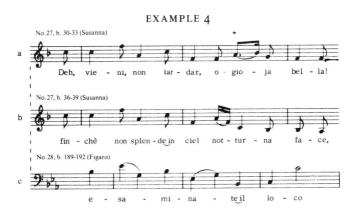

Figaro misses his mark. His parody is too gross to be properly understood by his wife. This enables Mozart to carry on the joke. When, after having been slapped, Figaro resumes the triadic arpeggio, it is adopted by Susanna who does not realize that she is parodying herself (b. 254ff.).

That the garden aria is the object of Figaro's quotation is not at all surprising. When hidden in the bushes, he imagined that Susanna's tender words were addressed to his rival. Although presently relieved, he makes a rather silly figure. Hence his eagerness to construct an analogous situation in which he plays the part of the seducer instead of the *cocu*. Moreover, he indulges in the idea that by courting a countess he considerably exceeds the bounds of his social class. He knows of course that everything is but a game. Susanna, however, does not share this knowledge, and it is precisely her anger which compensates for his previous sufferings. Thus Figaro is doubly satisfied: his wife unintentionally proves her faith – although in a rather high-handed way – and the stain of his unjustified mistrust is wiped out. Susanna herself offers him the opportunity to take his revenge.

But Figaro is unteachable. After a day of vicissitudes he has still to learn that it is the women who dominate. Not he, but Susanna shall have the last word.

IV. In his analytical study of the opera, Siegmund Levarie draws attention to the ingenious rhythmical transformations in the first G major section of the finale.[14] The Count's gay orchestral melody starts with a tonic triadic arpeggio (see Ex. 5a, b. 51). The same motif, in retrograde motion, accompanies the Countess' rejoinder (see Ex. 5b, b. 55). Through a rhytmical change, however, it has acquired a tense character and may serve now to underline Figaro's bitter comments (see Ex. 5c, b. 57ff.). Next we hear in the orchestra a variant in the minor mode (see Ex. 5d, b. 81–82), which is again adopted by Figaro (see Ex. 5e, b. 91–92). In the course of some fifty bars, the motif appears no less than twelve times but never succeeds in becoming a rounded theme. This is significant of Figaro's frustration. The social distance from his master keeps him from interfering. Only at the end of the G major section does his anger get the upper hand. He brazenly disturbs the rendezvous, and immediately the motif develops into a proper melody (b. 100–106).

Levarie's interpretation is certainly plausible. However, he did not notice that further on in the score the motif re-emerges in a new configuration. It is transformed into the principal theme of the scene in which Figaro and

---

[14] S. Levarie, *Le nozze di Figaro*, Chicago, 1952, pp. 222–224.

Susanna are reconciled (see Ex. 5f, b. 275ff.). This marks the end of the motif's development.

EXAMPLE 5

Mozart achieves the last transformation by (1) exchanging the first two notes, (2) equalizing the rhythm, (3) symmetrizing the melody (the last interval being the inversion of the first), and (4) adapting the motif to a new metre. Each of these factors contributes to relaxation.

Ex. 5f is not merely a transformed melody, it is also a quotation. Between the sections in G and B♭ we have witnessed two scenes (Figaro's short monologue and his duet with Susanna), both built on entirely different melodic materials. In an absolute sense, too, the distance is considerable (166 bars). But most of all, the textual relationship stamps the conciliatory tune as a quotation. Figaro refers to his sarcastic words: "Che compiacente femmina! Che sposa di buon cor!" ("*What a complacent woman. What a good-hearted wife.*") Recognizing his error he now sings on a new variant of the same motif: "Pace! pace! mio dolce tesoro!" ("*Peace, peace, my sweet treasure.*") The melodic and rhythmic transformation has clearly a dramatic function. It expresses the transition from tension and bitterness to relaxation and reconciliation.

V. Susanna still owes us a pin-prick. We find it in the second part of the B♭ section (b. 293—334), where Figaro gives a reprise of his grotesque court-ship; this time he does not parody Susanna but the Count. In accordance with the aristocratic *code d'amour*, he throws himself at the pseudo-Countess' feet and imitates in his way the style of opera seria. The trill in b. 314 reminds us of the arias of his masters, Count Almaviva's "Vedrò mentr 'io sospiro" (Act III, No. 17, b. 147, 150) and the Countess' "Dove sono i bei momenti" (Act III, No. 19, b. 123).[15] The 6/8 time, characteris-tic of the music used by the lower classes, does not suit this climate; hence Figaro tries to change it into 3/4 (b. 315–316). Equally unsuited is the major mode; he therefore modulates to G minor, in which key he produces a pathetically beseeching chord of the minor ninth (b. 320–321). Susanna's answer leaves nothing to be desired: "Io son quì, faccia quel che volete." ("*Here I am; do what you will.*") Yet the passage is ambiguous. While playing her part without the least reserve, she alludes at the same time to her husband's weakness. The melody is almost literally borrowed from Figaro's aria. With purely musical means she mockingly quotes the words: ["il resto nol dico,] già ognuno lo sa." ("*I won't say the rest, as everyone knows it.*") (ex. 6).

EXAMPLE 6

Strictly speaking Susanna cannot have heard this aria. Only in the follow-ing secco recitative does she learn from Marcellina that Figaro has been seen in the garden. But her ignorance could be feigned. Why should she

---

[15] It is characteristic of the parvenue-like Marcellina that, apart from the Count and Countess, only she makes use of the trill (No. 24, b. 73).

tell her ex-enemy Marcellina that she overheard the end of Figaro's complaint?[16]

The quotation illuminates Susanna's character which, though more homogeneous than Figaro's, shows a wide spectrum of human qualities. With all her tenderness, she rarely loses an opportunity to tease. Always alert in the eternal battle of the sexes, she never lapses into sentimentality. Susanna is no daughter of Pamela, no *buona figliola*. She exerts herself with energy and likes the good fight but uses her weapons in a most subtle way. And she is more sagacious than any person around her. Thus, in spite of the old dogma of man's superiority, the last word is hers.

VI. After the denouement there is no longer a place for individual acting. On the stage all the *dramatis personae* comment together on the events of the day. Only the distinction between the sexes is maintained. As if to symbolize the opera's feminist colour, the women take the lead, first Susanna and the Countess (b. 436, 439), then all the female characters together (b. 456ff.). Only towards the end do they comply with society's convention and yield the *pas* to the men (b. 487ff.). But before the opera is concluded by a vocal fanfare, Mozart has to correct a discrepancy in the last scene of the third act – the C major chorus of the Count's vassals, which came next to the wedding march in the Finale of Act III (No. 22, b. 61ff.) and was repeated in a shortened version after the fandango (No. 22, b. 186ff.). Its text gives expression to the most perfect harmony in human and social relations:

> Amanti costanti,
> Seguaci d'onor,
> Cantate, lodate,
> Sì saggio Signor.
> A un dritto cedendo,
> Che oltraggia, che offende,
> Ei caste vi rende,
> Ai vostri amator.
>
> *Faithful, virtuous lovers, sing*
> *to our wise master and praise*
> *him. Having renounced an offending*
> *right, he restores you chaste to*
> *your lovers.*

---

[16] In the libretto, inconsistencies and improbabilities are not exceptional, especially in the third act. No explanation is given, for instance, for the provenance of the ransom produced by Susanna in the sextet (No. 18, b. 26ff.). See however R. Moberly and Chr. Raeburn, *Mozart's Figaro: the Plan of Act III*, Music & Letters, vol. 46 (1965), p. 134–136.

Constant lovers, a wise master, contented and grateful subjects – this Utopian picture is faithfully rendered in music by Mozart. Melody, rhythm, and harmony are simple and cheerful. Relying exclusively on text and music, one cannot help thinking that this is the opera's end. But we know better. The actual situation is in flat contradiction to the ingenuousness of the peasant song. There are two couples to be married, Bartolo-Marcellina and Figaro-Susanna. The first are no *amanti*. Marcellina uses marriage to raise her social status; Bartolo is forced into it by the disclosure of his fatherhood. While it is true that Figaro and Susanna are faithful lovers, they do not altogether believe in each other's constancy. Finally the wise master tries to reobtain, through the backdoor, the abolished *droit de seigneur*. Thus the third act ends with an inaudible, but nonetheless strident, dramatic dissonance.

Now, in the last section of the fourth-act finale the chorus' initial motif is quoted (ex. 7).[17]

EXAMPLE 7

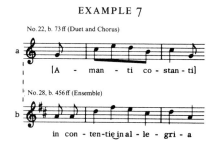

No. 22, b. 73 ff (Duet and Chorus)

a

[A - man - ti co - stan - ti]

No. 28, b. 456 ff (Ensemble)

b

in con - ten-tie in al - le - gri - a

As in most other cases, the quotation cannot be explained without knowledge of the context:

> Questo giorno di tormenti,
> Di capricci e di follia,
> In contenti e in allegria
> Solo amor può terminar.
>
> *Only love can conclude this*
> *day of torments, whims and*
> *folly, in content and*
> *cheerfulness.*

---

[17] The third note of Ex. 7a is played by the orchestra only.

The music closely follows upon these words. The first couple of lines are rendered by pathetic chords. A leap of an augmented fourth and a subdominant chord of the minor seventh clashing with the dominant pedal point effectively underline the word "tormenti" which seems to reverberate also in the following arpeggio of the D minor triad (b. 453–455). The passage covering the first half of the stanza may be interpreted as the postponed musical expression of the *real* situation at the end of the third act. Thereafter, the reminiscence of the peasant chorus, started by the women and answered by the men, comes as a true relief. The dissonance is resolved.

*   *
*

Our examination leads to several observations. In the first place all six quotations have a function in the dramatic structure. They contribute to the outline of the characters, stress tension or relaxation, elucidate situations on the stage, or draw the audience into the action. This is not as self-evident as it seems. Musical quotation also can be used very well as a non-dramatic device; for instance, as a simple pun. Da Ponte's libretto offers several occasions for this. When, in her second-act aria, Susanna dresses Cherubino, she tells him to stand straight and to stop looking at the Countess. Twice she says: "Madama qui non è." ("*Her ladyship is not here.*") (ex. 8).

EXAMPLE 8

No. 12, b. 38-40 (48-50) (Susanna)

Ma - da - ma qui non   è

If quoted in the E♭ duet of the last finale, this melodic fragment would have pictured quite a different situation (Figaro adressing the pseudo-Countess). Whether Mozart overlooked or rejected this possibility, we do not know. But it is obvious that he was not interested in mere joking. His musical witticism had to serve the drama.[18]

---

[18] It seems that Mozart only uses the non-dramatic quotation to connect two different works. A well-known example is Basilio's melody on the words "Così fan tutte le belle" (No. 7, b. 184–186), which is quoted several times in the Overture of *Così fan tutte* (b. 35–37, 43–45, etc.). See also Chapter 5, ex. 5–8.

A second, no less striking, characteristic of Mozart's quotations is the diversity of application. Each has its proper function. Figaro's reminiscence of his cavatina (I) expresses bitterness, camouflaged by buffo pathos. The once so resourceful barber faces a situation which he is unable to handle. The quotation is even retrodictive, for it belies his display of bravery in the first act. Quotations II and V are only seemingly of the same kind. The former is based on an instrumental motif. Obviously it is Mozart who addresses the audience, using the actors' voices merely as tools. On the other hand, Susanna's mocking hint at Figaro's *boutade* is a deliberate quotation on her part. Even though the libretto gives no indication that she actually heard the end of the aria, there can hardly be any doubt that this is what Mozart had in mind. While Figaro's abortive attempt at imitating Susanna's tenderness (III) turns out to be a parodying quotation, the correction of his own bitter words (IV) is realized through a melodic and rhythmic transformation. The latter example is particularly interesting because of the unusual application of the device. Normally one expects to find mockery or sarcasm in the quotation, because the subject itself is harmless. Quotation VI bears on the opera as a whole. It stresses the significance of the original title of Beaumarchais' comedy: *La folle journée*. The opera's subject is not a wedding, but a day of human folly. In the course of this day people have suffered, but everything has to end in perfect harmony. However skeptical we may be about the future (the Count's constancy, Figaro's insight into female conduct, Susanna's restraint of her coquetry, or Cherubino's becoming a man), within the framework of the drama the conflicts should be resolved once and for all. Therefore all the actors have to repeat the motif of the cheerful peasants, before the curtain is allowed to fall.

And last, the study of Mozart's quotation technique may lead to a reevaluation of the fourth-act finale. Since the publication of Abert's monograph, the 'first' finale is generally rated above the 'second'. This judgment is based upon the idea that, while the latter pictures external events the former expresses inner developments.[19] The antithesis of 'exterior' and 'interior' is a typical product of German Romantic aesthetics. When applied to Mozart's finales, it leads to misrepresentations. It is true, of course, that the fourth-act finale contains more 'action' than that of the second. People come and go, hide in bushes and bowers, reappear unexpectedly. But at the same time they act with individual emotion, and even in the most farcical situations their characters are delineated with utter refinement. As

---

[19] See H. Abert, *W. A. Mozart*, vol. II, Leipzig, 1921, p. 375ff.

one means of achieving this, Mozart uses the musical quotation. Its varied application as a dramatic device proves that the fourth-act finale contains much more than the mere painting of external events. The implication that 'exterior' and 'interior' are mutually exclusive is wrong. These concepts do not collide; they are dissimilar, not opposite. The 'exterior' deals with events, the 'interior' with characters. If one seeks an antithesis between these two great finales, then it will be found in the difference of dramatic development. The second-act finale starts with a simple situation; through the gradual extension of the number of actors and the cumulation of conflicts it ends in the utmost confusion. In the finale of the fourth act, the most complicated situation is at the beginning. In the course of this latter finale, conflicts, misunderstandings, and tensions are solved one by one, until a *lieta marcia* accompanies all persons to the wedding-feast.

In both finales Mozart expresses emotional undercurrents and psychological conflicts with amazing subtlety and great variety of means. But it is especially in the last act that he favours the musical quotation. With the aid of the device, he gives a finishing touch to the characters.

1967

CHAPTER 2

'LE NOZZE DI FIGARO':
SOCIAL TENSIONS

In the older operas a character such as Count Almaviva would have been presented with the main emphasis on his rank, and the personality of the character would have been a secondary consideration. Consequently his amorous affairs would appear as a cavalier's sport. Mozart's Count, however, is primarily moved by sensual passion which is constantly at odds with his awareness of himself. His aristocratic rank is of consequence only in so far as it represents the external expression of this awareness, the insistence on the ancient rights of the upper classes. In short, the primary factors are human, not social. Because of this, Mozart pays almost no attention to external trappings or surroundings. What intrigues him is the personality *per se* of the human being, not the external circumstances and relationships which produced it.

The above paragraph is quoted from Hermann Abert's monumental Mozart biography which appeared shortly after the First World War.[1] Today not everyone is ready to accept the image of Mozart as a man lacking interest in social matters; nevertheless the concept may be found in several recent studies.[2] A curious way of thinking underlies this opinion. Briefly it amounts to this: Mozart was not interested in politics but in human beings; since lack of interest in political affairs necessarily implies indifference to social questions, there can be no affinity between his operatic characters and contemporary society. This way of reasoning, already far from logical in itself, becomes completely incomprehensible if we think of Mozart's letters, which unequivocally indicate his lively interest in the social conditions of his time. Thus Abert and several biographers after him involuntarily created a dualistic image: a man who was an 'engaged' correspondent and at the same time a 'transcendent' composer. It is significant, however, that this artificial conception was not consistently elabo-

---

[1] *W. A. Mozart*, II, Leipzig 1921, p. 12.

[2] See for instance J.-V. Hocquard, *La Pensé de Mozart*, Paris, 1958, pp. 377–8, and D. J. Grout, *A Short History of Opera*, 2nd ed., New York, 1965, p. 283.

rated. Generally the 'romantic' image of the timeless genius over-shadows that of the historically conditioned man. Mozart belongs to all ages, and therefore not to his own.

Among post-war writings which give a more modern view is a little study on *Le nozze di Figaro* by Gunter Reiss; it elucidates the dramatic 'themes' of the opera by drawing attention to the conflicts between old and new tendencies in eighteenth-century society.[3] Reiss bases his research principally on the libretto, in which the composer undoubtedly will have had his say. In the present study the stress lies on the score. Mozart gave each of the characters a specific musical configuration, which remains recognizable during the whole drama. These sonorous individualities reveal themselves most clearly in their emotional response to the dramatic action. Our task is to discover whether latent social tensions do motivate these responses and determine their musical expression. Since social tensions cannot arise except in a community, the fundamental question is: what relationship exists among the characters of *Le nozze di Figaro*?

* *
*

The Family

The cast consists of eleven actors, four female and seven male. Their respective social positions at the beginning of the day cannot be determined with absolute certainty, but a rough division into three groups is possible with the aid of data provided by Beaumarchais' comedies and Pietrosellini's libretto of *Il barbiere di Siviglia*. The lowest social stratum is formed by the gardener Antonio, his daughter Barbarina and his niece Susanna. Figaro and Marcellina also belong to this group, although the former as an ex-barber might perhaps claim a slightly higher step on the social ladder. The middle class is represented by Bartolo, Basilio and Curzio. The latter two are called Don by Pietrosellini and Da Ponte respectively. This is not necessarily significant, because this title, which originally indicated noble birth, had gradually lost its standing in the course of time. In any case all three are professional men and therefore belong to a higher class than the servants. The Count, Countess and Cherubino form the upper-class group. Although little is known about the page's social background, the fact that he is sent to serve as an officer in the Count's regiment at Seville strongly points to his being high-born. It should be noted that on the strength of his youth Cherubino can permit himself more social liberty than the Count and the Countess. The same holds for Barbarina in the lowest group.

All the actors except one play a vital part in the drama. The exception is Don Curzio, who, as a character, is so little profiled that we have to recognize him by an external feature (he stammers in the recitatives). The question of why Da Ponte and Mozart should have reduced Beaumarchais' judge (Don Guzman) and clerk (Doublemain) to this meagre part has already occupied many a critic. It is generally assumed that the shortening of the French model was caused either by fear of the imperial censor or by the excessively long duration of the opera. Neither of these interpretations seems implausible, but they do not explain why it was precisely the most brilliant scene of Beaumarchais' comedy that fell victim to the curtailment. This scene would certainly have offered Mozart a splendid opportunity for writing a lively *buffo* ensemble. As for the censor, Da Ponte had no difficulty elsewhere in the libretto in allaying the suspicions of the imperial magistrate. It seems to me that a particular motive must have outweighed all others: Don Curzio does not belong to the 'family'.

Actually the quotation marks are superfluous. In English society about 1700 the concept of a family still embraced the whole patriarchally ruled household including not only grandparents, nephews, nieces, etc., but also all kinds of servants and other subordinates.[4] There can be little doubt that in the second half of the eighteenth century this situation was virtually unchanged in less progressive regions of Europe, such as the Iberian peninsula. The libretto of *Le nozze di Figaro* offers ample evidence for this. Figaro and Susanna are not allowed to marry without the Count's permission, and the latter has sufficient control over the organist Basilio to send him to Seville on an errand. Indeed Bartolo, Basilio and Marcellina are related to the Count's household by their antecedents. Only Don Curzio, as an independent judge, does not form a part of the family and therefore he plays but an insignificant role in the complex of intrigues. Thus the action is limited to the smallest social entity: the family. The essential difference with the family concept of our day is not the Count's unbounded authority, but the social heterogeneity of the group. It is this circumstance which strongly provokes tensions and conflicts.

How does the individual react to these tensions? Generally speaking, there are two courses open to him. Either he puts up with the actual sit-

---

[4] See Ian Watt, *The Rise of the Novel*, London, 1966, p. 145. The author refers to Gregory King, *Natural and Political Observations and Conclusions upon the State and Condition of England*, London, 1696.

uation, whether resigned or not, or he tries to break the bonds of his caste. Analysis of the social aspects of *Le nozze di Figaro* leads to the remarkable conclusion that all men choose the first course and all women the second.[5] Each of the characters has a different motive for his conduct, which will be examined further on. The reason why the women's reactions are diametrically opposed to those of the men must first be explored.

The following offers an explanation. The external attitude to life during the second half of the eighteenth century has, in so far as the upper classes are concerned, an undeniably 'feminine' colour. This is revealed in many social forms of expression, such as fashion, hairdress, dislike of beard growth, furniture, tone of conversation and epistolary style. In the minuet, perhaps the most refined dance of Western culture, the lady is the central figure. Moreover, in contrast to the seventeenth-century leaning toward systematic reasoning (implying scientific training denied to women) the eighteenth-century empirical way of thinking offers opportunities to the female for participation in intellectual life. Provided with a basic knowledge about various topics and a fair amount of common sense, she may go far. In this spiritual climate an intelligent female servant will not have too much difficulty in bridging, at least externally, the distance from her mistress. She daily observes the manners of the higher classes and soon succeeds in imitating them. This is something in which the male servant would fail. For him the feminine tone of high society forms an insurmountable barrier. It is anything but fortuitous that Susanna's aria "Al desio" (K. 577), which replaced "Deh vieni" in the Vienna performances op 1789, was considered for a long time to have been written for the Countess. In fact, there is, musically speaking, hardly any class difference between the Countess and Susanna. One forgets that Susanna is but the niece of a plain gardener in the third-act letter scene, and the same holds for her duet with the Count. A scene similar to the latter is simply unthinkable between Figaro and the Countess. The servant's courtship would turn into a parody, like the one in the B♭ section of the last finale.

The women's social mobility and the men's inertia or frustration confer on the drama a special dimension. This is principally Mozart's achievement, since the social tensions are expressed with purely musical means. It is Da Ponte's merit to have provided the composer with the opportunity.

* *
*

[5] Admittedly Figaro attempts to revolt in his cavatina, but this is due to his underestimating the situation. He soon finds out that he has no chance whatever. Socially he remains immobile, even when in the fourth act he is convinced that, in spite of being married to him, Susanna will not be secure from the Count.

The Individual Characters

We may now look at the actors separately and in their relation to each other. If we compare their individual reactions to analogous situations, we find considerable differences. The obvious explanation for this is the diversity of personalities. Basilio reacts differently from Antonio, and Figaro from Susanna, simply because each of them is an individual human being. But in an opera like *Le nozze di Figaro* such an explanation does not suffice. Since all the characters are 'normal' people – we do not encounter any exceptional figure like Don Giovanni or Donna Elvira – the motives for their emotional responses cannot be explained exclusively by their individuality. There are obvious external influences at work and because we are dealing with a social comedy we shall have to look for these in the social atmosphere.

The Count. All too often he is presented on the stage in an unsatisfying manner. We see a stupid, hot-tempered man who on the one hand is not funny enough to play a *buffo* part, and on the other lacks sufficient dignity and *allure* to pass for a paterfamilias. In such an interpretation his third-act aria will never be convincing to the audience. And it is precisely this aria which expresses the essence of his role: his personal tragedy. The Count is the victim of fate, which forces him to embody a feudal as well as an enlightened ruler. During the whole day he is tormented with the incompatibility of these two conceptions, and the aria "Vedrò mentr'io" is nothing else than the expression of his impotent anger against fate. Mozart pictures him as a lion jumping desperately against the bars of his cage (ex. 1).

EXAMPLE I

If we discern this as the Count's essential conflict, then there will no longer be a need to depict him as a savage oppressor or an erotomaniac. During one of the rare episodes when he feels detached he almost appears good-natured. This occurs in the scene of the second-act finale, where he calls Figaro to account for the letter denouncing the Countess's rendezvous (according to his promise given earlier in the finale we know already that Figaro will not be punished) (ex. 2).

No. 15 (Count)   EXAMPLE 2
Andante

Co - no - sce - te, si - gnor Fi-ga-ro, que-sto fo - glio chi ver - gò?

With this Haydn-like melody the master mockingly speaks his servant's language, reinforcing the irony of the title *signor*.[6] Here he is the feudal ruler who can afford to reprove his subordinate in a rather mild way. Unconscious of what there is still in store for him, he thinks he has reached his goal. Marcellina may arrive at any moment to claim Figaro as her *promesso sposo*, removing every obstacle to his affair with Susanna. It probably does not occur to him that he will destroy the happiness of two people, and therefore there is no question of real malignity. For him, as for others of his rank, a man like Figaro does not exist as a person but only as a servant. The same holds for his relationship to Susanna. It is not so much erotic passion which carries him to the lady's maid as the urge to convince himself of his unlimited feudal power. The third-act duet seems to contradict this explanation. There he looks across the boundaries of his social domain and recognizes Susanna as a human being. His words, although derived from the conventional amorous vocabulary, clearly spring from his heart. However this human tone during the encounter with Susanna is an exception to the rule. When in the fourth-act finale, he believes the difficulties have vanished, he is once more in his usual attitude. Susanna is merely the object of a frivolous affair. The affinity of his courting theme with the light-hearted melody through which the ladies of *Così fan tutte* are supposed to be seduced is striking. Even the key is the same, a particularity rarely without meaning in Mozart (ex. 3).

No. 28 (Count)   EXAMPLE 3
[Andante con moto]

a

'Così fan tutte', No. 15 (Guglielmo)
Andante

b

[6] The occurrence of the same passage (including the bass) in the Vienna duet of Leoporello and Zerlina (K. 540^b, b. 46–7 and 72–3) is evidence of the low-class character of the melody.

Here we see the Count in his true colours: a feudal nobleman parading with enlightened ideas which cover his frivolities.

The Countess. Opposed to the tragic role of the Count is the dramatic part of his spouse. This is all the more remarkable since she is predestined, by her sex and high position, to a passive attitude. Indeed, her first appearance seems to confirm this outlook. The cavatina in E♭ is actually nothing but the traditional *lamento* of the *sposa abbandonata*. Its text contains the standard formulae of such a piece ("O rendi il mio tesoro; o mi lascia almen morir"). But the following scenes show the Countess from a less conventional side. She is not insensible to Cherubino's charm, and the accusations of her husband provoke a resistance which is stimulated by Susanna. Like the Count, she is powerless within the frame of her social position but, in contrast to him, she decides to exceed its bounds, and this is possible in only one direction: downward. It is a decision which cannot be taken without inner struggle, and this is Mozart's reason for writing an aria with psychological action ("Dove sono i bei momenti"). Its preceding *recitativo accompagnato* shows how much the Countess feels the intended *travesti* as a real humiliation. There is no question of the traditional light-hearted atmosphere of the *commedia dell'arte*, from which this dramatic device is originally derived. On the contrary, the complaint at the end of the recitative clearly expresses class consciousness (ex. 4).

EXAMPLE 4

No. 19 (Countess)

fam - mi or cer-car   da u - - - na mia ser - va a - i - ta!

Almaviva, too, speaks in his aria about his *servo*, though in much cruder terms ("un vil ogetto"); this parallelism is symptomatic of the fixed social bond between Count and Countess.

Viewed in the light of the preceding recitative, the dramatic significance of "Dove sono" has been curiously undervalued. Even Dent and Newman consider the aria a set piece.[7] Actually, what happens here is, socially speaking, the most sensational scene of the opera. A lady of high birth decides to conspire with her maid against her husband, not as a frivolous pastime but in order to restore her domestic happiness. The consequences

[7] E. Newman, *Mozart and Da Ponte*, Sunday Times, 26 June 1939; E. J. Dent, *Mozart's Operas*, 2nd ed., London, 1962, p. 143.

of this brave decision appear in the letter duet. The metre is the 'low' 6/8 and the lady has the same melodic material as the servant. True, Susanna meets the Countess halfway, but the eighteenth-century public must nevertheless have strongly felt the self-humiliation of the mistress, since it had a basic awareness of her high, inviolable position. Today we are struck primarily by the spiritual *noblesse* and not by the dramatic conflict between class and humanity. For contemporaries, however, Rosina was first of all a countess and therefore classified *a priori*. Apart from this, Mozart conferred on her a high moral character and expressed her courage in such a convincing way that her violation of social convention became acceptable.

Susanna. Her leading role during the whole day makes us easily forget that she belongs to the lowest class of the 'family'. Her social mobility is remarkably strong. In each situation and with each antagonist she strikes the right note. Hence she asserts herself pre-eminently in the duets and ensembles. When, finally, she sings her "Deh vieni, non tardar", we have already received the impression of a many-sided personality, and the simplicity of this aria is therefore deceiving. Here Susanna plays a part within a part. From the beginning her interests run concurrently with those of the Countess. She, too, crosses the borders of her social class, naturally in an upward direction. If the Countess's step requires moral courage, Susanna's calls for intelligence and charm, qualities which she possesses to a high degree. Although she could easily turn the Count around her little finger, she does not use her talents to further any social position, but exclusively to secure her marriage with Figaro. This modest purpose paradoxically contributes most to her superiority. Like the Countess, Susanna shows traits which are borrowed from Rousseau's sphere of thought. The Countess's *noblesse* of mind exceeds the nobility of her birth; Susanna posseses a singleness of heart to which her innate refinement and coquetry remain subordinated.

Figaro. His lack of success might lead to the conclusion that he is not the same man as the hero of *Il barbiere di Siviglia*. Such an interpretation is hardly compatible with the popularity of Paisiello's opera, which shortly after its première (St. Petersburg, 1782) had been succesfully performed in Vienna. Moreover, the two comedies of Beaumarchais must have been fairly well known in upper- and middle-class circles of Central Europe. Both plays were available in print, and the interdiction of their performance by the censor must have stimulated their circulation. Mozart simply could not afford to create a different Figaro, and the idea probably never crossed his mind. A comparison of the scores of *Figaro* and *Il barbiere* shows his familiarity with Paisiello's opera buffa.[8] The musical affinity between these fragments, for example, is striking (ex. 5).

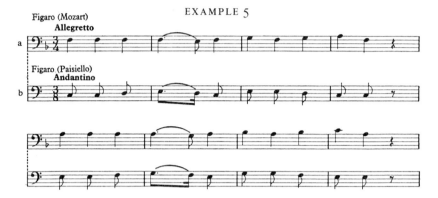

EXAMPLE 5

Le nozze di Figaro contains several scenes in which the insolence of Paisiello's hero is easily recognized (e.g. the recitative preceding "Non più andrai", where Cherubino is addressed with *tu* instead of *voi*; the 'military' aria itself; the dialogue with Antonio in the finale of the second act). If nevertheless Figaro gradually looses his grasp on events and, toward the end of the day, submerges into darkest pessimism, it is because in the present opera he faces situations which he cannot handle. *Il barbiere* required cleverness, while *Figaro* calls for insight. Figaro is undoubtedly clever, but his intelligence is too restricted to follow the subtle intrigues of the females. Moreover, his relation to the Count is quite different from what it was in the opera of Paisiello. There he was the ally and almost the companion of a young nobleman without responsibilities; here we find him as the lowly servant of a grandee of Spain.

Figaro is fully aware of the enormous social distance separating him from his master. Although at first he thinks he can manage the difficulties with his usual flair and impertinence ("Se vuol ballare, signor contino"), in the evening he has to admit that he has not the slightest chance against his high-born adversary ("Aprite un po' quegli occhi"). Hence the partiality of his diatribe, which only refers to the women: the Count is above the law. Figaro's frustration is clearly revealed in the first G major section of the last finale, where he witnesses the Count's rendezvous with the pseudo-Susanna. Hidden in the bushes, he repeatedly interrupts the couple with pent-up rage (ex. 6).

---

[8] The two composers had met in Vienna (1784).

EXAMPLE 6

No. 28 (Figaro)

Che com-pia-cen-te fem-mi-na, che spo-sa di buon cor!

Finally, with courage born of despair, he disturbs the meeting, and only then does this motif develop into a complete melody.[9] Figaro's inertia is diametrically opposed to Susanna's quick reactions in analogous situations. Twice in the course of the day she feels hurt by his supposed infidelity and both times he is promptly slapped (sextet and fourth-act finale). In the last act we see a bitter Figaro on the stage – a man who knows himself to be the victim of an unjust social system, to which, nevertheless, unconditionally he submits.

Antonio. The garderner's social immobility neither poses a problem to himself nor to us. What he wants is order, in his flower-beds as well as in the conduct of his daughter and niece. When this order is disturbed he becomes angry. For such a four-square character the Count is the symbol of all that is right; hence his scrupulous imitation of his master in the second-act finale (bars 472–3, 477–8, 524–8, 534–6). He is entirely devoid of imagination and his melodic range is very small. But he should not be shown as a stupid figure, since he repeatedly acts with common sense.[10] Even worse is the presentation of a drunken Antonio. Although Figaro, pushed against the wall, does accuse the gardener of drunkenness, nothing in the libretto nor in Mozart's music corroborates this insinuation. Antonio may be a rude fellow, but as a social conformist he knows better than to appear before his master in a state of inebriation.

Basilio. He is not so much a conformist as an opportunist. Because of his profession – he is a musician and serves the Count as organist of his chapel – his social position is less strongly fixed than those of the other characters. His 'confession' ("In quegli anni") is the only piece in the opera for which librettist and composer were at a loss. Da Ponte uses many words and Mozart many instruments to picture Basilio, but nevertheless he remains rather lifeless in this monologue. His appearance in the chair trio of the first act is much more convincing (ex. 7).

[9] The passage has been analysed in detail by S. Levarie, *Mozart's Le Nozze di Figaro*, Chicago, 1952, pp. 222–4, and in Ch. I of this book.

[10] The same holds true for Masetto, who is often presented as a dullard.

No. 7 (Basilio)   EXAMPLE 7

Ah, del pag - gio quel che ho det - to, e - ra so - lo un mio so - spet - to.

Toward the end of the trio Basilio resumes this musical phrase with exactly
the same words but in a completely different situation (Cherubino has
been discovered in the chair). First we hear cowardice, then malice.
Mozart's device is more than an ingenious pun: it is the sharp characterization of an opportunist.

Bartolo. His aria ("La vendetta") is difficult to understand without previous knowledge. Obviously Mozart and Da Ponte assumed that
Beaumarchais' *Barbier de Séville* was known to the public. Although in *Le
nozze di Figaro* Bartolo is involved in the plot, he is dominated above all
by his old grudge against Figaro. The reason for Bartolo's aggression does
not seem to be sufficiently explained by the previous story, since at the
time Bartolo aimed at Rosina's dowry rather than herself; and thanks to
Almaviva's generosity he finally succeeded in obtaining this dowry. A
stronger motive for his lasting enmity lies in the social atmosphere. In this
connection the following phrase is significant (ex. 8).

EXAMPLE 8

No. 4 (Bartolo)

Tut - ta Si - vi - glia co - no - sce Bar - to - lo, il bir - bo Fi - ga-ro vo - stro sa - rà

The difference in scansion between their names is symptomatic of the
doctor's feeling of superiority toward the barber. Here we see the professional man looking down on the artisan. The eighteenth-century public
must have understood this immediately. Today barbers no longer practise
medicine and Bartolo's animosity is therefore easily overlooked. When in
the third act Figaro turns out to be his son, the doctor is quite taken
aback. No wonder that, unable to show any paternal feelings, he merely
produces this inane melody (ex. 9).

EXAMPLE 9

No. 18 (Bartolo)

Re - si - sten - za   la   co - scien - za   far   non   la - scia   tuo   de - sir

Marcellina. Siegmund Levarie characterizes her aria ("Il capro e la ca-pretta") as mere entertainment.[11] This interpretation seems untenable: every scene in the opera has its dramatic function. Marcellina's monologue is undoubtedly less attractive than most of the other arias, but then she is also a less attractive person. Besides, æsthetic considerations do not in-validate the psychological and dramatic function of the piece in question. The aria does tell us a few things about Marcellina: her aspirations are bourgeois and she has a cold nature. The first of these particularities will be discussed later; as for the second, we should interpret the aria as the complement of Marcellina's characterization in the third-act sextet. There she revealed herself as a woman of empty sentimentality. Any trace of real human relationship between mother and son was lacking. Marcellina mere-ly enjoyed her unexpected social success: she would get married at last – and even better, with a physician, through whom her status will be raised considerably more than she had ever dared to hope. Marcellina is a fem-inist from purely interested motives. With her, feminism overshadows motherhood: as a mother she is almost a caricature. When in the fourth act Figaro complains about Susanna's supposed infidelity, one would ex-pect Marcellina to take her son's part; instead she sides with her daughter-in-law (sc. 4). Now, in the aria, Marcellina's character is rounded off. Like many sentimental persons, she is devoid of intense human feeling; funda-mentally she is icy cold. Mozart renders this characteristic through col-oratura interpolations in the regular phrases of the minuet tune (bars 8–11, 32–5) and the Allegro section (bars 68–73). The text contains no expla-nation of these interpolations: their function appears to be purely psy-chological.[12]

Marcellina's feminism differs essentially from Susanna's. What serves as a means for Figaro's bride is a purpose for Bartolo's former mistress. Susanna wants to marry the man of her choice; Marcellina aims at mar-riage with whomsoever. In her eyes matrimony is synonymous with social progress. She is ambitious, reads books and speaks a few words of French

[11] Levarie, *op. cit.*, p. 189.

[12] The metaphor ("Il capro e la capretta"), borrowed from Ariosto's *Orlando Furioso* (can-to 5, stanza 1; see Dent, *op. cit.*, p. 110, n. 1), sounds like a parody of a Metastasian text. But in spite of the coloratura the music has little affinity with *opera seria*. If Da Ponte aimed at a parodistic image of Marcellina, Mozart did not follow his intention.

(in eighteenth-century society erudition was not considered unbecoming in a woman, at least not in the middle and upper classes). Susanna easily sees through Marcellina's display of superficial learning. "Che lingua" is her mocking comment on the words "[l']argent fait tout" (Act I, sc. 4), and after her duet with the spinster she exclaims: "Va là, vecchia pedante, dottoressa arrogante! Perchè hai letti due libri ..." (*ibid.*, sc. 5). The use of the term "dottoressa" is ambiguously ironic; besides referring to Marcellina's display of learning it maliciously hints at her carnal relationship with Doctor Bartolo.

Barbarina. The twelve-year old Anna Gottlieb, who acted the first Barbarina, was faced with a difficult task. The gardener's daughter is certainly no longer a child; she performs (as a character) the part of a child – when it suits her. Barbarina borrows her affectations and little tricks from her cousin, whom she must have closely observed. The cavatina "L'ho perduta" is full of the half-tender, half-coquettish appoggiaturas which we frequently heard from Susanna. The whole piece is dominated by the semitones above and below the fifth. Naturally Barbarina lacks Susanna's variety of expression. This is clearly apparent from her restricted vocal range, which is exactly one octave, whereas Susanna has a compass of two octaves and a minor third. But the musical affinity in their response to difficult situations is conspicuous (ex. 10).

EXAMPLE 10

The first of these examples is taken from the chair scene, the second from Barbarina's cavatina. Melody, rhythm and words are almost the same, and both fragments are at the same pitch level. The variance in tempo is easily explained, if one compares the two situations: Barbarina is in trouble, Susanna in a crisis demanding immediate action. This difference also justifies the rise in the latter's melody; Barbarina's phrase, on the contrary, remains under the centripetal influence of the dominant.

Barbarina's social ambition is as yet concealed under the cover of her

playfulness. Nevertheless she succeeds in checkmating the Count by reminding him, in the presence of the Countess, Cherubino, Susanna,
Antonio and the peasant girls, of his promise to comply with her wish in
exchange for a kiss (Act III, sc. 12). She then asks for nothing less than
Cherubino to be her future husband; her social ambition seems to exceed
that of everyone else. Naturally none of those present takes this claim as a
serious one; it is simply ignored. But this does not alter the fact that many
a designing woman could still learn something from this clever young person.

Cherubino. Unlike the other characters, the page does not take an active
part in the intrigues. Instead he works for his own benefit. Like Barbarina,
he makes ample use of the social freedom which is the privilege of his age.
This might have been the reason why Kierkegaard pictured him as a Don
Giovanni *in statu nascendi*.[13] Kierkegaard's interpretation was the
starting-signal for the tracing of other camouflaged Dons: Alfonso,
Papageno, and even Mozart himself. The latest addition to the list, offered
by Brigid Brophy, is the Count:

It is not Cherubino who is Don Giovanni *in potentia* but Count Almaviva. There
was needed only one impetus to develop Mozart's conception of this insolent aris-
tocrat, who would like to take advantage of the *droit de seigneur* in order to seduce
Susanna, into the insolent privateer who would like to seduce every woman he sets
eyes on. And in point of fact ... it is possible to be exact about what the impetus
was: the death of Mozart's father, which took place between the composition of
the two operas.[14]

The reconciliation scene of the Count and the Countess already contradicts Miss Brophy's interpretation.[15] We have seen that the Count's
craving for amorous affairs is in large part motivated by his efforts to
maintain the way of living of his feudal ancestors. His class consciousness
is quite opposite to Don Giovanni's avowed denial of social order. In a
few years Cherubino, too, will respect the conventions of his class. The last
part of Beaumarchais' trilogy clearly testifies to this.[16]

[13] S. Kierkegaard, *Enten-Eller* (*Either/Or*), first part (1843). See *Complete Works*, vol. I,
Copenhagen, 1901, pp. 57–60 and 81.

[14] *Mozart the Dramatist*, London, 1964, p. 109.

[15] See J. Kerman, *Opera as Drama*, New York, 1959, pp. 107–8. Another essential difference between Count Almaviva and Don Giovanni is the latter's flexibility (e.g. in the first-act
quartet and in his dealings with Zerlina and Masetto).

[16] In *L'Autre Tartuffe ou La Mère coupable* (1789–90) we are told that the Countess has
given birth to an illegitimate child after having been seduced by Léon d'Astorga (Cherubino's
real name). Nevertheless she cuts loose from her lover, who, in accordance with the code of
honour, seeks and finds his death on the battlefield.

But Mozart does not stress so much Cherubino's social liberties as his passive function in the drama. Through his unappeasable appetite the page confuses the Count as well as the Countess and Susanna. In his way he imitates his master's game; and because Almaviva recognizes himself in the young man's behaviour, he is almost powerless to punish him efficiently. Both women are not unaware of their weakness with regard to the charming boy, and Barbarina, too, is clearly under his spell. This, perhaps, explains the affinities between the following fragments, in which the Countess, Cherubino, Susanna and Barbarina are more or less concerned (ex. 11).

EXAMPLE 11

No. 11 (Cherubino)

No. 21 (Peasant girls including Barbarina
and Cherubino *in travesti*)

No. 23 (Barbarina)

Thus Cherubino's function is of an indirect, rather than a direct order. Unintentionally he confronts the other characters with the consequences of their conduct. The page represents their social conscience.

*   *
*

The Minuet as Social Indicator

The opera contains five fragments which, for the sake of convenience, I shall refer to as minuets, although actually they are but minuet-like pieces. The only real dance is the *fandango* in the finale of the third act. The question arises: are these 'dance' sections related to the social climate and, if so, in what way?

During the last three decades of the eighteenth century the minuet gradually loses its significance as a specifically aristocratic dance. It shifts to the middle class, but even there it cannot hold its own against the fashionable country dances and the German 'waltz' (the so-called *Allemande* or *Deutsche*). The social displacement of the minuet affected its musical style.

This is clearly apparent in *opera buffa* and *Singspiel*, where it was maintained, either as a dance on the stage or as a purely musical form applied to arias and ensembles. Here two types may be distinguished: the aristocratic and the bourgeois. The former was usually written in a somewhat archaic style, i.e. in a slow tempo (Larghetto; Andante; Andantino) and often without initial upbeat. Its most characteristic feature is, however, the absence of melodic movement in the first bar, where, as in the sixteenth- and seventeenth-century *canzona*, only the rhythm is presented. The classical example of the aristocratic minuet is to be found in the first finale of *Don Giovanni*, where it is danced by the upper-class couple, Donna Anna and Don Ottavio (ex. 12).

EXAMPLE 12

'Don Giovanni', No. 13

The aristocratic minuet could also be used by the lower classes, for instance as a sincere or ironic expression of reverence (ex. 13).

EXAMPLE 13

Dittersdorf, 'Doktor und Apotheker', No. 6

The bourgeois minuet was influenced by symphonic and chamber music of the time. Its tempo is considerably faster (Andantino grazioso; Allegretto; Tempo di menuetto) and it starts with a real melody, either with or without an upbeat. This type served to underline the middle-class character of a person or group of persons (ex. 14).

EXAMPLE 14

Haydn, 'Die Feuerbrunst', No. 25 (Colombina and Hanswurst)

Naturally there are borderline cases, and one finds also numerous instances of minuets which defy sociological interpretation. In broad outline,
however, the distinction of two types answers to the practice of late
eighteenth-century opera.

Three of the minuets which occur in *Le nozze di Figaro* belong to the
aristocratic type. One would expect Mozart to assign these to the Count or the
Countess, as a musical expression of their high rank. But this is not the case.
Two are sung by Figaro and one by Susanna. In this way the aristocratic
minuet clearly assumes the function of a social weapon.

Figaro starts and concludes his cavatina with a minuet tune, illustrating
the metaphor in the text ("Se vuol ballare, signor contino"). The rather
quick tempo (Allegretto) derives from his emotional state: Figaro is much
more uneasy than he himself realizes. Susanna uses the minuet in a still
sharper way. When she appears on the threshold of the closet, instead of
Cherubino, she mocks the Count by using his 'own' dance (ex. 15).

EXAMPLE 15

The last minuet in the score – hitherto not identified as such – is Figaro's
short monologue in the finale of the fourth act (bars 109–21).[17] Here the
dance is not used as a weapon but as an expression of bitterness (Figaro
thinks himself defeated) (ex. 16).

---

[17] One reason why the minuet character of this piece has been overlooked may be a misin-
terpretation of its tempo (Larghetto). In the eighteenth century Larghetto was quite different
from Largo. In fact the term indicated a tempo faster than Adagio. Another possible reason
is the predominance of the left-hand triplets in the vocal score. Actually they belong to the
inner voices and are played by the violins.

No. 28 (Figaro)   EXAMPLE 16

Characteristic of Figaro's frustration is the irregular structure (the fourth bar is a contraction of two bars). The text illustrates the quasi-aristocratic atmosphere of the piece. The servant makes use of an image of classical mythology – Venus and Mars caught in Vulcan's net:

> Tutto è tranquillo e placido;
> Entrò la bella Venere,
> Col vago Marte prendere
> Nuovo Vulcan del secolo,
> In rete li potrò!

> *All is quiet and peaceful; the*
> *beautiful Venus has entered. Now I*
> *shall be able, as a new Vulcan, to*
> *catch her and the lovable Mars in*
> *my net.*

Abert's assertion that this piece and the following duet have only a key relationship is incorrect.[18] At the beginning of the duet Figaro repeats his minuet motif no fewer than six times (a little varied and naturally in a much faster tempo). Significantly, this melodic formula is maintained until the moment that he recognizes Susanna's voice.

[18] Abert, *op. cit.*, II, p. 360.

The remaining two minuets are middle-class pieces. The second section of Basilio's aria ("In quegli anni") contains but a vague allusion to the dance (without an upbeat, which, however, is added in the reprise); the melody soon gets lost in the orchestral painting of the thunderstorm and probably does not have any specific social meaning. Marcellina's aria, on the other hand, can hardly be misunderstood (ex. 17).

EXAMPLE 17

No. 24 (Marcellina)

Tempo di Menuetto

Il ca - pro e la ca - pret - ta son sem .- pre in a - mi - stà, ___

The bourgeois character of this minuet is explicit: middle class constitutes the height of Marcellina's social aspirations.

Finally the *fandango* requires an interpretation. Mozart's piece does not answer to the description of this dance in John Moore's epistolary 'novel' *Mordaunt*, published in 1800:

> They [i.e. the Spaniards] generally begin by dancing country dances, and finish with the fandango, which is performed in a most indecent manner by the common people, but in a style less reprehensible by the higher ranks. This information I had from the colonel. He introduced me into a large room, where nine or ten couples were dancing the fandango, every couple having a pair of castanets in each hand, which they rattled with great dexterity, and in exact time. The movements of this dance are more lively than graceful; and the dance, upon the whole, is such as a modest English woman would not choose to excel in. Some of the females whom I saw performing on this occasion were of an age which might have made them decline it, independent of any other consideration. Nothing can form a greater contrast than that between the serious and solemn manners of the Spaniards in general and this popular dance. I own it surprised me exceedingly to see, at the house of a woman of character, the sister of a bishop, an exhibition by ladies in respectable situations of life, which would certainly be thought reprehensible by an English bishop, even in opera-dancers.[19]

Although the *fandango* is described here as a popular dance, it seems rather to be a national dance of popular origin. Moore's description refers to a middle-class circle in a small provincial town near the Portuguese border (Bajados). A performance in a more distinguished gathering might perhaps have shocked him less. In any case, Mozart's *fandango* certainly suggests

---

[19] John Moore, *Mordaunt, Sketches of Life, Characters and Manners in Various Countries; Including the Memoirs of a French Lady of Quality*, new ed. by W. L. Renwick, London 1965, p. 60 (Letter no. 12).

the "less reprehensible" practice of the higher ranks. The composer borrowed the musical material from Gluck,[20] who probably knew the melody directly or indirectly from a Spanish source.[21] Mozart's dance sounds even more aristocratic than Gluck's, especially in his treatment of the bass, which gives an impression of archaism. The ceremonial character of the piece is easily accounted for by the presence of the Count and the Countess; on the other hand it stresses the disturbance of social order, because it is not the masters who are dancing but their servants. Of particular significance are the poignant dissonances in the inner voices (oboe and bassoon, e.g. bars 142 and 156). They illustrate the underlying tension in a seemingly unclouded atmosphere.

*   *
*

Humanity and Social Engagement

However clearly social tensions are expressed in the opera, they should not lead us to te conclusion that the composer intended to expose the oppression of the lower classes by a ruthless aristocracy. *Le nozze di Figaro* contains no message; it does not even propagate reform of the social order, let alone a revolution. Everyone who uses his eyes and ears must admit that Mozart only registers the social climate, without taking sides. His Count is no monster, nor is Figaro the people's hero. All characters show their weaknesses, at which we tend to smile. On the other hand, the traditional negation of the opera's affinity to contemporary society – illogically based on Mozart's deep humanity – should also be dismissed. It is founded on sentiment rather than on reason. To speak of Mozart's music as timeless is merely an expression of our admiration, since we are unable to imagine an age when people will feel indifferent to it. An obsolete 'Jupiter' symphony, G minor string quintet or *Nozze di Figaro* is simply inconceivable. But this does not mean that timelessness is a concept fit to be handled by musical scholarship. No piece of music, no drama is without relation to the time in which it was written. While it is true that a work of art creates its own world, still this world will as a matter of course be linked with the world outside, which in the present case is European society of the late eighteenth century.

[20] "Don Juan" (ballet), no. 19.

[21] See M. Schneider's article *Fandango* in MGG. Brian Trowell has pointed out that the tune is reproduced in Sir John Hawkins' *General History of the Science and Practice of Music*, London 1776. See his Letter to the Editor of *Music & Letters* (vol. 50, 1969, pp. 427–28) and my reply (vol. 51, 1970, p. 346).

Does the truth lie midway between these two extremes? I do not think so. It lies on a higher level. The humanity of the characters and the time-bound social tensions are both constituents of the drama, each of them reinforcing and raising the other. What would remain of the Count without his tragic social conflict? At his best an amusing *basso buffo*, at his worst a bloodless *parte seria*. On the other hand, how could we believe in the Countess's denial of her rank, had not Mozart given her a viable character? Here lies the essential difference between the opera and its French model. True, Beaumarchais' social engagement is beyond question and his characters are full of life. But they create less tension on the stage, and much wit is needed to keep the public's attention. Mozart discarded most of the Frenchman's *esprit;* he could afford to write the third-act sextet as an understatement. Nevertheless the social tensions are more strongly felt in his music than in Beaumarchais' text; and this is because of his deep insight into human nature.

1968

CHAPTER 3

'DON GIOVANNI':
MUSICAL AFFINITIES AND
DRAMATIC STRUCTURE

As the curtain rises we see a sulking servant who envies the freedom of his libertine master. – Noise is heard, the master appears, harangued by a young lady who seems to accuse him of assault. She leaves the stage at the moment her father arrives. The latter challenges the assailant; a duel follows during which the old man is severely wounded. He dies. The servant protests but his words are stifled by his master's threats. Exeunt both. The lady returns with her fiancé; she discovers her father's body and faints. When brought round she first mistakes her lover for the ravisher and then forces him to vow vengeance. The curtain falls and for the first time in the opera we hear a closing cadence in the orchestra. The opening scenes have lasted only twelve minutes, little more than the duration of a sonata movement.

Few people in the audience will be aware of this. The more happening on the stage, the more one looses touch with time. What was called by Gounod "the most beautiful opening scene of any opera" is also the most overwhelming one. A sequence of unusual and exciting events presented in a breathtaking dramatic rhythm naturally produces sensation. When measured by the standards of the eighteenth century stage, *Don Giovanni* is an extremely sensational opera. Tempo and extravagant action are maintained throughout the two acts, although not always with the same dramatic intensity.[1] Another exceptional feature is the opera's darkness. The word should be taken in its literal meaning, as the great majority of scenes are enacted in the open air during the evening or at night. In this respect,

---

[1] For instance, the beating undergone by Masetto in the second act produces sensation for its own sake. This scene as well as the next (Zerlina's 'medicine') are merely fillers supplied by Da Ponte who could no longer paraphrase Bertati's libretto. In the latter's opera, set by Gazzaniga, the episode corresponding with Don Giovanni's courtship of Zerlina and Elvira's rebuke (nrs. 7 and 8) is immediately followed by the cemetery scene.

too, *Don Giovanni* is unique among operatic master-pieces of the eighteenth century and perhaps of all times.

A series of sensational episodes lacking fluency and visual clarity offers special problems to the composer. Such a libretto calls for a musical setting which strongly furthers the dramatic coherence and unity. To say that Mozart has fulfilled his task in an admirable way is merely a truism. Much more intriguing is the question of *how* he achieved it. Even if we admit that the creative process never discloses its secrets entirely, this should not discourage us from attempting to solve its mysteries. Close examination of the score will reveal the use of certain devices by which disconnected scenes are linked and dramatically unified.

One means applied to this purpose is in no way exceptional since Mozart uses it in all his operas from *Idomeneo* on. I refer to the maintenance of the musical physiognomy of the individual actors, not only in the arias but also in most of the ensembles. For example, the difference in character between Donna Anna and Donna Elvira is scrupulously observed in Mozart's melodic treatment of their respective parts. Donna Anna, who fundamentally is a conventional young woman, expresses her feelings dutifully with elegant turns – even in situations which strongly arouse her emotions. Donna Elvira, on the contrary, continually stresses her nonconformist attitude by nervous rhythms and extravagant melodic lines. When occasionally she seems to borrow a gracious formula from the commander's daughter, the ressemblance is only superficial; her true character betrays itself by the irregular context in which the motif is placed (ex. 1).

EXAMPLE I

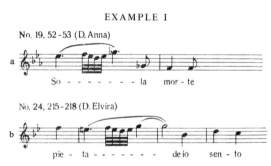

No. 19, 52-53 (D. Anna)

a   So - - - - - - - la   mor - te

No. 24, 215-218 (D. Elvira)

b   pie - ta - - - - - - - de io   sen - to

Of all the characters, Don Giovanni himself seems to be musically the least homogeneous. If we compare his melodic language in various episodes, such as the *Introduzione* (no. 1), his two encounters with Zerlina (no. 7 and no. 13, b. 92–121), his own exuberant aria (no. 11), his duet with Leporello (no. 14), the balcony scene (no. 15), his management of the peasants (no. 17) and Elvira's interruption of the banquet (no. 24), we hardly recognize him as an individual. This was undoubtedly Mozart's intention. The kaleidoscopic picture of the Don is merely the negative application of the principle of individual characterization. Our hero lacks the others' homogeneity simply because he adapts himself subtly to every situation. Sometimes he even changes face during a single scene, as in the quartet of the first act. Flexibility is his main weapon for obtaining power. A consistent Don Giovanni would fail to dominate his opponents and to convince us, his audience.

Other devices used for the purpose of achieving dramatic coherence require a detailed examination. For the sake of clarity, these will be divided into two categories: the musical relationships that serve the continuity and secondly, the affinities between distant scenes. Finally a curious example of the latter kind, a sort of 'Leitmotiv', will be treated separately.

*   *
*

Continuity

It is hardly surprising that Mozart never fails to accept the opportunities offered by Da Ponte to further the musical continuity. A clear instance of this is found in the beginning of the 'catalogue' aria (no. 4). Leporello summarizes the contents of the register and naturally does it in a reciting style, establishing in this way a link with the preceding *secco*. In the course of the piece his wish to identify himself with his master leads him to imitate the latter's tone of bravura and gradually he adopts a true aria style. At the beginning of the first finale (no. 13) we encounter a similar example of smooth transition prepared by the libretto. The preceding dispute between Zerlina and Masetto is simply pursued and the latter's snappish words do call for a recitative-like style. In point of fact, this finale starts, unlike Mozart's other finales, as if it were an *accompagnato*.

More revealing are the transitions that are not dictated by the text, but only realized with musical means. Several arias start with a melody which seems to be derived from the closing formula of the preceding secco recitative.[2] A typical example is found in the beginning of Zerlina's second aria (the practice of singing an appoggiatura on the penultimate note of the recitative should be taken into account) (ex. 2).

[2] Relationship between an aria and its preceding *accompagnato* (for instance Donna Anna's scene, no. 23) does not constitute a specific Mozartian feature. It is quite common in eighteenth-century Italian opera.

EXAMPLE 2

Sometimes the relation between *recitativo secco* and aria is obscured by retrograde motion (ex. 3 and 4).

EXAMPLE 3

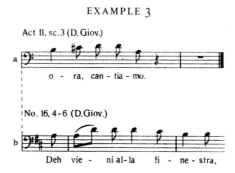

EXAMPLE 4

Don Ottavio's aria is particularly interesting in this respect because it shows not only a 'crab' relation to the recitative but also an affinity in *motu recto*: the descending thirds which dominate the first section (b. 1–29) and its reprise (49–70) (ex. 5).

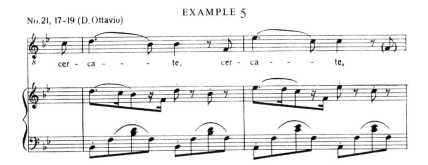

In this case the relationship is undoubtedly determined by the words, since, in contrast to the aria's second part which deals with 'vengeance', the first section treats of 'pity' and 'affection'.

The Viennese score (1788) contains an additional *secco* which, unlike the former examples, is linked with the preceding piece (Leporello's apology, no. 20) instead of the material which follows. It takes up the canonically treated triadic arpeggios which occurred in the middle of the aria (b. 72ff; see also 9ff and 96ff) (ex. 6).

This unusual handling of a recitative can only be explained by the composer's wish to further the continuity. It is clear that in this instance the recitative must have been modeled upon the aria since the former was added a year after the Prague première. The same may be assumed with

regard to examples 2–5, quoted above, although in the score they occur in
reverse order.

A curious example of musical affinity linking consecutive sections is encountered at the beginning of the second finale (no. 24), where a relationship between the music of two different composers is involved. We
know that Mozart's idea of inserting operatic fragments borrowed from
Martin y Soler and Sarti originated during the rehearsals at Prague and it
is very likely that the preceding introduction, written in common time (b.
1–46), was composed only after the selection from *Una cosa rara* and *Fra i
due litiganti* was made. But if proof were needed for this assumption, it
could be found in the score. The entire initial section is dominated by two
basic motifs, a descending arpeggio on the tonic chord, consisting of three
or four notes, and an ascending scale of four or six steps (ex. 7).

EXAMPLE 7

No. 24, Melodic materials of initial section

These two contrasting motifs are the very elements of which Martin's melody is constituted (ex. 8).

No. 24, 47-52   EXAMPLE 8

In spite of the composer's ability to sustain dramatic élan throughout the whole work, he cannot use melodic relationship to bridge the gap between the two acts.[3] Instead Mozart and Da Ponte apply a device which is less explicit but which succeeds in giving the public the impression that during their absence there has been no break in the drama. The second act starts with a rejoinder rather than a question. We are clearly in the middle of a dialogue that must have started long before the curtain rose, a kind of dialogue that no one could foresee (Don Giovanni adopting Leporello's *buffo* tone). After the uproarious ending of the first act we are carried back into the atmosphere of the unexpected.

One more example of relationship between consecutive items may be mentioned. It concerns the first two sections of the *Introduzione*, Leporello's monologue (no. 1, b. 1–70) and the dispute of Donna Anna and Don Giovanni (no. 1, b. 71–134). The dramatic contrast between these scenes is clearly reflected in the music. Leporello's *boutade* in F major is simple and outspoken. The servant's melody contains very few notes not belonging to the underlying chords; the melodic rhythm is elementary, the harmonic rhythm slow. In contrast to this the B♭ fragment has a nervous rhythm, full of dotted notes, and especially in the beginning the harmonic rhythm is considerably faster than that of the preceding section. Moreover, the parts of Donna Anna and Don Giovanni are less dependent on chordal notes. Still, in spite of the contrast between the two scenes, they are musically connected in a most refined way. Toward the end of his section (b. 57ff) Leporello hears noise: people are arriving. Suddenly the atmosphere becomes tense. The harmonic rhythm doubles its speed, but remains subordinated to the metre: |♩♩|. On the other hand, the rhythmic motif (an anapaest) and its orchestration (alternately strings and winds) straddles the barline (♪♪|♩), forming a syncopation with the harmony. This anapaestic motif anticipates rhythmically both the beginning of Donna Anna's melody (b. 74ff) and the Don's reply in the lower octave (b. 79ff) (ex. 9).

EXAMPLE 9

No. 1, 74 - 75 (D. Anna)

Non spe - rar,

---

[3] According to Dent's convincingly argued hypothesis the opera was originally conceived in four acts, the first closing with Donna Anna's aria (no. 10), the third with the sextet (no. 19). See E. J. Dent, *Mozart's Operas*, 2nd ed., London 1962, p. 138.

Here we have an instance of perfect co-operation between librettist and composer. By inserting the line "ma mi par che venga gente" Da Ponte offered Mozart an opportunity to tie together two contrasting scenes. The rhyme ("ma mi par" – "non sperar") may be fortuitous but the intention is clear beyond doubt. Another striking example of Mozart's dramatic technique is the final reprise of Leporello's refrain. This, too, was prepared by Da Ponte. Only a very slight change in the words (leaving their sound virtually unaltered) expresses the change in the situation:

e non voglio più servir   non mi voglio far sentir

By using the same music for both lines, Mozart prevents a break in the rondo-like form of the F major section. Thus two seemingly conflicting aims have been realized: Leporello's monologue is unified as well as connected with the next scene.

Lastly a word should be said about the function of syncopation. From the overture on the score swarms with syncopes. Their dramatic significance is easily determined: they are closely related to the magic atmosphere of charm, tension and terror radiating from Don Giovanni. Only in the marginal episodes of the plot is the music free from syncopation. Characteristically, Zerlina's arias addressed to Masetto, unlike her encounters with the Don, virtually lack syncopes. The same holds true for the *scena ultima*, in which liberation from terror is negatively expressed by the absence of syncopation.

Although syncopation has primarily a psychological function in the drama, it serves also to intensify continuous movement. Many of Mozart's syncopes level to a certain degree the natural contrast between strong and weak beats; they belong to the type of *fluent* syncope.[4] Continuity is most clearly furthered by their use as melodic anticipation. Donna Anna's duet with Don Ottavio (no. 2, b. 63ff) is linked in this way with the preceding *accompagnato*. Equally smooth is the transition from the *secco* (I, sc. 12) to the quartet (no. 9) sung by Elvira, and another example is found at the beginning of Leporello's apology (no. 20). In all three cases, the initial bars are also melodically related to foregoing materials; the anticipating syncopes obviously function as reinforcement of the relationships.

---

[4] It is not true, of course, that syncopation is *eo ipso* a means of obliterating metrical beats. No one listening to the second movement of Beethoven's cello sonata op. 69 (a syncopated scherzo) will receive the impression of a particularly fluent melody. On the contrary, the piece in question strikes us rather as a 'revolt' against established metre, by which, paradoxally, this very metre is consolidated. Another type of syncopation is encountered in Hugo Wolf's setting of *Peregrina I* (text by Mörike). Here, the result is a relatively metrical independence of voice and piano part.

Other characteristic examples are met with in the duet "Là ci darem la mano" (no. 7, b. 24–25; 38–39; 42–43), where the music speaks more truthfully than the text. In spite of her words ("Presto non son più forte"), Zerlina has already surrendered to Don Giovanni and her anticipating syncopes suggest that she is urging him as much as he her (ex. 10).

EXAMPLE 10

No. 7, 24-26 (Zerlina)

Pre - - sto non son più for- te

The latter example clearly shows the disturbance of social order in *Don Giovanni*. In eighteenth-century operatic scores fluent syncopation generally belongs to the refined language of the upper classes. In this opera, however, we find it in the part of a simple peasant girl. Enchanted by a nobleman, she instinctively adopts a tone far above her class. The same goes for Leporello who, in the catalogue aria (no. 4, b. 61–68) speaks the idiom of his master (ex. 11).

EXAMPLE 11

No. 4, 61-63 (Leporello)

ma, ma, — ma in I - spa - gna,

Wherever the Don casts his spell, the syncope appears, dominating the melodic language of the actors and creating an atmosphere of nervous restlessness.

* *
*

Distant relationships

While the dramatic significance of musical affinity between consecutive items is self-evident, the relationship of distant scenes necessarily calls for an interpretation. Once the connection has been established and interpreted, other questions arise: how far do the two fragments differ? Is the distinction between them also dramatically explicable? And finally, is it possible to classify the various instances of musico-dramatic affinity?

The most unequivocal type of musical connection is naturally that of melody. But similarity of rhythm may also suffice to establish a relationship, provided that a logical explanation is available. Thus, the link between the two first scenes of the *Introduzione*, discussed above (ex. 9), is merely rhythmical, because the emotional dispute of Donna Anna and Don Giovanni is expressed by a melody that would not fit Leporello's buffo language. Harmony and orchestration may equally serve as a means to connect two fragments; their function, however, is generally limited to reinforcement of a melodic or rhythmic relationship. Here, too, the characters involved in the dramatic situations should be taken into account. Donna Anna's harmonies, for instance, are far more expressive and therefore better suited to 'quotation' than Leporello's. Another element of secondary value is the key; its importance, however, should not be underestimated. In the case of an affinity which is musically doubtful but dramatically clear identity of key may settle the matter.

Evaluation of the differences occurring between related fragments is again dependent on the dramatic interpretation. Instead of weakening the effect, they may stress the dramatic intensity and the development of the action. Moreover, if 'subject' and 'quotation' are sung by different persons, the variance is logically explained by the composer's wish to preserve the individuality of each actor.

Mozart's versatility makes it virtually impossible to establish a typological list of relationships. It is true that different kinds, such as the reminiscence, the quotation, and the *topos*, can be discerned, but the way in which they are applied is so varied that classification is out of the question. The fifteen instances discussed below are therefore presented in chronological order.

(1) No. 1, b. 40–42 (Leporello)   "... and I am to play the sentinel"

    No. 6, b. 10–13 (Masetto)   "I bow my head and shall go."

EXAMPLE 12

No. 1, 40-42 (Leporello)

ed io far la sen - ti - nel - la

No. 6, 10-13 (Masetto)

chi - no il ca - po e me ne vò.

The musical affinity between these two passages, taken from the opening scene and Masetto's aria, is primarily melodic; in addition there is similarity of key and tempo (molto allegro and allegro di molto). The fact of Masetto's phrase being written in double note values is easily accounted for: the time signature of his aria is *alla breve*.

The dramatic connotation lies on the surface. In both fragments text and situation refer to enforced subordination. More interesting are the differences. Masetto's language and its orchestral accompaniment (virtually in unison) is more primitive than Leporello's. This holds also for the instrumentation: Leporello is accompanied by strings, oboes, bassoons and horns, Masetto only by strings. Obviously this points to the social distinction between the servant and the peasant. Both actors express feelings of social frustration, yet there is an essential difference between their respective situations. While Leporello is merely sulking about his lack of freedom, Masetto is threatened and therefore forced to incline. Hence the bitterness of his tone. Leporello, on the other hand, makes a bit of a show of his complaint and gives it a buffo turn by twice repeating the word "sentinella" (the second time with an emphatic fermata on the first syllable). It should be noted, by the way, that these repeats (no. 1, b. 42–44) are practically identical to the first motif of Masetto's aria (no. 6, b. 4–5).

(2) No. 1, b. 57–60 (Leporello)	"But it seems that people are coming; I won't let myself be seen."
No. 19, b. 13–16 (Leporello)	"The more I seek, the less I find this cursed door."
No. 19, b. 157–161; 202–206 (Leporello)	"If I save myself in this tempest, it will be truly a miracle."

Leporello's motif, already mentioned above as a means of connecting the first two sections of the *Introduzione*, reappears twice in the E♭ sextet of the second act. The affinity is more clearly determined by the orchestra than by the voice part. The decisive elements are the metrically subordinated rhythm and its orchestration (regular alternation of strings and winds). The dramatic connotation is the servant's fear of becoming a victim of his master's ventures. Different phases of this are shown. In the opening scene he is merely afraid of getting involved in something yet unknown; in the first section of the sextet (Andante) he tries to escape, before it will be too late; in the second section (Molto allegro) he has been caught but still wonders if there is a way to save his skin. Comparison of

EXAMPLE 13

No. 1, 57-61 (Leporello)

Ma mi par, che venga gen-te. ma mi par, che venga gen-te;

str.   winds   str.   winds

No. 19, 13-16 (Leporello)

Più   che   cer-co,   men   ri - tro-vo   que - sta   por-ta

winds   str.   winds   str.

No. 19,157-161 and 202-206 (Leporello)

se mi sal-vo   in tal tem - pe -sta,   è pro - di - gio   in ve-ri - tà,

winds   str.   winds   str.

the three fragments reveals a gradual deterioration of situations. Nevertheless there is practically no change in Leporello's vocal idiom; only the alternating harmonies become more tense (respectively triads, dominant seventh and diminished seventh chords). This is characteristic of the servant's limitations in the expression of his emotions.[5]

(3) No. 1, b. 101–107; 109–125 (Donna Anna, Don Giovanni)

"As a desperate fury I shall persecute you"

"This desperate fury wants to ruin me"

No. 1, b. 177–181 (Don Giovanni)

"Ah, there he lies already, the miserable man; I see his soul part from his gasping, agonizing body."

EXAMPLE 14

While watching the dying Commendatore, Don Giovanni resumes the melody heard at the height of his dispute with Donna Anna. This musical phrase (including its rhythm) is so well profiled that the lack of other connective elements does not invalidate the relationship. Indeed everything else (key, tempo, harmony and orchestration) is different. These differences

---

[5] The pathetic diminished sevenths produced by Leporello right after having been caught (no. 19, b. 107–113: "viver lasciate mi per carità") are nothing but a clumsy imitation of upper-class language. They certainly do not belong to his own idiom.

are, of course, amply justified by the contrast between the two dramatic situations.

How should we interpret the reminiscence? While Hermann Abert considered the musical similarity as fortuitous, Chantavoine spoke of Don Giovanni's sadism ("trait essentiel de tout voluptueux blasé").[6] Both explanations are equally unconvincing. The melody is much too conspicuous to have been repeated merely by chance; some intention must be presumed. The idea of brutal sadism, however, is quite incompatible with the oppressive atmosphere of the F minor trio. Both master and servant are taken aback by what has happened. And besides, quite apart from the question of whether Don Giovanni is really a blasé voluptuary, nothing in the drama points to his being a sadist.

I believe the quotation to be unconscious on Don Giovanni's part, but certainly not on Mozart's. The resumption of the melody has a prophetic meaning. Fate will take its course. The libertine will be persecuted and meet his ruin. Here Mozart subtly gives us information about the issue of the drama.

(4) No. 1, b. 178; 180 (Don Giovanni)   "the miserable . . . agonizing"
     No. 1, b. 181–183; 186–188 (Don   "already from his gasping body"
     Giovanni)
     No. 9, b. 66–68 (Donna Anna,   "I begin to doubt"
     Don Ottavio)
     No. 10, b. 91–92 (Donna Anna)   "Remember the poor man's
                                               wound; do not forget the
                                               ground covered with blood."

The harmonic tension of the scale descending from the dominant ninth to the tonic is hardly felt as such in ex. 15a, because here the Db has rather the function of an ornamental note. But in the following bar (181) the minor ninth appears unprepared on a strong beat; the same holds for the fragments taken from the quartet and Donna Anna's aria, each of which has a key relationship to the trio for male voices (Bb and F). Between ex. 15b and 15d there is also a relationship in the orchestration (solo bassoon and violas); furthermore all four examples have the same bass rhythm (interrupted by rests).

[6] H. Abert, *W. A. Mozart*, vol. II, Leipzig 1921, p. 479, footnote 4; J. Chantavoine, *Mozart dans Mozart*, Paris 1948, pp. 75–76.

EXAMPLE 15

No. 1, 179 -181 (D.Giov.)

No. 1, 181-183 (D. Giov.)

No. 9, 66- 68 (D. Anna, D. Ott.)

No.10, 90-92 (D.Anna)

This melo-harmonic formula could be called an endogenous symbol,
namely that of blood (or a bleeding wound). Its intensity is 'regulated' by
the instrumentation. The bassoon underlines the most acute feeling
(ex. 15b and d). Leporello who sings a melody descending from the minor
ninth in steps of a third (No. 1, b. 186–188) is also accompanied by the
bassoon, but less conspicuously than Don Giovanni and Donna Anna. In
the quartet (ex. 15c), where the quotation is only implicit, the bassoon is
absent.

Throughout the death scene the Commendatore never touches the dominant ninth nor any other note discordant with the bass. It seems
therefore that this musical symbol pictures the bystanders' impression of
physical violence, rather than the physical suffering of the victim himself.

(5)   No. 2, b. 63–64 (Donna Anna)   "Flee, cruel man, flee"
      No. 13, b. 173–177; 182–186   "The affair requires courage"
      (Donna Elvira, Don Ottavio)   "Our friend is right"
      No. 19, b. 46–47 (Donna Anna)   "Leave this small comfort to my
                                          suffering"

EXAMPLE 16

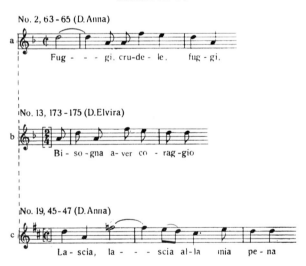

While the musical affinity between these initial melodies is obvious, the
dramatic connotation is far from clear. Abert interpreted the motif as the

EXAMPLE 17

symbol of Donna Anna's sufferings,[7] but this does not explain its use by Donna Elvira and Don Ottavio with a text pointing to the Don's exposure. The notion of vengeance, implied in ex. 16b, is supported indeed by the revenge aria of the Queen of the Night from the second act of *Die Zauberflöte;* this piece – equally in D minor – begins with exactly the same melodic intervals (A – D – A – F – E – D). In our opera, interpretation as a vengeance motif is, however, contradicted by Donna Anna's mood in the Sextet (ex. 16c), which is plaintive rather than vindictive. Since Mozart uses this triadic arpeggio also in instrumental works, it may have no specific meaning at all within the frame of the drama. Still, a twofold interpretation (suffering *and* vengeance) is not to be excluded.

(6) No. 2, b. 17–25 (Donna Anna)   "This blood ... this wound ... this countenance ... covered with the pallor of death"

    No. 10, b. 10–15 (Donna Anna)   "O God! O God! *He* is the murderer of my father."

From a dramatic point of view Donna Anna's first aria is a sequal to her duet with Don Ottavio. No wonder then that musically both pieces are also closely related. The duet as well as the aria is governed by appoggiatura motifs and syncopated rhythms. The two examples quoted above are taken from the preceding *recitativi accompagnati;* both show a sequence of ascending appoggiaturas alternating with orchestral motifs.

The words of the two fragments leave no doubt as to the dramatic significance of the relationship. It is the notion of violent death, this time not used in the way of an impersonal symbol but as an individual feeling of Donna Anna.

(7) No. 2, b. 221–222 (Donna Anna, Don Ottavio)

    No. 24, b. 600–602 (Commendatore, Don Giovanni, Leporello)

The affinity between the final chords of the vengeance duet and the damnation scene in the second finale is fairly obvious. Nowhere else in the score does a piece close with a similar rhythmic formula; furthermore the two fragments share the key of D minor.

The relationship touches upon the essence of the drama. While the duet's ending emphasizes the vow of vengeance, the last chord of the finale

---

[7] H. Abert, *op. cit.*, p. 528.

EXAMPLE 18

No. 2, 221-222

No. 24, 600-602

section seals the requital. The murderer does not perish by Don Ottavio's hand, however. He is punished by a supernatural power. Hence the Picardy third which has a traditional bearing on matters of heaven and eternity.

(8) No. 4, b. 115–120 (Leporello)	"the little one, the little one"
No. 13, b. 504–508 (Don Giovanni, Leporello, Don Ottavio)	(D.G.:) "Die, villain!"
	(Lep.:) "O, what are you doing?"
	(D.G.:) "I say, die!"
	(D.O.:) "Relinquish no hope!"
No. 13, b. 514–518 (Don Giovanni, Donna Elvira, Don Ottavio, Donna Anna, Zerlina, Masetto)	(D.G.:) "Donna Elvira!"
	(D.E.:) "Yes, rascal!"
	(D.G.:) "Don Ottavio!"
	(D.O.:) "Yes sir!"
	(D.G.:) "Donna Anna!"
	(D.A.:) "Traitor!"
	(All:) "Traitor!"

The musical relationship between these fragments taken from the 'catalogue' aria and the exposure scene of the first finale is primarily melo-harmonic. In both cases the bass descends by thirds covering in total a distance of one octave and a fourth. Some differences are to be noted. In contrast to Leporello's melody which is accompanied in unison, the finale

EXAMPLE 19

fragment is not only harmonized but also elaborated with secondary
dominant-tonic relationships underlining Don Giovanni's words (see b.
504–506; 514–516). Moreover the aria's rhythmic fluency (melodic as well
as harmonic) is replaced in the ensemble by dotted notes and accelerated
harmonic rhythm with a characteristic crescendo. These differences need
no comment; the dramatic situations speak for themselves.

By connecting one of the most striking passages of the 'catalogue' aria
with the exposure of Don Giovanni, Mozart establishes a link between the
'abstract' *picina* and an individual person: Zerlina. The dramatic connotation is the concept of betrayal. It is not only the seduced woman who

-na, la pi-ci-na, la pi-ci-na, la pi -   ci-na, la pi-ci-na, la pi-ci-na, la pi - ci - na

D. Ott.

Nol   spe - ra - te,   nol   spe - ra - te!

- te !

cresc.

is betrayed, but also society, towards which a *cavaliere* has his obligations
(cf. Don Ottavio's words in I, sc. 14: "How can I believe a gentleman to be
capable of such a grave crime?").[8]

[8] As for the subtle differences between the finale fragment (ex. 21b) and its repeat (b.
514–518; not reproduced here), the reader is referred to the score. It concerns a number of
details, all of which are explained by the reversal of the situation (D. G. who first played the
part of the accuser, now becomes the accused). Special notice should be taken of the reversal
of the alternating instrumentation (winds-strings) and the dynamics (*p–f*); besides, there is
a slight but very characteristic change in the secondary dominant chords: when D. G. is the
accuser, the supporting chords are in root position; as the accused his dominant seventh
chords are presented in first inversion.

(9) No. 5, b. 17–20 (Zerlina)   "Young girls, you who are in love, don't let time pass. If you feel desire in your heart, see here the remedy. What a pleasure it will be!"

No. 13, b. 287–289 (Don Giovanni, Leporello)   "Then continue with your follies, with your larks and dances."

EXAMPLE 20

No. 5, 17 - 20 (Zerlina)

Gio - vi - net - te che fa - te all'a - mo - re, che fa - te all'a - mo - re,

No. 13, 287 - 289 (D. Giov., Lep.)

Tor - ne - re - te a far pre - sto le   paz - ze.

The duet with chorus and the ballroom quartet from the first finale are closely related by a tarantella-like rhythm which in the first of these pieces pictures the sprightly and innocent atmosphere of the peasants. Innocent indeed: not a trace of obscenity is contained in the text which unequivocally alludes to the wedding-night.[9] The simple three-note motif that dominates the whole duet and chorus reappears in the first ballroom scene of the finale, now sung by Don Giovanni seconded by Leporello. It is a typical example of the Don's power of adaptation. By adopting a low class tone he tries to gain the peasants' confidence. There is no question of a deliberate quotation, however, since neither Don Giovanni nor Leporello were on stage when the duet with chorus was sung.

(10) No. 5, b. 37–39; 61–63; 79ff (chorus)   "la la la la la!"

No. 13, b. 317–319; 323–325 (Don Giovanni, Leporello)   D.G.: "You are pretty, precious Zerlina"

Lep.: "You are lovely, Gianotta, Sandrina"

---

[9] Cf. Masetto's text in the second strophe: "the rollicking fun doesn't last long but for me it hasn't yet begun."

EXAMPLE 21

Another instance of affinity between the same two peasant scenes may be noted. The phrases shown in example 21 include the three-note motif mentioned above; in the wedding chorus this motif started not only on the third (b. 17ff) and the tonic (b. 40ff), but also on the sixth (b. 28ff; 33ff; 52ff; 57ff; 71ff; 75ff).

Once more Don Giovanni (followed by Leporello) cleverly adopts the peasant idiom, but this time he moves farther. By flattering Zerlina he elicits from her a coquettish rejoinder and from Masetto a sarcastic comment. The sudden increase of tension in the ballroom atmosphere is expressed through an interruption of the bass' steady movement (a pedal point of no less than fourteen bars: 317–331). It should be noted that the other remarks made by Masetto in the course of the quartet are equally underlined by interruption of the tarantella rhythm in the orchestra; besides they are stressed by a change of instrumentation (winds instead of strings: b. 298–299; 304–305; 336–337; 342–343).

(11) No. 9, b. 40–44 (Donna Elvira)	"Within my soul I feel horror, dismay, wrath and rage, telling me innumerable things about this traitor that I am unable to understand."
No. 9, b. 64–66 (Donna Elvira)	"Liar, liar, liar!"
No. 9, b. 81–85 (Donna Elvira)	"Do not hope, I have lost my caution; do not hope, O villain; I shall disclose your guilt and my situation to everyone."
No. 24, b. 275–278 (Donna Elvira)	"Treacherous heart!"

No. 24, b. 322–332 (Donna
Elvira)

"Stay then, barbarian, in the
pool of iniquity, horrible paragon of sin!"

EXAMPLE 22

Twice in the course of the opera Donna Elvira addresses Don Giovanni
repeatedly in the crudest terms of hate and contempt: during the first act
quartet and during her interruption of the banquet in the second finale.
Each time she sings her imprecations on a single note with emphatic octave

leaps that express her emotion. These rhetoric passages are the musical counterpart of her melodic outbursts occurring throughout the score and consisting mostly of chordal arpeggios (no. 3, b. 92ff; no. 8, 34ff; no. 9, 44ff; no. 13, 258–259 and 266ff; no. 15, 46–48; no. 19, 184ff). From a dramatic point of view, however, these triadic arpeggios are not on a par with the tone repetitions. They bear on Elvira's emotional character in general and therefore have no mutual key relationship. On the other hand, the recitative-like passages, most of which form part of ensemble fragments, are dramatically related by their words (flying out at Don Giovanni). Besides they are all sung on the note of F, either as the tonic of that key or as the dominant of B♭. They do not occur in the so-called masked trio (no. 13, 251–272), although the key of this piece (B♭) offers opportunity for it. The reason is obvious: Don Giovanni is absent from the stage.

(12) No. 13, b. 52–54; 56–58; 70–72; 75–77 (Don Giovanni, four servants) "Come along, lively and gay! Come, cheer up, good friends!"

No. 13, b. 541–543; 547–549 (Leporello) "He is losing his head, he doesn't know what to do."

EXAMPLE 23

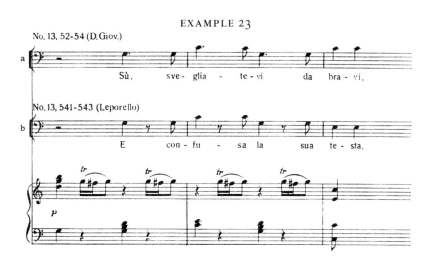

Of these two fragments of the first finale, one is taken from scene 17 (Don Giovanni and his servants encouraging the peasants), the other from scene 20 (the exposure). Both phrases and their orchestral accompaniment are similar to such an extent that in this case a single musical example may suffice. In scene 17 the melody is sung solo (ending with a double C) as well as in combination with an upper voice; in scene 20 this upper voice is given to Don Giovanni with a slightly altered text ("I am losing my head", etc.).

Since during the initial scenes of the finale Leporello is not on stage, the rather malicious quotation is not his but Mozart's. Part of Leporello's comment (and Giovanni's complaint) is covered by the heated words of the five other actors. The relative obscurity of the passage may account for the fact that I have been unable to find any mention of the close relationship between these two scenes in the literature on the opera.

(13) No. 15, b. 35ff (Don Giovanni)   "Descend, o my precious jewel; come and you'll see that you are the one my heart adores. You will find me repentant."

No. 16, b. 4ff (Don Giovanni)   "O come to the window, my treasure, to allay my pain."

EXAMPLE 24

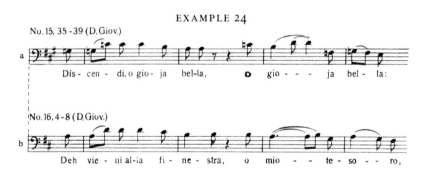

The well-known relationship between the seduction theme of the balcony trio and the mandolin canzonetta has given rise to varied comments. Abert believed that in the first piece Don Giovanni does not address himself to Donna Elvira, but to the female in general. Therefore the return of the melody in the canzonetta (with a dance-like rhythm and accompanied by a plucked instrument) sounds like selfmockery.[10] Chantavoine's comment, although rather vague, once more seems to point to the Don's supposed sadism.[11] The most astonishing explanation, however, stems from

[10] H. Abert, op. cit., p. 520.
[11] J. Chantavoine, op. cit., p. 94–95.

an anonymous article that appeared in a German periodical in 1857.[12] There it is argued that as early as the balcony scene Don Giovanni is already courting Elvira's maid. Only the words, not the music are addressed to the lady. Two years later Otto Jahn clearly demonstrated that this interpretation would imply a dramatic inefficiency of which Mozart was certainly incapable.[13] Nevertheless it was subsequently adopted by several other authors, including Arthur Schurig.[14]

One must wonder if the supporters of such a far-fetched theory ever studied the score. Even a superficial look at the C major fragment and the serenade theme suffices to note essential differences characteristic of the social distance between Donna Elvira and her maid. The first melody shows several 'irregularities', such as the contraction on "bella" in bar 37, the ecstatically syncopated contour on "o gioja", and the fivefold repetition of the notes C–B in bars 39–43, which has a particularly 'urging' effect. Every detail in this phrase speaks of Don Giovanni's efforts to pacify Donna Elvira's mood and to revive her love. In contrast to this, the canzonetta is a rather conventional piece giving the impression of something 'known' and therefore well suited to captivate a female servant. Since in Mozart's time serenades were the order of the day, she is of course familiar with that type of music, although she has probably never been the object herself of this form of courtship. Thus in spite of its simplicity the canzonetta would certainly be as effective as the seductive melody addressed to Donna Elvira, were it not that Don Giovanni is interrupted by Masetto and his friends.

In opposition to the above mentioned explanations, I would suggest that by cynically addressing both an upper and a lower class female with the aid of variants of a single melody Don Giovanni once more brilliantly displays his power. This *tour de force* confirms his mastership in handling people and situations.

(14) No. 19, b. 184–192 (Donna Anna, Zerlina, Donna Elvira, Don Ottavio, Masetto)	"A thousand turbid thoughts run through my head."
No. 20, b. 1–6 (Leporello)	"Ah, mercy, my lords, have mercy!"

---

[12] *Fliegende Blätter für Musik*, vol. III (1857), p. 11ff. The author was probably Johann Christian Lobe.

[13] O. Jahn, *W. A. Mozart*, Leipzig 1859, p. 408–409 (footnote 109).

[14] A. Schurig, *Wolfgang Amadeus Mozart*, vol. II, Leipzig 1913, p. 147.

No. 22, b. 34–44 (Leporello)   "Sir, my master ..., mark you,
                                      not I, ... wants to dine with
                                      you."

EXAMPLE 25

While the reprise in Leporello's aria of a theme from the sextet is mentioned in several Mozart studies, its appearance in the cemetary scene has been overlooked. The melody's essential features are the initial syncope, the range of the descending scale (a sixth or a seventh), the instrumentation (flutes, bassoons), and the tempo (allegro or even faster). The dramatic connotation is the concept of fear, but in this case again the differences are more revealing than the similarities. In the sextet it is the terror exercised by the absent Don Giovanni, causing blind confusion and panic. Leporello's aria shows another kind of fear. He is physically threatened, but at least his situation is clear and he understands the nature of the danger.[15] In the cemetery scene Leporello is again frightened; this

[15] If it is true that 'Mozart originally conceived the sextet as the finale of the third act (see above, footnote 3), then Leporello's apology must have been composed after this idea was rejected. It is obvious that, in spite of the intervening *secco* (sc. 9), he wanted to establish a link between the sextet and the aria in order to promote the continuity.

time, however, he faces a power beyond his world. When, after two fail-
ures, he finally succeeds in inviting the statue on behalf of his master, the
flutes and bassoons express his mortal fear by suspensions causing sharp
dissonances (ex. 26).

EXAMPLE 26

The fact that the descending melody is not sung but played by the orchestra could point to its having a wider purport: not only Leporello but
man in general is frightened by the statue.

Thus a single musical phrase serves to depict three different situations.
In the sextet it is society that is terrorized through the power of an individual who threatens to disturb its order; in the aria it is a weak and
fundamentally conformistic individual who fears to be punished by society; finally in the cemetery scene, stage and public are completely be-
wildered by the appearance of the supernatural.

EXAMPLE 27

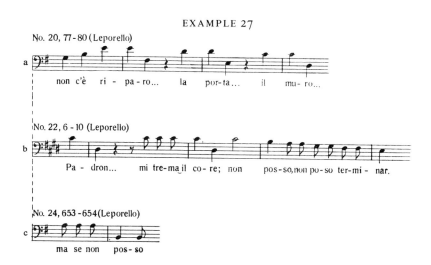

(15) No. 20, b. 77–80 (Leporello)	"There's no recourse ... the door ... the wall ..."
No. 22, b. 6–10 (Leporello)	"Master, ... my heart trembles; I cannot, I cannot finish."
No. 24, b. 653–654 (Leporello)	"But I cannot"

The downward leap of a seventh belongs to the stock of current *buffo* formulae. In the present context it is connected with the notion of fear (more specifically: with the inability to proceed) and therefore musically related to the previous item of our list (14). The juxtaposition of both motifs in ex. 27b is anything but fortuitous. Yet a slight but essential distinction between the descending scale and the leap should be observed. The latter being exclusively sung by Leporello lacks the varied application of the former; it shows us only the comic aspect of fear. The servant's bewilderment persists well into the final sextet; trembling in his shoes he feels himself unable to proceed with the account of the Don's fate.

*   *
*

A 'Leitmotiv'

When after the opening scenes Donna Elvira makes her entrance, she complains about being abandoned by Don Giovanni. The first strophe of her aria ends with the line "che mi mancò di fè", the three last words of which are set to the notes Eb – A – Bb, a conventional closing formula. From here on this motif will symbolize a fundamental element of the drama: the concept of betrayal. As a simple cadential turn, the motif is far too common to be connected with a specific dramatic idea; hence its use as a *tradimento* motif is subject to a number of restrictions. The first and most important of these is its limitation to the key of Bb. Secondly, although the interval of the minor fifth may be filled up, the intervening notes never will exceed the Eb. Thirdly, whether sung or played, the motif always appears at the end of a phraseological entity (this holds for the music as well as the text). And finally, the notes are invariably harmonized by the dominant and the tonic chords.

Nowhere in the score does the motif appear in the key of Bb without an unequivocal connotation of betrayal,[16] whereas the many instances of its occurrence in other keys only rarely reveal a (vague) connection with the

---

[16] As has been pointed out before, the concept of betrayal is not limited to the relation between individuals, but also refers to man in his relation to society.

idea of break of faith; the vast majority either refer to other elements or seem to have no specific dramatic meaning.

Twice in Elvira's first aria (no. 3) the motif occurs in its most elementary form, *viz.* with dotted rhythm and lacking any intervening or additional notes (ex. 28a). At the end of the *secco* preceding the quartet (I, sc. 12) we hear a slightly different version: Donna Elvira interrupts the conversation of Donna Anna and Don Giovanni, addressing the latter in the most fierce terms ("perfidious monster!"). A fermata on the first syllable emphasizes the exclamation, raising it above the level of a routine recitative ending (ex. 28b), and establishing a link with the following quartet (no. 9). This ensemble, the only one in the opera in which all four upper-class characters are alone on the stage, is dominated by the *tradimento* formula; in the course of the piece it occurs no less than eighteen times. The motif is exposed in the first phrase, sung by Donna Elvira: "Do not trust, O un-happy lady, this villainous heart. The monster has already betrayed me, he will betray you too." (ex. 28c) Both Donna Anna and Don Ottavio are impressed by Elvira's "noble aspect", but only in the former's part does the motif resound, prepared by a threefold repetition in the orchestra (b. 9–19). From the dramatic point of view this is perfectly logical: while Don Ottavio merely sympathizes with the unknown lady, Donna Anna's feel-ings are mixed with suspicion. When the motif is taken up by Don Giovanni himself (b. 25–28), it underlines his lie ("this poor girl is men-tally disturbed, dear friends; leave me alone with her, and perhaps she will calm down."), illustrating the very act of treason. Toward the end of the quartet, the key of Bb is reached again. Now Donna Anna doesn't need orchestral preparation anymore. Convinced as she is of Don Giovanni's guilt, she strikes up the motif on the word "(che mi) determinar", followed by violins; the motif also serves as a closing turn (flute and clarinet).[17]

We next encounter the formula in Don Giovanni's aria "Fin ch'han dal vino" (no. 11). Its reference to 'betrayal' cannot be explicit in this instance, because the libertine does not recognize his behaviour as treacherous.[18] First we hear the three notes played by flute and violins at the end of a prolongued phrase (ex. 28d), illustrating the true meaning of the rather harmless words ("Meanwhile in another corner, I will court a few of

---

[17] The fact that Don Ottavio has the same words as Donna Anna ("This whispering, this changing of colour are clear indications that convince me") is one of the small inconsistencies in the libretto. (Don Ottavio will be only convinced in act II, sc. 10, preceding his aria, no. 20). This is another instance where Mozart's music proves dramatically more trustworthy than Da Ponte's text.

[18] Cf. the first secco recitative of the second act (sc. 1).

EXAMPLE 28

No. 3, 21-22 (D. Elv.)

man-cò   di   fè?

Act I, sc. 12 (D. Elv.)

per- fi- do mo-stro?

No. 9, 8-9 (D. Elv.)

te   vuol tra-di- re an - cor

No. 11, 68-69 (D. Giov.)

No. 11, 93 - 97 (D. Giov.)

[me-]nar. —————————— Ah

No. 13, 264 - 266 (D. Elv.)

il   mio, il   mio tra- di - to a-mor

Ah non la-sciar- mi!

No. 21, 71- 74 (D. Ottavio)

Di - te - le, che i suoi tor- ti   a ven-di - car   io   va-do,

No. 24, 209 - 212 (D. Elv.)

Più non ram - men- to   gl'in-gan - ni   tuo - i,

No. 24, 314-322 (D. Elv., D. Giov., Lep.)

them"). The whole phrase is in B♭ minor and harmonically supported by a dominant pedal point, provoking sharp dissonances on the twofold repetition of the words "vo'amoreggiar". This too stresses the implied collision with social order. When the aria reaches its climax (b. 86–97), Don Giovanni himself takes up the motif, which is elaborated with a written-out fermata on E♭, an ornamental G and a trill on the leading tone (ex. 28e). The text is more forthrightly shocking than in the previous instance ("If you find some girls on the square, try to take these along with you too."), especially in connection with the following reference of the famous catalogue ("Ah, to-morrow you will add ten names to my list"). Don Giovanni uses the motif here as an unequivocal challenge to society.

In the second masked trio (no. 13, b. 264–266), Donna Elvira applies the formula in a way which greatly contrasts with Don Giovanni's bravura. By the insertion of three notes the leap of the diminished fifth has become a descending scale; thus the motif has developed into a short phrase that barely betrays its original configuration (ex. 28f). Besides, Elvira's part is overshadowed by the much more conspicuous melody of Donna Anna, displaying her elegant language. The commander's daughter seems to have almost forgotten about revenge; not only the musical but also the textual difference between the parts is significant:

Donna Anna, Don Ottavio: "May the justice of heaven protect the zeal of my love."

Donna Elvira: "May the justice of heaven avenge the betrayal of my love."

The first half of the second act deals with matters offering no opportunity for the use of the motif. Although Donna Elvira is once more betrayed, she does not realize this until Leporello's unmasking in the sextet. Still, during her stroll with the pseudo-Don, she feels something to be wrong and at the end of the *secco* preceding the sextet (II, sc. 7) she expresses her unconscious suspicion by using the three notes for the exclamation "Do not abandon me!" (ex. 28g). In the sextet the motif fails to appear; it seems that everyone is much too confused to pronounce an explicit accusation. Only after Leporello's attempt at justification and his escape (no. 20), do the Don's opponents realize the enormity of his deceit, and it is actually Don Ottavio – now at last convinced – who twice uses the motif for the text "Tell her that I am going to revenge his outrages" (no. 21, b. 71–74; see ex. 28h). It is typical of Don Ottavio's inertia that this musical phrase does not occur until the last section of the aria; besides, his words do not refer to the deceived Donna Elvira (in whom he does not take the slightest interest), but to Donna Anna, his legal betrothed. For Don Ottavio it is quite inconceivable to show any emotion that is not entirely subordinated to social convention.

Lastly the motif plays an important part in Elvira's interruption of the banquet (no. 24, b. 200–348). First (b. 209–212; 229–230; see ex. 28i), the music ironically contradicts the words ("No longer I'll remember your deceits" and "For its faith this oppressed heart requests some reward from you") but after Don Giovanni's cynical reply, text and melody are in agreement again. Donna Elvira's curse surpasses all her former emotional outbursts: "Stay then, barbarian, in the pool of iniquity" (b. 314–320). However, the most striking part in this scene is Leporello's. By imitating Elvira's melody (which includes the three-note motif), he finally abandons his usual ambivalent attitude: "If her sorrow doesn't touch him, he must have a heart of stone" (ex. 28j). The servant has chosen the side of Don Giovanni's opponents.

Apart from the discussed examples two additional instances may be noted; these are however rather doubtful as to their dramatic significance. At the end of the *secco* following the *Introduzione* Leporello submits to the will of his master with the following melody (ex. 29).

Not only the inversion of the most characteristic interval (the diminished fifth), but also the non-harmonic function of the B♭ deprive the mo-

EXAMPLE 29

Act I, sc. 2 (Lep.)

Si-gnor, non par - lo più.

tif of its dramatic purpose. Besides, the text does not refer to betrayal. More interesting is the use of the three-note formula in Don Giovanni's little monologue after the first-act quartet (I, sc. 12):

EXAMPLE 30

Act I, sc. 12 (D.Giov.)

a - mi- ci, ad- di- o.

Although the underlying chords are the same as in example 29, the B♭ falling on the relatively strong beat is not harmonized. The word "amici" could be interpreted as evidence of implied betrayal. On the other hand this explanation is questionable from the viewpoint of Don Giovanni's philosophy. The dons and donnas (as well as the Zerlinas and Masettos) are his tools, not his enemies. Why should he not be sincere in calling them friends? At any rate a dramatic interpretation of this recitative ending is far from self-evident.

The *accompagnato* preceding Donna Elvira's 'Viennese' aria (K. 504c) ends with a cadential turn that closely resembles the final bar of the recitative leading to the E♭ sextet (see ex. 28g):

EXAMPLE 31

Act II, sc. 10d (D.Elv.)

e que- ste am-ba-scie?

Both scenes are also dramatically similar, as they show us Elvira in an unsteady mood (an appoggiatura on the first B♭ is quite appropriate here). It is possible that during the composition of the Viennese recitative Mozart still had the motif in mind; this, however, should in no way justify the usual insertion of this scene in a performance based on the original Prague score.

If we look back on the different applications of the *tradimento* motif, its dramatic function can be easily determined as that of an endogenous symbol. The formula is neutral in itself and is used by various persons. To speak of a 'Leitmotiv' is merely a matter of convention. Naturally it has nothing to do with the Wagnerian meaning of this term. The fact that dramatic use of the motif is restricted to a single key already constitutes an essential difference. Besides, unlike Wagner, Mozart does not use the device as part of a preconceived structural system. Still, it is interesting to note that the practice of linking dramatically related situations by a certain melodic motif preceded Wagner not only in *opéra-comique* (as has been recognized for some time in the works of Grétry and others), but also in *opera buffa*.

*   *
*

Conclusion

The libretto of *Don Giovanni* shows many traces of having been written – or rather compiled – in a great hurry. Though often exquisite in detail, it lacks the unity of *Le nozze di Figaro* and *Così fan tutte*. Even Mozart could not entirely remedy the incoherence; nevertheless he succeeded in compensating to a high degree for Da Ponte's shortcomings. Examination of the musical affinities found in the score give us an idea of his approach to the plot and his dramatic technique. Out of the turbulent sequence of events he appears to have chosen a number of basic elements such as the concepts of 'violence', 'fear' and 'betrayal', which he subsequently translated in his own sonorous language. Although neutral in themselves, these motifs gradually adopt a dramatic dimension in the course of the opera. Some of them express an idea and are therefore impersonal, while others are related to special persons, reinforcing the viability of their characters. All serve to intensify the dramatic action. Never is a motif repeated automatically in order to connect two scenes; small differences are always dramatically determined.

Moreover, the basic idea itself may be treated in a complex way. Thus the concept of 'betrayal' elaborated by the B♭ 'Leitmotiv' has various moral aspects. Donna Elvira feels betrayal primarily as violation of a *human* value, she is individually hurt and reacts by personal accusations. With the exception of Leporello who during the interruption of the banquet chooses her side, no one else shares this conception.[19] For Donna Anna and Don Ottavio 'betrayal' has the exclusive meaning of conscious disturbance of social convention. Neither of them shows the slightest interest in the real nature of Elvira's sufferings, because they are unable to recognize moral standards detached from social order. This is also the case with Don Giovanni, but in addition he denies the existence of 'social' betrayal, which in spite of being based on convention rather than on ethics is still a moral concept. As a character the Don is not immoral but amoral. Nowhere in the drama does he show the slightest awareness of any ethical values. Hence his use of the 'betrayal' motif has only an implicit meaning. In the quartet (no. 9, b. 19–28) he infringes on Elvira's human standards, in his aria (no. 11, b. 69–70 and 93–97) on the social order (disrespect for the ancient right of hospitality). The latter infraction is also referred to in the quotation from the *picina* fragment in the first finale (see ex. 19); Donna Anna and Don Ottavio do not protest against the assault of a person (Zerlina), but merely against the violation of a principle.

The question of whether the musical relationships discussed in this study stem from a *conscious* effort to promote the coherence and unity of the drama must be left unanswered. Some of the affinities interpret the dramatic situations so cleverly that one must consider Mozart to have been fully aware of what he was doing. Others that are extremely subtle and refined could very well have emanated from his unconscious engagement with the drama and its implications. It is this engagement which may explain his extreme concentration and care for the smallest details. During the greater part of 1787 Mozart must have virtually lived in the world of Don Giovanni.

1970

---

[19] Toward the end of the balcony trio (no. 15) Leporello already expresses his concern: "May God protect her against her credulity."

CHAPTER 4

'DON GIOVANNI': AN INTERPRETATION

Any attempt to interpret a drama should start from data supplied by its author. This may sound like a truism; still it seems that in the case of *Don Giovanni* the rule is often disregarded. Here are a few pronouncements made by distinguished scholars and critics during the last decade or so:

> "*Dramma giocoso*, this disputed concept, is it not explained by the very reasoning of the Enlightment? An 'amusing drama' is presented here, no more and no less! The word *giocoso* does not mean only 'gay' and 'joyful', but includes the quality of pleasant edification. How close these amusing dramas could come to the border of tragedy is shown by Molière's *Misanthrope* and Lessing's *Minna von Barnhelm*." (Christof Bitter.)[1]
>
> "The fable of the punished libertine is a tragedy whose hero is dragged down to hell by a marble statue. Yet Da Ponte and Mozart described their work as a *dramma giocoso*. The tragic hero never appears without the comic Leporello hovering somewhere near like a shadow. Two other figures, the rustic couple Masetto and Zerlina, are buffoons. The intensely dramatic close of the action proper is followed by a moralizing final sextet in gay *opera buffa* style." (Hans Stuckenschmidt.)[2]
>
> "*Don Giovanni* is not an *opera buffa* but a *dramma giocoso*, a tragi-comedy." (Donald J. Grout.)[3]

Apparently Bitter considers the words *dramma* and *giocoso* contradictory. In order to remedy this discrepancy he projects the notion of edification onto the adjective *giocoso*, an interpretation which I have been

---

[1] Chr. Bitter, *Wandlungen in den Inszenierungsformen des "Don Giovanni" von 1787 bis 1928*, Ratisbon 1961, p. 39. The original text reads: "Dramma giocoso", dieser umstrittene Begriff, klärt er sich nicht aus dem aufklärerischen Denken von selbst? Ein "ergötzliches Drama" wird hier vorgestellt, nicht mehr und auch nicht weniger. "Giocoso" ist nicht nur "heiter", "fröhlich", sondern schliesst den Charakter des auf angenehme Art Erbaulichen mit ein. Wie nah an den Rand der Tragödie solche "ergötzliche Dramen" gehen können, dafür sind Molières "Misantrop" und Lessings "Minna von Barnhelm" beste Beispiele."

[2] The passage is quoted from a booklet accompanying the DGG recording (LMP 18267–69) of *Die Zauberflöte*, conducted by Ferenc Fricsay (1964).

[3] D. J. Grout, *A History of Western Music*, New York 1960, p. 468.

unable to find in any Italian dictionary. Actually the 'educational' aspect of Enlightment is a typical concept of Northern and Western Europe, and therefore not applicable to an Italian operatic libretto. Moreover, the references to *Le Misanthrope* and *Minna von Barnhelm* are irrelevant. The former is a *comédie*, the latter a *Lustspiel;* neither of these typological indications is synonymous with *dramma giocoso.*

Stuckenschmidt's remark about Don Giovanni never appearing without his shadow Leporello is at variance with the facts (cf. Act. I, sc. 9–12 and 17–18, Act. II, sc. 3–5), and his characterization of Masetto and Zerlina as buffoons seems rather inept. His main error, however, lies elsewhere. Starting from the (questionable) basis that the legend of Don Juan is a fable and besides a tragedy, he assumes too easily that Mozart's Don is a tragic hero and that the mere inclusion in the cast of three low-class characters accounts for the adjective *giocoso.* Finally, he asserts that the *dramma* closes with the damnation scene, and that what follows is but an additional bit of *giocosità.*

Grout's erroneous statement has at least the advantage of being simple and clear: the concepts of *opera buffa* and *dramma giocoso* are mutually exclusive and the latter term has to be translated as 'tragi-comedy'.

All three authors seem to have unconsciously manipulated facts in order to suit their preconceived interpretations. These facts and some others that have been generally overlooked or ignored should be stated here once and for all. If they do not give us a direct clue to a plausible interpretation of the opera, at least they will help to avoid basic errors.

First, Mozart never used the term *dramma giocoso.* His autograph manuscript has no subtitle, but on October 28th, 1787 he wrote in his own thematic catalogue: "Il dissoluto punito o, il Don Giovanni; *opera buffa.*" It is therefore wrong to speak of "Mozart's *dramma giocoso*" (Bitter)[4] or to suggest that Da Ponte *and* Mozart described their work in these terms (Stuckenschmidt).[5] The subtitle *dramma giocoso* occurs only in Da Ponte's libretto.

Secondly, the importance of both terms, irrespective of their exact meaning, has often been overestimated. Mozart had very little choice. He could not possibly have called his work an *opera seria.* The contemporary action, the inclusion of low-class characters and the abundance of comical scenes precluded such a denomination. On the other hand the cast of an *opera buffa* could very well contain a *serio* character like Don Ottavio; equally

[4] *Op. cit.*, p. 133, 135.
[5] *Loc. cit.*

common in this genre was the inclusion of gripping, pathetic scenes. Mozart cannot have hesitated, then, to call his work an *opera buffa*.[6]

Da Ponte had considerably more choice. An Italian librettist of the late eighteenth century could select from a great variety of typological indications: *dramma*, *dramma per musica*, *dramma serio*, *dramma tragico-comico* or *tragicomico*, *comedia per musica* (often used when the libretto was based on a play, a spoken comedy), *dramma comico*, *dramma giocoso*, *dramma buffo*, and several others. It is conspicuous that Da Ponte did not choose for *Don Giovanni* the subtitle *dramma tragico-comico*, as he did for *Axur* (Salieri). This denomination was by no means exceptional in connection with the subject of the legendary libertine, as is shown by the anonymous libretto of Vincenzo Righini's opera *Il convitato di pietra ossia Il dissoluto*, *dramma tragicomico* (first performed at Prague 1776).[7] The same holds for the neutral term *dramma per musica*, the subtitle of Bertati's libretto for Gazzaniga's one-act opera *Il Don Giovanni, ossia Il convitato di pietra*, which served as a model for Da Ponte's text. Therefore there can be no doubt that the explanatory title *dramma giocoso* was a deliberate choice on the part of Mozart's librettist.

Finally, it should be pointed out that there is nothing ambivalent, paradoxical or mysterious about the term *dramma giocoso*. Unlike the French word *drame*, the Italian noun *dramma* has a neutral meaning. It does not imply the slightest connotation of tragedy or any other special type of play. *Dramma* means "action on the stage, developed through words" and the adjective *giocoso* merely adds that this action is gay, joyful, amusing.

For those who distrust definitions found in dictionaries the following selection of librettos should offer conclusive evidence. All of them, including the indisputably comical *Così fan tutte* and *Il barbiere di Siviglia*, were called *dramma giocoso* by their authors (see the opposite page).

To summarize: both the nouns *dramma* and *opera* indicate a dramatic action, respectively expressed through words and music. The adjectives *giocoso* and *buffa* tell us that this action is principally gay. In Mozart's day *dramma giocoso* as well as *opera buffa* permitted a very wide scope. Therefore these denominations do not in themselves lead to an interpretation of *Don Giovanni*. All we can be sure of is that the work is neither a tragedy nor a semi-tragedy.

[6] Theoretically he could have used the term *opera semiseria;* however, this typological indication is rarely met with in Mozart's time.

[7] The preserved libretto was printed for the Viennese performances of 1777. The title belies Bitter's remark that before Da Ponte only Goldoni (1760) called his hero a *dissoluto* (Bitter, *op. cit.*, p. 38).

Title	Librettist	Composer	First performance
La cantarina	Goldoni	Galuppi	1756
Le contadine bizzarre	Pietrosellini	Sacchini	1766
L'amore soldato	Tassi	Sacchini	1777
I filosofi immaginari	Bertati	Paisiello	1777
I finti nobili	Palomba	Cimarosa	1780
Il barbiere di Siviglia	Pietrosellini	Paisiello	1782
Fra i due litiganti il terzo gode	Goldoni	Sarti	1782
Il ricco d'un giorno	Da Ponte	Salieri	1784
Una cosa rara	Da Ponte	Martin y Soler	1786
Così fan tutte	Da Ponte	Mozart	1790
Il matrimonio segreto	Bertati	Cimarosa	1792
Il mondo all' rovescia	Mazzolà	Salieri	1795

So we start with a clean slate. Or do we? Every attempt to lay bare the dramatic essence of this opera is hampered by the burden of nearly two centuries of misinterpretations. Even Mozart himself contributed to this. His usual lack of interest in a new performance of his own work resulted in a too-farcical staging at the Viennese Court Opera (1788), where, moreover, the parts of Donna Elvira and Don Ottavio were considerably weakened. It is curious to note that this dramatic enfeeblement was caused not by omissions, but by additions, i.e. the scenes 10a–10c of the second act, including the *buffo* duet of Zerlina and Leporello, and the beautiful but dramatically colourless aria written for Catarina Cavalieri, who acted Donna Elvira in Vienna. Don Ottavio's "Dalla sua pace" may also be considered an addition, since this lyrical aria did not really replace the discarded "Il mio tesoro", but was interpolated between the first-act arias of Donna Anna and Don Giovanni, causing a serious break in the dramatic élan. As for the omission of the *scena ultima*, this question is still being disputed. While Bitter is convinced of its inclusion in the Vienna performance of 1788, the editors of the latest Complete Edition have some doubts.[8]

The subsequent stage history of *Don Giovanni*, until about 1930, has been investigated and admirably described by Christof Bitter. The titles of his chapters dealing with the first hundred years are most revealing: *Don Juan – eyn Singspiel* [1789–1800]; *Don Juan – eine romantische Oper* [1800–1850];

---

[8] Cf. Bitter, *op. cit.*, pp. 57–64; W. Platt and W. Rehm, Introduction to vol. II/5/17 of the *Neue Ausgabe sämtlicher Werke* [*von W. A. Mozart*], Kassel, etc. 1968, pp. xii–xiv.

Don Juan – ein musikalisches Drama. The author deals with staging in Germany and Austria only. While descriptions of performance practice in other countries would probably have complicated his historical survey, there is no reason to believe that such an extension would bring fundamental changes into the general picture.

A few particularities of this German stage history may be noted. During the *Singspiel* period (before 1800), the opera was virtually transformed into a play in which arias and ensembles functioned as interpolations. The character of the performances was chiefly determined by the German adaptations of the text. Thus Don Juan becomes either a sentimental sensualist (Mainz, Frankfurt, 1789) or an ordinary criminal (Hamburg, 1789), but in both cases the whole is sauced with unshaded bourgeois moralization, depriving the final sextet – still maintained – of its irony. This play-like staging persisted well into the first half of the nineteenth century, but the part of the felonious Don Giovanni became more sharply profiled by its opposition to a 'pure' Donna Anna.

The impulse of this romantic development did not come from a stage director or conductor, but from the writer E. T. A. Hoffmann. In his novella *Don Juan*, this author inflated the role of the Commander's daughter into that of a tragic heroine who, bewitched by "the fire of a superhuman sensuality," is seduced and therefore fated to die. (She asks Ottavio to postpone their wedding, in the consciousness that she will not survive the year's delay.) Don Giovanni also becomes a tragic hero. Basically he is as 'ideal' as Donna Anna, that is, far too exceptional for this trivial world. Hence his eternal *Sehnsucht* that no woman can ever fulfill, with the exception of Donna Anna. But it is precisely this woman to whom he gives the consciousness of sin. Therefore she is forced to hate him and the result for both of them is tragic. Hoffmann's interpretation has a strongly sexual accent, but understandably during his time and long afterward, no one could afford to admit this. It should be noted that Hoffmann explicitly stated that his interpretation was based on Mozart's music. This music, he said, is entirely alien to Da Ponte's unpoetic text. On its own, Hoffmann's description could easily furnish material for a convincing tragedy. However, if we take him seriously, with regard to his pretention to interpret an existing opera, then it is difficult to consider his arguments as anything but nonsense. The writer himself must have felt this; hence his rejection of Da Ponte's text from which he nevertheless frequently quotes. Besides, Hoffmann could always say: I have written a fiction, not a scholarly treatise; this of course leaves us without rebuttal.

As we move from the Romantic and Biedermeier era into the Victorian age, the painful, indecent position of Donna Anna is increasingly felt. What really happened to her shortly before she first appeared upon the stage? True, in the middle of the first act she does recount in great detail what had happened in her bedroom, but with the exception of Don Ottavio, no one in the theatre believes a word of this highly improbable story. And the Victorian spectator will think: if this Donna Anna was really seduced by Don Giovanni, then this drama is morally unfit for viewing by us, let alone by our wives and daughters.

Happily there is Richard Wagner to solve the Victorian's dilemma. Did this astonishing dramatist not accomplish the presentation of an incestuous relationship to the most prudish society of Western history? Compared to the behaviour of Siegmund and Sieglinde, the misstep of Donna Anna is but child's play. The magic word which solves the moral problem of the audience is Idea. The antithesis Donna Anna – Don Giovanni remains, but instead of two people of flesh and blood who shock our inborn or acquired sense of virtue, now we are served with two mutually opposing ideas. Don Giovanni incorporates the bodily, Donna Anna the spiritual world. The opera has become a drama of ideas, whose protagonists have taken on mythological dimensions. In the universe of the Idea much more is permitted than in the everyday world. Because of this, the opera does not merely maintain itself during the Victorian period, but even reaches new heights of popularity.

The reaction set in toward the end of the nineteenth century, but the way leading back to a 'human' Don Giovanni proved to be a difficult one. Persistent operatic traditions impeded the reformative attempts. Still, the Munich performance of 1896, directed by Ernst von Possart and conducted by Hermann Levi, restored Mozart's score to its original form, stripping it of all additions and alterations. Possart presented the opera as a rococo *Lustspiel;* the work once again became a 'play' staged in a rather naturalistic manner.

The first quarter of the new century saw a great variety of performances, such as Alfred Roller's and Gustav Mahler's (Vienna 1905), which taking a step back towards a Hoffmann-like view could be called a neo-romantic interpretation; Ernst Lert's (1917–18), which showed Don Giovanni as a demoniac sensualist; and Franz Ludwig Hörth's (Berlin 1923), which presented the work as an intoxicating sequence of exuberant scenes and the Don himself as a paradoxical demoniac-gay character. As a reaction to the latter interpretation the opera was performed by Otto Klemperer in an icy-cold, neo-classical staging (Berlin 1928).

Not only operatic stage-tradition and contemporary movements in the arts and literature (like naturalism, expressionism, neo-romantic and neo-classical styles) have hampered the work's restoration, but also the many other Don Juans that were created during the nineteenth and early twentieth centuries by poets, playwrights and composers, among them Byron, Grabbe, Lenau, Pushkin, Baudelaire, Tolstoy, R. Strauss and Shaw. Although these Dons have little to do with the hero of Da Ponte and Mozart, they have undoubtedly exercised an influence on the opera's stage-history and on the image of Mozart as an operatic composer. The same holds true for great philosophers like Goethe and Kierkegaard. A typical example is found in Ernst Bücken's *Musik des Rokoko und der Klassik*, which some thirty years ago was considered an authoritative textbook of eighteenth-century music.[9] Referring to Goethe's well-known words in connection with *Don Giovanni* ("Mozart should have set *Faust* to music" and this music "should have been in the manner of Don Juan, where on surface events go on merrily, while in the depths gravity rules"), the author attacks Edward Dent who had called the work an unequivocal *opera buffa*: "In spite of Goethe's pronouncement, which should crush a thousand contrary opinions, to this day the voices of those who consider the work a real *opera buffa* have not been silenced."[10] This belligerent rebuke is followed by a Pan-Germanic argument on the superiority of the Teutonic sense of the comical as compared with the Latin. Bücken wrote this, of course, at a time when German scholarship was subordinated to political ideology and therefore the dissolute Jew Da Ponte had to be clearly separated from the pure, divine, and of course thoroughly Germanic Mozart. Today no one automatically stands at attention when Goethe's name is mentioned, but the fact that his statement dates from thirty-six years after the Prague premiere, i.e. when *Don Giovanni* was already being performed as a romantic work, is still generally overlooked.

For nearly two centuries, then, the true image of the opera *Don Giovanni* has been obscured or even falsified by interpretations based on views that have no relation whatsoever to the work conceived by Da Ponte and Mozart in 1787. One wonders whether the history of Western music offers any other examples of operas that have been mistreated to the same extent. Excellent editions based on the autograph score are easily available; nevertheless,

---

[9] E. Bücken, *Musik des Rokoko und der Klassik* (Handbuch der Musikwissenschaft), Potsdam 1935, pp. 214–216.

[10] "Trotz des Ausspruchs Goethes, der tausend Gegenansichten niederzuschlagen fähig sein sollte, sind die Stimmen, die in dem Werke eine echte opera buffa sehen, bis heute nicht verstummt." If read without prejudice, Goethe's words are not at all contradictory to the concept of *opera buffa* in Mozart's time.

indisputable facts and even Da Ponte's simple but very efficient stage directions are disregarded again and again. Not only local but also international festival performances suffer from this treatment. Obviously the opera has become an object solely for the private pleasure of stage directors and conductors.

*   *
    *

The present interpretation of the opera *Don Giovanni* as drama is based on a study of historical data and on a close reading of the full score. Musicological aspects, particularly with regard to structure, have been discussed elsewhere.[11] In this chapter, the stress lies on the characters, their interrelations, and their respective attitudes toward society. Needless to say, anachronisms stemming from nineteenth- and early twentieth-century interpretations have been totally discarded.

The first question to be raised is the meaning for Mozart's contemporaries of the traditional Don Juan legend. For them the story was a sort of folk tale that was consequently sneered at by enlightened people of the middle and upper classes. If within the framework of comedy a theme like *Le nozze di Figaro* could be called highbrow, then *Don Giovanni* was certainly lowbrow. In Vienna the story of the libertine who is drawn to hell by a statue was frequently performed as a farcical puppet show. In these performances the moral aspect was of course emphasized and evil always met its just punishment.

Was it because of its popularity that Mozart chose the subject? I cannot possibly believe this. Although he was certainly not an irreligious or even a sceptical person, it is difficult to imagine Mozart as the composer of a drama which opposes Good to Evil and takes its essential meaning from a divine judgment. The supernatural hocus-pocus is in flat contradiction to the spirit of Enlightment, of which he, as well as his librettist, are true representatives. Even a 'natural' version like Goldoni's play, in which Don Juan is destroyed by lightning rather than by a marble statue, could hardly have suited the composer's taste. Why, then, did he accept this libretto? Undoubtedly because he saw the subject as quite another kind of drama, the possibilities of which attracted him so strongly that he was willing to take the obligatory damnation scene as part of the bargain. It is even possible that he was attracted to this scene as a challenge for a musical tour de force. As we know, he brilliantly succeeded in overcoming the difficulties, but this does

[11] See Chapter 3.

not alter the fact that the damnation scene occupies a rather strange position
in the totality of the drama. Not until the final sextet do we return to the
familiar atmosphere, namely, that of a social drama in the form of a comedy.

This final sextet – during the nineteenth century nearly always omitted in
performances that stressed the assumed tragic character of the work – fur-
nishes a clear example of Mozart's personal treatment of the subject. The
situation is the following: At the opening of the scene the five adversaries of
Don Giovanni rush into the room to deliver him to justice. Leporello tells
them that they are too late and, still trembling with fear, relates what has
happened. This closes the action proper, but not the drama; what follows is
a strongly revealing characterization of the survivors. First we hear a duet
from Donna Anna and Don Ottavio, showing that neither has learned
anything from the experience. In the elegant, impersonal style of opera seria,
full of conventional melodic formulae, the two aristocratic characters express their mutually fictitious love. Zerlina and Masetto announce their decision to go home and treat themselves to a jolly good gorge. It would be
difficult to find anything more vulgar. Thereupon both of them, together
with Leporello, reveal their hypocrisy in a passage which produces a comical
as well as an unveiling effect through the use of mythological image and a
slightly archaic musical accompaniment.

> Resti dunque quel birbon
> Con Proserpina e Pluton!
>
> *Then let this rascal stay*
> *with Proserpine and Pluto!*

But hypocrisy climaxes in the following passage, in which according to
tradition all actors address themselves to the audience:

> E noi tutti, o buona gente,
> ripetiam allegrammente
> l'antichissima canzon:
> "Questo è il fin di chi fa mal,
> e di perfidi la morte
> alla vita è sempre ugual."
>
> *And, good folks,*
> *let us all joyfully*
> *take up the ancient song:*

This is the end
of the evil-doer.
The criminal always
dies as he lived.

Mozart expresses these words by a pretentious fugal exposition, which, however, does not debouch in a true fugue, but in a mere homophonic ensemble. In this way he pictures the hollow presumption of the established social order and the sanctimoniousness of virtue. Had the curtain fallen right after the destruction of Don Giovanni, the opera would have ended as a melodrama; now the work ends as a true comedy.

My thesis that the opera is a social drama may be clarified by comparison with another work of Mozart. In *Le nozze di Figaro*, we encounter a number of people who, though not always observing the rights and duties of their respective social classes, nevertheless submit to the conventions of society. Consequently they are often forced to act in secrecy because the established social order, which is basically accepted by all of them, has to be maintained.

In *Don Giovanni* the situation is essentially different. Here we find a man who challenges social order in its totality. The Don is a Prometheus-like figure; this, however, does not mean that the opera presents a myth. On the contrary, the work is a realistic drama in that it faithfully reflects the social conditions and tensions of the late eighteenth century. At that time, doubts regarding the fairness and justice of current social principles were as widespread as today. If in such a situation a man arises who is far superior to his fellowmen, and who in his behaviour flouts both written and unwritten laws of social order, then a struggle results between the individual and society, the outcome of which will depend on the strength of both parties. As we have seen, in Mozart's drama this outcome is ambiguous. Like every real comedy this one, too, ends with an implicit question mark. True, Don Giovanni is defeated and punished – not, however, by the power of the existing social order, but by a supernatural force. And the secular order does not come out so favourably that we could conclude that the Establishment has justified itself.

How does Mozart characterize his hero? Actually by a negative device. Every other actor possesses a very clear musical physiognomy; even if they would not appear on the stage, we could easily recognize them from the score. Don Giovanni, on the contrary, has no consistent delineation. Adaptability is his strongest weapon. In each scene he smoothly adjusts to the relevant situation and in this way manipulates persons of all classes quite effectively. With Zerlina he uses a melodic language different from the one with which he addresses Donna Elvira; Masetto and his friends are musically handled otherwise than Leporello. Don Giovanni's aim is gratification of power, to be achieved by destruction of the strongest obstacle he finds in his path: the laws of society. It should be stressed that Don Giovanni is no erotomaniac; nor is he the impotent character who, driven by a latent mother-fixation, unconsciously hates the female and strives for her destruction. These interesting Freudian explanations may fit other Dons, but not Mozart's. The fact that Don Giovanni directs his tactics of disturbance primarily at women is easily explained. Every man who tries to beat an adversary will logically attack the weakest link of his defense. The Don's adversary is not a single person but a total social system, and the weakest link of this system is undoubtedly the relation between the sexes. (Although this may not hold for every society in the world, it certainly applies to occidental Christian society.) Therefore it is on this particular point that Don Giovanni avails himself of the opportunity to effect a breach in the bulwark of social order. This does not imply that he is a sexomaniac, however. True, he feels physically attracted to women – so does about half the world's population – but his essential goal is power, or perhaps rather the consciousness of power. The proof of the Don's *indiscriminate* appetite for power is shown by his relation to the drama's male characters, Don Ottavio, Leporello, Masetto; these he dominates as effectively as the females. Actually Don Giovanni is an existentialist hero *avant la lettre*; he is a man who tries for total freedom to justify his existence, freedom that can only be realized by obtaining total power. In this respect there is undoubtedly a certain psychological affinity between Mozart's Don Giovanni and Camus' Caligula.

Thus the drama's fundamental theme is: Don Giovanni versus Society. The individual weaknesses and shortcomings of the characters who represent social order contribute considerably to the interest of this theme. Let us therefore take a close look at the Don's opponents.

First we have the aristocratic couple Donna Anna-Don Ottavio. In their behaviour both are completely conditioned by the conventions of their social stratum. Although decidedly temperamental, Donna Anna does not possess a strong personality. From a dramatic point of view her role is practically finished after the middle of the first act; for the rest she does nothing but complain about her father's death. Don Ottavio is the slave of social convention to such an extent that he moves on the stage as a character without any human dimension. Almost every word of his is predictable. Characteristically it is only towards the end of the drama that he becomes convinced of Don Giovanni's guilt. He simply cannot imagine a gentleman who rides roughshod over the rules of his social class. If there is *any* element of tragedy in this opera, it is embodied in the role of Don Ottavio. In him we see a man who, by being totally dependent on a social system, has practically dehumanized himself.

Zerlina and Masetto are also captives of the class to which they belong. Still, the situation of this rustic couple is essentially different, since their dependency on the social system is compulsory. This does not influence their human nature so much as their character. Masetto is not simply the type of the clever peasant, he is strongly intelligent. He sees through Don Giovanni even more clearly than Leporello. But in spite of his insight he is utterly powerless with the Don, who uses the privileges of his class to divest himself easily of this lowly adversary. "I'll bow my head and go away" sings Masetto in his first-act aria. He cannot do otherwise; but later in the drama we hear him mockingly imitating Don Giovanni's elegant melodic contours, which had impressed Zerlina so much.

It is a typical example of dramatic irony that this intelligent Masetto is no match for Zerlina. In spite of all efforts, especially undertaken in Germany, to idealize Zerlina as a paragon of rural innocence, she is nothing but a dull goose. True, by means of her innate coquetry she easily turns Masetto round her little finger, but nevertheless this Zerlina is decidedly dull. The way in which she allows herself to be caught by Don Giovanni does not precisely point to an intelligent mind. Besides, she is corrupt. Although she tries to retain a modicum of decency (she does not want to hurt Masetto), she actually sacrifices him to her material and social ambitions. And, when after Don Giovanni's exposure, she joins the others as a mouthpiece of respectable virtue, she strikes us as a particularly hypocritical creature. How far Zerlina's consciousness goes is uncertain. Within her own world she may perhaps be considered honest to a certain degree. But however ambiguous Zerlina's attitude may be, one thing is sure: her character is a product of social pseudo-morals.

By far the most interesting figure among Don Giovanni's adversaries is Donna Elvira. Superseded by the unjustly romanticized Donna Anna, she remained more or less in the background during the nineteenth century. Obviously our ancestors did not know what to do with this extravagant lady. Nevertheless it is Donna Elvira and not Donna Anna, who is Don Giovanni's principal antagonist. She is the only character in the cast who might understand him because, like him, she moves independently of the reigning social rules and conventions. There is little doubt that Donna Elvira (with or without the assistance of Don Giovanni) has escaped from a nunnery in Burgos. In Molière's *comédie* this is explicitly told, in Da Ponte's libretto only vaguely hinted. Like the man she loves, Donna Elvira may therefore consider herself a social outcast, although for motives quite different from those of the Don. Most characteristic is Donna Elvira's moral outlook as compared, for example, with Don Ottavio's. Both of them accuse Don Giovanni of treason, only they do not have the same meaning in mind. For Don Ottavio, treason has the exclusive meaning of breach of social rules; for Donna Elvira it means violation of human values. Elvira is the truly noble character in the drama. Like Ilia in *Idomeneo* and the Countess in *Le nozze di Figaro*, she belongs to those female roles in Mozart's operas, which develop in the course of the drama and only unfold toward the end. This process can be followed by comparing the three terzettos, three pillars on which, so to speak, her role is founded.

In each of these terzettos Donna Elvira sings together with Don Giovanni and Leporello. The first is not designated as such but as *aria*, obviously because it consists of Elvira's monologue, overheard and commented upon by Don Giovanni and his servant. Neither the two men nor the audience know anything about this new figure on the stage. She sings her complaint about the treason of her lover in the style of opera seria, and with her extravagant melodic leaps, sudden pauses and exaggerated accents she almost makes an impression of hysteria. Actually she is presented as a ridiculous person and this effect is reinforced by a detail that must have been better understood by Mozart's contemporaries than by present-day audiences. Donna Elvira makes her entrance in travelling-dress. Try to imagine what sort of impression this will make on the eighteenth-century operagoer, accustomed as he is to see the heroines of opera seria in luxuriant aristocratic attire. Here he beholds a lady trivially clad in travelling-dress, through which her outward appearance strongly contrasts with her style of singing.

I realize that the entrance of a 'ridiculous' Elvira is difficult for today's audience to accept. Most of us are acquainted with the rest of the plot and thus have a more or less preconceived image of her character in mind. Besides, unlike the eighteenth-century public, today we no longer have any feeling for the comical contrasts of opera seria and opera buffa, especially since the former genre has practically disappeared from the stage. Still, to ignore the comical character of this scene as many a stage-director does, is a falsification of Donna Elvira's part and therefore inexcusable.

The next ensemble of the three characters, the famous balcony terzetto (although Da Ponte mentions only a window), occurs shortly after the opening of Act II. In the meantime we have become better acquainted with Donna Elvira. She is no longer ridiculous. On the contrary, we know now that of all the actors, this woman is the only one who possesses great moral courage and a warm heart. Nevertheless we see her here again in a comical, or rather bitter-comical scene. It is different from the terzetto in the first act in that Donna Elvira is not ridiculous as a person anymore, but because of the situation in which she finds herself. The scene is in three parts. In the first section Elvira expresses her internal conflict: her hatred and love for Don Giovanni. Then, in the second section the Don addresses her and once more gives proof of his extraordinary adaptability. With an enchanting melody he shows his repentance as well as his love (both pretended, of course), and in this way he successfully regains his former status as a lover. We in the theatre know that Donna Elvira is listening to Don Giovanni's voice, but that the man she sees is no other than Leporello dressed in his master's cloak. This, of course, produces a comical effect. But at the same time the scene is particularly moving. Elvira's defeat is a matter of course. In the last section, her words still express doubt and hesitation, but Mozart's musical language convinces us that she has already forgiven the libertine. Here, Da Ponte transmits Donna Elvira's reason, Mozart the voice of her heart.

Finally the three characters meet in the finale in this situation: Don Giovanni, seated at a well-spread table, is served by Leporello while his domestic musicians are playing fragments from popular operas (including Mozart's own *Figaro*). Suddenly the excited Donna Elvira rushes into the room. She gives Don Giovanni the ultimate proof of her love by renouncing him if only he will reform and save his soul. But the Don treats her with cynical mockery, whereupon she rejoins with these words:

> Restati, barbaro
> nel lezzo immondo,
> esempio orribile
> d'iniquità!

> *Stay then, barbarian,*
> *in the pool of iniquity,*
> *horrible paragon*
> *of sin!*

This is certainly no elegant language. Donna Anna would never express herself in this way, even in moments of strongest emotion. But under the present circumstances, Donna Elvira is unable to observe the tone which she owes to her class. In hatred her feelings express themselves as sincerely as in love.

Apart from the Don himself, Elvira is undoubtedly the richest character of the cast and by far the most modern. Only *she* breaks through the barriers of the eighteenth century and takes on the dimensions of a true heroine. Paradoxically it was the utterly conventional Donna Anna who, under the impact of nineteenth-century taste, became the 'official' antagonist of Don Giovanni. Today, Donna Elvira is more or less restored to her proper position in the drama; still, she seems to remain an embarrassing person to many stage directors.

Finally a few words should be said about Leporello. In the course of time he has been rather constantly interpreted as belonging to the established social order. True, he generally functions as the shadow of Don Giovanni, but he clearly lacks his master's capacities and mentality. His first appearance on the stage, right after the overture, fully characterizes him: he would like to be a Don Giovanni, yet he is only a Leporello. He borrows the impertinence and cynicism from his master and mixes them with his own vulgarity. In reality, however, he dwells in a world which is essentially alien to him.

While agreeing with this interpretation, I would like to add a few remarks. Leporello is an ambivalent character who, as such, suits a comedy very well. Every true drama contains elements of ambivalence or ambiguity. In a tragedy these elements are often rationally elaborated, in a comedy they reveal themselves more implicitly. During the greater part of the opera we see Leporello hesitate between Don Giovanni's free universe and the closed frame of social order, but finally it becomes evident that he belongs to the Establishment. I believe, however, that in another respect Leporello does function as a link, namely, between stage and audience. We, too, would like to be Don Giovannis; still most of us are only Leporellos. Let no one feel offended by this remark. Fundamentally this Leporello is not a bad chap. A review of his words in the three terzetto-scenes may prove this. In the first terzetto he merely comments comically on Don Giovanni's intention to console the seemingly unknown lady. Leporello's attitude to Donna Elvira is clearly demonstrated in the next item, the famous 'catalogue' aria. Especially at the end of this piece Leporello shows himself in his most vulgar mood. During the greatest part of the balcony scene he holds his sides with laughter ("se seguitate io rido"), but toward the end one perceives some sympathy in his words for the first time:

> Deh proteggete, o Dei,
> la sua credulità.

May God protect her
against her credulity.

In the third terzetto, Leporello refuses to play his master's game any longer. The Don has gone too far and the servant's human feelings get the better of his loyalty. Moved by Elvira's words, he sings:

> Se non muove
> Nel suo dolore,
> Di sasso ha il core.

> *If her sorrow*
> *doesn't touch him,*
> *he has a heart*
> *of stone.*

Although Leporello's words are quite unequivocal, they could be taken as a gratuitous outburst of pity not really affecting his behaviour. But here again the music speaks more intensely than the text: at this very moment Leporello takes up Elvira's melodic motif. The servant has definitely dissociated himself from his master.

The path followed by Leporello is also the way of the audience. Since he is the only character with whom we can easily identify ourselves, we too, have gained an experience. The same cannot possibly be said of the two couples in the cast, Donna Anna-Don Ottavio and Zerlina-Masetto.

* *
*

The use of the indefinite article in the title of this paper is anything but fortuitous. *The* interpretation of a drama – or, for that matter, of any true work of art – does not exist. It should be pointed out, however, that the room left for interpretative freedom is much more restricted in music drama than in verbal drama. According to a widespread opinion, music is too vague a language to fit dramatic interpretation. I believe this to be incorrect. Music is certainly an irrational means of expression, but nevertheless it may communicate the gist of a dramatic action in a more exact and penetrating way than words are ever capable of. In opera, this 'communication' is embedded in the score as "transmitted enactment", which cannot be adapted to the time-bound views of later generations. To 'modernize' a music drama without damaging the original conception is virtually impossible. If today a faithful performance of *Don Giovanni* strikes us as 'modern', then this can only be explained by the affinity between the social and moral climate of the late eighteenth century and our own.

1970–'71

CHAPTER 5

'COSÌ FAN TUTTE':
DRAMATIC IRONY

Like *Don Giovanni*, Mozart's last opera buffa carried the burden of its own myth for a long time. Yet the stage history of *Così fan tutte* differs essentially from that of its predecessor. While audiences all over Europe were invariably fascinated by the theme of the legendary libertine, the subject matter of 'The School of Lovers' was simply rejected. In order to save the music, many nineteenth- and early twentieth-century performances presented the work with considerable modifications or even with entirely new plots that involved omission, displacement and arrangement of arias and ensembles. *Les peines d'amour perdues* (based on the plot of *Love's Labour's Lost*) by Barbier and Carré was perhaps the most extreme of these 'revisions', but Treitschke's *Zauberprobe* (which transformed the work into a 'magic opera') and Scheidemantel's *Dame Kobold* (after Calderon) were hardly less radical alterations of the original.[1] The reason for this kind of mistreatment was of course the supposed frivolity and immorality of the opera's subject, which in turn fostered the false tradition that the composer disliked the libretto and even his own music. To devotees of Mozart it was inconceivable that their idol could have accepted the theme of *Così fan tutte* except with extreme reluctance. Thus the work was rated considerably lower than *Figaro* and *Don Giovanni*, not only on moral grounds but also because of its alleged dramatic and musical weakness.[2] This was of course an *a posteriori* reasoning, a rationalized justification of the 'estrangement' felt by a nineteenth-century audience vainly trying to engage in the drama. The true

---

[1] Nineteenth- and early twentieth-century revisions of the opera are discussed in H. Abert, *W. A. Mozart*, vol. II, Leipzig 1921, pp. 641–644.

[2] That this myth seems ineradicable is shown by Alfred Orel's statement that Mozart wrote *Così fan tutte* merely "to keep the pot boiling" (a "*Brotarbeit*"). Ironically the argument misses its mark, since the composer hardly ever wrote any music except to make a living. Cf. A. Orel, *Mozarts Schicksalsweg zwischen den grossen Musiknationen*, Mozart Jahrbuch 1965/66, Salzburg 1967, p. 69.

reason for this alienation may have been that Mozart fell short of the audience's expectations. The composer's unusual handling of two essential dramatic elements, rhythm and colour, must have played an important role in this respect.

Those who expected Mozart and Da Ponte to equal or exceed the extremely fast sequence of events occurring in *Don Giovanni* were certainly disappointed. In *Così fan tutte* dramatic rhythm is considerably slower than in previous operas. The betting at the beginning of Act I takes three terzetti, and the farewell scene requires a quintet, a duet, a chorus, another quintet followed by a shortened repeat of the chorus, and a terzettino. The resultant general impression of slowness is strengthened by secondary factors: the restricted number of characters, their grouping in pairs, and the absence of any trace of subplot. Dramatic tempo is not steady throughout the work; in accordance with *buffo* tradition the action accelerates in the first finale, but this also holds for *Figaro* and *Don Giovanni*. The leisurely dramatic rhythm of *Così fan tutte* is reinforced by frequent interruptions of musical rhythm. The opera contains a total of 150 fermatas, compared with 45 in *Figaro* and 35 in *Don Giovanni*.

Another characteristic unusual for Mozart is the importance of the drama's visual aspect. While in the two previous works outdoor scenes are enacted in darkness or dusk, *Così fan tutte* offers the spectator bright daylight scenes in colourful surroundings. No other mature opera of Mozart makes use of 'nature' as much as this one. It is not the Rousseau-like concept of wild nature, but nature as modified by man: ornamental gardens with turf-seats, a barque adorned with flowers, actors entwined with garlands, vases filled with bouquets. Even the weather contributes to the 'controlled' ambiance ("il vento soave" and "l'onda tranquilla" in the first-act terzettino; the "aurette amiche" in the duet with chorus, no. 21 of Act II). There is no functional difference between outdoor and indoor decoration, nor between the dressing of the barque with flowers and the rich livery of the servants. For a Victorian audience who chanced to see the opera more or less in its original form, this splendid but fundamentally unromantic stage setting was easily associated with stereotyped notions of *ancien régime* frivolity. If frivolity and libertinage were censured and punished in *Figaro* and *Don Giovanni*, how could one accept *Così fan tutte*'s idealization of immoral behaviour?

Visual colour is matched by audible colour. The range of tonalities is much wider than in the earlier operas, extending from four sharps to four flats and leaving the work's central key (C major) exactly in the middle. No less than four pieces are in E major (the terzetti, nos. 2 and 10 in Act I,

Fiordiligi's Rondo, no. 25, and the finale section starting with scene 17 in Act II); on the 'flat' side we have Alfonso's first aria in F minor (no. 5), and a long section of the second finale in A♭ major ("Tutto, tutto, o vita mia", followed by the canon). In contrast to this, *Le nozze di Figaro* has only a short cavatina in F minor (IV, Barbarina), while in *Don Giovanni* the sole piece in a key with more than three sharps or flats is the cemetery scene in E major.

In some instances Mozart uses tonal colour for special dramatic purposes. The *secco* recitative at the beginning of scene 8 in Act II is a clear example of this. Ferrando's account of his failure to seduce Fiordiligi ("Amico, abbiamo vinto!") modulates constantly through sharp keys: A major, D major, G major, F♯ minor, B minor, etc. Although the tonalities occasionally touch C major or A minor, they never proceed beyond this limit. After 37 bars Ferrando asks Guglielmo about the latter's *tête à tête* with Dorabella, and immediately the music turns to flat keys: F major, B♭ major, E♭ major, F minor, G minor, etc. Thus in this recitative the positive outcome (for Guglielmo) is expressed by sharps, the negative (for Ferrando) by flats.

Occasionally the harmony also contributes to the opera's colour. Although the work's harmonic language is not more advanced than that of *Figaro* and *Don Giovanni*, still a few unusual chords and chord progressions are surprising: the chromatically ascending augmented triads in the first finale (b. 99ff; text: "d'un disperato affetto/mirate il tristo effetto"), and the astonishing 'Schubertian' chord E♭ – C♯ – G – A that occurs soon after in the same scene and pictures the simulated agony of the young men ("nè può la lingua o il labbro accenti articolar").

Finally, a special device of orchestration should be mentioned in connection with audible colour. The score includes a number of pieces and finale-sections in which the horns are replaced by trumpets, producing a quality of timbre not found in previous operas. I do not refer to those ensembles without horns where the trumpets are accompanied by timpani, such as the terzetto, no. 3, the soldiers' chorus, no. 8, the sextet, no. 13, the first section of Finale II, and the Allegro "Giusto ciel" of the *scena ultima*. In these fragments the trumpets function more or less as they do in the Maestoso-section of the first finale of *Don Giovanni* (containing the famous words: "Viva, viva la libertà"), that is, as trumpets and not as horns. In other more intimate and expressive pieces, however, the trumpets appear without percussion: Fiordiligi's B♭ aria (no. 14), the Andante-section of the first finale (no. 18, b. 429–484), Ferrando's "Ah lo veggio quell' anima bella" (no. 24), and the quartet (no. 22). Although sparingly used, they add a new colour to the orchestral palette by adopting the role of the missing horns. Since the trumpet, unlike the horn, cannot blend easily with the woodwinds, its presence adds spice to the orchestral sound. Moreover the absence of the horns in a number of pieces provides the composer with the opportunity to use them elsewhere in the score as *concertante* instruments (Fiordiligi's second aria, no. 25).

Although in several respects *Così fan tutte* differs essentially from the two earlier comic operas, there are also strong resemblances, especially in the matter of musical and dramatic coherence. Since the question of coherence has been amply discussed in a previous chapter, I need only mention a few examples.[3] Despina's first-act aria (no. 12) is in two parts, both marked Allegretto but with different time signatures (2/4 and 6/8). Continuity between the two sections is guaranteed by the triplets occurring in the last three bars of the first, where they establish the slightly faster tempo of the second Allegretto. Another continuity device, already known from *Don Giovanni*, is the smooth transition from recitative to aria. At the beginning of Despina's aria, the second violin resumes the vocal part of the preceding *secco*'s final bar, while the continuo bass reappears in the first violin (ex. 1).

EXAMPLE I

Despina's musical image is one of those most clearly depicted in the drama. The descending pentachord in example 1 is a recognizable feature, not only in the second section of the first-act aria, but also in other fragments (aria, no. 19, and the doctor's scene in the first finale, b. 292ff). In

[3] See Chapter 3.

addition the gradually shrinking interval[4] and the downward arpeggiated chord[5] should be mentioned. Occasionally these motifs are taken over by Don Alfonso,[6] pointing to the musical characterization in pairs that is a special structural device of the opera. With respect to the two sisters, for the greater part of the drama Mozart seems to have deliberately abstained from characterizing them as individual persons. They are conspicuously interdependent, clinging to each other and exchanging each other's melodies. The two present the image of a single person, notably in their three duets, nos. 4, 18 (first section), and 20, which moreover are musically interrelated by various melodic and rhythmic motifs. Paradoxically in Fiordiligi's Rondo (no. 25) a reminiscence from one of these duets (no. 20) stresses a departure from the dependent attitude. Not only the text but also the wide disparity of keys (Bb and E) indicates that from this point her personality will unfold (ex. 2).

EXAMPLE 2

The two young men are presented with more differentiation. The third of the initial terzetti already opposes Guglielmo's prosaic 'sense' to Ferrando's 'sensibility'. At the end of the preceding *secco* Ferrando chuckles over the prospect of having a good laugh at the expense of Don Alfonso; for Guglielmo, however, the 'expense' has a more material meaning: "But what are we going to do with the hundred ducats?" His own answer to this question characterizes him aptly: "I will have a banquet in honour of my Venus." Ferrando, on the other hand, shows his sensibility by his intention of offering his goddess a beautiful serenade. The distinction between the two

---

[4] See for instance no. 12, b. 10–12, and 14–16 (orchestra); no. 13, b. 27–30 ("Vallachi, Turchi . . ."); no. 18, b. 311–315 ("so il greco e l'arabo . . ."), and 402–407 ("tenete forte . . .").

[5] See no. 12, b. 67ff; no. 13, b. 44ff ("io non so se son Vallachi . . ."); no. 18, b. 500–505 ("Secondate per effetto di bontate"), repeated in 571–576; no. 19, b. 45ff ("Par ch'abbiam gusto di tal dottrina, viva Despina che sa servir"); no. 22, b. 55–56 ("rompasi omai quel laccio").

[6] See, for example, no. 16, b. 18–22 ("Se risentissero, se vi scoprissero, si guasterebbe tutto l'affar").

characters is found in the music as well as in the text. Ferrando's melody has a broader swing than Guglielmo's; it climaxes three times (on the words "serenata", "Dea" and "voglio"), each climax attaining a higher pitch than the previous one. In contrast to this Guglielmo starts on his highest note, which by recurring twice in the middle of the melody weakens the climax at the end. The varied harmonic rhythm in Ferrando's phrase also points to his being more emotional than Guglielmo, whose harmonies change almost regularly with each bar. The distinctive musical design of each of the young men is however recognizable only in situations in which the sisters are absent. Wherever the sexes are opposed, the 'boys', like the 'girls', act and sing almost as a single character. We must wait till the second finale to see Guglielmo disrupt their (superficial) unity; but this happens at a moment when the opposition of males and females has been dissolved (the canon "E nel tuo, nel mio bicchiero").

The image of Don Alfonso resembles that of Don Giovanni in that it lacks a clear musical physiognomy. The only consistent element is the absence of wind instruments in the accompaniment to his arias; for the rest these pieces are written in a remarkably eclectic style. In the F minor aria (no. 5) Don Alfonso is hardly able to show his true self, since here he acts a role within a role. One would expect him to commit himself in the short aria ending of the *secco* monologue succeeding the farewell scene, but instead we hear him quoting an adage with a particularly unusual orchestral accompaniment: the slow harmonic rhythm – only three chords in eleven bars – is counterbalanced by a rapid change of texture, each of the three harmonies being presented in a different style ('arioso', contrapuntally archaic, and 'contemporary'). The *Andante* (no. 30) gives the same impression of indeterminacy by juxtaposing characteristics of archaic and modern style. As already remarked, the sonorous image of Don Alfonso reminds us of Don Giovanni in a negative sense; this of course does not imply similarity of character. In the case of the libertine the lack of a consistent musical design results from his adaptability. Don Alfonso, on the other hand, strikes us as a deliberately elusive person, hiding under the cover of a superficially philosophical attitude.

*   *
*

The concepts of parody and irony have been discussed many times in connection with *Così fan tutte*. In a paper dealing with the opera, Delores Jerde Keahey clarifies the terminology:

"Parody and its technique [refer] to a humorous or burlesque imitation of opera buffa or opera seria techniques and forms; irony [refers] to a technique which may or may not use means identical to parody, but which [has] a deeper meaning than parody because of the context in which it is placed. Irony needs the knowledge of context to achieve its effect; parody may exist purely for its own sake, apart from any perspective. Thus techniques of parody may be used to produce an ironic effect, but not vice versa."[7]

In the opera under discussion Mozart uses parody either as a *buffo* concomitant or as self-mockery. The notary, for instance, belongs to the stock of caricatured types in comic opera; whether he is a sham notary (as in *Così fan tutte*) or a real one (as in *Don Pasquale*), he is invariably presented as a ridiculous figure in accordance with the audience's expectation. The same holds for the doctor. Mozart parodies him in the first finale by means of a musical archaicism: the 'baroque' hemiola cadence with a trill on the dominant (no. 18, b. 380ff). This, however, does not suffice as a caricature, and therefore the cadence itself is parodically disproportioned and adorned with a second trill. Instead of singing the usual formula

EXAMPLE 3

Despina stretches the end of her phrase over two additional bars. Thus the implicit time signature of 3/2 is replaced by an implicit 3/1 metre:

EXAMPLE 4

No. 18, b. 380–385 (Despina)

che poi si ce — le – bre là in Fran – – cia fù.

The comic effect of this passage is reinforced in the second finale, when the young men quote the cadence after their *démasqué* (no. 31, b. 509–518). This kind of quotation is also a well-known device in opera buffa, occurring as

---

[7] Delores J. Keahey, *Così fan tutte: Parody of Irony?* in 'Paul A. Pisk, Essays in his Honor', Austin (Texas), 1966, pp. 116–130.

late as *Falstaff* (the "Reverenza" theme cited by Mrs. Quickly in the
Windsor Park scene).

Conventional parody is not always used in such an unambiguous way.
Fiordiligi's "Come scoglio" (no. 14) is a parody of opera seria with regard to
both text and music. At the same time the aria expresses ironic discrepancy
between action and emotional response. After a not too serious challenge of
her virtue by two burlesque persons in the preceding sextet, Fiordiligi reacts
as if she had to withstand a Lovelace.

Mozart's self-mockery is revealed by a number of parodied fragments
from *Don Giovanni*; hidden in the score they seem to have been inserted
solely for the composer's own pleasure. All of these 'quotations' refer to
dramatic situations infinitely more serious than those in which they now
occur. In Don Alfonso's first aria, for instance, the 'blood' motif from the
scene of the dying Commendatore suggests to the young women the perils of
war (ex. 5).

EXAMPLE 5

Fiordiligi's concern for the 'agonizing' lovers ("At a moment so painful,
who could forsake them?") is closely related in melody and key to Don
Giovanni's interruption of Elvira's complaint, the interruption itself being
an instance of dramatic irony (ex. 6).

EXAMPLE 6

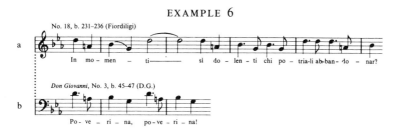

Another quotation from ''Ah chi mi dice mai'' is found in the second finale. Fiordiligi accuses Don Alfonso and Despina of cruelty and seduction; exactly the same reproaches were made by Donna Elvira (ex. 7).

EXAMPLE 7

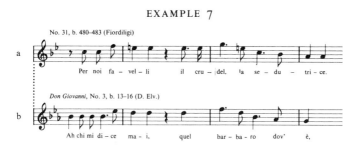

'Seduction' also connects the beginning of the first-act sextet with a well-known passage from *Don Giovanni*. The tender 6/8 section of ''Là ci darem la mano'' is parodically transformed into a march-like melody with a concluding *forte* chord (ex. 8).

EXAMPLE 8

In all four examples the parodical effect results from the use of an originally 'serious' motif or theme in a comic situation; only in ex. 8 is this effect reinforced by distortion of the musical material itself.

Dramatic irony in opera may be defined as the sharing by composer and audience of secret intelligence which contradicts the explicit words of one or more characters. Although admittedly narrow, this definition is quite compatible with Miss Keahey's observations: the 'secret' cannot be understood without contextual knowledge. In semiotic terms[8] dramatic irony is communicated through a sign process (semiosis); both the syntactic and semantic dimensions of this process enable the composer to use irony as a structural device.[9]

The fact that in opera the composer must be considered the dramatist does not preclude incidental use of verbal irony. The recitatives of *Così fan tutte* contain several witty examples. Fiordiligi chooses Ferrando's uniform to join Guglielmo on the battlefield (II, sc. 12); and Guglielmo, infuriated because of his fiancée's betrayal, wants to pluck out his beard, forgetting that it is a false one (II, sc. 13). Still, musical contradiction of a text generally provides a more subtle means for the disclosure of the underlying truth. But in order to contradict, music must first adopt a meaning. A connection is therefore established between a dramatic concept or attitude (expressed through words) and a musical unit (an interval, motif, phrase or chord). Then in a later scene this unit recurs but associated with quite different words. Which of the two is speaking the truth, text or music? Of course it is the music that belies the words and not vice versa. Thus music ironically reveals the dramatic truth.

The device can be applied in various ways. The orchestra may contradict the actor, or the actor may contradict himself (vocal melody versus words). Retrospective irony occurs when the later scene discloses the inner contradiction of the earlier one. And irony itself may become ironic, that is, by its ambiguity. The interpretation is then left to the audience. It goes without saying that the device needs to be applied with a certain frequency in order to be communicable. As a result, not only an actor's attitude in a particular scene but even a character *in toto* may be ironically 'exposed' long before the dénouement.

In the score of *Così fan tutte* some ironic signs recur so often that they function in themselves as structural elements of the drama. Other more

---

[8] See Ch. Morris, *Foundations of the Theory of Signs*, Chicago 1938; included in his *Writings on the General Theory of Signs*, The Hague-Paris 1972. See also Appendix I.

[9] It is true that parody also may be understood as a sign. However, unlike irony it refers to matters lying outside the drama and therefore cannot easily be used as a structural means.

sparingly used formulae are semio-semantically interrelated by serving the same dramatic purpose. The signs not only designate the attitudes or moods of certain persons, but also disclose emotional links between opposed characters, of course by contradicting their words. Generally the musical sign vehicles do not refer to a particular dramatic concept, as in *Don Giovanni*.[10] An exception is the melodic interval of the diminished third (with or without an intermediate passing note), which invariably refers to the idea of pity, notably self-pity. Because of his inborn sensibility Ferrando easily identifies himself with the role he has to act in the plot, and therefore the expression of pity accompanying his pathetic "Addio!" in the second quintet (E♭ – C♯) has overtones of sincerity. In the sextet (no. 13) the situation is different. The disguised lovers start their courtship in a clearly burlesque manner. Together with Despina they fall on their knees before the sisters, asking for forgiveness. The words convey a feigned appeal for pity:

> Ah Madame perdonate!
> Al bel piè languir mirate
> due meschin, di vostro merto
> spasimanti adorator.

> *Ah, ladies, pardon!*
> *See at your lovely feet*
> *two wretches languishing,*
> *adorers of your virtues.*

EXAMPLE 9

[10] See Chapter 3, various examples including ex. 28.

The musical setting of these words includes several diminished thirds (ex. 9). The ladies' reaction is violent:

> Giusti Numi, cosa sento,
> dell'enorme tradimento
> chi fu mai l'indegno autor?

> *Great heavens! What do I hear?*
> *Who was the shameless instigator*
> *of this vile betrayal?*

Nevertheless the interval reappears in Dorabella's part; its more specific relationship with the augmented sixth chord formed by the 'trio' a few bars earlier is evident (ex. 10).

EXAMPLE 10

No. 13, b. 113–116 (Desp., Fer., Gugl.)

a

Deh cal – ma – te,   deh cal – ma – te

Deh cal – ma – te,   deh cal – ma – te

No. 13, b. 118–121 (Fior., Dor.)

b

chi fu   mai l'in – de-gno au – tor?

As an example of dramatic irony the last fragments would hardly be convincing were they not followed by other more explicit applications of the formula. In the first finale Don Alfonso asks the girls to show some sympathy for the 'agonizing' lovers:

> Giacchè a morir vicini
> sono quei meschinelli;
> pietade almeno a quelli
> cercate di mostrar.

Since these unfortunates
are near to death,
at least try to show them
a little pity.

The word "pietade" is underlined by a diminished third (ex. 11).

EXAMPLE 11

No. 18, b. 141–143 (Don Alfonso)

pie – ta-de al – me-no a quel–li

The ironic effect of this fragment results from the quiet flow of the strings supported by clarinets and bassoons, which not only contradicts Don Alfonso's pathos, but forms a striking contrast with the highly emotional character of the preceding G minor section. However, Alfonso's plea is successful; when left alone with their 'victims', the sisters' pity is roused. The meaning of the orchestral motif dominating this scene (ex. 12a) is explicated in a phrase of Guglielmo (ex. 12b):

Più domestiche e trattabile
sono entrambe diventate:
sta a veder che la pietade
va in amore terminar.

Both have become
calmer and more gentle;
we shall see if their pity
will turn into love.

EXAMPLE 12

No. 18, b. 222–224

a

No. 18, b. 271–273 (Gugl.)

b

so – no en – tram-be di – ven – ta – te:

In the course of the second act the young men become victims of their own actions. Informed of Dorabella's infidelity, Ferrando now earnestly asks for sympathy (II, sc. 8) (ex. 13).

EXAMPLE 13

During the monologue preceding Ferrando's cavatina the motif of the diminished third repeatedly indicates his mood of self-pity (ex. 14).

EXAMPLE 14

Finally at the 'return' of the real fiancés, the sisters are seizes by panic and implicitly cry for pity (ex. 15b). The irony of this passage results from the occurrence of the same musical formula in the initial duet of the first finale, where it expressed the torments caused by the lovers' 'absence' (ex. 15a).

EXAMPLE 15

Text (a):   Ah, che un mar pien di tormento
             è la vita ormai per me!

             Ah, what a sea of torment
             is life henceforth for me!

     (b):   Barbare stelle!
             In tal momento
             che si farà?

             Ye cruel stars!
             What's to be done
             at such a dire moment?

Several motifs recurring fairly often in the score function as an undermining force in the drama; they gradually impair explicit professions of love, constancy, attachment, etc. For example the following lines are sung by Fiordiligi and Dorabella in their first duet (no. 4):

Se questo mio core
mai cangia desio,
Amore mi faccia
vivendo penar.

If ever my heart
changes its affection
may Love make me
live in pain.

The end of this quatrain is set to a *sospiro* motif (ex. 16a) which reappears in the second duet (ex. 16b), connected with the words:

Finchè meco il caro bene
mi lasciar le ingrate stelle,
non sapea cos'eran pene,
non sapea languir cos' è.

So long as the cruel stars
left my dear one with me,
I knew not what grief was,
I knew not what it was to languish.

Lastly the motif recurs in the third duet (no. 20), illustrating the prospect of flirtation with the new lovers ("Sighing, I'll imitate the other's sighs") and the general anticipatory delight ("And meanwhile what sport and pleasure I'll have" (ex. 16c and d).

EXAMPLE 16

The ironic effect of ex. 16c and 16d is caused by their textual and situational contrasts with the earlier duets. The same device is applied to two other motifs, the first of which originally seems to express Ferrando's adoration of his fiancée in the third terzetto (ex. 17), and the second the girls' despair in the farewell scene (ex. 18).

EXAMPLE 17

EXAMPLE 18

No. 6, b. 37–38 (Fiordiligi)

Both motifs frequently recur in the score, sometimes with minor modifications, but always clearly recognizable. Not only are they exchanged between the male and female but they are also used in connection with the amorous 'cross-relation'. Thus their original meanings become completely invalidated.

The most effective use of dramatic irony is found in the relationship of the two 'romantic' characters in the cast: Fiordiligi and Ferrando. At the beginning of the drama we already hear Fiordiligi imitating Ferrando's syncopated melody; the passage is prospectively related to their love duet in the second act (ex. 19).

EXAMPLE 19

Actually it is Ferrando who in the quintet adapts himself to the sisters' idiom; the fluent syncopes, which strongly contrast with Alfonso's and Guglielmo's dotted rhythms, originate in the A major duet (no. 4).[11]

Shortly afterward Ferrando seems to betray an unconscious affection for Fiordiligi. The passage may speak for itself (ex. 20):

EXAMPLE 20

[11] The fact of Ferrando's absence from the stage when the duet was sung is of no importance. Not he but the composer gives the sign to the audience.

EXAMPLE 21

In the last section of the first finale Fiordiligi's and Ferrando's coloraturas contrasting with the others' syllabic parts once more point to an emotional relationship. As in previous instances, words and visual action are undermined by the music.

Ferrando's explicit courtship in the second act seems at the outset totally unsuccessful. The *accompagnato* in scene 7 shows a striking resemblance to the recitative preceding Fiordiligi's "Come scoglio" (no. 14). Yet the slow tempo and the 'hesitant' motifs of the strings seem to indicate a process of weakening: Fiordiligi is no longer as firm "as a rock" (ex. 21).

The most striking examples of dramatic irony are found in the complex love duet, no. 29. Its musical 'epigraph' is virtually identical to that of Ferrando's first-act aria, "Un aura amorosa" (ex. 22).

EXAMPLE 22

The affinity of aria and duet is not confined to their initial motifs. The motif on which the aria's vocal part is built (an ascending third or fourth with anticipation of the second note) reappears in Ferrando's interruption of Fiordiligi's soliloquy (ex. 23).

EXAMPLE 23

Another fragment of the duet is closely related to the beginning of the third terzetto, i.e. the phrase by which Ferrando expressed the wish to serenade his fiancée (ex. 24).

EXAMPLE 24

How should we interpret these recurrent signs? Since all three of them refer unequivocally to Ferrando, it may be safely assumed that they are semio-semantically interrelated. In addition, each of the sign vehicles is determined by a particular tonality, respectively A major (ex. 22), E major and minor (ex. 23), and C major (ex. 24).[12] Finally there is a clear parallelism of context: all three signs first occur in connection with Ferrando's

[12] The key relationships are formal properties of the signs in question and therefore must be considered as belonging to the syntactical dimension of the sign process. Still they may also be interpreted in terms of semantics. Mozart often connects the key of A (including its dominant E) with real or shammed seduction scenes, e.g. the Count-Susanna duet and the beginning of the last finale of *Le nozze di Figaro*, and the duet "Là ci darem la mano" in *Don Giovanni*. As for the middle section in C occurring in A major pieces, I refer to the 'balcony' terzetto in the latter opera (the renewed seduction of Donna Elvira).

profession of love for Dorabella (terzetto and aria), and the second time in connection with his attempt to seduce Fiordiligi (duet).

The interpretation apparent on the surface is that by addressing two different females with the aid of the same musical material Ferrando is being depicted as a cynical character. However obvious this explanation may seem, on second thought it must be dismissed. Ferrando is anything but a Don Giovanni, who achieves this feat in two consecutive scenes.[13] Instead we have come to know him in the course of the drama as a young man who immaturely indulges his emotions and is virtually incapable of feigning love. Ferrando cannot take his role of a disguised lover for what it is: a game. From the moment he is separated from his companion and has to act for himself, that is, to seduce his friend's fiancée, the role becomes an emotional reality. However, this reality is not love for Fiordiligi but simply the blissful state of 'being in love.' Ferrando is hardly capable of loving a woman; instead he is continually in love with Love. Once we take this as the signs' designatum, then several details in the terzetto and aria are clarified. The melismatic emphasis in the terzetto on the words "serenata" and "voglio" points to the serenade being more important than its addressee. And in the aria the words "nostro tesoro" (not "*mio* tesoro") betray an unsubstantial emotion; the "aura amorosa" actually emanates from Ferrando himself.

Basically Guglielmo is as immature as Ferrando, though for opposite reasons. While Ferrando's love lacks an object, Guglielmo's object is deprived of love. Guglielmo's concept of love is *possession* and the social codification of this possession is called honour. Only a threat to his honour may arouse his emotions; otherwise he remains a quite unromantic person who indulges in materialistic self-satisfaction (twice during the drama he speaks about a meal).[14] Guglielmo is better able to play the game than Ferrando, although in the end it is he who proves to be a bad loser (in the canon "E nel tuo, nel mio bicchiero" he is the spoil-sport). His prosaic character matches the superficial Dorabella, whose seduction is a rather unemotional affair that can be dispatched in a secco recitative. The fact that the couple's ensuing duet is one of the most exquisite pieces in the opera may be taken as an instance of almost perverse dramatic irony. For the rest Guglielmo's character and behaviour do not offer much opportunity for ironic exposure. While the amorous clichés occurring in Ferrando's text are often belied by the music, there are no such contradictions in his companion's part. The latter contains but a few recurrent motifs and these

---

[13] The terzetto no. 15, and the *canzonetta* no. 16 in Act II.

[14] No. 3 (terzetto) and the secco recitative preceding no. 17.

serve to confirm earlier statements rather than to deny them.
Characteristically Guglielmo reveals himself most clearly in a piece belonging to the stock of *buffo* conventions: a *boutade* on the unreliability of the
female in general (no. 26: "Donne mie le fate a tanti").[15] The aria includes a
musical confirmation of Don Alfonso's words from the second terzetto
(ex. 25).

EXAMPLE 25

Although Guglielmo, blinded by his conceit, is convinced that the rules
do not apply to his fiancée and himself, he still adheres fundamentally to
Don Alfonso's philosophy. The text of his aria is nothing but an elaboration
of the opera's title, thus explaining a witty quotation hidden on the last page
of the score in the orchestral accompaniment (ex. 26).

EXAMPLE 26

*   *
*

---

[15] See, for example, Figaro's aria, no. 26: "Aprite un po'quegli occhi".

And so the composer takes leave of his audience with a reminder: "Così fan tutte". Is this the opera's subject or merely the title? Most of Mozart's dramatic works bear titles referring either to the plot (e.g. *La finta giardiniera; Die Entführung aus dem Serail; Le nozze di Figaro; La clemenza di Tito*) or to a leading character (e.g. *Mitridate, Re di Ponte; Idomeneo; Don Giovanni*). The title *Così fan tutte* however, being a maxim, does not confine its import to this drama alone but suggests a generally valid truth: "Thus do they all".

Everyone familiar with Mozart's mild feminism, traceable in *Die Entführung, Figaro*, and *Don Giovanni*, will be puzzled by his laying the blame entirely on the female. One plausible explanation would be that the opera's title has little to do with the subject matter. Da Ponte simply borrowed it from Basilio's cynical line in the 'chair' terzetto of *Le nozze di Figaro* ("Così fan tutte le belle") and the quotation of its melody in the overture of *Così fan tutte* points to Mozart's acceptance of his librettist's choice. This explanation does not necessarily exclude another. If understood as irony, the words "così fan tutte" may very well refer to the drama's subject. The maxim (addressed to the male) could be read as: "Thus do they all – if you treat them in that way."

The latter view implies that the drama should be interpreted as a social comedy dealing, like *Le nozze di Figaro* and *Don Giovanni*, not only with personal relationships between men and women, but with their general positions in society. Each of the three works stresses a particular theme. *Figaro* treats the tension among the various strata within a basically-accepted social framework, while *Don Giovanni* considers the challenge of the entire social order. *Così fan tutte* differs from the two earlier dramas in its lack of social frictions; instead the opera shows us men and women as victims of social conventions which impede their maturing as human beings.

Among the drama's characters only Don Alfonso seems to be aware of this, although his shallow philosophy never touches the roots of the evil. He merely accepts the fact that human nature may occasionally prove stronger than social code, and instead of questioning the justice of the code he advises the young men to accept the unpleasant consequences of its inadequacy (II, sc. 13). As for Despina, her cynical attitude to life may result from dissatisfaction with her inferior social position (I, sc. 8). She has a low opinion of men and tries to take advantage of them whenever the opportunity arises. Clever rather than intelligent, Despina functions as Alfonso's agent, and so her role seems less important in terms of drama than in terms of plot.

Although in *Così fan tutte* the female is ruled by the male, the latter is no less victim than the former. Both Ferrando and Guglielmo strike us as particularly immature. Even their first musical phrase (terzetto, no. 1) contains an allusion to this: the repeated descending thirds which are a feature of children's songs. Neither young man is capable of a truly human relationship with the girl of his choice, nor is either aware of the fact that such a relationship might be possible. Each of them looks upon his *sposa* as one of life's ornaments: Fiordiligi for Guglielmo's possessions, Dorabella for Ferrando's emotions.

In their first recitative (I, sc. 2) the sisters unconsciously reveal their weak position in society: they must wait patiently till it will please the young men to marry them. Living in a world which has turned moral concepts into social conventions, Fiordiligi and Dorabella, like Ferrando and Guglielmo, are the slaves of those conventions to such an extent that they are no longer aware of their dependence. The moment they face an unforeseen situation they are seized by panic and become wax in the hands of Don Alfonso, the success of whose stratagems is a matter of course. The girls cling to each other in utter helplessness and soon Dorabella embraces Despina's cynical 'philosophy', which provides her with new rules and inner security. Fiordiligi, on the other hand, offers some resistance and even reaches a crisis of conscience which, although expressed in textual clichés, is rooted in something deeper than convention. Because of her moral courage her final defeat touches us deeply. It is typical of Fiordiligi's emotional sincerity to accept the new situation without the slightest reserve; instead of merely following (as in the B♭ duet, no. 20) she now takes the lead in the melodic 'chains' (ex. 27).

EXAMPLE 27

In his study, *Opera as Drama*, Joseph Kerman points to a discrepancy between Da Ponte's concept of *Così fan tutte* and Mozart's.[16] According to Kerman's view, the composer spoiled an impeccable libretto by taking emotion seriously. As a result, the reunion of the former couples is deprived of its wittiness, and becomes improbable if not immoral. Kerman considers the lack of an explanation for the abrupt lowering of the imaginative level in the finale as "quite undramatic". Of course the blame is laid on Da Ponte who "should have known by this time that Mozart would pounce upon any feasable emotional matter, in however dry a book, and turn it to account."

Kerman's argument raises several questions. First, is it possible to distinguish two equivalent concepts of the drama, one by the librettist, the other by the composer? Further, does the "lowering of the imaginative level" apply to all four characters involved? And lastly, is the second half of the opera's finale really unsatisfactory or even undramatic?

To answer the first question: Da Ponte did not write a drama but rather provided the composer with material for a drama. In this connection we may quote Kerman's own recurrent statement that "the composer is the dramatist." Whether or not Da Ponte wanted to expose the girls' feelings as meaningless is of little importance; what does count is that Mozart wanted to define their quality. The librettist's own ideas about the characters in his text are irrelevant in connection with our evaluation of the drama as it unfolds in the music. Let us look briefly at the reconciliation scene of *Le nozze di Figaro*:

CONTE: Contessa perdono!
CONTESSA: Più docile io sono,
            e dico di sì.
TUTTI: Ah tutti contenti
            saremo così.

COUNT: *Forgive me, Countess!*
COUNTESS: *I am more gentle,*
            and say 'yes'.
ALL: *Thus we shall all*
            be delighted.

Are not the feelings transmitted through these lines as meaningless as those described in the words of Dorabella and Fiordiligi? Referring to this very

---

[16] J. Kerman, *Opera as Drama*, New York 1956, Ch. 4, no. 3.

scene, Kerman speaks of the "miserable material" on which Mozart "built a revelation".[17] One could hardly consider this revelation to contradict the librettist's concept of the scene. Dramatically speaking there is no such concept, only an extremely banal piece of conversation, transformed by the composer into meaningful drama. Therefore, in evaluating the last finale of *Così fan tutte* we should not judge the verbal material as self-contained dramatic substance, but instead concentrate on the music built on this material.

As for the question of the lowered level of the finale, I believe clear distinctions should be made among the characters. Throughout the drama Guglielmo has always stayed on a low plane of imagination. Only the threat to his cherished honour could rouse his emotions, and even that Mozart considered unworthy of being depicted in an *accompagnato* or aria (see II, sc. 13). Now that he can take possession of Fiordiligi again, the matter is settled and thus from his point of view the solution is most satisfactory. Dorabella, too, has reached her goal: marriage and henceforth safety in her unimaginative existence. Ferrando simply recovers the old peg upon which to hang his self-centered feelings; soon he will hardly remember that he ever exchanged it for another one. Thus for three out of four characters the return to the old pairing-off is painless and offers no problems. To censure their behaviour in terms of morality would imply that we consider them mature persons, which they are not.

But what about Fiordiligi? Surely *she* had an emotional experience which raised her far above the level of her sister. Kerman believes that in the finale this experience goes up in smoke; from a dramatic point of view her un-explained return to Guglielmo is considered an anticlimax.

Contrary to this opinion I hold that the dénouement *is* explained – not by a particular scene or phrase, but by the drama as a whole. If the duet gave us a glimpse of how human a relationship could be, the finale shows how persons are united in society. Fiordiligi's return to her old lover is a matter of course; regardless of her feelings it is simply the 'right' thing to do. The audience, however, knows that Fiordiligi has gone through an experience which, though incompatible with the social code, cannot be undone. Why, then, is there no allusion to her inescapable inner conflict?

Had Mozart wanted this, Da Ponte would have promptly provided the text. But obviously he did not want it; and if the idea ever crossed his mind, he must have realised immediately that such an allusion, however slight, would spoil the comedy. Let us not forget that since *Così fan tutte* is an

[17] *Ibid.*, Ch. 4, no. 2.

opera buffa, it has to obey the rules of comedy, one of which prescribes the
final solution of all conflicts – solution on the surface of course, but nevertheless solution. As we leave the theatre we may wonder about Fiordiligi's
future life. Is it possible for her to return to her former state of social
marionette? And if not, how will she stay married to a man like Guglielmo?
But these questions concern a new drama lying outside the scope of the
present one. The *buffo* ending of *Così fan tutte* is dramatically as indispensable (and satisfactory) as that of *Don Giovanni*. Enacted on the dominant
imaginative level of the opera it closes the circle and allows the actors to
address the audience with a piece of Don Alfonso's philosophy. Considered
in musical terms, the comedy has to end in C major. Nevertheless the key of
A reverberates in our minds. This is the drama's final irony.

*   *
*

The above interpretation certainly leaves more than one problem unresolved. The opera's slow dramatic rhythm has been mentioned but not
explained. Another untreated question is Mozart's departure from the realism found in *Figaro*, and *Don Giovanni* (improbabilities occur in all three
plots, but only in the present work are actions and situations presented in
caricatured form). In the second of the initial terzetti, Alfonso's surprising
turn to the minor mode (no. 2, b. 9ff and 45ff) seems of vital importance, but
is still difficult to explain; one perceives an undercurrent of melancholy in
the drama. Does this reflect the composer's basic pessimism? A thorough
examination of the score leaves us not only fascinated and puzzled but also
with the conclusion that *Così fan tutte* is an opera that will always elude
complete understanding. In this connection the title of another Italian
drama comes to mind: *Così è (se vi pare)*.[18]

1974

---

[18] Title of a play by Luigi Pirandello; it is known in English-speaking countries as: *Right you
are (if you think so)*.

CHAPTER 6

SEMANTICS OF ORCHESTRATION

Like any other kind of art, that of musical drama is conditioned by restrictive factors. Although the dramatist may change or disregard certain rules and conventions, his creation will always be determined by limitations of time, space and medium. Because of this he can hardly afford to neglect any resources which are at his disposal. In terms of music this means that in principle every sonorous parameter will be made subservient to the drama, including that of instrumental timbre.

Although in Mozart's operas timbre as compared to melody, rhythm or harmony is of secondary structural importance, it has its own function with respect to the dramatic idea. By means of its tone colour the orchestral instrument may reveal, transmit, reinforce or clarify a dramatic element, such as a particular mood, attitude, situation, character or action.

Before beginning a discussion of the dramatic 'meaning' of various instrumental timbres, a few observations should be made about elements of orchestration defying semantical interpretation. The orchestral accompaniment of large ensembles and choruses rarely offers an opportunity to establish a meaningful relationship between the use of one or more instruments and dramatic substance. In these pieces only the conspicuous absence of certain instruments may reveal something. For example, the missing clarinets in the soldiers' chorus of *Così fan tutte* (I, no. 8) point to their incompatability with military matters.

Another non-interpretable category is that of the *concertante* aria. Here the dramatist temporarily yields pride of place to the musician. The interplay of timbres in these arias functions in about the same way as in the *symphonie concertante*, the genre which enjoyed so much popularity in public concerts of the late eighteenth century. Any attempt to interpret dramatically the solo parts in the accompaniment of Ilia's "Se il padre perdei" (*Idomeneo* II, no. 11) or Constanze's "Martern aller Arten" (*Die Entführung* II, no. 11) would be fruitless. The same holds for pieces which contain only one or two solo parts, like Fiordiligi's Rondo "Per pietà" (*Così fan tutte* II, No. 25) and Sesto's "Parto, parto" (*La clemenza di Tito* I, no. 9). The only relevant point is that these pieces stress the importance of the character involved. A *concertante* written for Arbace, Marcellina, Publio or Monostatos would be almost unthinkable. In addition it should be noticed that in Mozart pieces of this kind are usually assigned to female voices.

Instruments generally used on a 'neutral' level include the separate strings and the horn. Since the strings form the backbone of the eighteenth-century orchestra, only their absence might denote something dramatically explainable. With Mozart this is hardly the case however. The scoring of the duet with chorus, no. 21 of *Così fan tutte*, for wind instruments merely enhances the effect of outdoor music. The B♭ 'masked' terzetto in the first finale of *Don Giovanni*, which has a similar orchestration, expresses a climax of emotional tension and is of the highest dramatic importance. This, however, does not lead to a semantic interpretation of its unusual scoring. The only reasonable explanation of the absence of strings in the terzetto is an aesthetic one: the principle of variety which requires an interruption of the continuous use of the strings throughout the opera.

The horns, which since the middle of the century had partially taken over the function of the former *continuo*, also occupy a central position in the orchestra. Occasional deviations from their neutral role may be noted (e.g. the famous 'pun' in Figaro's fourth-act aria "Aprite un po'quelgli occhi"), but this holds also for the strings.

In contrast to the neutral elements in the orchestra are those instruments which by tradition or extra-operatic usage designate a dramatically applicable concept. Mozart uses some of them exclusively in this capacity (e.g. the 'serenading' mandolin in *Don Giovanni;* the 'Turkish' triangle, cymbals and big drum in *Die Entführung;* the trombones associated with the supernatural in *Idomeneo, Don Giovanni* and *Die Zauberflöte*). Other instruments function semantically in more than one way (e.g. the trumpets and timpani which denote the imaginary battlefield in Figaro's "Non più andrai", imperial majesty in the march of *La clemenza di Tito*, and nothing special in the final sextet of *Don Giovanni*). Since Mozart research has dealt extensively with these devices of instrumentation, they do not require further discussion.

Another category is that of the string orchestra. Although generally the separate stringed instruments do not designate rationally perceivable concepts, as a group they may indicate something tangible – if not by virtue of their presence, then by the conspicuous absence of winds and percussion. Pieces accompanied by strings alone occur in all operas. Some of these belong to the type of *recitativo accompagnato* and function as introduction to the ensuing colourful aria or duet. Others may have been scored for strings merely for the sake of variety (e.g. Elettra's second aria in *Idomeneo*). However, the great majority of string accompaniments denote dramatically relevant features. Thus the absence of wind instruments and percussion may allude to the inferior social position of the character in question (e.g. Serpetta's and Nardo's arias in *La finta giardiniera*[1]) or indicate the fact that we are dealing with a secondary role in the drama (Arbate in *Mitridate, Re di Ponto*). The string accompaniment of Barbarina's cavatina in *Le nozze di Figaro* seems to point to her tender age, rather than her social inferiority as a gardener's daughter. Nor do the strings in Marcellina's aria denote a social position – she has shortly before been married to a doctor and is therefore raised to the middle class stratum. Instead the restricted orchestral scoring could ironically refer to the emptiness underlying Marcellina's presumption. The string orchestra may also contribute to achieve a mild parody. Donna Elvira's warning of Zerlina (*Don Giovanni* I, no. 8) assumes a severe accent by its being scored for strings alone (in this case an allusion to late Baroque music).

In most of these examples the denotation is rather weak and needs reinforcement by other musical elements. Many of the 'low class' arias are in 6/8 metre, occasionally preceded by a 2/4 section.[2] Barbarina's small vocal range confirms her youth, and Marcellina's cold coloraturas strengthen the impression that she lacks any true feeling. As for Donna Elvira's aria, its style marked by dotted rhythms, contrapuntal devices and hemiola cadences is decidedly archaic.

Mozart's most original and effective use of timbre for the sake of revealing dramatic truth is found in the woodwind parts. Three woodwind instruments, the flute, the oboe and the clarinet, are related to various extramusical concepts. The fourth, the bassoon, lacks these connotations, but generally reinforces the dramatic function of each of the other instruments.[3]

Among these three, the oboe plays the least conspicuous part. The instrument is often used to express the idea of companionship and, more partic-

---

[1] Nardo's first aria is scored for strings and two horns.

[2] The 'low class' connotation of the 6/8 time signature is only valid in operatic genres which contain roles of different social strata, i.c. opera buffa and *Singspiel*. A rare exception is Dorabella's aria "È amore un ladroncello" (*Così fan tutte* II, no. 28), which is in 6/8 metre. The obvious explanation is that Dorabella, though belonging to the upper class, identifies herself with Despina's frivolous ideas.

[3] Pieces and fragments scored for strings and bassoon(s) are rarely met with in Mozart's operas. Neither the scoring for strings and two bassoons of Ramiro's aria "Dolce d'amor compagna" (*La finta giardiniera* II, no. 18) nor that of the C minor fragment in the first finale of *Così fan tutte* (for strings and one bassoon) lend themselves to semantic interpretation.

ularly, fidelity in love, friendship or servitude. Arbace's "Se il tuo duol"
(*Idomeneo* II, no. 10a), Fiordiligi's "Come scoglio" (*Così fan tutte* I, no. 14),
and Annio's "Tu fosti tradito" (*La clemenza di Tito* II, no. 17) are clear
examples of arias that express the concept of fidelity. Ferrando and
Guglielmo act on a lower level; nevertheless they are companions, if not
friends, as is shown in the first and third of the initial terzetti of *Così fan
tutte*.[4] In all these pieces the flutes are missing, and therefore the oboes have
a prominent part in the orchestra.[5] Prospective and ironic use of the oboe
timbre is found in the duet no. 14 at the beginning of Act II of *Don Giovanni*.
Here Leporello threatens to leave his master, but the oboes contradicting his
words tell us that he will stay. Sometimes the oboe goes beyond its illustrative or revealing function. In the aria "Dove sono i bei momenti" (*Figaro*
III, no 19), the instrument almost functions as an actor in the drama by
helping the Countess to overcome her depressive mood and her reluctance
to conspire with her servant Susanna. In the letter duet (no. 20) the 'linking'
function of the oboe supported by the bassoon is particularly obvious
(ex. 1).

EXAMPLE 1

[4] The second terzetto is dominated by Don Alfonso.
[5] In general the dramatic relevance of a woodwind instrument is conditioned by its occupy-
ing the highest part in the score.

Another striking example of the instrument's 'helpful' role is found in *Così fan tutte*. With the aid of the oboe Fiordiligi surrenders to Ferrando (ex. 2).

EXAMPLE 2

Generally the oboes together with the bassoons refer to determination, mental force or *noblesse*. In this connection they stand opposite to the clarinets, which usually indicate soft and gentle feelings, sometimes even degenerating into spinelessness. In other contexts the clarinet points to a character not (yet) involved in the plot. Examples include the Countess' cavatina in *Figaro* (II, no. 10), Donna Elvira's first aria (*Don Giovanni* I, no. 3), the sisters' A major duet in *Così fan tutte* (I, no. 4), and Tamino's aria (*Die Zauberflöte* I, no. 3), all scored for clarinets, bassoons and horns. A character who fundamentally fails to understand what is really going on may also be pictured in this way. Don Ottavio's "Il mio tesoro" (*Don Giovanni* II, no. 21) is particularly revealing in this respect; despite his words in the preceding *secco* ("dopo eccessi si enormi dubitar non possiam"), the accompaniment is written for the same instruments as in the pieces mentioned above.

The flute is Mozart's most effective orchestral tool. The instrument functions as the disturber of balance, serving the intrigue and often revealing subconscious desire. While both the oboe and the clarinet may express feelings of love, the flute acts as the mouthpiece of eroticism and is particularly dominant in seduction scenes. A clear example of a disruptive role is that of Elettra in *Idomeneo*, as is illustrated by the flute arpeggios in her aria "Tutte nel cor vi sento" (I, no. 4). A more specific connotation in this piece is the concept of vengeance. Dorabella's "Smanie implacabile" (*Così fan tutte* I, no. 11) also contains an allusion to this idea (the mention of the Eumenides, which is accompanied by two flutes and one bassoon). As for scenes of seduction, the bassoon frequently acts as counterpart to the flute, doubling the voice of the seducee, while the flute itself goes in unison with the seducer. I refer to two examples, "Là ci darem la mano" (*Don Giovanni* I, no. 7) and the Count-Susanna duet (*Figaro* III, no. 16):

EXAMPLE 3

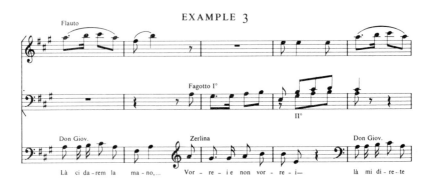

EXAMPLE 4

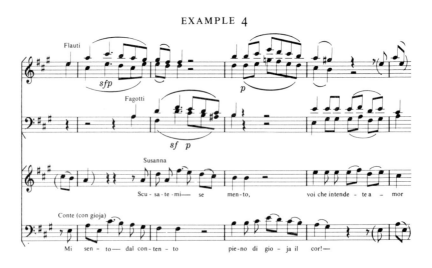

In the last-quoted example the seduction is feigned on the part of the seducee. Another scene shows us a seducer who wants to fail rather than succeed, and therefore turns his effort into a parody (Guglielmo's aria "Non siate ritrosi", *Così fan tutte* I, no. 15, scored for one flute and one bassoon). Unintended seduction occurs in Pamina's lament "Ach, ich fühl's" (*Die Zauberflöte* II, no. 17), where, as regards orchestration, plot prevails over drama. In view of Pamina's gentle character and rather passive role in the opera, one is surprised to hear the flute in the orchestral accompaniment, but it is the situation which requires its presence: unknowingly Pamina tempts her lover to break the injunction to remain silent.

As may be expected, Don Giovanni rarely sings without a flute in the orchestra. In his capacity of seducer he acts in accordance with his own intentions. But not always are intentions and actions to be assigned to a single person. Surprisingly, neither of the two seduction duets in *Così fan tutte* (nos. 23 and 29) are accompanied by the flute. A meaningful explanation is that, instead of Guglielmo and Ferrando, Don Alfonso and, more specifically, Despina must be considered as the real seducers. The maidservant has the flute as an almost constant companion (I, no. 12, and finale, sc. 16; II, no. 19, the quartet, no. 22, and the notary scene in the second finale). As for Don Alfonso, his most revealing piece is the second of the initial terzetti, "E la fede delle femmine come l'araba fenice", scored for one flute and one bassoon.

Other 'amorous' pieces that are characterized by the missing flute include Cherubino's first aria (no. 6) and the initial section of the last finale of *Le nozze di Figaro*. Both deal with scenes which principally involve Susanna (or the pseudo-Susanna). On the other hand, the page's relationship to the Countess is marked by the flute's presence in the score (II, *canzona* no. 11, and aria no. 12). Although no definite conclusions can be drawn from these facts, still they may contribute to an interpretation of Cherubino's feelings and attitude toward each of the two females.

At the end of the same opera the sudden interruption of the flute parts (and the change of tempo) is most revealing. The Count's humble plea for forgiveness and the Countess' gracious answer are accompanied by oboes and bassoons, underlining "the core of decency" which transcends the comedy as a whole.[6] In contrast to this an unexpected entrance of the flute may disclose disturbing undercurrents and even suggest verbal ambiguity. In the farewell terzettino of *Così fan tutte* (I, no. 10) a harmless phrase addressed to the wind and the waves suddenly adopts an ambiguous meaning with the

[6] See J. Kerman, *Opera as Drama*, New York 1956, p. 104.

EXAMPLE 5

flute starting on the second syllable of the word "desir" (bar 22). The
impression is reinforced by the strongly dissonant harmony (ex. 5).

*   *
*

Many more examples could have been chosen in support of these observations on the semantic aspects of Mozart's orchestra. The evidence, however, could easily lead to the idea that the composer's instrumentation
contains a built-in mechanism of semantics, providing us with unequivocal
answers to all questions regarding dramatic details. Such a view is, of
course, untenable. As a means of communication the orchestral 'sign' is a
rather weak one and consequently difficult to grasp – hence its occasional
reinforcement by other musical elements. Moreover, the various dramatic
genres do not require the same degree of orchestral 'engagement': semantic
use of tone colour is more frequent and also more subtle in opera buffa than
in opera seria. Furthermore, the fact that the connection between orchestra
and drama is occasionally rather loose may arise not only from purely
aesthetic considerations on the part of the composer but also from practical

limitations (e.g. before *Idomeneo*, Mozart never had the opportunity to use the clarinet in his operas).

And yet Mozart's handling of orchestral timbres is illuminating with regard to his overall image as a musical dramatist. His instruments do not function as self-supporting means to transmit the dramatic idea; they are the bearers of musical material that in itself is dramatically relevant. Whether the relevance is explicitly demonstrable or not is a problem which concerns the researcher who examines the scores on his desk. But it is in the theatre that we learn to know Mozart for what he truly is: a creator of total drama.

1974

PART TWO

VERDI

CHAPTER 7

OTELLO: DRAMA THROUGH STRUCTURE

For Charles Warren Fox on his seventieth birthday

Since the beginning of the nineteenth century, opera in Italy is often called *melodramma*, the term simply meaning that the drama in question is realized through music. Nevertheless, a connection with the concept of melodrama in its more popular sense should not be excluded, even in cases where the libretto is based on spoken tragedy.[1] Certainly no Italian operagoer would call Verdi's *Giovanna d'Arco*, *Luisa Miller*, *I Masnadieri*, or *Macbeth* trage-dies.[2] Even *Otello*, which is claimed to follow its model more closely than any other work of Verdi, is basically different from Shakespeare's work. In the latter, characters develop in the course of the play, often expressing themselves in an ambiguous way, and leaving room for more than one interpretation. In contrast to this, Verdi's characters show less development and may seem flat. Their words and actions are unequivocal, if not to each other, certainly to the audience.

Do these qualities identify *Otello* as a melodrama? This is difficult to accept. As a dramatic genre, melodrama has a bad name because of the excesses generally associated with it, but even if this low reputation is disregarded, one must admit that next to Jago (the 'perfect' villain) and Desdemona (the 'perfect' angel), Otello himself is difficult to place. He is surely not the hero in the traditional melodramatic sense. We may accept him as a hero because the idea is presented to us at the beginning, but we invariably *see* him in actions which contribute to his downfall. Lodovico, the envoy from Venice, expresses our feelings:

---

[1] In order to avoid misunderstandings about the English term 'melodrama' it should be observed that in the present chapter the word has exclusively the meaning of: "a dramatic genre characterized by heavy use of suspense, sensational episodes, [and] romantic sentiment" (cf. *The American Heritage Dictionary of the English Language*, Boston etc., 1969, entry "Melodrama"). See also: Eric Bentley, *The Life of the Drama*, New York, 1967, Chapter 6.

[2] Verdi's librettists, however, sometimes did. The librettos of *Alzira*, *La Battaglia di Legnano* and *I due Foscari* designate them as *tragedia lirica*.

Quest'è dunque l'eroe? Quest'è il guerriero dai sublimi ardimenti?

So this is the hero? This is the warrior of sublime courage?

In the opera everything concerning Otello's glory is conveyed to the audience solely through his memories; but in his own mind those memories gradually lose their value. This may be seen as early as the second act, where he complains:

> Ora e per sempre addio sante memorie,
> addio sublimi incanti del pensier!
> Addio schiere fulgenti, addio vittorie,
> dardi volanti e volanti corsier!
> Addio vessilo trionfale e pio!
> E diane squillanti in sul mattin!
> Clamori e canti di battaglia, addio!
> Della gloria d'Otello è questo il fin.

> *Now and forever farewell, sacred memories,*
> *farewell, sublime enchantments of the mind!*
> *Farewell, shining legions, farewell victories,*
> *swift spears and flying steeds!*
> *Farewell, standards triumphant and holy*
> *and reveilles ringing in the morn!*
> *Clamours and songs of battle, farewell!*
> *This is the end of Otello's glory.*

Herein lies a basic difference between the opera and the play. In the first act (omitted by Boito and Verdi) of the latter, we witness Othello's great moral courage in defending himself before the Venetian Duke and Senators against Brabantio's accusations. There we see the whole man on the stage and this enables us to *share* his memories in later moments of despair (e.g. III, sc. 3, v. 347–359). In the opera, however, these memories merely refer to information that has been given in quite a different context, principally in the last scene of the first act. The information is more or less abstract and therefore cannot arouse our pity (an essential element of tragedy) to the same degree as the scene witnessed in Shakespeare's play.

Another important difference concerns the dramatic approach. Since the characters in the opera are simple, unequivocal, and compared to those of Shakespeare basically not very interesting, the stress lies instead on situations. These are realized in a way which might be expected from an operatic composer, namely with emphasis on purely musical expression of mood. In opera, lyricism and dramatic action do not exclude each other: 'outer' or 'inner' action (or both) proceed during scenes dominated by the expression of feelings. The second-act quartet, for example, is a piece of strong emotional intensity (Desdemona's melodic line prevails over the other parts), but it contains a good deal of action; similarly, the singing of the Willow Song is a human act, indispensable for the fulfilment of the drama. As will be shown below, even such items as the mandolin chorus (II, sc. 3), which seems to be no more than a set piece, are fully integrated in the drama's development.

If in *Otello* we watch the actors with fascination, it is for what they do, rather than for what they are. And because nearly every action stems from Jago, it is he who may appear to determine the structure of the drama. Before we assign the work to a particular dramatic category, we should investigate its general structure, as well as the role of Jago and of the other principals. Are not the theoretical observations which might lead one to label *Otello* a melodrama contradicted by our experience in the theatre? Who would, at the final curtain, still speak of flat characters?

*　*
*

General Structural Features

Otello is known as a continuous opera. This, however, does not alter the fact that quite a number of 'pieces' may be discerned: the tempest scene, the fire chorus, the drinking song, and the love duet of Act I; Jago's *Credo*, the mandolin chorus, the quartet, and the vengeance duet of Act II; the Otello-Desdemona duet, the terzetto, and the great septet with chorus of Act III; the Willow Song and the *Ave Maria* of Act IV. It is conspicuous that most of these items are choruses and ensembles; the few solo pieces are written either in a recitative or arioso-like style, or have the characteristics of songs. Actually *Otello* is an opera without true arias. Furthermore, it may be noticed that many ensembles and choruses are linked with operatic tradition: tempest, drinking song, chorus of vassals, vengeance duet and prayer are all old acquaintances from early nineteenth- or even eighteenth-century opera.[3] But they differ from their models in being fully integrated in the drama.

---

[3] Significantly one Verdian stock item is missing: the *battaglia*. In *Otello* everything concerning battles and glory on the battlefield refers to the past and is only revealed through memories.

Consider, for example, what is generally held to be the most 'separate'
piece of the opera, the mandolin chorus in the second act. Its function is
clear; the homage of the Cypriots to Desdemona serves to illuminate her
angelic character. The offering of the lily (a traditionally pure and sacred
flower), the allusion to the Blessed Virgin, and the comparison to "a holy
image" are particularly significant. Toward the end of the chorus,
Desdemona repeats its final melody on the words:

> Splende il cielo, danza l'aura, olezza il fior...
> Gioa, amor, speranza cantan nel mio cor.

> *The heavens shine, the breeze dances, the flowers smell sweet...*
> *Joy, love and hope sing in my heart.*

while watching her, Otello utters, "sweetly moved":

> Quel canto mi conquide.

> *This song quite overcomes me.*

Not only the text, also the music expresses Otello's appeasement and confirms the strong bonds of love between man and wife. His melody is merely a
simplified version of Desdemona's (ex. 1).[4]

EXAMPLE I

Thus the mandolin chorus does not function only as indirect characterization of Desdemona, it also paradoxically maintains the tension by tipping
the scale in favour of her conjugal fidelity. From a dramatic point of view
the chorus works as a *recul pour mieux sauter*; when in the next scene

---

[4] Musical examples are quoted from the newly revised edition of the full score (FS) published
at Milan in 1954 by Ricordi (plate number P.R. 155). For practical reasons I also refer to the
vocal score (VS), edited by Mario Parenti, and published by Ricordi in 1964 (plate number
51023). Since the bars in both scores lack numbering, only page numbers are given.

Desdemona makes her unfortunate plea for Cassio, Otello will be upset once more. Finally, the insertion of the homage chorus serves the aesthetic needs of both drama and music (which indeed cannot be separated even in analysis). The work abounds in dialogues or duets (Jago-Roderigo, Jago-Otello, Jago-Cassio, Otello-Desdemona, Desdemona-Emilia); although logical in terms of the plot, this structural feature contains the danger of monotony, and therefore the insertion of contrasting ensembles was necessary.

Other ensembles are integrated in an analogous way. They are subtly related to foregoing or following materials, in this way simultaneously establishing musical and dramatic links. The choruses of the first act are especially striking in this respect. Although there is little demonstrable connection between the storm scene and the fire chorus, these pieces have an affinity of atmosphere, due to the extremely brilliant orchestration. Moreover, a small motif (chordal arpeggios in contrary motion) occurring at the breathing spaces of Otello's first sentence (ex. 2a) reappears in the bonfire scene, equally as orchestral interruption of speech (ex. 2b). A variant of this formula (ex. 2c) persists into the following scene of Jago, Cassio and Roderigo (ex. 2d); another variant (ex. 2e) forms a link with the introduction of the drinking song (ex. 2f). Finally a rhythmically changed version (ex. 2g) not only recurs in the same introduction, but dominates the accompaniment of the brawl scene which follows the drinking song (ex. 2h).

EXAMPLE 2

a   (FS 36, VS 22)   b   (FS 61, VS 37–38)

c   (FS 60, VS 36)   d   (FS 82–84, VS 55–56

e   (FS 61, VS 38)   f   (FS 88, VS 59)

g   (FS 74–75, VS 49)   h   (FS 123ff, VS 81ff)

However unimportant these connections may seem, they clearly testify to Verdi's conception of the major part of Act I as a whole, the parts of which are unified in spite of their inner contrasts.[5] The fact that *Scena I* of the first act is excessively long cannot be explained by a mere formal reason (i.e. the Cypriots remaining on the stage). It has a deeper meaning: from the beginning the plot must be clear and simple, and no separate scenes must divert our attention. Besides, the scene's length contributes to making Otello's reappearance and his first fatal step (the degradation of Cassio) dramatically effective.

EXAMPLE 3

---

[5] *Scena I* runs to 88 pages of the vocal score, i.e. more than four fifths of the first act and nearly one fourth of the whole opera. In the full score, indication of scenes is omitted.

The score contains numerous instances of relationship between consecutive items. In some cases the melodic material of a piece is anticipated in previous sections. An example of this device is provided by the vengeance duet at the end of Act II. Its melodic kernel, a descending fourth (ex. 3a), dominates the whole piece, including the astonishing series of parallel triads in the orchestral postlude (ex. 3b). During the preceding section (a short monologue by Otello ending with the "Sangue!" exclamation) this descending fourth is already announced in the triplets of the orchestral accompaniment (ex. 3c). The last quoted example also anticipates another detail of the vengeance melody, the emphatic minor sixth resolving in the dominant (cf. ex. 7, p. 144).

The opposite device, the 'reverberation' of material into the following section, may be illustrated by an example from the *Credo*. The pentatonic interruptions of Jago's speech (ex. 4a) dissolve into a series of three-note rhythmic motifs (ex. 4b), which are maintained during the beginning of the next scene (Jago watching Cassio and Desdemona, ex. 4c), and reappear in its final bars (ex. 4d).

EXAMPLE 4

The autograph manuscript of *Otello* shows that originally the last variant of the motif (octave leaps of the first horn: A – a – A) persisted even into the following scene (dialogue Jago-Otello), during which it interrupted Jago's words: "Cassio? no ... quei si scosse come un reo nel vedervi." Verdi noted the motif twice, first to be played by a horn and a bassoon (FS p. 194, b. 5;

VS p. 124, b. 9), and then by a horn alone (FS p. 194, b. 7; VS p. 125, b. 2). Later he tried to erase the motif in both bars; nevertheless the first version is still legible, giving an insight into his original intention: to connect three consecutive items (the *Credo*, the watching scene and the dialogue) by means of a single motif. That the rhythmic formula refers to Jago's machinations is proved by its previous occurrence in the first act. There it dominates the scene in which Jago induces Cassio to drink (FS p. 82–84, VS p. 55–56).

The tight and logical building of the drama by Boito and Verdi has always been admired. Its construction reminds us that in Latin countries romantic trends have never destroyed classical tradition. Each of the first three acts represents a phase of Jago's machinations and Otello's decline. In Act I the ensign induces the general to degrade Cassio; in Act II he successfully upsets his master's peace of mind; in Act III Otello accuses Desdemona, Jago plays his last card, showing the handkerchief in Cassio's possession, and finally Otello's mental disintegration is shown in front of all his subordinates as well as the Venetian envoy. This leaves Act IV as a structural problem.

During the first three acts we have seen Jago almost continuously on the stage.[6] Now that his work is completed he disappears and our attention is drawn to Desdemona. Verdi must have felt the danger of a break in the unity of the work, especially with regard to the first half of the last act, which from a dramatic as well as a musical point of view (the two solo songs) seems essentially different from what we have seen and heard before. Probably for this reason he establishes musical links with the previous acts. The first and most important of these is his special use of the English horn. This instrument appears at only four places in the score: the love duet (Act I, sc. 3), the Willow Song (Act IV, sc. 1), Otello watching the sleeping Desdemona (*ibid.* sc. 3) and finally, after he has stabbed himself, as he stands by er corpse (*ibid.* sc. 4). In the love duet the instrument plays but a subordinate part; in the prelude of Act IV and the Willow Song, however, its dark timbre determines the atmosphere. Furthermore, in both scenes 3 and 4, the English horn melody precedes the famous *bacio* theme. The instrument therefore functions psychologically and dramatically as a common denominator of these four scenes, expressing the double concept of love and death.

In this respect, Otello's words in the love scene are significant:

> Venga la morte! e mi colga
> nell'estasi di quest'amplesso
> il momento supremo!

---

[6] Jago is only absent during the two Otello-Desdemona duets (Act 1, sc. 3; Act III, sc. 2).

Let death come! And may
the supreme moment take me
in the ecstasy of this embrace.

The text of the Willow Song is equally revealing

Egli era nato per la sua gloria,
io per amarlo e per morir.

He was born for his glory
And I to love him and to die.

whereas the two scenes later in Act IV speak for themselves. In three of these
instances the use of the English horn is closely tied to the kiss theme. Its
specific function, however, is that it integrates the Willow Song in the
totality of the drama.

EXAMPLE 5

Other connections between the Willow Song and foregoing scenes are of a melodic nature. The entire song is governed by *descending* minor thirds, either as a leap (ex. 5a and b), or filled with an intervening note (ex. 5c). A second melodic characteristic is the use of the leading note as a *cambiata*, leaping downwards to the fifth (ex. 5d) Both of these features have already appeared in the great third-act ensemble. The following examples, all from Desdemona's part, hardly need any commentary (ex. 5e, f and g).

Finally, it should be noted that in the *preghiera* immediately following the Willow Song, the dominating interval is the *ascending* minor third (C – Eb) which we hear immediately at the beginning, and which is repeated several times in the course of the piece. In other respects, too, the *Ave Maria* forms a dramatically efficient contrast to the Willow Song. Both songs have a short 'refrain' which is thrice repeated: the one is sung on unaccompanied dissonant notes ("salce!"); the other, of purely instrumental origin, is harmonized by simple subdominant and tonic triads. There is in addition a striking difference in orchestration. The prelude to the fourth act is written exclusively for woodwinds and one horn; during the Willow Song itself the same instruments dominate the accompaniment as well as the interludes. The *Ave Maria*, on the other hand, is scored exclusively for strings.

Desdemona's prayer is not without affinity to other scenes of the drama. In both her duets with Otello (I, sc. 3; III, sc. 2), she refers to her religious feelings and thoughts:

DESD: Disperda il ciel gli affani
        e amor non muti col mutar degli anni.
OT: A questa tua preghiera
        Amen risponda la celeste schiera.
DESD: *Amen* risponda . . .

DESD: *May heaven drive away care, and love not change with changing*
        years.
OT: *To this your prayer let the celestial host answer* Amen.
DESD: *May it answer* Amen.

                                                                    (I, sc. 3)

Desdemona's exclamations during the third act duet ("Iddio m'aiuti!" and "No ... no ... pel battesmo della fede cristiana..."[7] should therefore be taken in their literal sense. Like many Verdian heroines, she is a deeply religious woman.

---

[7] "God send me aid" and "No ... no, by the baptism of Christian faith ..."

As love and religion are closely related in this opera, it is not surprising to find in the *Ave Maria* not only a textual reference but also a musical quotation of the first act love scene (ex. 6a). Its words referring to Otello are significant: "e pel possente, misero anch'esso, tua pietà dimostra."[8] The motif first occurred in the violoncello quartet which leads to the duet (ex. 6b). But we have heard it in several other scenes too, such as the love duet itself (ex. 6c), Jago's first direct 'attack' (II, sc. 3), where it twice underlines the last moments of Otello's peace of mind (ex. 6d), the end of the second Otello-Desdemona duet (ex. 6e), bitterly illustrating the words "quella vil cortigiana ch'è la sposa d'Otello,"[9] and finally the last scene of the drama when Otello, after the truth has been revealed to him, looks at the lifeless Desdemona (ex. 6f).

EXAMPLE 6

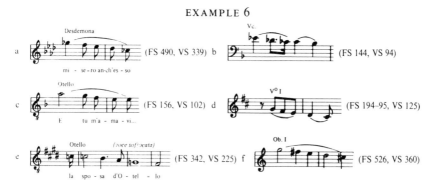

Love, religion and death, these interrelated concepts, constitute a spiritual atmosphere to which Jago has no access.

Two other motifs repeatedly found in the score draw our attention. Students of Verdi's operas will be familiar with both of them, since they occur in most of his works. The first, the emphatic minor sixth, has already been mentioned in connection with the vengeance duet (see ex. 3a and c above). This is the common use of the motif, known from such famous examples as the B♭♭ of Lady Macbeth's sleepwalking scene and the Fate melody in *La Forza del Destino*. In *Otello*, however, the motif is used also in a more specific way, as a *repeated* 'appoggiatura', shown in example 7.

Strictly speaking not all of these examples are appoggiaturas; nevertheless they are closely interrelated. This holds especially for examples (a) and (b), taken respectively from the introduction of the drinking song and the end of the brawl (Act I, sc. 1); here we have one more proof of Verdi's striving for

[8] "... and to the mighty, wretched also, show thy pity."
[9] "... that vile whore who is Otello's wife."

EXAMPLE 7

a  (FS 88, VS 59)

b  (FS 134–35, VS 87)

c  (FS 178, VS 115)

d  (FS 250–51, VS 171–72)

e  (VS 241, FS 372)

f  (FS 377, VS 244)

g  (FS 463, VS 323)

h  (FS 468, VS 326)

i (FS 495, VS 343)

unity. Example (c), occurring in Jago's *Credo*,[10] obviously comments on the preceding words "vile son nato,"[11] the melody of which consists of the same notes (Ab – G – F). The next three examples refer to various stages of Otello's fury and despair: (d) "M'hai legato alla croce! ... Ahimè! ..." (II, sc. 4);[12] (e) "Le parole non odo ... Lasso! e udir le vorrei! Dove son guinto!"[13] (III, sc. 5 during which Otello, hidden behind a pillar, watches Cassio and Jago); (f) "È quello! è quello! Ruina e morte!"[14] (the same scene after Otello has seen the handkerchief). Example (g) is from the final bars of Act III; it seals the complete breakdown of the Moor and is in bitter contradiction to the off-stage cheers of the Cypriots ("Viva! Viva! Viva Otello!"). The last two examples are seemingly of a gentler tone, but the dramatic situations in which they occur are no less moving than the foregoing. Example (h) comments on Desdemona's request to be buried in her bridal garment (IV, sc. 1), and example (i) is the melody of Otello's entrance into his wife's bedroom, where he watches her as she sleeps (IV, sc. 3). The common element in the frequent use of this motif is the high degree of emotional tension. Although the motif itself has no specific meaning, it functions structurally within the framework of the drama.

In contrast to the first, the second motif, which can be traced in nearly all of Verdi's operas, does possess a special connotation. It refers to death, and occurs here in two versions, one played by wind instruments, the other by a kettle-drum (ex. 8).[15]

EXAMPLE 8

As in previous operas, Verdi employs the death motif in *Otello* in an implicit and prospective way. Since it is connected with 'fatal' rather than with 'natural' death (which includes death on the battlefield), the occurrence of the motif (a) in connection with Otello's war memories in the love duet (I, sc. 3; FS p. 147–50; omitted in VS) and with his monologue, "Ora e per sempre addio", quoted at the beginning of this chapter (II, sc. 5; FS p. 257–259) may seem ambiguous. In both scenes it does not refer to the battlefield, however, but to the ultimate fate of Otello. The same anapaestic motif,

[10] In the vocal score the reading is inaccurate.
[11] "Base am I born."
[12] "You have bound me to the cross ... Alas!"
[13] "I can't catch the words ... O misery! I would hear them! To what have I come!"
[14] "That's it! That's it! Death and damnation!"
[15] See Ch. 8.

softly played by brass and bassoons, accompanies Desdemona's words in
the third-act duet:

> Esterrefatta fisso lo sguardo tuo tremendo;
> in te parla una Furia, la sento e non l'intendo.

> *Terrified, I fix your terrible look. A fury speaks in you;*
> *I feel it, but understand it not.* (III, sc. 2).

Here, too, the motif is used in a prospective way; Otello's fury will ultimately lead to Desdemona's destruction.

In order to illustrate actual death, Verdi uses the motif (b). It occurs in the
scene where Otello speaks to Desdemona's corpse:

> Fredda come la casta tua vita, e in cielo assorta.

> *Cold as your chaste life, and gathered to the skies.*

These words are accompanied by plucked strings which alternate with the
drum playing motif (b).[16]

Most of the structural material thus far discussed consists of short motifs.
Themes, defined here as periodic musical sentences, never function as reminiscent or associative melodies. Even the best known orchestral melody of
the opera, the *bacio* theme, is not a complete phrase, since it starts with an
appoggiatura on a six-four chord. There are indeed very few 'regular' themes
in *Otello*. They occur in choruses like the drinking song (I, sc. 1), the
homage of the Cypriots to Desdemona (II, sc. 3), and in other 'ceremonial'
scenes, such as the vengeance duet (II, sc. 5), the beginning of the second
Otello-Desdemona duet (III, sc. 2), and the two fourth-act songs. But the
great majority of scenes are written in a free melodic style, full of exclamations, unfinished phrases and interruptions, which almost extinguish the
differences between aria, arioso and recitative. It is in this respect that the
opera varies most widely from its predecessor, composed sixteen years before. *Aida* was not only commissioned for a ceremonial occasion, but is also
in itself a ceremonial opera. Since ceremony essentially depends on control,
the actors express themselves in regular phrases, however strong their emotion may be. The structural materials of *Aida*, i.e. the themes of the titular
heroine, of Amneris, of the priests, and the melody of rivalry, all of which

---

[16] In the vocal score the drum motif has been omitted.

recur several times in the course of the drama, never deny their original periodic structure, even in those cases where they are only partially quoted. If we compare the death scenes of *Aida* and *Otello*, the difference becomes perfectly clear. Aida and Radamès sing in regular phrases, supported by simple harmonies. Their death is not only the consequence of a ceremony (the trial) but also forms part of it. The death scenes of Desdemona and Otello, on the other hand, are for the most part depicted by musical disintegration. There is no question of themes, only of exclamations and bits of phrases, supported by tremolos or a paratactic sequence of chords (see for instance FS p. 510–11, 525; VS p. 352–53, 360). It may be argued that Aida dies of her own free will, whereas Desdemona does not. But this is only true in terms of the plot; from a dramatic point of view they are both victims of Fate.

The underlying reason for the structural differences between the two operas is that in contrast to the ceremonial character of *Aida*, the essential dramatic quality of *Otello* is the dissolution of ceremony. Even before the crucial moment in the third act, when, in the presence of the Venetian envoy, Otello strikes out at Desdemona and throws her down, we have already witnessed disorder in previous scenes. The drinking song (in itself a sort of ritual) degenerates into a brawl, and at the end of the second duet with Desdemona, Otello is unable to maintain even a sarcastically courteous tone; his voice is suffocated (FS p. 342, VS p. 225). *Otello* is the drama of a human passion that proves stronger than social order and convention.

*   *
*

The working of the poison

Verdi's Jago: a born villain with not half the motivation of his Shakespearean namesake. Jago professes villany as a gratuitous occupation, as the natural consequence of his existence. In themselves, pure villains, like pure saints, hardly provide interesting human material for the dramatist; on the stage, both soon become boring. Verdi's achievement seems to contradict this rule, however. His insistence on the continual reworking of the *Credo* proves that from the beginning it was this kind of Jago he had in mind. And he certainly succeeded in bringing him to life. The question is therefore, how did he do it?

Jago sets himself a task, the destruction of Otello. He holds no personal grudge against Desdemona, nor even against Cassio. In view of his self-revelation in the *Credo*, one might even question his genuine hatred for the Moor; to be disappointed in military advancement seems hardly sufficient explanation for his perfidious conduct. However this may be, Verdi has clearly marked the beginning and the end of Jago's path. It is done by a melody which we first hear as an aside to Roderigo during the storm scene ("May the frantic belly of the sea be her tomb")[17] and then at the moment of his triumph ("Who can now prevent me from pressing this forehead beneath my heel?") (ex. 9).

EXAMPLE 9

Jago has several musical attributes which already appear in his first dialogue with Roderigo: the downward leap of an octave with short appoggiatura, the vocal or orchestral trill, the *unisono* accompaniment, and the descending chromatic scale. All of these are shown in the following fragment (ex. 10).

EXAMPLE 10

[17] The words refer to Otello's ship.

(FS 58, VS 35)

The octave leap which seems to have the connotation of sneering occurs twice in the Jago-Roderigo dialogue, both times in the orchestra. It also closes the introduction to the drinking song (FS p. 89, VS p. 59), while during the song the motif is taken up by Jago himself, characteristically in a changed 2/4 metre which interrupts the flow of 6/8 bars (FS p. 90; 100; VS p. 60; 65;). In the *Credo*, the four leaping bassoons sneer at the "honest man" whose tears, kisses and sacrifices are said to be no more than lies (FS p. 183, VS p. 117). The octave leap appears again in the fifth scene of Act III, which shows another instance of Jago's manipulation of Cassio and is therefore dramatically related to the drinking song. Here, too, the orchestral interruption leaves the impression of a sneering aside.

The trill which occurs more frequently in connection with Jago's part often leaves the impression of a jeer but also pictures gentle persuasion. In the drinking song and in the third-act terzetto it may have the ambiguous meaning of both playfulness and devilry. Other scenes in which the vocal or orchestral trill appears are the *Credo* (passim), the *idra* fragment (FS p. 203, VS p. 131) and its elaboration as introduction to the third act (FS p. 305, VS p. 204), the dialogue preceding Jago's relation of the faked dream (FS p. 270, VS p. 184), and his final exclamation with a gesture of horrendous triumph; "Ecco il Leone!" (III, sc. 9; FS p. 461–62, VS p. 322).

The arioso-like passages accompanied in unison are not numerous but

they express Jago's most pregnant words. Apart from the fragment quoted
in example 10 above, all of them are addressed to Otello (II, sc. 3: FS p. 203,
206; VS p. 131, 133; and III, sc. 9: FS p. 459, 460–61; VS p. 321, 322). The
descending chromatic scales are equally connected with Jago's most perfidious manipulations, especially in those cases where they are assigned to
the voice. A striking example is found in the dream fragment, where a
chromatic passage of parallel sixth chords proceeds in the no man's land
between two keys, underlining the fictitious words put in Cassio's mouth
(ex. 11a). The melisma on "beva" in the drinking song shows another instance of this device (see below, ex. 12). Moreover, at the moment that
Otello hurls himself against the crowd (Act III, sc. 9), Jago's hypocritical
words ("A malady which deprives him of all sense now assails him") are
rendered by a chromatic melody (ex. 11b). The use of descending chromat-

EXAMPLE 11

(FS 129–30, VS 85)

(FS 168, VS 109)

(FS 287–89, VS 195–96)

icism in the orchestra only may be interpreted as an indirect picture of his perfidy (see ex. 10 above, and also passages from the brawl scene, i.e. the asides addressed to Roderigo, from the introduction to Act II, and from Jago's strophe of the vengeance duet) (ex. 11c, d and e).

Finally it should be noted that melodies and motifs in triple time or in triplets form an important musical feature of Jago's language, especially in his dealings with Otello and Cassio. During the first act this is apparent only in the drinking song in which Jago plays a leading part, but from the second act onwards the triplets or ternary metres dominate nearly all his dialogues with the two men he wants to destroy. The first bars of Act II are characteristic in this respect: the triplets played *forte* by four bassoons and the violoncellos picture Jago in all his ferocity, but later they underline his gentle persuasion of Cassio. The motif persists into the *Credo* which, in spite of being written in common time, is full of triplets. Key-points of the drama, like the *idra*-arioso (FS p. 203, VS p. 131; see also the prelude of Act III), the dream fragment (FS p. 272ff, VS p. 186ff), the vengeance duet (FS p. 283ff, VS p. 193ff), and the third-act terzetto (FS p. 363, VS p. 236) are all written in simple or compound triple metre. Generally Jago addresses Otello or Cassio in common time only in recitative-like passages.

Jago keeps some of his musical attributes for himself (the octave leap, the trill and the unison accompaniment); other characteristics, however, creep into the parts of Otello and the Cypriots. This is done by what I consider the most important structural feature of the opera: the working of the poison. Twice in the course of the work Jago pronounces: "il mio velen lavora,"[18] first after the second-act quartet, later at the moment of Otello's complete collapse (end of Act III). The poison works indeed, not only in the text and in the visible action on the stage, but also and even more subtly in the music.

A characteristic example of this device is found in the drinking scene of Act I. Verdi conceived the song in the traditional 'bar' form, consisting of two strophes and an *abgesang*, which are unified by a common refrain. Moreover the song is preceded by an orchestral introduction, and its three sections are separated by short interludes (asides of Jago and Roderigo). This form type particularly suited his dramatic purpose: what begins as an orderly situation (the two strophes) deteriorates into disorder (the *abgesang* in which Cassio is mocked at, followed by the brawl). But at the same time Verdi stays within operatic tradition; the refrain guarantees the unity of the song as a musical entity. It is in this refrain that the poison works. Jago exposes his melody, which contains the descending chromatic scales that are so typical of his musical language (ex. 12).

EXAMPLE 12

(FS 93-94, VS 61)

Subsequently the melody of the refrain is taken up by the chorus, characteristically *without* the chromatic passages. These are sung by Jago who is shortly afterwards joined by Roderigo, his spineless tool (ex. 13).[19]

EXAMPLE 13

(FS 97-98, VS 63-64)

[18] "My poison works."

[19] Only the last four notes of the longest chromatic scale are doubled by the male voices of the chorus.

In the second strophe this procedure is repeated with the sole difference that all the actors sing *con voce soffocata*, obviously as a result of intoxication. Not until the refrain of the *abgesang* section does Jago succeed in bringing the people over to his side; the whole chromatic scale descending a ninth (from F to E) is doubled by tenors and basses of the chorus. It is clear that in this instance chromaticism has worked as a poison, inducing the people in the tavern to mock at Cassio and to provoke him.

Many instances of the contaminating force of Jago's chromatic melodies occur in Otello's part. During his initial private encounter with the ensign

EXAMPLE 14

(Act II, sc. 3), his words "... nel chiostro dell'anima ricetti qualche terribil mostro"[20] are sung on a melody which seems to be borrowed from Jago's spiritual atmosphere (ex. 14a). Otello's exclamation "la prova io voglio!"[21] is supported by a similar melody (ex. 14b); in this instance the example is the more conclusive since the melody is played by a bassoon and low strings, instruments that are often encountered in connection with Jago. Other examples are found at the end of the monologue "Ora e per sempre addio" (ex. 14c), in the second Otello-Desdemona duet (III, sc. 3) and its postlude (ex. 14d), in the unison passages of the following scene (ex. 14e), and at the moment of his breakdown (a chain of parallel sixth chords, chromatically descending from A″ to D′; ex. 14f).

Examples of descending chromaticism appear also in the parts of Desdemona and Lodovico; these however have a plaintive character and are far removed from Jago's realm. Nor does Cassio undergo Jago's influence, but the latter's chromatic scales are heard when the degraded captain tells him about the *fazzoletto* (FS p. 370–71, VS p. 240–41).

Equally efficient is the working of the poison by means of orchestral triplets. Derived from a phrase of the *Credo* (ex. 15a), they first appear in Otello's rhetorical monologue "Ora e per sempre addio" (ex. 15b); covered by the dull *pizzicato* of the divided double basses,[22] they are hardly perceptible. But in the following section (FS p. 26off, VS p. 176ff), which ends with his assault of Jago, these triplets dominate the orchestral accompaniment. They reappear after Jago's relation of the dream and, as has already been shown, provide not only the material of the vengeance duet (another rhetorical piece), but also of its pathetic introduction written on the text: "Jago, ho il cor di gelo" (see above, ex. 3a and c).

EXAMPLE 15

[20] "In the cloister of your mind you house some fearful monster."
[21] "I want proof!" (II, sc. 5)
[22] Verdi may have borrowed this orchestral device from Berlioz (*Symphonie fantastique*, 4th movement, "Marche au supplice").

Thus the triplets entirely dominate the last part of Act II. The complete text of the melody from which they are derived is significant:

Credo con fermo cuor, sicome crede
la vedovella al tempio,
che il mal ch'io penso e che da me procede,
per mio destino adempio.

I believe with a firm heart, as ever
did widow in church,
that the evil which I conceive and which from me proceeds,
I will achieve by my destiny.

Another motif from the *Credo* (the semiquaver triplet) reappears in Otello's Ab minor monologue "Dio! mi potevi scagliar tutti mali della miseria, della vergogna" (III, sc. 3; FS p. 346ff, VS p. 226ff).[23] Finally the *unisono* orchestral accompaniment to Otello's discovery of the handkerchief in Cassio's possession ("È quello!")[24] is clearly reminiscent of the *Credo* (FS p. 377, VS p. 244).

A third means by which the poison infects Otello is a special four-note formula that may be called Jago's designing motif. It appears in different forms but invariably retains the shape of three stepwise ascending notes followed by a descending interval. The latter may vary from a minor second to a double octave plus a major third. Sometimes it is a dissonant interval (diminished fifth, minor or diminished seventh); when it is consonant the motif is often repeated with emphasis (ex. 16).[25]

However numerous, these examples are far from complete. The orchestral beginning of the *Credo* (F – Gb – Bb) and several vocal phrases of this piece ("... e che nell'ira io nomo")[26]; "Credo che il giusto è un istrion beffardo ..."[27]; "E credo l'uom gioco d'iniqua sorte ..."[28]) are certainly related to the motif of designing.

The motif is first used to characterize Jago and his manipulation of Cassio (ex. 16a–e). From the moment the ensign speaks the fatal words "ciò

---

[23] "Oh God! Thou mightest have heaped upon me all the ills of misery, of shame."

[24] "That's it!" (III, sc. 5)

[25] Repeat signs indicate reiteration of the motif (at least twice).

[26] "... and whom, in hate, I name."

[27] "I believe that the honest man is a jeering buffoon ..."

[28] "And I believe man to be the sport of a malign fate."

EXAMPLE 16

m'accora ...",[29] it begins to serve its main purpose: the destruction of Otello's peace of mind (ex. 16f–j). During the third and fourth acts the motif functions as a reminder. When Desdemona asks why she is the innocent cause of Otello's grief, the four notes significantly interrupt her speech (ex. 16k); in the terzetto the motif underlines Otello's despair (ex. 16l) and Jago's ambiguous words: "Questa è una regna dove il tuo cor casca, si lagna, s'impiglia e muor"[30] (ex. 16m). The last two examples (ex. 16n and o), occurring just before and immediately after the strangling of Desdemona, remind us once more of the man who is the source of the catastrophe.

Thus the poison works in a threefold manner, by means of descending chromatic scales, by triplets, and by the use of a special motif. The importance of this structural device is clear: our whole attention is drawn to what is really happening, not on the level of the fable, but on that of the drama. It may be that the device was not new. One thinks of other operas in which the spell of one person over another is shown by musical means (for instance, the relationship Fiordiligi-Ferrando in *Così fan tutte*, where the influence is particularly evident, although unconscious from the two characters' point of view). But I wonder if before or after Verdi a composer ever used the device in such a penetrating way, making it the structural essence of his work.

*　　*
*

Desdemona

Desdemona is Jago's antipode, not only as a person, but also as to her role in the plot. Her passivity is set off in sharp opposition to his machinations. Desdemona's sole active contribution to the development of the

---

[29] "I like not that" (cf. *Othello* III, sc. 3, v. 35). In the opera the words are found in II, sc. 3 (FS p. 193; VS p. 124).
[30] "This is a web wherein your heart stumbles, cries out, entangles itself and dies."

plot is her repeated plea for Cassio; but even this can hardly be considered a free act, since it is both the result of Jago's intrigue and the compelling consequence of her innate goodness. Without the contrasting villain, a personality like hers would certainly bore us. The viability of her role rests on the interdependence of the leading characters, which is so essential to the structure of this opera. Still, the Desdemona-Jago relationship reveals a curious paradox; in a drama which is virtually enacted by no more than three persons, two of them never really speak to each other.[31] Strange as this may seem, on second thought it becomes perfectly logical. Only by keeping Desdemona apart from Jago does Verdi succeed in making her purity acceptable. While it is true that by means of their contrasting characters the drama opposes good to evil, nevertheless a *direct* confrontation of these embodied concepts is almost systematically avoided.

As might be expected, Desdemona's musical physiognomy is also the complete opposite of Jago's. In contrast to the latter's slithery ariosos written in triple metre, she sings her quiet, expressive melodies in common time. Only the second-act quartet and the middle section of her third-act duet with Otello are exceptions to this rule; in the former ensemble, however, her part contains a characteristic descending scale in duplets (ex. 17).

EXAMPLE 17

(FS 240–41, VS 164)

The same example shows another feature contrasting with Jago's musical language: the descending *diatonic* scale.[32] In Act III, shortly after the arrival of the Venetian ambassadors, Desdemona sings the following words, indirectly addressed to Otello (ex. 18).[33]

EXAMPLE 18

(FS 403, VS 263)

[31] In Act III, sc. 7, Desdemona's words referring to Cassio's return to grace ("Jago, I hope so; you know I feel true affection for Cassio") do not form part of a dialogue but rather of a conversation in which several persons are involved (Lodovico, Jago, Desdemona). Actually the words are addressed to Otello, who is reading the Doge's letter but listening at the same time.

[32] When, under the pressure of her deep sorrow, Desdemona exceptionally sings a chromatically descending melody, the expressive accompaniment with its accelerating harmonic rhythm is completely alien to Jago's style (see III, sc. 8; FS p. 417–18; VS p. 272–73).

[33] "I think he will return to grace."

A few moments later this melody is taken over literally by Jago who only substitutes the word "forse"[34] for "credo". Here, by changing his habitual chromatic scale to a diatonic one, the ensign slyly adapts himself to Desdemona. The opposite would be impossible, since Otello's wife is virtually incapable of imitating the true Jago. Besides having no idea of the kind of man he really is, she forms part of a world of unassailable values, and is therefore immune from the poison.[35]

Generally the accompaniment to Desdemona's singing underlines her mental equilibrium with steadily repeated chords in slow harmonic rhythm. The following phrase from the love duet is a characteristic example (ex. 19).

EXAMPLE 19

(FS 151, VS 99–100)

Similar instances are found in Act II, sc. 4 (Desdemona's first plea for Cassio, FS p. 228ff, VS p. 99ff), Act III, sc. 2 (her complaint in the middle of the second duet with Otello, FS p. 329ff, VS p. 218ff), and the great ensemble in Act III, sc. 8 (FS p. 416, 422; VS p. 272, 277). The harmonies, which especially in the two great duets show a certain French influence, are very expressive and compensate for the lack of rhythmic variety.

---

[34] "Perhaps".
[35] One could hardly be as sure of Shakespeare's Desdemona.

Nowhere in the opera has Verdi shown more clearly Desdemona's curiously distinctive function than in the second-art quartet. The piece in question is a typical specimen of operatic ensemble in which each of the characters involved simultaneously expresses his or her own feelings. Like its famous forerunners (e.g. the quartets from *Idomeneo*, *Fidelio*, and *Rigoletto*), it forms a dramatic climax in the work, realized by a device of which verbal drama is incapable. This is the situation: Jago urges Emilia to give him Desdemona's handkerchief. Emilia does not understand why he wants it. Although she has no idea of her husband's machinations, she suspects him of evil intentions and refuses; finally Jago wrenches the handkerchief from her. At the same time Desdemona addresses Otello in the following terms:

> La tua fanciulla io sono
> umile e mansueta;
> ma il labbro tuo sospira,
> hai l'occhio fiso al suol.
> Guardami in volto e mira
> come favella amor.
> Vien ch'io t'allieti il core,
> ch'io ti lenisca il duol.

> *I am your handmaiden*
> *humble and submissive;*
> *but your lips sigh,*
> *your eyes are bent on the ground.*
> *Look me in the face and see*
> *how love does speak.*
> *Come, let me cheer your heart*
> *let me assuage your pain.*

But Otello does not listen; instead he soliloquizes:

> Forse perchè gl'inganni
> d'arguto amor non tendo,
> forse perchè discendo
> nella valle degli anni,
> forse perchè ho sul viso
> quest'atro tenebror,

ella è perduta e irriso
io sono e il core m'infrango
e ruinar nel fango
vedo il mio sogno d'or.

Perchance because I do not understand
the subtle deceits of love,
perchance because I have passed
the heyday of my years,
perchance because I have upon my face
this sombre hue,
she is lost and I am mocked
and my heart is broken
and ruined in the mire
I see my golden dream.

The structural problems of this ensemble could have been solved in various ways. A division into two simultaneous duets would seem logical, since the 'lower' couple is dealing with a specific matter which is far removed from Otello's and Desdemona's preoccupations. Even more acceptable would have been a division into two plus one plus one, since only Jago and Emilia are having a real dialogue; Otello's soliloquizing sets both him and Desdemona apart. Verdi, however, chose a solution which, although contradicting the 'superficial' dramatic situation, actually underlines an essential element of the drama: Jago's hold on Otello. Naturally the parts of Jago and Emilia are closely connected but they are also rhythmically and melodically linked with Otello's soliloquy. A motif of Jago (ex. 20a) reappears in Otello's part, is again taken up by Jago (ex. 20b) and is finally quoted in the third-act ensemble (ex. 20c).[36]

Over and against this 'terzetto' stands Desdemona's beseeching melody which, compared with the rhythm of the other parts, is written in approximately doubled note values.[37] She is the one person who has not the slightest idea of what is going on, not only because of her innocence, but also because she is incapable of understanding anything evil. The fact that she sings in large melodic curves, dominating the other actors' parts and

---

[36] The motif also serves to connect the quartet with the next scene. It provides the musical material for the transition, appearing first in semiquavers, then in demisemiquavers, and finally as triple appoggiaturas (slides) of the initial chords of *scena* 5 (see FS p. 247–50, VS p. 169–71).

[37] The respective numbers of semiquavers (practically the shortest note value in the quartet) are significant: Jago (103), Emilia (61), Otello (71), Desdemona (2).

EXAMPLE 20

consequently the whole piece, is particularly significant. Unknowing and passive, she is nevertheless the main figure on the stage.

Another famous Verdian ensemble, the first-act terzetto of *Aida*, seems to me to have served as a structural model for this quartet. The situation is somewhat analogous. Aida is completely ignorant of the tension between Amneris and Radamès; she has her own emotional problem, the conflicting love for her native country and its main enemy. Her part, too, is written in double note values and therefore widely differs from the other two.[38] In *Otello*, however, this structural device has a deeper meaning. One might say of the quartet that while its text furthers the development of the plot, its music truly serves the drama.

*   *
*

Otello

The old question of whether Otello – either Shakespeare's or Verdi's – is a jealous man cannot be answered unless there is agreement about the concept of jealousy. Unfortunately this consensus is lacking. 'Jealousy' may have different meanings varying from "envious attitude" to "watchfulness,"[39] but Otello is certainly not jealous in either sense. Envy which deprives a man of his dignity could perhaps serve as theme for a comedy, but surely not for Shakespeare's tragedy or Verdi's opera. On the other hand, to call Otello merely 'watchful' would be equally unconvincing. Jago's cunning advice to beware of *gelosia* certainly does not refer to 'watchfulness'. Whatever the meaning of 'jealousy' may be in the drama one thing is certain: it is a human passion. And being 'watchful' is not exactly a passionate state of mind. In order to understand the real nature of Otello's attitude, it is necessary to

---

[38] The respective numbers of quavers (the shortest value) are: Amneris (54), Radames (61), Aida (1).

[39] See: *The American Heritage Dictionary of the English Language*, entry "Jealousy".

analyze the text of his part; the monologues and soliloquies prove particularly revealing.

In his first line Otello already speaks about "pride and glory". Since these
words refer to the victory over the Mussulman there is nothing exceptional
in them. Still, in the course of the drama the term 'glory' acquires a specific
and personal meaning. Otello's glory is not just the renown of a brave
soldier; it is the fruit of a lifelong struggle against handicaps. Two of these
are referred to in the love duet: "the life of exile" and "the chains and grief
of the slave". But Otello is much more explicit in his soliloquy during the
second-act quartet, the text of which has already been quoted above. First,
he is a black man; secondly, he is incapable of understanding fashionable
and subtle frivolities in love; and finally he marries the youthful Desdemona
at middle age. The relationship of all these drawbacks with the concept of
glory and its loss is emphasized repeatedly in the course of the drama. In the
love duet Otello recalls the time of courting, when he told his beloved of his
previous sufferings:

> Ingentilia di lagrime la storia
> il tuo bel viso e il labbro di sospir;
> scendean sulle mie tenebre la gloria,
> il paradiso e gli astri a benedir.

> *Your lovely face ennobled the story*
> *with tears, and your lips with sighs;*
> *on my darkness glory,*
> *paradise and the stars descended with a blessing.*

Desdemona takes up this thought:

> Ed io vedea fra le tue tempie oscure
> splender del genio l'eternea beltà.

> *And from your dusky temples I saw*
> *the eternal beauty of your spirit shine forth.*

"The subtle deceits of love" (see Otello's text in the quartet, quoted
above) seem to refer to Cassio, who is a fashionable Florentine bachelor of
noble birth (Jago sneeringly characterizes him as "dressed up"; see FS p. 57,
VS p. 34). Like Jago and Roderigo he is considerably younger than Otello;
the latter is incapable of understanding Cassio's frivolities, not only because

of his age but also because of his totally different background and the sufferings of his youth. This may explain the naiveté through which he is ensnared by Jago; Otello is unaware of the fact that the seemingly frivolous Cassio is his own and Desdemona's most loyal friend. Conspicuously, a musical phrase of Cassio sung in the course of the third-act terzetto is very much akin to the melodic language of the Cypriots in the homage chorus of Act II and thus underlines his innocence and loyalty (ex. 21).

EXAMPLE 21

Cassio
Mi – ra – co – lo va – go del - l'a-spo e del - l'a – go—— che in rag – gi tra-mu – ta le

fi – la d'un vel, più bian – co, più lie – ve che fioc-co di ne – ve,—— che

(FS 379–382, VS 246–47)

nu – be tes-su – – ta dal - l'au – re—— del ciel.

The explicit proof of Cassio's love and esteem for his general is his cry "Ah ferma!"[40] at the moment that Otello stabs himself, while Lodovico and Montano only exclaim "Sciagurato!"[41] In spite of all that has happened, the captain still wants Otello's life to be saved.

But the Moor's fate is sealed. He believes his *gloria*, of which the marriage with Desdemona is not only an integral part but the very crowning, has been destroyed. And since in the course of his life 'glory' has become the basis of his existence, Desdemona's supposed unfaithfulness destroys the past as well as the present. Hence the monologue "Ora e per sempre addio", quoted at the beginning of this chapter. Life becomes vacuous to Otello: "L'alma mia nissun più smuova".[42]

Musically the Moor's sufferings are pictured by alternation of 'disintegrating' and 'rhetorical' monologues. His outburst following Jago's first move (FS p. 197–99; VS p. 127–29) already contains the characteristics of his later breakdown: irregular phraseology and tonal instability. After the quartet, Otello's despair cries out in stronger terms. Especially at the end of this section, in which he expresses the torments of doubt and suspicion, a chain of dissonant chords reveals his unstable state of mind. This is followed

[40] "Oh! Stop!"
[41] "Wretched man!"
[42] "Nothing can touch my soul any more" (FS p. 377–78, VS p. 244–45).

rather suddenly by the rhetorical monologue "Ora e per sempre addio" which, in spite of the soft triplets in tremolo reminding us of Jago's poison (see ex. 15b above), is firmly supported by consonant chords. At the end of the second act Otello expresses himself in a similar way by means of two contrasting sections. After Jago's mention of the handkerchief seen in Cassio's hands, the Moor is very close to a breakdown ("Jago, ho il cor di gelo", ending with the triple exclamation of "sangue!"; FS p. 280–82, VS p. 191–93). This is followed by the rhetorical first strophe of the vengeance duet, a mode of expression which is cunningly adopted by Jago in the second.

In the third act 'disintegration' gets the upper hand of 'control'. After the great E major duet, which begins and ends in a bitterly sarcastic ceremonial style, Otello's true state of mind is pictured by a short but violent orchestral interlude. This is followed by a monologue in A♭ minor in 'bar' form, which still maintains the character of a 'controlled' piece of music. Each of its three sections is preceded by a solemn chromatic scale in double-dotted rhythm and descending from the dominant to the tonic (see above, ex. 14e). But Otello is no longer capable of controlling his voice; "con voce soffocata" he sings a complaint which is perhaps the most moving piece of the whole opera.

After the septet there is no longer any trace of rhetorical style in Otello's language. He has become unable to utter anything but separate bits of phrases and single words referring to previous scenes: "Sangue!"; "ciò m'accora!"[43]; "il fazzoletto!" – The breakdown is complete.

Otello's steadily growing despair and loss of control does not imply the disintegration of his relationship with Desdemona. The bond between man and wife remains insoluble throughout the drama and even transcends death. The kisses (I, sc. 3; IV, sc. 3 and 4) are the visible symbols of this union; perhaps not by chance the accompanying theme is the best-known melody of the opera. Apart from this, another structural element underlines the unbreakable ties between Otello and Desdemona: two special keys, or rather chords.[44]

As has been pointed out, Otello's marriage with Desdemona forms an integral part of his 'glory'. This is the reason why the two concepts of 'union' and 'glory' are constantly interwoven. Verdi symbolizes them by the major triads of C and E, appearing at crucial points of the drama. Though it seems

---

[43] Jago's 'first' words (II, sc. 3; FS p. 193, VS p. 124).

[44] I am deeply obliged to my friend and colleague Pierluigi Petrobelli for drawing my attention to this structural aspect, as well as for his interest in various matters dealt with in this chapter.

at first that the chord of E major serves to stress exclusively Otello's military exploits and renown, it soon appears that both triads are coupled or used individually to emphasize Otello's past as well as his relationship with Desdemona. It should be observed, however, that these chords are by no means Otello's or Desdemona's 'property'; Jago's tale of the dream is in C, the fire chorus in E.

The cry "È salvo!" (FS p. 30–31, VS p. 18) and the exclamation "Vittoria!" (e.g. FS p. 44–45, VS p. 26), both on an E chord, refer to Otello's exploits prior to the drama. More pregnant is the use of both chords in the love duet. The fragments preceding the *bacio* theme ("Disperda il ciel gli affanni", and "Ah! la gioia m'innonda si fieramente"; FS p. 158–61, VS p. 104–105) are both in C, while the theme itself is in E with a turn to C in the seventh bar. In Act II, the choice of E major for the homage chorus is anything but fortuitous, since it stresses the meaning of Desdemona's words ("Splende il cielo", etc.) as well as Otello's appeasement ("Quel canto mi conquide"; see above, ex. 1). The final bars of Otello's monologue, "Ora e per sempre addio", seem to turn to E major (actually it concerns the Neapolitan chord of the key of E♭); the text of this passage is particularly revealing:

> Clamori e canti di battaglia, addio!
> Della gloria d'Otello è questo il fin.[45]

Bitter ironic use of the key of E major is emphasized by Verdi in the third-act duet. At its end, the initial section is repeated in a shortened version, as if nothing has happened between. Desdemona, however, now remains silent, and Otello's true state of mind is indicated by the stage direction "mutando d'un tratto l'ira nella più terribile calma dell'ironia."[46] In the course of the third act the irony is reinforced in various ways. The fanfares announcing the arrival of the Venetian ambassadors are in C (FS p. 387ff, VS p. 251ff); the cries of the Cypriots, "Evviva il Leone di San Marco!", end in the same key (FS p. 398, VS p. 259). Towards the end of the act the ironic bitterness reaches its climax. While the off-stage Cypriots exclaim "Evviva Otello! Gloria al Leon di Venezia!" (mostly in unison on the note C), Jago triumphantly points to the inert Moor: "Ecco il Leone!" The final measures underline this image: the third act concludes with the chords of E and C (ex. 22).

---

[45] See the translation on p. 134.
[46] "Changing suddenly from anger to the even more terrible ironic calm."

EXAMPLE 22

(FS 463, VS 323)

During the last act the two chords are mostly coupled. Otello's entrance into the bedchamber is accompanied by a motif built on the notes of the E major triad with a characteristic appoggiatura on the sixth. A few moments later the motif reappears in the key of A (FS p. 493, VS p. 341), introducing the *bacio* theme. This is played a fourth higher than in Act I but, at the moment of the third kiss, the melody turns again to E, the chord of which is followed by the six-four chord of C (as in the love duet).[47] Yet the expected cadence in the key of E fails to appear; instead Desdemona's awakening is accompanied by a sudden modulation to F minor, the key that announces her fate.[48]

Any remaining doubt about the dramatic and psychological meaning of the two chords is removed when we hear the accompaniment to Otello's words while he is standing by Desdemona's corpse: "Ecco la fine del mio cammin . . . Oh! Gloria! Otello fu." (ex. 23).[49]

EXAMPLE 23

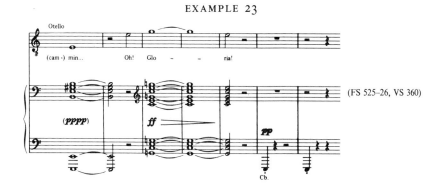

(FS 525–26, VS 360)

[47] It should be noted that in Otello's vocal part Verdi has scrupulously indicated the exact moments and duration of the three kisses.

[48] This 'silent' scene has been brilliantly analysed by Joseph Kerman in his *Opera as Drama* (New York 1956, pp. 9ff), especially with regard to the possibilities and impossibilities of musical and verbal drama.

[49] "This is my journey's end . . . Oh glory! Otello's day is done."

The final reprise of the *bacio* theme, virtually identical with its appearance in the first-act love scene,[50] hardly needs any comment. The fact that the opera ends in the key of E major is significant. Jago may have driven Otello and Desdemona into death, but he has failed to destroy their union.

*   *
*

Melodrama or Tragedy?

In his invaluable study entitled *The Life of the Drama*, Eric Bentley discusses a number of the elements present in tragedy: reality, pain, guilt, anxiety, awe, compassion and death.[51] If we test Otello's character, actions and experiences against the first of these criteria, it is immediately apparent that his situation, struggle, failure and ultimate crisis are *real* beyond any doubt. They are not at all products of an artificial world of daydreaming, but belong to this world and could be the lot of the man behind some *faits divers* recounted in today's newspaper. With some changes, of course, but essentially of the same type. The racial problem comes to mind first, but Otello's experience could in fact be that of any person who because of something in his background is only partially accepted by society, and therefore destined to occupy an unstable position.

Once we have recognized Otello's reality, we understand and even feel his pain, his guilt and his anxiety.[52] Of course, our feelings cannot be identical with his. Otello's guilt, for example, stems from his social inferiority; hence his staking of his whole existence on a single chance (the 'glory'), hence his hidden insecurity, his susceptibility to Jago's fomentations, and his lack of faith in Desdemona and Cassio. Our own guilt, on the other hand, is less easy to determine. If we do not identify entirely with Otello, we at least have some empathy with him and perhaps to varying degrees feel somehow responsible for his suffering, so that we cannot ignore him or his fate. Nor can we disregard death, which Otello desires. (In the first-act love scene, he even calls it the supreme moment.) We may not share his death wish, but since death is something which constantly confronts each of us, when it is presented on the stage in a framework of reality we cannot but be moved by it.

In melodrama, on the contrary, the emotions and experiences of the heroes and heroines are basically *unreal*, so that we cannot participate in

---

[50] I, sc. 3.

[51] E. Bentley, *The Life of the Drama*, New York 1967, pp. 257ff.

[52] "Reality gives pain. (...) Reality makes us feel guilty, and so arouses anxiety." (Bentley, *op. cit.*, p. 258).

them. We may fool ourselves briefly by imagining that we share their feelings, because we want a vicarious thrill. But neither the villain's guilt and death, nor the hero's virtues and final happiness can arouse anything but superficial emotions and these will vanish as soon as we leave the theatre.

These considerations lead to the inescapable conclusion that Otello is a tragic hero. But what of Jago, is he a melodramatic villain? And if so, which of the two is the real protagonist and determines the nature of the drama? In the case of Jago, categorization is particularly dangerous; he seems to possess all the characteristics of the typical scoundrel of melodrama. Unlike Otello he has neither past nor future, and this condition is significant. Verdi and Boito let him go unpunished, as did Shakespeare. Jago just vanishes and we in the audience do not care, because our attention is focused on Otello.[53]

Nevertheless, one can hardly deny that on the stage Jago has at least the outward appearance of reality and thus seems to contradict the melodramatic nature of his role. During his performance Jago strikes us as a very real human being, however monstrous his machinations may be. The explanation lies in the fact that he represents iniquity *in* a tragedy and since in principle tragedy does not deal with villainy, it follows that Jago is not the protagonist, despite his almost continuous presence on the stage during the first three acts. He merely functions as a melodramatic agent for the fulfillment of the drama. This explains his absence in the fourth act, during which it becomes apparent that we are watching (and taking part in) a tragedy. Jago's dramatic significance is that he dominates the *plot*. Otello, however, dominates the *drama* and by being a tragic hero identifies the drama as tragedy.

The question remains as to why Verdi needed melodramatic means to create a musical tragedy. The answer is that he had no intention of breaking with tradition. The relationship of *melodramma* to melodrama is rooted not only in his own work from *Oberto* to *Aida*, but in all Italian opera of the *Risorgimento*.[54] Emotions are transferred with a 'melodramatic' immediacy of which only music is capable, while ambiguity, an important feature of higher dramatic forms, is rejected. This does not mean that *melodramma* is identical or even analogous to melodrama. Study of Verdi's earlier operas

---

[53] It may be argued that, since he dies, Otello has no future either. But this is paradoxically the very reason why he "lives on" after the final curtain. It is through death that his existence is transcended.

[54] See Luigi Dallapiccola, *Words and Music in XIXth-Century Italian Opera*, Italian Institute in Dublin, 1964.

may similarly reveal their character as tragedies realized through melodramatic devices. But only with *Otello* did he raise the genre to a level which, up to the present, appears unrivalled.

1971

CHAPTER 8

THE MUSICAL FIGURE OF DEATH

Every student of Verdi's dramatic art is acquainted with the impressive anapaestic motifs which announce tragic death in the "Miserere" of *Il trovatore* and in the final scene of *La traviata*. Péter Pál Várnai included this figure in his excellent short study of Verdi's 'negative' devices.[1] When I started to investigate the use of this rhythmic formula, I realized that the device did not belong exclusively to Verdi, but had already been applied in similar situations by his predecessors in both Italy and France. Actually, the musical figure of death was common property for at least a century and a half, and may therefore be designated as a *topos*.

A *topos* was originally a device of ancient rhetoric, an aid for oratorical elaboration. Quintilianus calls the *topoi* the *argomentorum sedes*,[2] which we may freely translate as "the gold-mine of thought". Medieval literature adopted this rhetorical device and in the course of time the *topos* became a cliché or a commonplace (words that should not be applied here in their pejorative sense, however). Since the publication in 1948 of Ernst Robert Curtius' invaluable study of European literature and Latin middle ages, extensive *topos* research has been done not only in the literature of the past but also in art history, notably in iconology.[3] Pre-war studies in musical 'topology' by Gurlitt and Schering were restricted to the renaissance and baroque periods. It is evident, however, that during the eighteenth and nineteenth centuries *topoi* were still used by composers, especially in connection with certain texts or dramatic situations.[4]

---

[1] P. P. Várnai, *Contributo per uno studio della tipizzazione negativa nelle opere verdiane; Personaggi e situazioni*, in "Atti del I° Congresso internazionale di studi verdiani" (1966), Parma 1969, pp. 268–275.

[2] M. F. Quintilianus, *Institutio oratoria*, V, 10, 20.

[3] E. R. Curtius, *Europäische Literatur und Lateinisches Mittelalter*, 6th ed., Bern-München 1967.

[4] See for instance: A. A. Abert, *Bedeutungswandel eines Mozartschen Lieblingsmotivs*, in "Mozart-Jahrbuch 1965/66", Salzburg 1967, pp. 7–14.

Although a musical *topos* may have a descriptive or imitative configuration, it generally communicates in a purely intellectual way, i.e.,
through persistent association with a certain idea, situation or concept. It
is even possible to create a *topos* within the structure of a single work; in *Don
Giovanni*, for instance, a neutral and very common cadential formula
gradually assumes the connotation of the concept of treason.[5] Normally,
however, a musical *topos* does not belong to a single composer but is
transmitted from one generation to the next.

The *topos* which I call "the musical figure of death" appears in three
interrelated versions which may be described in terms of ancient metrics
(ex. 1).

EXAMPLE 1

(a)   ♫♪ (an anapaest)

(b)   ♬♬ ♪ (a double resolved iambic)

(c)   ♬♬ ♪ (a paeon)

These three motifs are purely rhythmical and therefore are restricted to
notes of the same pitch; the last note of each motif is not only the longest but
is also stressed. Notation varies of course according to the given tempo.

It should be observed that in addition to the death connotation the motifs
may call up other associations. The anapaestic formula, for instance, is
often used in connection with battle and war, while Motif-b may refer to
strong emotion, fear and trembling. This multiplicity enables the composer
to handle the figure in an ambiguous way: it may implicitly point to tragic
death, although the actual situation in which it occurs does not give any clue
to a fatal issue.

Since I have not done any systematic research into the origins and history
of this musical *topos* (nor has anyone else, as far as I am aware), the
examples discussed below do not lead to any definite conclusions.
Nevertheless they may give us at least an impression of how the musical
figure of death was used in the period from the late seventeenth to the early
nineteenth centuries.[6]

*   *
    *

[5] See Chapter 3.

[6] The fact that the list of examples starts with an opera of Lully by no means implies that he
is the 'inventor' of the *topos*. Undoubtedly the device is considerably older; its origins may most
likely be sought in execution rituals and funeral ceremonies.

In Act II, sc. 3 of Lully's opera *Amadis*, Arcalaus expresses his hate and his wish to destroy Amadis with the words:

> Dans un piège fatal
> Son mauvais sort l'amène.

His evil fortune leads him into a fatal trap.

The ritornel of this air is dominated by Motif-a. In Act III, sc. 2, Arcabonne announces death to the prisoners and again the ritornel of the scene is built on Motif-a. The same holds for Arcabonne's air: "Toi qui dans ce tombeau n'es plus qu'un peu de cendre", and the prelude preceding scene 4, which illustrates the text:

> Non, rien n'arrêtera la fureur qui m'anime;
> On vient me livrer ma victime.
> Meurs!...

No, nothing can abate the fury which inspires me. My victim is delivered into my hands. Die!

Act II, sc. 5 of *Armide* (1686) contains the famous monologue of the titular heroine: "Enfin il est dans ma puissance". Armide's intention to kill Renaud is depicted in the orchestral introduction by anapaestic motifs. In Act III, sc. 3, we find an implicit application of the death concept in the air of La Haine and the chorus of her attendants; both orchestral and vocal parts make frequent use of Motif-a.

Rameau's first opera *Hippolyte et Aricie* (1733) is particularly rich in death formulae. The underworld scene in Act II (sc. 2) is announced by a triple occurrence of Motif-c, which is then twice repeated in its entirety. The triplicity points to a ritual use of the *topos*. The first "air infernal" (II, sc. 3) is dominated by (a) and (c), the "trio des Parques" by (a) only. Aricie's fear for Hippolyte's fate (IV, sc. 3) – he fights against a monster emerged from the sea – is pictured by Motif-a and so is Phèdre's remorse when she is told of the hero's death (IV, sc. 4). Thésée, too, is conscience-stricken (V, sc. 1); his monologue is accompanied by (c) and his supplication to Neptune by (a):

> Après le plus noir des forfaits,
> Ouvrez-moi pour tombeau vos demeures profondes!
> Que la mort que je cherche au milieu de vos ondes
> Soit le dernier de vos bienfaits.

*After the blackest of crimes, bury me in your deep dwellings! May
the death which I seek amongst your waves be your final gift.*

Dardanus (1739) also contains some interesting examples of the *topos*. In
the first scene of the Prologue, the dance of *Les Plaisirs* is disturbed by *La
Jalousie et sa suite*, and immediately Motif-a appears. After the disrupters
are tied up, the implication of death becomes clear in an air of Vénus:

> Quand l'aquilon fougueux s'échappe de sa chaîne,
> Sur les mers qu'il ravage, il fait régner la mort.

> *When the fiery north wind escapes its chain,*
> *it ravages the seas and makes death reign.*

Act II, sc. 3 deals with magic. Isménor, the priest of Jupiter, consults the
forces of the Underworld, which are pictured by Motif-a, not only in the
usual slow tempo, but also in a rapid movement. The chorus "Obéis aux lois
des enfers / Ou ta perte est certaine", which concludes this scene, again
applies the device in a ritual way. Three times – in the beginning, the middle
and the end – the voices are interrupted by a triple appearance of the
anapaestic motif in the orchestra.

An exceptional instance of ritual usage is found in Gluck's *Alceste*
(French version). In the "air d'un dieu infernal" (Act III, sc. 4), the 3 × 3
formula of Motif-a is given to the horns as a direct illustration of the words:
"Charon t'appelle, entends sa voix!". The fast sections between these sum-
monses also make use of anapaestic motifs; they are played by a trombone
and other wind instruments in stepwise ascending motion (ex. 2):

EXAMPLE 2

The subterranean chorus of the "divinités infernales" in the next scene is
accompanied by the same motif in *ostinato*.

Gluck's Italian followers seem to have introduced the variant (b). In Act
IV, sc. 3 of Salieri's *Les Danaïdes*, for example, this motif underlines
Hypermnestre's threat of suicide. Sacchini's opera *Evélina* (also known as
Arvire et Evélina) is based on a *Norma*-like plot which includes a scene in a
magic cave, "destinée aux mystères secrets des Druides" (Act II, sc. 3). The
invocation of the priest Modred:

Sortez du gouffre des tombeaux,
Venez à nous, Dieux infernaux!

Arise from the depths of the grave,
come to us, infernal Gods!

is accompanied by Motif-b in the horns and strings; the fact that it is played twelve times (a multiple of the number 3) hardly seems fortuitous.

During the Revolution and Napoleonic era, the death figure occurs in operatic scores even more frequently than before. The reason may be that plots become more realistic. Although the optimistic revolutionary philosophy shall more or less require a happy ending, 'negative' scenes are no longer presented in the abstract manner of the ancien régime. Death on the stage is now much more acutely experienced by the audience, obviously as a result of the terror and the wars they have known. This remains true even for classical subjects like Spontini's *La Vestale* (Paris 1807), an opera which contains several instances of the use of the *topos*, including the first-act "Hymne du matin", sung by the high priestess, the duet Licinius-Julia, the finale of Act II, and the funeral march in Act III. The figure occurs much less frequently in the same composer's historical opera *Fernand Cortez* (1809). Motif-b appears in the strings however, when the Spaniards complain about the fate of Cortez' brother Alvar, who has fallen into the hands of the Mexicans (II, sc. 5), and when Amazily sacrifices herself for Alvar (III, sc. 3).

Cherubini's first French opera *Démophoon* contains a ritual application of the device. The last three words of a choral fragment (I, sc. 3) are illustrated by a sixfold occurrence of Motif-b:

Au moment que l'urne terrible
reçoit les noms, soumis au sort,
dans ce moment pour nous horrible,
où va sortir l'arrêt de mort ...

Just when the dread urn
receives those names, obedient to fate,
at that moment, so horrible for us,
when the sentence of death will emerge ...

Opéra-comique of the ancien régime still lacks the *topos*. I have found no clear instance of it in Grétry's works, except for *Andromaque* (Paris 1780), which has no spoken dialogue.[7] Cherubini, however, uses the figure in *Médée* (1797) and *Les deux journées* (1800). The latter work is particularly remarkable, since it offers one of the earliest examples of the *topos*' prospective dramatic function. The situation is this: Constance has planned a meeting with her fugitive husband Armand. As he does not answer her signal she sings: "Que ce silence est effrayant ... se serait-il laissé surprendre?", words that are interrupted by Motif-c in the strings. She is then captured by two soldiers and this scene is continuously accompanied by the same death motif. The explanation follows somewhat later, when Armand is actually arrested.

Lesueur, another important composer of the Napoleonic period, applies the device in several operas, of which *La mort d'Adam* (1809) contains the most striking examples. In Act I, sc. 8, the Angel of Death announces Adam's end:

> Homme de terre,
> Voici l'arrêt d'un Dieu vengeur:
> Avant que le soleil ait fini sa carrière
> Tu mourras de la mort ...
>
> *Earthly man,*
> *here is the sentence of a vengeful God:*
> *before the sun has run its course,*
> *death will strike you down.*

The last two lines are preceded by Motif-a, played by horns and trumpets. Still more impressive is Adam's prophecy of mankind's destiny in Act III, sc. 6:

> De morts et de mourants je vois les champs couverts.
>
> *I see the fields covered with the dead and dying.*

This line, too, is preceded by Motif-a in the horns. Finally the motif appears repeatedly in the scene of Satan and the demons (III, sc. 9), e.g., as an illustration of the words: "Mort! C'est le chant des enfers" (trumpets, horns and woodwinds).

---

[7] See p. 222 (Act II) and pp. 342–343 (Act III) of the full score published in the Complete Edition.

The examples thus far discussed are taken from works written for the Paris stage. In all probability it was Giovanni Simone Mayr who introduced the musical figure of death in Italy. From a historical point of view Mayr is generally considered the link between eighteenth-century opera and the *melodramma* of the *Risorgimento*. In view of this fact the absence of a comprehensive study and edition of his works is particularly regrettable. Fortunately I have been able to consult some of the early editions and manuscript scores in Italian libraries, and they seem to confirm his role in the transmission of the device.

Ginevra di Scozia (Trieste 1801), one of Mayr's early successful operas, is remarkable for the fanfares in anapaestic rhythm which form part of the plot and are commented upon by the actors. In the fourth scene of the first act, Ginevra's words "Suoni marziali rimbombano d'intorno" do not seem to have any death connotation, but a few moments later the same formula repeatedly interrupts Ariodante's text:

> Per voi, fra l'armi intrepido;
> La morte cimentai.
> Di Marte i fulmini l'ire sfidai . . .

> *Fearless on the field of battle,*
> *I risked death for you.*
> *I defied the angry thunderbolts of Mars.*

Another trumpet fanfare occurs in the second-act duet of Ginevra and Ariodante (no. 13), preceding these words:

GINEVRA   Qual suono!. . .
ARIODANTE Ecco la tromba, . . .
           Addio . . . vado a pugnar, a morir.
           La tromba mi chiama
           per te a morir!

GIN.:   *What sound do I hear!*
AR.:   *It is the trumpet . . .*
           Farewell . . . I am leaving to fight, to die.
           The trumpet summons me
           to die for you.

In the same duet a phrase of Ginevra is illustrated in the strings by the paeon-motif (twelve times):

E così mi togli a morte . . .

And thus you carry me away towards death . . .

Number 6 of the first volume of Mayr's *Ariette e duettini per cembalo e canto* (Vienna, Cappi, 1803), includes an ambiguous example of the *topos*. The text

Morir mi sento,
Ah, ah, non so dirti addio;
Mi trema il labbro, il core . . .

I feel death upon me,
ah, I cannot say farewell;
my lips and my heart tremble.

is accompanied by four b-motifs; it is uncertain whether they refer to "morire" or "tremare".

The curious subtitle *farsa sentimentale* of the one-act opera *L'amor coniugale* (Padua 1805) is not meant to suggest a sentimental opera buffa. The libretto closely resembles the plot of Beethoven's *Fidelio*, the first version of which was performed in Vienna the same year. Mayr's sinfonia already makes use of variant (b) of the death figure, forming an impressive crescendo in the low strings (bars 25–29); the same motif appears in bars 32–38 in the violoncellos. Moroski's first appearance – he corresponds to Beethoven's Pizarro – is underlined in the violins by Motif-b, ambiguously illustrating not only his words ("Oh! Che palpito . . . il cor mi trema in petto"), but also his murderous intentions. The latter interpretation is supported by the motif's occurrence in the next scene, where it continuously accompanies Moroski's text, including the lines:

Pressa il tempo ed il periglio
Che farò? Qual consiglio? . . .

Time presses on, and danger is near.
What shall I do? What shall I decide?

The beginning of Amorvano's ("Florestan's") *accompagnato* in the dungeon is again stressed by variant (b) in the violas and cellos; later the motif sinks to cellos and double basses. In the aria which follows ("Cara imagine") the figure does not appear; its role seems to be taken over by the English horn, an instrument which in the eighteenth and nineteenth centuries often expresses feelings of death. Nor does the *topos* illustrate the critical moment, when Zeliska ("Leonore") prevents the murder of her husband. Motif-c does not appear until the next quartet, once more in an ambiguous context (Moroski: "trema . . . che smania orribile . . . qual funesto palpito . . . il cor mi scuote"). The governor being condemned to a slow death by Ardelao ("Fernando") comments on his fate in the final sextet. These words as well as the rest of his text are underlined by Motif-a, played by the wind instruments.

In the duet "È deserto il bosco intorno" from *La rosa bianca e la rosa rossa* (Genua 1813), Mayr combines the death figure with the sound of a bell, a device subsequently adopted by various younger composers, e.g. Mercadante (*Il giuramento*, II, sc. 4) and Verdi (*Il trovatore*, IV: "Miserere"). During twelve bars the words

> Giusto ciel! ma più tempo non ti resta;
> Suon di morte, oh Dio, non odi?
>
> *Merciful heavens! your time has run out.*
> *O God, can you not hear the sound of death?*

are accompanied by Motif-b and reinforced by the tolling of the bell. Further on in the duet Motif-a, played by trumpets and strings, underlines the words:

> Fin che resta in tal periglio
> Sento in seno il cor tremar.
>
> *While he is in such danger,*
> *I feel my heart tremble within me.*

Mayr's *Medea in Corinto*, based on an excellent libretto by Felice Romani, was written for the San Carlo in Naples (1813). This tragic opera combines in a superior way the musical heritage of three nations: French declamation and choral writing, German symphonic elaboration of thematic material, Italian bel canto and dramatic poignancy. The climax in this brilliant score is Medea's incantation, the *Scongiuro* (Act II). Here, the eighteenth century ritual scene is presented in a romantic atmosphere, full of passion and horror. The trombones which invariably support the voices of the Furies no longer symbolize the dignity of a supernatural power (like Gluck's oracle or Mozart's statue), they express brutal destruction, i.e., the murder of the innocent Creusa. The death figure is used in connection with her husband Jasone, for whom Medea has something worse in store: "A lui morte fia poca pena; io voglio farlo, Ismene, più misero di me. Vita peggiore dargli di morte" (namely, through the loss of both his future wife and his children). The words "morte fia poca pena" are paradoxically accompanied by Motif-b, in a stepwise ascending repetition (C, Db, E, F). The rising motion expresses Medea's fury, which was already pictured by the same device in her first-act duet with Jasone.

In view of the opera's subject, it is hardly astonishing that the score is very rich in death motifs. During the first act these have mostly a premonitory dramatic function. Medea's reproaches:

> E tradir chi t'ama
> onor da te si chiama?
> Ah, questo, ingrato,
> questo è il maggior
> de' delitti tuoi!

> *Do you call it honour*
> *to betray one who loves you?*
> *Ah, ungrateful man,*
> *this is the worst*
> *of your crimes.*

are accompanied and followed by Motif-b, and so is Jasone's answer. The overthrow of the wedding altar also provides an opportunity for the insertion of this motif; it is played ten times during the comment of the Corinthians:

> Contaminato è il tempio!
> Che giorno! oh dei! che orror!

> *The temple is defiled!*
> *Oh unhappy day! Oh gods! Oh horror!*

But the most striking examples are found in Act II. While awaiting his death in prison, the Athenian King Egeo hears someone coming: "Ma qual fioco rumor ... Pallida luce ferisce gl'occhi miei ... Ah! qui giunge alcuno ...

L'ultimo di mia vita istante è questo!'". These pathetic words are repeatedly interrupted by Motif-b. The visitor, however, is Medea, who has come to liberate him. Therefore the *topos* has an ambiguous meaning: it pictures Egeo's explicit anticipation of death, as well as Medea's implicit murderous intentions.

Equally effective is the insertion of the motif in the middle of Medea's line

> Cerco col sangue mio la mia vendetta

> *I seek revenge with my own blood.*

which is immediately followed by her first attempt to stab her (and Jasone's) children.

Mayr's contemporaries were already starting to use the figure of death in a rather routine way and this 'automatic' treatment became fairly common in Italy during the third and fourth decades of the century. The early works of Ferdinando Paer still contain a few interesting examples (in *Camilla*, 1799, the first-act scene in which the Duke enters the dungeon that hides his imprisoned wife; in *Achille*, 1801, the impressive funeral scene following Patroclo's death, where motifs (b) and (c) are played by the kettledrum). But the composer's later operas (e.g. *Agnese*, 1809) show a rather careless application of the device. Many of Rossini's serious operas abound with death figures. Most of these are a matter of routine, but a few instances have rare dramatic poignancy. In Act II, sc. 14 of *Aureliano in Palmira* (1813), Motif-b comments upon something worse than death (as in Mayr's *Medea*), namely the life of a slave in Rome: "Poca pena, indegni, è morte. Voi vivrete in pianto amaro; del rossor che vi preparo sarà il Tebro spettator!". In the quartet of the first finale of *Elisabetta, regina d'Inghilterra*, the words are stressed by the *ostinato* use of (a):

> Il gelo della morte tutto s'aduna in me.

> *Death's cold hand caresses me.*

Leicester's bitter reflections in the dungeon (II, sc. 12) are pictured by (b) and so is the Queen's sentence condemning the treacherous Norfolc (*sic*) in the last finale. In *Otello* (1816), death figures subtly prepare the ultimate catastrophe. The Jago-Otello dialogue in Act II, sc. 5 is characteristic in this respect:

OTELLO   Tu m'uccidi così. Meno infelice
         sarei, se il vero io conoscessi.
JAGO   Ebbene, il vuoi? t'appagherò . . .
         [Orchestral interruption: twice Motif-b]
JAGO   Che dico! io gelo!

OTELLO   *You are killing me like this. I would be less*
         unhappy if I knew the truth.
JAGO   *All right then, you want it? I'll satisfy you . . .*
         What am I saying! I freeze with terror!

In a dialogue in the first-act of *Guillaume Tell* (1829), the death figure is used in a particularly ironic and foreboding way. While Guillaume speaks about his "bonheur d'être père", Motif-b is heard in the orchestra, obviously pointing to the famous archer-scene in Act III.

Such subtleties are rare, however. It seems that the more the old *topos* is used, the less interesting it becomes within the framework of the drama. In most cases the death figure merely functions as an illustration of certain words or situations, and since librettists indulge in the romantic fashion of tragic endings, the motif's occurrence at the moment of final catastrophe is almost predictable. Thus we find death motifs in Bellini's *Il pirata* (delirium scene), *La straniera* (last finale), *Norma* (drums in the scena ultima); in Donizetti's *Anna Bolena* (second finale), *Parisina* (third finale), *Maria Stuarda* (aria del supplizio), *Lucia di Lammermoor* (III, sc. 7, 8 and finale), *Lucrezia Borgia* (nuovo finale II, written for La Scala in 1840), *Maria di Rohan* (III, sc. 7), *Dom Sébastien* (scena ultima); Mercadante's *Il giuramento* (passim), *Il bravo* (scena ultima), *La Vestale* (passim); and in Pacini's *Saffo*, which seems to surpass all records (in Act III, scena ed aria finale, Motif-b occurs no less than 117 times). This is only a small selection from a seemingly endless profusion. The convention maintained itself during several decades, as witnessed by Enrico Petrella's *I promessi sposi* (Lecco 1869; libretto by Ghislanzoni after Manzoni's novel). In the "Introduzione" of this opera, the threat by two bravos of the old priest Don Abbondio is illustrated by Motif-a in the timpani.

Meanwhile Paris composers showed more restraint in the application of the device. In Meyerbeer's scores the death figure is found only rarely. The first bars of *Les Huguenots*, however, contain a particularly effective example. The opera starts with Motif-a, twice played by the kettledrum and immediately followed by the Lutheran chorale in the wind instruments. Thus the composer makes it perfectly clear that his drama deals with death and religion. Halévy's *La juive* (IV, duet no. 21, and Eléazar's aria, no. 22) also contains some instances of effective use of the death figure. Berlioz applies the device in his dramatic symphony *Roméo et Juliette*. Motif-a interrupts Padre Lorenzo's words (after "mystère" and "cadavre"):

> Je vais dévoiler le mystère:
> Ce cadavre, c'était l'époux
> De Juliette . . .

> *I will unveil the mystery:*
> *this corpse was Juliette's husband.*

EXAMPLE 3

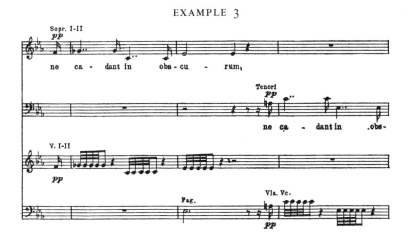

In this connection another non-operatic genre may be mentioned: the Requiem Mass. Both Requiems of Cherubini contain examples of the death figure. In the C minor Requiem (for mixed voices) the words "Tuba mirum", "per sepulcra regionum" and "rex tremendae maiestatis" (all from the "Dies irae" section) are underlined by (a). The "Offertorium" makes use of the same motif in *ostinato* to illustrate the words "de poenis inferni" and "libera de ore leonis". The most interesting passage occurs with the text "ne cadant in obscurum"; here, the composer combines the device with word painting (ex. 3).

In the "Dies irae" of his second Requiem (for male voices), Cherubini uses Motif-b as an *ostinato* figure.

As might be expected, Berlioz too applies the device in his *Grande messe des morts*. The figure occurs in one of the most impressive pages: the opening measures of the Andante maestoso in the "Dies irae". Motif-a appears in three of the four brass ensembles and is treated in a gradually accelerating motion.

To summarize this historical sketch: before 1780 the death *topos* was principally used in French *tragédie lyrique* and *opéra*, with a clear predilection for motifs (a) and (c). Italian Gluckists and the German-born Simone Mayr added to this Motif-b and transmitted the device to Italy where, in the course of several decades, the figure's application became a matter of routine. French composers, on the other hand, kept to a more sparing use of the three motifs, applying them only in special cases.

The fact that the death figure is rarely met with in German speaking countries reconfirms its character of a *topos*. The device essentially belongs to tradition, i.e., tradition in the sense of a specific cultural custom transmitted from generation to generation. This implies a geographical (or social) limitation. It was this limitation which kept the *topos* alive.

*   *
*

In his first opera, *Oberto, conte di San Bonifacio*, Verdi uses the death formula almost exclusively in connection with the concept of vengeance. Motif-a occurs in the introduction to Leonora's cavatina (text: "Nozze? ... Con altra donna? ... Inaspettata io pur sarovvi! ... anch'io reco a quell'ara il giuramento mio", and "Ma vendicato sarà l'oltraggio, e questo è il giorno in cui la mia vendetta appresto!") and is repeated in the following father-daughter scene. Their encounter with Cuniza again stresses the *vendetta* idea, e.g., through the chromatically ascending use of Motif-a preceding Oberto's words "Son io stesso!" and the same figure at the beginning of the terzetto ("credilo al mio furor"). The finale primo, too, makes copious use of this motif. Cuniza's complaint in Act II includes an orchestral interruption which shows more dramatic imagination. The words

Oh! soavi memorie! oh caro affetto!
Chi vi toglie al mio petto?

Oh! sweet memories! oh dear tenderness!
Who drags you from my breast?

are underlined by (a), played sforzando on the lowered sixth degree of E major. The chorus of knights philosophically comments upon the situation ("son compagne in questa vita / la sventura e la virtù"), but its orchestral accompaniment already anticipates disaster (Motif-a). Oberto's C major scene is again marked by the vengeance formula, this time dramatically reinforced by the instrumentation: horns, trumpets, trombones and timpani (the text "niun asil può sottrarlo al brando mio" speaks for itself). The approaching catastrophe is clearly perceptible in the quartet, in which a combination of (a) and (c) accompanies not only Riccardo's words ("La vergogna ed il dispetto / combattono il mio seno") but also Leonora's ("Egli è infame, è traditore") (ex. 4).

EXAMPLE 4

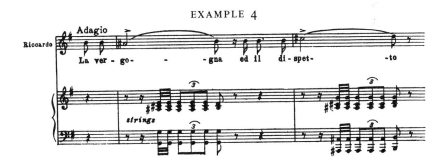

The duel itself, which takes place off-stage, is not commented upon by the death figure, but the opera ends with Motif-a, twice played by the full orchestra as if confirming the first-act terzetto which ended in the same manner. The similarity with *Don Giovanni* (endings of first-act vengeance duet and second-act damnation scene) is striking indeed.

Un giorno di regno offers less material for discussion. During the first act Motif-a occurs several times in connection with military matters, although there is not the slightest threat of violence. The only clear instance of death connotation is found in the scene in which the baron challenges the treasurer. Here Motif-a underlines the words of both buffos ("ahi, soccorso! aiuto! ah son morto", and "sangue io voglio!"). The baron in his turn expresses fear by (b) at the 'King's' sudden entrance. Act II contains but a single example of the figure's use: anapaests picture the amorous war between the marchioness and Belfiore.

In *Nabucco* the vengeance concept adopts a scriptural dimension. Zaccharia's prayer (II, sc. 2) is preceded by Motif-a played by the strings ("Di novel portento me vuol ministro Iddio!"), and (c) announces his prophecy in the third finale ("sul mio labbro favella il Signor"); the prophecy itself is stressed by anapaestic motifs ("del leone di Giunda il furor" etc.). This image of the *deus vindex* is also present in *I Lombardi alla prima crociata* (the words "Dio lo vuole" in Pagano's second-act scene). Although in both operas the death figure occurs rather frequently, only a few passages are worth mentioning: Abigaille's threat to Fenena in the first-act terzettino ("Talamo la tomba a voi sarà . . . "), the decision to have her killed (II, sc. 1: "Ah sì! cada Fenena" etc.) and the third-act scene of Nabucco and Abigaille ("Morte qui sta pei tristi [. . .] Soscrivi!" etc.) followed a few moments later by the trumpet signal announcing the execution. Interesting examples in *I Lombardi* include the scene of Sofia and her son Oronte (Act II), where Motif-b accompanying the latter's words "Mortal di me più lieto non ha la terra" expresses dramatic irony, which is reinforced in the following cavatina ("dove mortal non va"); also the encounter of Oronte and Giselda (Act III), in which (b) ambiguously pictures the (false) tidings of his death as well as his future fate; and finally Giselda's vision in the fourth act (*ostinato* use of the same motif). However effective these examples are from·a dramatic point of view, they stay within the bounds of convention. Verdi may have felt this; in the following operas (*Ernani, I due Foscari, Giovanna d'Arco, Alzira* und *Atilla*) relatively few instances of the death formula are found. The composer seems to have gradually lost interest in the application of the device. Even the mention of the "Dio vindice" is no longer stressed by the old figure (trial scene in *Giovanna d'Arco*, finale II).

The great change came with *Macbeth*. The essential difference between this musical drama and the preceding works is that it deals with death in a direct way. Death is no longer the (mostly unwanted) consequence of mere violence stirred by feelings of vengeance, jealousy or rivalry; it is the compelling result of thirst after power. Only by means of brutal murder will Macbeth be able to reach his goal. It follows logically that the death figure permeates the whole score and almost adopts the function of a structural device in the drama. Verdi restricts the use of the *topos* as an explicit illustration of violence, murderous intentions or mourning; instead he lays stress on what is happening in the minds of his actors, often in contradiction to their words. The death figure expresses the unspoken thought.

After the opera's prelude and the witches' chorus, the first scene already gives a clear example of this new dramatic technique. The price to be paid for the realization of the witches' 'predictions' is indicated beforehand through a dry anapaestic motif, played in unison by the strings (Macbeth: "Or via parlate!"). Equally revealing is the orchestral answer to Banco's question: "Tremar vi fanno così lieti auguri?" (the same motif twice). Throughout the score replies to questions or thoughts that cannot be explicitly answered or expressed by the actors are supplied by the orchestra. When Lady Macbeth reflects upon thirst for power combined with lack of strength

> [. . .] e mal per lui che il piede
> Dubitoso vi pone, e retrocede!

> *. . . and woe betide he who steps forward*
> *uncertainly, and then draws back!*

the instruments unequivocally picture what she means by a "piede fermo": the death figure interrupts her speech. More explicit is the unison Motif-a at the end of her cavatina ("Che tardi?"), but it is only after she has learned of Duncan's intended stay at the castle that she openly expresses her thoughts in the cabaletta:

> Or tutti sorgete, ministri infernali,
> Che al sangue incorate, spingete i mortali!
> Tu, notte, ne avvolgi di tenebra immota;
> Qual petto percota non vegga il pugnal.

> *Now rise up, all you infernal ministers,*
> *who inspire murder, and encourage mortal men!*
> *Come, night, envelop us in unmoving shadows,*
> *so the dagger does not see the breast it strikes.*

Paradoxically the *ostinato* Motif-a, which accompanies these words in the violoncellos, double basses and bassoons, is now covered by the rest of the instruments.

Macbeth's scene preceding the first-act duet with his spouse also contains a striking example of the orchestra's new function. His words

> Ma nulla esiste ancora . . . Il sol cruento
> Mio pensier le dà forma, e come vera
> Mi presenta allo sguardo una chimera.

> *But nothing has happened yet . . . Only my bloody*
> *thoughts gave it shape, and placed before*
> *my eyes a horrible illusion made real.*

are belied by the instruments; the interrupting Motif-a tells us that far from being a phantom, the thought will be followed by the deed.

When Macduff appears from Duncan's room he is almost speechless and just able to cry "Orrore!" Banco asks: "Che avvenne mai?" and immediately the orchestra answers by the death figure (a); a moment later, the same anapaests explain the meaning of Macduff's incoherent words ("Là . . . là dentro contemplate voi stesso . . . io dir nol possa! . . ."). The passage is the more poignant since both times the motifs first appear pianissimo in the horns, bassoons and low strings and then fortissimo in all wind instruments and percussion.

The second-act scene of the hired murderers bears witness to the death figure's increased importance as a structural device. Part of the melodic material is derived from (a), which in its original form comments upon the words "Con suo figlio ei [i.e., Banco] qui verrà". The accompanying timpani-figures in the chorus clearly recall motifs (b) and (c).

As might be expected, the off-stage murder of Banco is not stressed by any special death formula. Remember that Verdi uses the device to disclose what is going on in the human mind, rather than to illustrate visible or audible action. Banco's preceding words, however, are underlined by (c):

> In notte ugual trafissero
> Duncano, il mio signor.

> *On such a night as this,*
> *my Lord Duncan was stabbed.*

Here, the death figure has an explicitly retrospective, as well as an implicitly prospective function; it refers to the slaughter of both Duncan and himself. Also dramatically anticipatory is Motif-a, played by the strings as an introduction to Macbeth's soliloquy during the banquet scene ("Sangue a me quell'ombra chiede"). It points to the terror which from now on will reign in Scotland. The second act closes with the rhythmical figure known from the quartet of *Oberto*, namely a contraction of (a) and (c).

It is hardly astonishing that in the great scene of the ghosts we come across various death formulae. The anapaests that support the witches' question

> Dalle incognite posse udir lo vuoi,
> Cui ministre obbediam, oppur da noi?

> *Would you hear it from the unknown powers,*
> *whose commands we obey, or from us?*

obviously picture the spectres: the head of a warrior, the bloody child and the crowned child with a bough, each of which appears as a symbol of violence. Their invocation is accompanied by (c), played by strings supported by trombones. Motif (b) twice interrupts Macbeth's words

> La caldaia è sparita! perché?

> *The cauldron has vanished! Why?*

and seems to mark the end of the 'negative' prophecy. What follows is the procession of kings, which is accompanied by woodwinds from underneath the stage (in his letter of 23 November 1848 to Cammarano, Verdi categorically forbids the addition of the death-connoting trombones and trumpets).[8] Both the accompaniment to Macbeth's reflection on the vision and the music of the kings recall the death figure, however; the anapaests and paeons have developed into melodic motifs. When Macbeth regains consciousness, the infernal atmosphere is still present in his mind: the words "Ove son io!" are followed by Motif-b.

The introduction to the famous sleepwalking scene of Lady Macbeth includes several traces of the death figure, notably (b) and (a). As for the rest of the final act, the *topos* is found mainly in pieces that occur only in the Florentine version, as for example the beginning of the chorus "Patria oppressa!" (ex. 5).

---

[8] G. Verdi, *I copialettere*, ed. G. Cesari and A. Luzio, Milano 1913, p. 62.

EXAMPLE 5

Macbeth's own death scene – totally discarded in the Paris score – marks the dramatic climax in the treatment of the device. For the first time we hear the gripping orchestral sound that will reappear in *Il trovatore* and later operas. During the breathing spaces appearing in the soliloquy of the ago-nized King, the following motif stresses the inevitability of his fate (ex. 6).

EXAMPLE 6

The motif is played very softly by two bassoons, three horns, one trumpet, three trombones and timpani, and it is precisely because of the dull sound of instruments usually associated with braying signals and fanfares that we receive the impression of something quite new. Besides, the dramatic re-lationship with a previous scene in the opera is easily found. Trombones played a dominant part in the invocation music of the spectres in the third act, and it was these phantoms who prophesied the ultimate fate of Macbeth. He himself even refers to their predictions:

> Mal per me . . . che m'affidai . . .
> Ne' presagi . . . dell'inferno.
>
> *Woe is me . . . I put my trust . . .*
> *in the prophecies . . . of hell.*

If it was the intrinsic dramatic quality of *Macbeth* that challenged Verdi to renew this technique, then the 'lapse' in the following works is easily explained. Neither *Jérusalem*, *I masnadieri* nor *Il corsaro* offered possibilities comparable to those of the Shakespearean play. Nevertheless it would be incorrect to say that in these three operas the treatment of the death figure drops back to the former level. The composer handles the motifs more freely than before and something remains of the effectiveness and expressive force found in *Macbeth*. Both *Jérusalem* and *I masnadieri* contain trial scenes in which the death figure plays an essential part. The "marche funèbre" of the former opera (finale III) is entirely dominated by anapaestic motifs, played first by a *tamburo solo*, then by horns, trombones, ophicleide and percussion, and finally by the full orchestra.[9] The subsequent disgrace of Gaston is announced through Motif-b (strings followed by a kettledrum solo). The last judgment in the fourth act of *I masnadieri*, which in spite of being no more than the relation of Francesco's dream is a dramatically very impressive scene, has also the traditional characteristics of a ritual. Toward the end, the words "e primo il mio nome fra nembi tuonava" are stressed through Motif-a, played fortissimo by oboes, clarinets and all brass instruments, while scales ascending ferociously are heard in the strings and flutes. The foreboding Motif-b in the kettledrum appearing in the prelude to *I masnadieri* is also something not found in the scores written before 1847.

It must be admitted that *Il corsaro* is much less interesting with regard to our subject. Here, the use of death formulae is in general dramatically conventional, e.g., in the expression of Gulnara's hatred for the sultan (II, cavatina and bridge-passage to the cabaletta), the *vendetta* feelings of Seid (II, duettino), and the death sentence announced to Corrado (II, finale). However, the prospective function of Motif-b accompanying Medora's words at the moment of Corrado's departure is worth mentioning (I, duetto):

MEDORA   Dove, perché ten vai?
CORRADO   Un dì forse il saprai.

MED.:   *Where, then, are you going?*
COR.:   *One day perhaps you will know.*

While imprisoned in Seid's tower, Corrado reflects upon his situation and the fate of his mistress: "il fero annunzio l'ucciderà ...", words that are followed by (a). In the final terzetto both formulae (a) and (b) reappear, illustrating Medora's text: "Il mio Corrado non è più ... Fra poco con lui sarò ... già nel mio seno è morte! ...".

---

[9] In the autograph score (Paris, Bibl. Nat.), the piece is called "Marche lugubre". Later the adjective was deleted.

One could say that in *Il corsaro* the death figure has a structural function
with respect to the role of Medora. This function, however, is not very
important: Medora's part in the drama is rather peripherical and the motifs
themselves are conventionally handled. The same device is much more effective in *La battaglia di Legnano*. During the scene preceding her first-act
cavatina, Lida asserts her patriotic feelings, but complains of the price to be
paid for victory: "Voi lo diceste, amiche, amo la Patria, immensamente io
l'amo! Ma dove spande un riso la gioia, per me loco ivi non è. Sotterra
giacciono i miei fratelli, ambo i parenti, e … troppe in sen m'aperse or-
rendo fato insanabili piaghe! …". The reference to her dead parents and
brothers is underlined by this motif, heard four times in the strings (ex. 7).

EXAMPLE 7

Significantly Lida does not mention her former lover Arrigo whom she also
believes dead; it is more than probable, however, that the motif particularly
refers to her mourning for him. The audience already knows that Arrigo is
still alive, and in the course of the opera the emotional relationships of three
persons (Lida, her husband Rolando and Arrigo) provide a much-needed
human conflict against the merely theatrical setting of a patriotic war.
Verdi's insistence in a letter to his librettist on the importance of Lida's role
was probably due to a realization of this need.[10]

At the end of the opera, the march of the Lombards (which was already
heard in various preceding scenes) announces the victory obtained by the
patriots. The piece is accompanied by anapaests played by an on-stage
drum. The audience will not immediately connect these motifs with death;
on the contrary, they fit the atmosphere of triumph. Only when the arrival of
the mortally wounded Arrigo is preceded by a *mesto suon di tromba* does
their ambivalence becomes apparent: Lida's words and the chorus' commentary are supported by the figure of Lida's first-act scene. Even the key
(D minor) is the same; the addition of a kettledrum to the strings confirms
the inevitability of Arrigo's fate. Here the *topos* really determines the structure of Lida's part in the drama.

[10] G. Verdi, *I copialettere*, p. 60.

Compared to *Macbeth*, *La battaglia di Legnano* is certainly not a sophisticated work; nevertheless the opera may be considered one of Verdi's most accomplished creations. The score is full of death motifs and not one of these lacks dramatic effect. The anapaest heard during the first-act encounter of Lida and Arrigo is as ambiguous as the figure discussed above, i.e., its function is prospective as well as retrospective. Other examples illustrate situations on the stage in a particularly poignant or impressive way, e.g., the sudden appearance of Barbarossa in the second act ("Ah, da Pavia qui l'inferno lo guidò!"), the trumpets playing Motif-a pianissimo during the terzetto of the two Lombard leaders and the Teutonic emperor, and the third-act "giuramento" scene of the "cavalieri della morte" (Motif-b played by a drum and (a) by a trumpet). Unlike *Macbeth* and *I masnadieri*, the score contains no examples of the death figure in connection with villainy. Obviously Marcovaldo is considered too insignificant; he does not reach the stature of Francesco Moor, let alone Macbeth.

The domestic dramas *Luisa Miller* and *Stiffelio* make ample use of the death figure, functioning in both works not only to illustrate specific situations, but to create or stress an ominous atmosphere. The sinfonia to *Luisa Miller* opens with a theme accompanied by constantly repeated anapaests; these clearly belong to the latter category. The same holds for Motif-b which in the second act of *Stiffelio* precedes the dialogue of Stankar and Raffaele; the dialogue itself is supported by Motif-a. Notable examples of the figure's illustrative use are found in the first-act passage dealing with the subject of Stiffelio's sermon ("Dell'empio il vil tradimento"), in Lina's impressive cemetery scene ("Qui della morte è il regno"), and in the Stiffelio-Lina duet (Act III). In the latter instance, the idea of legal divorce substitutes for the death concept:

> Dal dritto sciogliere tal nodo è dato.
> Quest'atto il frange . . .
>
> *To untie such a knot is permitted by law.*
> *This act breaks it . . .*

Luisa Miller contains even more poignant examples, e.g., Motif-b, played by the timpani and emphasizing the stage direction: "Un sorriso diabolico spunta sul labbro di Wurm" (II, sc. 2); the anapaests explaining the true meaning of Luisa's aside "Ma in terra!" (III, after the introductory chorus);[11] the poisoning scene, in which Motif-a points to the breaking of a

---

[11] Miller: "All'amor tuo per me rinunziasti?" – Luisa: "È ver (ma in terra!)".

union as well as to death; and Luisa's faltering in the final scene (Motif-b), which played in unison by violoncellos and double basses on the low E♭ accompanies her words: "La man, Rodolfo ... sento mancarmi ...".

It is curious to note that in a superb score like *Rigoletto* Verdi once more submits to convention. Monterone's malediction and Rigoletto's dialogue with Sparafucile are dutifully underlined by Motif-b; so is Rigoletto's stupefaction when he hears the voice of the supposedly murdered duke. Even the actual murder of Gilda is announced through anapaests played by the brass instruments. In Gilda's own part the device is more delicately handled however. Her denial to her father that she ever went out is accompanied by (b), and the same formula is heard when she speaks of her remorse to Giovanna (I, sc. 4). Gilda's question: "Patria, parenti, amici voi dunque non avete?" touches Rigoletto's social background; here the death figure subtly points to a connection between his handicaps and the ultimate catastrophe. For the rest the opera contains very few death motifs.

This holds also for *Il trovatore* and *La traviata*. In the former work nothing is found before the finale of the second act, in which Leonora is introduced by (a) in the strings (she believes Manrico dead). The motif is heard again in the *scena* preceding Manrico's third-act aria ("Ah sí, ben mio"); here Leonora's sombre foreboding ("Di qual tetra luce il nostro imen risplende!") is supported by anapaests that anticipate the "Miserere" in the last act. Their dramatic function is explicitly prospective. In the "Miserere" itself, Motif-a, played by the full orchestra, continuously accompanies Leonora's words. The novelty of the sound is due to the combination of extreme softness (*ppp*) and dark tone colour (no instrument plays higher than E♭ above middle C), as a result of which brass and percussion dominate the quality of the sound. The tolling of the death-knell contrasts impressively with the dull colour of the orchestra. As indicated earlier, this device already occurs with Simone Mayr, Mercadante and other composers, but before Verdi none had succeeded in producing such a poignant effect.

In *La traviata*, the few appearances of the *topos* serve the sole purpose of preparing directly or indirectly the final scene. It was undoubtedly the simple and tightly constructed libretto that enabled Verdi to handle the device in this classical way.

When in the first finale Violetta asks herself "Saría per me sventura un serio amore?", the orchestra answers by means of Motif-b. Alfredo's discovery of his mistress' money troubles and his subsequent decision to go to Paris mark the end of the rural idyll (II, sc. 2); this passage is continuously accompanied by (a). The same formula stresses the dramatic significance of

her letter to Alfredo, written after her encounter with Germont: by returning to her ruinous life in town, Violetta will precipitate her end. The motif is
also heard at the moment when Alfredo receives the letter. During the
meeting of the lovers in Flora's salon, the continuously-played anapaests
seem to refer to either Douphol's or Alfredo's death (Violetta foresees a
duel). But this holds only for the plot; on the level of the drama it is
Violetta's death which is once more prophesied by the orchestra. In the last
act foreshadowing is replaced by fact: when Violetta proves unable to rise
from her seat, Motif-b is heard in the strings. The death scene itself strongly
resembles the "Miserere" from *Il trovatore*. Anapaests are played continuously by all instruments, although towards the end they are heard only
during the breathing spaces of the dying Violetta (cf. the analogous scene in
the 1847 score of *Macbeth*). If the effect is less powerful but more touching
than that of the "Miserere", then it is because of the realistic situation: for
the first time Verdi has created a drama in which death results from an
internal rather than external cause.[12]

By now it should be evident that there exists a correlation between the
quality of an operatic plot and the structural function of the death figure in
the musical drama built on this plot. The libretto of *Les vêpres siciliennes*
offers much theatre and little drama. I feel sure that Verdi's objections to
this Scribian book – he complained about the absence of moving scenes –
must be understood in a dramaturgical sense; the libretto lacks the possibility of bringing to life undercurrents of truly human emotion.[13] The main
theme of the work is *vendetta*; hence the opera swarms with anapaestic
motifs. They dominate a great part of the overture and occur in the cavatina
of Hélène, the first as well as the second finale, the prelude and *scène* at the
beginning of Act III, the subsequent aria of Montfort and his duet with
Henri, the duet Hélène-Henri and the finale of Act IV, and the terzetto of the
last finale. Basically this treatment of the motif is not different from that in
Oberto. The instrumentation is of course more developed and more personal
than in the *opus primum*, but dramatically the death figure functions at a lower
level than in any other opera written after *Macbeth* (notably *La battaglia di
Legnano*, in which Verdi had shown that a patriotic libretto could very well
generate a viable drama). This does not alter the fact that *Les vêpres* contains
superb music; it only proves that once a composer is prevented from bending
a librettist to his will, he is unable to display his full force as a dramatist.

[12] The death of Lady Macbeth can hardly be attributed to a natural cause. Nor is this the
case with Jacopo (tortured in prison) and his father Francesco (collapsed after his forced
abdication) in *I due Foscari*.

[13] See the letter to Louis Crosnier (Paris, 3 January 1855), in *I Copialettere*, pp. 157–159.

A totally different picture emerges from *Simon Boccanegra*. Although this libretto too has its flaws (not entirely removed in the 1881 revision), it certainly cannot be said to lack dramatic substance. Three of the four principal male roles (none of them a tenor) provide interesting, even fascinating characters: the deeply human Doge, the noble, adamant Fiesco, and the opportunist Paolo. Amelia, too, has some interesting traits; only Gabriele is a rather conventional role. Not since *I due Foscari* had Verdi treated the rich and difficult theme of politics and human relationships in such a serious way. Although we are still far from *Don Carlos*, a comparison with the work of 1844 shows that *Boccanegra* is a great step forward.

The death figure is handled with more variety than in previous operas. As in *Macbeth* (1847 version), *Il trovatore* and *La traviata*, its treatment climaxes at the end of the drama. In the duet with Fiesco, Motif-a twice pictures the Doge's agony. First we hear the anapaests in the bassoons, trombones and timpani, alternating with melodic formulae of the same rhythm in strings and clarinet. This happens when according to a stage direction the lights on the square gradually begin to weaken, until at the moment of the Doge's death they are fully extinguished. When Fiesco reveals to Boccanegra that he has been poisoned, Motif-a reappears, this time homophonically combined with a melody in the lower region (trombones) (ex. 8).

EXAMPLE 8

In the Prologue, the death figure refers of course to Amelia's mother Maria. Fiesco's mourning ("Il lacerato spirito") is stressed through Motif-c, slowly played by the timpani and plucked violoncellos. In the first-act scene of Amelia and Gabriele, both motifs (a) and (b) occur with an equivocal death connotation, but the latter certainly points to the girl's anxiety and the fact that she feels threatened. Anapaests in the trumpets picture Gabriele's fury in the second act (aria "Sento avvampar nell'anima"), and the poisoning scene is accompanied by Motif-b, thrice played by low strings and once

by a kettledrum solo. Before Boccanegra empties the poisoned cup, anapaests were already heard in the violoncellos and double basses (second
version only); since these, however, start on a strong beat, they differ metrically from the traditional death motifs. Melodic figures of both metrical
types are found at various places in the score (e.g., in the Prologue Paolo's
aria, its transition to Fiesco's romanza, and the latter's scene with
Boccanegra; in the first act Amelia's "Orfanella il tetto umile", and the little
dialogue of Paolo and Pietro preceding the finale; in the second act
Gabriele's scene and his duet with Amelia; in the last act the entrance of the
Doge). The question of whether these melodic motifs also refer to death is
difficult to determine; however, in a sombre drama like *Boccanegra*, it is
equally difficult to disprove the connotation. An unmistakable instance of
the death figure (and one of the most ingenious in Verdi's works) occurs in
Act I in connection with Amelia's revelation of her true identity. Between
her phrases "Vo' svelarti il segreto che m'ammanta ..." and "Non sono
una Grimaldi! ...", Motif-b is played very softly by a solo kettledrum.
Only later do we realize that this was a key point in the plot. The discovery
that Amelia is the Doge's daughter guarantees her freedom of choice and
destroys all hope for Paolo. At this moment Paolo is still Boccanegra's
friend, however, and so the death figure informs the audience about a
murder that has not yet been planned by the murderer himself.

No new modes of dramatic application are explored in *Un ballo in maschera*. But the various death motifs are so effectively integrated in the brilliant orchestration of this opera that any idea of convention would seem an
absurdity. As in *La traviata*, the libretto's construction is simple and well-
organized. Riccardo is at the center of both the main plot (the love-conflict)
and the subplot (the conspiracy). In the course of the work these two plots
are naturally fused, enabling Verdi to use the death figure throughout in a
prospective way, implicitly as well as explicitly. Melodic variants, still rather
indeterminable in *Boccanegra*, now appear with unequivocal death connotation. There is a striking increase in the use of Motif-c, and anapaests
with inverted accent also occur more frequently than in previous operas. As
an example of the great variety in the application of the device, all death
formulae found in the second part of Act I (the scenes in Ulrica's dwelling)
are listed here (ex. 9).

Example 9a precedes the words of the women's and girl's chorus: "Zitti
... l'incanto non dèssi turbare ... il dimonio tra breve halle a parlare!"; ex.
9b accompanies Ulrica's subsequent invocation, and ex. 9c announces the arrival of the "re dell'abisso". Ulrica's ecstasy ("È lui! è lui! ne' palpiti /
come risento adesso / la voluttà riardere / del suo tremendo amplesso!") is stressed

EXAMPLE 9

(a) ♫ ♪ (full orchestra, 4x)

(b) ♪♪♪ ♪ (timpano, 5x)

(c) ⁷ ♫ ♩· ♪ (ob., clar., violini, alternating with vla., vc., cb., 12x)

(d) ♫♩ (corni, 32x)

(e) ♪♪♪♪ ♪ (timpano, 3x)

(f) ♪♪♪ ♪ (trombe, 4x)

(g) ♫♩ ♩· (various instruments, full orchestra, 8x)

(h) ♫♩ ♩ (timpano, gran cassa, 2x)

(i) ⁷♫♩ ♩ (fag., tromboni, cimbasso, vc., cb., 4x)

(j) ♫♩ ♩ (violino secondo, vla., 5x)

by ex. 9d, her words "La face del futuro nella sinistra egli ha" by 9e.
Amelia's departure (Am.: "Stanotte ... Addio!"; Ulr.: "Presto partite!";
Ricc.: "Non sola: ché te degg'io seguir!") is marked by ex. 9f; here Motif-c
undoubtedly refers to Riccardo's fatal decision to follow her. Ex. 9g comments upon the latter's request to the fortune-teller, while Ulrica's horrible
prophecy is emphasized by 9h. Samuel's and Tom's words "tutto costei risà"
are significantly doubled by bassoons, trombones, cimbasso, violoncellos
and basses (ex. 9i). The last example (9j) seems ambivalent, since it accompanies two different stanzas, one sung by Ulrica, the other by the con-
spirators:

ULRICA: Non crede al proprio fato
              Ma pur morrà piagato;
              Sorrise al mio presagio,
              Ma nella fossa ha il pié.
COSPIRATORI: Chiude al ferir la via
              Questa servil genía,
              Che sta lambendo l'idolo,
              E non sa il perché.

UL.:   *He does not believe in his own destiny,*
              but will nevertheless die violently;
              he smiles at my prophesy,
              but is already half in the grave.
CONS.:   *This servile rabble*
              have prevented the assassination;
              they worship their idol
              without knowing the reason.

Although both deal with death, a prospective interpretation of the motif unequivocally points to Ulrica's stanza.

The second act, too, contains numerous instances of the death figure. Amelia's vision at the gallows – she sees a human head emerging from beneath the ground – is conveniently illustrated through Motif-a played by all instruments but the flutes, against the background of a drum roll and tremolos in the low strings. Motif-b in the kettledrum and strings accompanies the words "e m'affisa e terribile sta!", and is followed by a melodic variant in the bassoons, trombones and cimbasso. Soft anapaests in the strings ironically confirm Riccardo's jubilant words:

      Astro di queste tenebre,
      A cui consacro il core:
      Irradiami d'amore,
      E più non sorga il dì.

      Guiding star of this darkness,
      I dedicate my heart to you:
      make me radiant with love,
      and let the day never dawn.

Amelia's text in this duet is significant, too:

> Ahi, sul funereo letto
> Ov'io sognava spegnerlo,
> Gigante torna in petto
> L'amor che mi ferí!
> Ché non m'è dato in seno
> A lui versar quest'anima?
> O nella morte almeno,
> Almen addormentarmi qui?

> *Alas, on the very deathbed*
> *where I dreamt of its eclipse,*
> *the love which wounded me*
> *returns more powerful in my breast.*
> *Why can I not pour*
> *out my soul to it?*
> *Or at least*
> *find here my rest?*

Renato's reaction to the disclosure of his wife's identity ("Che! ... Amelia! ...") is followed by a melodic version of the anapaest (A♯ – B – B), played by bassoons, trumpets, trombones and cimbasso. Finally the orchestra reveals by means of (c) the true significance of Renato's request to Tom and Samuel for a rendezvous. The first part of Renato's aria in the last act speaks of vengeance and is constantly accompanied by (b). Motif-c sets the atmosphere for the drawing of the lot; it is played very softly by the death-connoting trombones and cimbasso, supported by bassoons. The same motif is heard *fff* and *ppp* when Renato orders his wife to draw a card from the vase, and again in brass and percussion at the moment when Samuel reveals the name written on it.

The last words exchanged between Amelia and Riccardo in the ballroom are continuously accompanied by a figure which is a combination of two Verdian formulae: the ascending Motif-a and the dissonant minor sixth (in a major key) resolving in the dominant (ex. 10).

EXAMPLE 10

(pp)

The effect resembles that of Lady Macbeth's sleepwalking scene, which is in the same key. Renato's unmasking and his exposure as the murderer is emphatically pictured by strings, low brass and percussion playing a melodic variant of (b). As usual Verdi does not apply the death figure to stress the actual moment of expiration.

Whatever the positive qualities of Piave's book for *La forza del destino*, the libretto is certainly not a balanced piece of work. Never before had Verdi written an opera that contained so many 'distracting' scenes and 'superfluous' roles. Neither the gypsy Preziosilla nor the two buffos Fra Melitone and Mastro Trabuco are really involved in the plot, and the numerous choruses of soldiers, "mulattieri", beggars etc. create an atmosphere which, instead of serving as a colourful background, overshadows the essence of the drama. Because of this the death figure cannot function in the same way as it did in *La traviata* and *Un ballo in maschera*. From a dramatic point of view the various motifs are used incidentally rather than structurally. The only example of a 'directional' application is found in the third act. Before the *battaglia*, Carlos' and Alvaro's mutual profession of friendship ("Uniti in vita e in morte") is ironically accompanied by four anapaests. When towards the end of the act Carlos challenges Alvaro, the earlier scene is recalled in a repetition of the figure:

> La morte disprezzo, ma duolmi inveire
> Contr'uom che per primo amistade m'offría.
>
> *I distain death, but it pains me to revile*
> *a man who at first offered me friendship.*

Carlos' answer ("No, no, profanato tal nome non sia") is stressed by four similar anapaests. There are however a few revealing differences between the two episodes. In the friendship scene, the motifs are softly played and harmonized with simple dominant and tonic chords; in the challenge scene, they appear *forte* as diminished seventh chords. The differing dynamics and harmonizations obviously are involved with the contrasting implicit and explicit use of the device.

The other death motifs found in the score are less interesting from a structural point of view. They all explicitly illustrate certain scenes or text fragments. Sometimes their pictorial function is presented in a rather crude way, as for instance in the last finale of the St. Petersburg version, where orchestral anapaests underline the duel on the stage ("si battono furiosamente"). This scene was discarded and replaced by a completely different

finale in the revision made for the Scala performance in 1869. The new
version, too, contains an example of the figure's illustrative function; this
time, however, the dramatic intensity is of a much higher quality. At the
moment when the fatally wounded Leonora appears on the stage, Verdi
gives us a new variant of the device known from *Il trovatore*, *La traviata* and
Simon Boccanegra: the ostinato anapaests (with inverted accents) alternately played by the full orchestra and the strings alone. Each of the 'tutti'
sections starts fortissimo and with a sharp decrescendo leads to a subsequent
string section which is played *ppp*. The impact is extremely forceful and there
is no need to understand Alvaro's words ("... o vendetta di Dio! ...
Maledizione!") in order to grasp the dramatic meaning of the passage.

The complications contained in the plot of *Don Carlos* are essentially
different from those of the preceding work. In this case there is no question
of superfluous or irrelevant characters and scenes;[14] on the contrary, within
the scope of the work, time is simply lacking to present some of the leading
roles in their full dimensions (Eboli, for instance). It has been said that the
opera is too long. The truth is that it is too short, not in terms of theatrical
convention, but in proportion to its rich dramatic substance. No other work
of Verdi has so many leading characters, each of whom represents his own
special background and contends with his own emotional problems.
Throughout the drama actors as well as audience are almost continuously
aware of death, which is presented in both an explicit and implicit manner.

Dark, indeterminate threats are already heard during the Fontainebleau
act. In the prelude preceding the wood-cutters' chorus (both sections deleted
before the first performance and still unpublished), Motif-b is played thrice
by the kettledrum (bars 29–31).[15] The same formula occurs in the Carlos-
Elizabeth duet ("Cet hymen, c'est l'exil! L'infant m'aimera-t-il? ...", and
further on with dramatic irony: "Vers mon nouveau pays j'irai joyeuse et
pleine d'espérance!"). Don Carlos' words "Ne tremble pas, reviens à toi"
are accompanied by (c) played by the timpani. In the course of the drama
this motif will reappear several times in the percussion.

Although still implicit, the meaning of the death figure becomes clearer in
the first finale. Under the sound of the gay march (clarinets and bassoons),
the words of the lovers:

---

[14] Only the third-act ballet may be considered dramatically superfluous.

[15] See U. Günther, *Le livret français de Don Carlos: Le premier acte et sa revision par Verdi*,
in "Atti del II° Congresso internazionale di studi verdiani" (1969), Parma, 1971, pp. 90–140. I
am very much obliged to Dr. Günther for having put at my disposal the complete manuscript of
the passages cut before the Paris performance. Her edition of this important material will be
published shortly.

C'en est donc fait! Fatales destinées,
A d'éternels regrets nos âmes condamnées
Ne connaîtrons jamais
Le bonheur ni la paix!

Thus it is finished! Fatal destiny;
our souls, condemned to eternal regrets,
will never know
happiness or peace.

are stressed by the timpani-motif (c), which recurs at the end of the finale:

DON CARLOS

L'heure fatale est sonnée,
La cruelle destinée,
Brise mon rêve si beau!
Et de regrets l'âme pleine,
Je m'en vais traîner ma chaîne
Jusqu'à la paix du tombeau!

The fatal hour has struck,
cruel fate
shatters my beautiful dream!
I must drag along my fetters
until the grave grants me peace!

A striking example of Carlos' weakness and inborn pessimism occurs in Act II, sc. 3 of the original Paris score, when the Infante reveals to Posa his secret love for Elisabeth. Posa's reaction ("Ta mère! Dieu puissant!") immediately evokes doubt of his loyalty and friendship:

Tu pâlis! ton regard, malgré toi,
Fuit le mien ... Malheureux! mon Rodrigue lui-même,
Rodrigue, avec horreur, se détourne de moi!

You grow pale! You cannot help
avoiding my glance ... Unhappy man! Even my Rodrigue
turns from me in horror!

These words are accompanied by Motif-b, played eight times by the kettledrum on B♭.[16] The semiconscious wish for death which obsesses Don Carlos is expressed in his second duet with Elisabeth through Motif-c, played six times by kettledrum and low strings. Carlos' words are revealing:

> A ma tombe fermée
> Au sommeil éternel
> Pourquoi m'arracher, Dieu cruel!
>
> *Cruel God!*
> *Why snatch me from eternal slumber,*
> *from my closed tomb?*

Posa's description of the misery of Flanders ("Un lieu d'horreur, un tombeau!") is illustrated by the drum-motif (c), while (a) picturing Philippe's reaction to these words ("La mort, entre mes mains, peut devenir féconde!) is played by brass, bassoons and kettledrum.[17] The same formula appears in the drum when the King starts to speak about the supposed relationship between his wife and his son: "La Reine ... un soupçon me torture ... Mon fils! ..." (only in the 1884 version). Here the death figure implicitly points at a threat.[18]

The auto-da-fé scene (Act III, part 2) is particularly rich in death motifs. During the people's chorus ("Ce jour est un jour d'allégresse!") the orchestra contradicts the words with rather crude irony (Motif-b in brass; (c) in the kettledrum). The monks are accompanied by the big drum (Motif-c), while the three trombones playing in unison naturally reinforce the death connotation ("Ce jour est un jour de colère, un jour de deuil, un jour d'effroi", etc.). Both passages reappear in a shortened version after the incident between Philippe and Don Carlos, and the Infante's arrest.

Act IV opens with two sombre scenes, Philippe's monologue and his duet with the Grand Inquisitor. Upon the latter's entrance the timpani start playing Motif-c. The middle section of the duet, in which the high priest reproaches the King for his lack of ruthlessness, illustrates the barely hidden threats by (b), first appearing in the violoncellos and then in the drums. The text speaks for itself:

---

[16] In the 1884 revision of the opera, this passage was rewritten.

[17] Only in the Paris score; see page 409 of the autograph (Paris, Bibl. Nat.).

[18] For a study of the different versions of this duet, see the excellent paper by D. Rosen, *Le quattro stesure del duetto Filippo-Posa*, in "Atti del II° Congresso internazionale di studi verdiani", pp. 368–388.

> O Roi, si je n'étais ici, dans ce palais
> Aujourd'hui: par le Dieu vivant, demain vous-même
> Vous seriez devant nous au tribunal suprême!

> *O King, if I were not here in this palace*
> *today, by the living God, tomorrow*
> *you would be in front of us at the supreme tribunal!*

Philippe's failing effort to make peace with the Inquisitor is again bitterly marked by (c): "L'orgueil du roi fléchit devant l'orgueil du prêtre!".

In the Paris score, the subsequent scene between Philippe and Elisabeth also contains an example of the death figure functioning as a threat. Motif-a is played by the brass instruments and interrupts these words:

> Parjure!
> Si l'infamie a comblé la mesure,
> Si vous m'avez trahi . . . par le Dieu tout-puissant
> Tremblez! Je verserai le sang! . . .

> *Perjurer!*
> *If dishonour floods over you,*
> *if you have betrayed me . . . by the all-powerful God,*
> *tremble! I will shed blood!*

The original version of the Elisabeth-Eboli duet included a fragment which was cut before the Paris première of 1867.[19] Here Eboli's words

> L'affreux remords, enfer au feu vengeur,
> Brûle mon âme misérable . . .

> *Hideous remorse, a hell of vengeful fires,*
> *burns my miserable soul . . .*

are reinforced by Motif-b in the kettledrum.

Since in the course of the drama formula (c) played by the kettledrums has adopted a close connection with the Inquisition, it is only logical for Posa's death scene to be illustrated by this motif. Various passages following the

---

[19] See Dr. Günther's forthcoming edition. The passage starts after Eboli's words: "L'Infant m'a repoussée".

marquis' death were cut before the première.[20] Originally Carlos' words
"Mes royaumes sont près de lui! ..." were followed by a few other lines:
Ph.: "Qui me rendra ce mort" etc., interrupted by (c) in the timpani (the
motif refers to the King-Inquisitor duet and has therefore a retrospective
function); furthermore there was an ensemble of Philippe, Carlos and the
courtiers, each part with its own text. The last line of the Infante (speaking
to Posa's corpse) was set to the rhythm of the well-known friendship theme,
here deprived of its melody; this musical 'impoverishment' is explained
logically by the fact that one of the friends is now dead (ex. 11).

EXAMPLE 11

The next scene (the rebellion) was also shortened before the first performance. In the original version the King challenges the revolters:

> Frappez! frappez! Me voilà! Du courage!

> *Strike! Strike! Here I am! Have courage!*

while at the same time the people sing:

> Ah cette voix, ces regards!
> Dieu lui-même a parlé;
> Sur nos fronts va tomber
> L'anathême ...

> *Ah! that voice, those looks!*
> *God himself has spoken;*
> *the curse will fall upon*
> *our heads ...*

---

[20] See Dr. Günther's edition.

This passage is stressed by four anapaests played by the timpani.[21] After the entrance of the Inquisitor and the submission of the people, the words of the ensemble – only in the 1884 version – are significantly underlined by motif (c) in the percussion:

COURTISANS ET LERMA	Vive le Roi!
GR. INQ. ET PHILIPPE	Grand Dieu! gloire à toi!
PEUPLE	Pardonnez-nous!

COURTIERS AND LERMA	*Long live the King!*
GR. INQ. AND PHILIP	*Glory be to you, O God!*
PEOPLE	*Pardon us!*

The last act contains but few instances of the death figure. Motif-a appears eight times in the allegro agitato introduction to Elisabeth's soliloquy (cornetti, trumpets, trombones), obviously referring to the tomb. The Queen's words "Pour moi, ma tâche est faite, et mon jour est fini!" are illustrated with four anapaests in the timpani, and finally the figure shown in example 12 is played twice fortissimo by the full orchestra at the supernatural ending of the drama (only in the 1884 score) (ex. 12).

EXAMPLE 12

In *Don Carlos*, the complex function of the musical figure of death reflects the complexity of the drama as a whole. Three functional aspects of the death concept dominate the score: (1) Illustration of death scenes (e.g., the auto-da-fé, the murder of Posa). (2) Implicit threat (e.g. with regard to the Inquisition or the King's honour). (3) Conscious or subconscious wish for

[21] *Ibid.*

death (Carlos, Elisabeth). Dramatically the last aspect is by far the most interesting. In the fifth act Elisabeth realizes that she no longer has any future, she is at "the end of her day". As for Carlos, his death wish is repeatedly expressed in the course of the drama, both in words and music. Although the Infante is an idealist, he is fundamentelly weak and frustrated in his relationships with other human beings. Because of the complete lack of understanding between his father and himself, and the loss of his substitute father (Posa), this tormented young man has but one wish: everlasting peace which means death. At the beginning of the drama he already speaks of "la paix tu tombeau", and the setting of both the second and fifth acts (the tomb of Charles V) symbolizes the ultimate solution of his problems. Contrary to general opinion I therefore believe the opera's supernatural ending to be entirely satisfactory from a dramatic point of view. Carlos at last finds his real father in death.

No complications in *Aida*. Its classical libretto is tightly constructed and the few death motifs occurring in the score are easily explained. As in *La traviata* and *Un ballo in maschera*, nearly all of them point to the final scenes. In the first-act terzetto of the three principal characters, Motif-c is heard continuously in the timpani, expressing the meaning of Amneris' aside:

> Trema, o rea schiava, ah! trema
> Ch'io nel tuo cor discenda! ...
> Trema che il ver mi apprenda
> Quel pianto e quel rossor!

> *Tremble, o guilty slave, ah! tremble*
> *that I delve into your heart ...*
> *Tremble that your tears*
> *and blushes teach me the truth.*

The kettledrum also reveals Amneris' true state of mind when she addresses Aida with false kindness (II, *scena e duetto*): "Fu la sorte dell'armi a' tuoi funesta, povera Aida!". Here Motif-b is heard thrice as a hidden threat.

In Amonasro's part the death figure is logically connected with vengeance. The horns precede and interrupt with anapaests his encouraging words to Aida:[22]

---

[22] Second finale. The same motif occurs in his third-act dialogue with Aida: "No! ... se lo brami la possente rival tu vincerai. E patria, e trono, e amor, tutto tu avrai".

Fa cor: della tua patria
I lieti eventi aspetta:
Per noi della vendetta
Già prossimo è l'albor.

Take heart: you will see
your homeland in happier times.
The dawn of our revenge
is at hand.

Aida's fatal proposal to Radamès to flee (Act III) is significantly accompanied by Motif-c, played *ostinato* by the violins. In the fourth-act duet of Amneris and Radamès, the variant (a) heard in the strings has an ambivalent function. On the text level it illustrates Radamès conviction that Aida has died (which is denied by Amneris); on the level of the drama, however, it points to the ultimate fate of the lovers. This is confirmed by the figure's recurrence in the postlude (after Radamès' refusal to be saved by Amneris); here the motif is played five times by the full brass section and the drums.

The climax of the score is the trial scene. This is a model of a Verdian ritual, examples of which are already found in *Giovanna d'Arco* and *Jérusalem*.[23] The composer ingeniously uses the scansion of Radamès' name to express the concept of death (ex. 13).

EXAMPLE 13

The occurrence of the death figure in Verdi's Requiem forms a logical continuation of the tradition. Apart from a few exceptions (e.g., the beginning of the "Sanctus"), the motifs appear only in the "Dies irae" and the "Libera me" but used in both movements with great variety. In the initial section of the "Dies irae", motifs (b) and (c) alternately played by timpani

---

[23] See Chapter 10.

and two low trumpets are followed by (a) in the trombones, trumpets and drums. The anapaests of the percussion lead to a special effect of the "Tuba mirum" music (Allegro sostenuto); here the free imitation of Berlioz' device is obvious (cf. the latter's Andante maestoso written on the same text; both composers make use of Motif-a). There is no need to refer to every appearance of the death figure in the two movements mentioned. It should be understood that Verdi uses the device with moderation, both with regard to quantity and quality. The 'understatement' at the beginning of the "Libera me" is particularly characteristic in this respect; the words "quando coeli movendi sunt et terra" are only underlined by soft anapaests of clarinets, bassoons, horns and drums.

If Otello, like Don Carlos, has the wish to die, then it is for entirely different reasons. His words "Venga la morte!" in the first-act love duet are the expression of complete saturation, of a *non plus ultra* in happiness. Characteristically there is no trace of a death motif in this passage. Verdi uses the *topos* only in connection with tragic death. During Otello's reference to his war memories (earlier in the duet: poco più agitato), anapaests alternately appear in the woodwinds and brass however. As they refer to the future (the hero's ultimate fate) as well as to the past (the battlefield), their function is ambivalent. The same holds for Otello's soliloquy "Ora e per sempre addio" (II, sc. 5), in which the motif reappears.

In the second duet of Otello and Desdemona (III, sc. 2), Motif-a is used in a particularly poignant way. Desdemona's words

> Esterrefatta fisso lo sguardo tuo tremendo,
> In te parla una Furia, la sento e non l'intendo.

> *I stare at your dreadful gaze, terrified;*
> *a Fury speaks within you, – I feel it but cannot understand.*

are accompanied by soft anapaests in the usual orchestration (bassoons, trombones, horns, timpani). Here the motif has a clearly foreboding function: Otello's fury will ultimately lead to catastrophe.

After the truth has been revealed to him, Otello speaks to Desdemona's lifeless body:

> Fredda come la casta tua vita, e in cielo assorta.

> *As cold as the chastity of your life, and now raised up to heaven.*

The words are underlined by plucked strings alternating with a drum playing motif (b).

It is well-known that Verdi wrote *Falstaff* to "amuse himself" and "to pass the time". The opera is full of self-mockery and in view of the considerable number of people the composer had killed on the stage during his long career, it is hardly astonishing that the musical figure of death has its fair share in the fun. Most of the motifs refer to traditional scenes in Italian operas. In *Falstaff*, however, the death connotation is consciously understated; sometimes the instruments presenting the figure are nearly inaudible, covered as they are by the rest of the orchestra. The sole exception to this rule is Dr. Cajus' solemn oath in Act I, part 1:

Giuro

Che se mai m'ubbriaco ancora all'osteria
Sarà fra gente onesta, sobria, civile e pia.

I swear that if ever I get drunk at an inn again,
it will be amongst fellows who are honest, sober, refined and pious.

These words are interrupted by (b) and (a) in the trumpets and trombones, obviously referring to the traditional *giuramento* scenes which always involved death. The equally traditional 'vendetta' idea is expressed through (a), played seven times by trumpets and drums in the combined quartet of women and quintet of men (I, part 2). The motif reappears after the two brief encounters of Fenton and Nannetta in a reinforced orchestration (brass and percussion). Ford's bitter exclamation (II, part. 1):

O matrimonio: Inferno!
Donna: Demonio!

O marriage: Hell!
Woman: Demon!

is stressed by Motif-b, played by horns, trumpets, trombones and timpani.

Another object of parody is the conjuration scene, known from many eighteenth- and nineteenth-century operas. It occurs in the second part of the last act:

Si faccia lo scongiuro!

. . . .

Spiritelli! Folletti!
Farfarelli! Vampiri! Agili insetti
Del palude infernale! Punzecchiatelo!
Orticheggiatelo!
Martirizzatelo
Coi grifi aguzzi!

Let's begin the conjuration!

. . . .

Sprites! Elves!
Pixies! Vampires! Swift-moving insects
of the infernal mire! Goad him!
Sting him!
Torment him
with your sharp snouts!

The last four lines marked by (a), are played fortissimo with inverted accent
by the kettledrum. The scene contains a choral fragment reinforced by the
same motif (horns and trombones). It illustrates the text of the Spiriti,
Folletti e Diavoli:

Scrolliam crepitacoli,
Scarandole e nacchere!
Di schizzi e di zacchere
Quell'otre si macoli.
Meniam scorribandole,
Danziamo la tresca,
Treschiam le farandole
Sull'ampia ventresca.

Let's shake our rattles,
clappers and castenets!
Splash the old drunkard with mud!
Let's lead the advance,
let's step out our dance,
let's do the farandole
over his great belly.

In the opera's final scene Ford asks mockingly:

> Sir John, dite: Il cornuto
> Chi è?

> *Tell me, Sir John:*
> *who is the cuckold?*

words that are accompanied by Motif-b in the violoncellos. Soon, however, Falstaff obtains his small revenge:

> Caro buon Messer Ford, ed ora, dite:
> Lo scornato, chi è?

> *My dear Master Ford, tell me now:*
> *who is the figure of fun?*

Naturally these words, too, are underlined by the violoncello-motif.

The most poetic example of self-irony is found in the second Fenton-Nannetta scene of Act I (part 2). The trumpets playing Motif-b comment upon the amorous battle:

NANNETTA	Il labbro è l'arco.
FENTON	E il bacio è il dardo
	Bada! la freccia
	Fatal già scocca
	Dalla mia bocca
	Sulla tua treccia.

NANN.:	*The lips are the bow.*
FEN.:	*And the kiss is the arrow.*
	Take care!
	A fatal dart has already shot
	from my mouth
	to your hair.

Like many other examples given in this chapter, the motif (referring to the "freccia fatal") is not to be found in the vocal score, but then such scores have long since proved their inadequacy for research purposes.

*   *
*

Verdi's treatment of the death *topos* may be summarized in a few words. In his first operas he adopts the routine-like application found in the works of his Italian predecessors and contemporaries. But he soon tires of this; between 1844 and 1847 the motifs almost disappear from his scores. In *Macbeth* he discovers the possibilities of a new and more personal treatment of the device, and from then on he no longer handles the formula as a mere illustration but as a dramatic means, determined by the structure of the plot and the nature of the leading characters. In addition, its function becomes more and more dependent on orchestration and dynamics. Finally, the last two operas reveal a restricted use of the death figure in combination with extreme dramatic subtlety.

By dealing with convention unconventionally Verdi re-established the *topos* as a traditional element, i.e., a device that constantly demands its own renewal.[24] Thus is his genius revealed, setting him apart and above the minor composer who submits to convention because he cannot master it.[25]

1972

[24] See the discussion Gossett-Von Fischer-Ringer in "Acta musicologica" XLIII, (1971), pp. 192–193.

[25] Although the Figure of Death appears only rarely in eighteenth- and early nineteenth-century German opera, it plays an important part in the works of Wagner, notably in the *Ring* tetralogy. I have discussed this subject in my forthcoming article, *Das exogene Todesmotiv in den Musikdramen Richard Wagners*, which is scheduled for publication in "Die Musikforschung", vol. 30 (1977) or vol. 31 (1978).

CHAPTER 9

'SIMON BOCCANEGRA': ONE PLOT, TWO DRAMAS

On 12 March 1857, Verdi's twentieth opera, *Simon Boccanegra*, had its first performance at La Fenice theatre. Beyond any doubt it proved to be a fiasco. One could very well term this the greatest defeat in the composer's career, because unlike the failure of *La traviata* four years previously on the same stage, it was not followed by a successful revival. Despite the rather favourable opinion of the critics, the public attitude in Florence and Milan was not really different from that of Venice.[1] After 1861 the work almost disappeared from the major Italian stages.

Today *Simon Boccanegra* is known only in its revised version, prepared in collaboration with Arrigo Boito during January and February 1881 and enthusiastically applauded at La Scala on 24 March of the same year. This was almost exactly 24 years after the Venetian première. When compared with Verdi's other revisions, the case of *Boccanegra* is a special one. Not only is the interval between first and second versions much longer than those of *Macbeth* (18 years) and *Don Carlos* (17 years), but the changes are by far the most extensive the composer ever made – about one third of the score was rewritten. Moreover, as I shall explain below, the opera became virtually a new drama in which not only the characters of several protagonists but also the attitude of the Genoese people have been put in a different light.

In order to understand and interpret the second *Boccanegra* it is necessary to study the first. As far as I am aware, the sole attempt in this direction has been made by Wolfgang Osthoff in an excellent article which appeared in 1963.[2] By comparing several fragments written on the same text, the author throws light on Verdi's revisionary technique and on characteristics of his late style. In the present study the emphasis lies rather on structural differ-

---

[1] Only in Reggio Emilia, Naples and Genoa did the work meet with a fairly satisfactory reception.

[2] *Die beiden "Boccanegra"-Fassungen und der Beginn von Verdi's Spätstil*, Analecta Musicologica, vol. I (1963), pp. 70–89.

ences between the two versions and the interpretative conclusions that may be drawn from them. Speculation about the reasons why the 1857 performance was a failure and the 1881 a success is meaningless. One cannot simply say: "it is because the second version is better than the first", as it seems very doubtful whether the most important change in the work (the replacement of the *festa* by the Council Chamber scene) would have pleased a mid-century Venetian public. But what we *can* do is make an inventory of the differences between the two versions, examine the discarded pieces, take into account Osthoff's conclusions about the rewritten fragments on Piave's text and study the structural characteristics of both scores. In this way it may be possible to understand in some measure why Verdi cherished *Simon Boccanegra* and why after long hesitation he undertook the hazardous task of revising a work written in a style that lay far behind him.

Osthoff's study must have been hampered by the fact that he was unable to see an orchestral score of the original version. In the early 1960's this score was still considered lost but thanks to the untiring labour of Pierluigi Petrobelli during the period when he was working as a librarian in the Verdi Institute at Parma, three manuscript copies have since been located: one in the archives of La Fenice at Venice, the second in the Noseda collection of the Milan Conservatory, and the third in the Conservatory Library at Naples. For the present study I was able to use a microfilm of the Milan copy.[3] A comparison with three extant editions of the vocal score proves this manuscript to be fairly reliable.[4]

*   *
*

Inventory of the two versions

Venice (1857)   Milan (1881)[5]

PROLOGO

1.	*Preludio* (E)	Lacking
2a.	*Recitativo*	Almost entirely new setting in *scena* style of the original text.

[3] Call number: Noseda I 208. I am indebted to Professor Guglielmo Barblan who provided me with the microfilm.

[4] Milano, Ricordi (plate numbers 29431–29455); Napoli, Presso del Monaco e G°. Vico S. M. delle Grazie, no. 24 e 25 (various plate numbers); and Paris, Léon Escudier. All three editions are undated but must have appeared shortly after the first performance.

[5] Page numbering in the right column refers to the most recent edition of the vocal score (VS), revised by Francesco Bellezza and published by Ricordi in 1968 (plate number 131142).

b.	*Racconto* (A–F♯)	New, but based on first version material (G–E).
c.	*Coro* (F♯)	Slightly changed, with a, prolongued epilogue (E).
3.	*Romanza* (Fiesco) *con coro* (F♯)	Unchanged
4.	*Recitativo e duetto* (Simone, Fiesco)	Partly new (VS 34 till Andantino and VS 45 from "Coll'amor mio" till VS 46).
5a.	*Scena*	Unchanged
b.	*Coro* (F)	Unchanged

ATTO 1°

6.	*Scena e Cavatina* (Amelia), consisting of an orchestral introduction (G, 22 bars); first strophe (E♭); an intermediate section (lo stesso movimento); second strophe (E♭); a short *scena* (Allegro); the first strophe of Gabriele's off-stage *romanza;* another short *scena;* the second strophe of the *romanza;* and finally Amelia's cabaletta (G, two strophes).	New orchestral introduction (G, 28 bars); new accompaniment to the strophes of Amelia's cavatina; melodic changes in the intermediate section; 'coda' added to the cavatina, on a new text replacing the first short *scena;* the two strophes of Gabriele accompanied by harp instead of *fisarmonica;* slight changes in the second short *scena* ("Ciel … la sua voce!"); cabaletta replaced by short Allegro agitato ("Ei vien!").
7.	*Scena e Duetto* (Amelia, Gabriele), consisting of a *scena*, the duet proper, another *scena* involving Amelia's maid and Pietro, and finally a cabaletta in G (two strophes).	Unchanged from Allegro moderato (VS 71, "Pavento …") till 76 ("Angiol che dall'empireo"); slight changes till VS 79 (Allegro); unchanged till last three bars of VS 82; cabaletta replaced by *stretta* using its musical material (G).

8. *Duetto e Giuramento* (Andrea, Gabriele). The duet is actually a *scena* which includes the off-stage trumpet signal announcing the arrival of the Doge. *Giuramento:* Andante mosso (E).

    Changes of text and music of the '*scena*'; no trumpet signal; *Giuramento* replaced by Sostenuto religioso section (VS 91–93, bar 6).

9. *Scena e Duetto* (Amelia, Doge). The *scena* starts with the second trumpet fanfare. The duet is a complex piece, ending with a cabaletta.

    Trumpet fanfare differing from that of the original, and more elaborated. Text and music unchanged from Allegro giusto (VS 97) till Poco più mosso (99); from Andantino (102) till 105 ("quante volte"); from Allegro moderato (108) till 110 (bar 5: "Ah! stringi al sen"); and from 110, bar 10 till 112, bar 7. The 'cabaletta' is considerably shortened and followed by a *stretta* (VS 115, bar 4–118, bar 8).

10. *Scena* (Doge, Paolo, Pietro)

    Slight changes in the first six bars; unchanged from Allegro (VS 118) till the end.

11. Finale: (a) *Coro di populo* (E)
          (b) *Barcarola* (A)

12. Finale: *Inno al Doge* (A)

13. Finale: *Ballabile di corsari africani con coro* (E)

14. Finale: (a) *Scena*
          (b) *Sestetto [con coro]*

15. Finale: (a) *Racconto* (Amelia)
          (b) *Stretta*

    Finale: plot partly different; new text and music with the exception of seven bars (VS 147, Moderato, till 148, bar 5) which correspond to a passage in No. 15 (a) of the first version.

ATTO 2°

16.	*Scena* (Pietro, Paolo, Fiesco)	Unchanged till Molto meno mosso (VS 180); new monologue of Paolo; slight melodic changes from Allegro sostenuto till the end (VS 187)
17a.	*Scena* (Paolo, Gabriele, Amelia)	*Scena:* unchanged
b.	*Aria* (Gabriele)	*Aria:* unchanged
18a.	*Recitativo* (Amelia, Gabriele)	New from VS 200, bar 3, till Andante (10 bars).
b.	*Duetto* (Amelia, Gabriele) in F♯, consisting of the duet proper (Andante), a short *scena* (Allegro assai vivo) and a *stretta* (Più mosso).	Unchanged till VS 203, bar 5; new music for the 10 bars preceding Allegro assai vivo. The next section and the *stretta* unchanged.
19a.	*Scena* (Amelia, Doge)	*Scena:* unchanged till Andante (VS 215), followed by 21 newly composed bars. The nine bars preceding the *Sogno* are identical to those of the first version.
b.	*Sogno del Doge*	*Scena* (continued): no changes.
20a.	*Scena* (Amelia, Gabriele, Doge)	*Scena* (continued): unchanged.
b.	*Terzetto* (E – E♭)	*Terzetto.* At the beginning one transitional bar added (VS 220, bar 4–5). No changes till VS 227, bar 3 ("morte"). New setting based on first version material till the end (38 bars).
c.	*Coro finale*	*Coro finale:* text and music slightly changed.

ATTO 3°

21. *Coro d'introduzione* (the hymn to the Doge)

Orchestral introduction based on the final chorus of Act II (No. 20c). The chromatic accompaniment is borrowed from the 1857 *Preludio* to the Prologue (No. 1). Short victory chorus with new text and music, followed by dialogue (Capitano, Fiesco, Paolo).

22. *Coro nuziale*

Off-stage but unchanged; combined with continued dialogue of Fiesco and Paolo.

23. *Scena* (Fiesco, Paolo)

New (soliloquy of Fiesco)

24a. *Scena* (Doge, Pietro, Fiesco)

This section is preceded by the captain's proclamation on the balcony. Part of the first version music is retained in the Doge's soliloquy (replacing his dialogue with Pietro). The Moderato and the subsequent 6/8 sections are unchanged and so is the Doge's short dialogue with Fiesco preceding the duet (11 bars).

b. *Duetto* in E♭ (Doge, Fiesco)

Unchanged but for five bars (VS 268, bar 6 – 269, bar 3).

25a. *Scena*

Five transitional bars replacing the recurrence of the hymn in the first version orchestra. From VS 271, bar 9 onwards unchanged.

b. *Quartetto finale* in A♭ (Amelia, Gabriele, Doge, Fiesco, with chorus)

New music from VS 275, bar 11, till 286, bar 1, but based on first version material.

*   *
*

Discarded pieces

In a letter to Giulio Ricordi of 20 November 1880, Verdi exposes his ideas about the revision and his intention to rewrite the first act: "But it is necessary to revise the whole of the second[6] act, to give it more relief, variety and animation". Although in the next sentence this is somewhat reduced (he wants to retain a cavatina and two duets), the entire finale was actually discarded and replaced by the Council Chamber scene. Moreover the composer deleted the *giuramento* duet and Amelia's cabaletta. Thus the bulk of abandoned material is to be found in the first act of the 1857 version. In addition, Verdi expunged the prelude to the opera.

This *Preludio*, which according to the practice of the time was almost certainly written after the completion of the work, consists of materials borrowed from no less than six items. It starts with a *staccato* version of the Hymn to the Doge (Finale I and introductory chorus to Act III), which is followed by two small fragments (the interjections "è morta" and "miserere") taken from the choral accompaniment to Fiesco's *romanza*, "Il lacerato spirito". Next the melody of the father-daughter cabaletta is quoted (Act I, no. 9: "Figlia! a tal nome io palpito"). An Allegro agitato section anticipates the final chorus of the second act ("All'armi!") and is linked through a transitional passage alluding to the accompaniment in the Prologue's finale ("viva Simon": see VS 56, bars 3–4 and 7–8) with the quotation of a phrase occurring in the second Simone-Fiesco duet (Act III, no. 24b): "Anco una volta vo' benedirla"). The prelude ends with a third motif taken from Fiesco's *romanza*.

This patchwork is anything but a feather in the composer's cap. Possibly he was pressed for time, but even in such circumstances Verdi had proved that he could do better. For example, when a few days before the first performance of *Alzira* (Naples, 12 August 1845) the impressario Flauto commissioned an additional *Sinfonia*, Verdi wrote a delightful piece, scored for an unusual combination of orchestral instruments.[7] The word "Amen" written in big letters at the end of the autograph score still bears witness to his efforts in carrying out the task during the few hours left to him between rehearsals. Unlike this sinfonia the *Boccanegra* prelude seems merely a

---

[6] See *Copialettere*, pp. 559–60. Verdi speaks of the second act because in this letter he counts the Prologue as the first. Original text: "Ma bisogna rifare tutto il second' atto, e dargli rilievo e varietà e maggiore vita".

[7] The orchestra of the main section (Andante mosso) consists of 2 flutes, piccolo, 2 oboes, 2 clarinets, (no bassoons), one horn, (no other brass instruments), timpani, tamburro, triangle, (no violons, no altos), one violoncello, and one double bass. The ensuing short Prestissimo and Allegro brillante are scored for the usual Verdian orchestra. The *Sinfonia* was commissioned because the opera was considered to be too short.

matter of routine and the piece was surely dropped without any hesitation when the composer started work on the revision. One element he retained however: the chromatically running bass to the "All'armi" tune, which reappears in the new introduction to Act III.

In November 1880 Verdi still wanted to keep the three first-act cabalettas: "From a musical point of view, we could retain the young lady's cavatina, the duet with the tenor and the other duet between father and daughter, in spite of the cabalettas! (Open O earth!)".[8] Less than two months later he had changed his opinion and wanted to drop Amelia's cabaletta: "In the first act I would cut the cabaletta to the first piece, not because it is a cabaletta but because it's very ugly."[9] Whether the music is really ugly or not is a matter of taste, but undoubtedly its style no longer fitted Verdi's dramatic conceptions. The rather conventional text

> Il palpito deh frena,
> o core innamorato,
> in questo dì beato.
> No, non vorrei morir.

> *O loving heart,*
> *restrain your palpitation*
> *on this blessed day.*
> *No, I wouldn't want to die!*

is matched by conventional exuberance of the voice, which has ample opportunity to display its virtuosic qualities. In each of the two strophes the high C is reached three times, followed first by descending arpeggios, then by diatonic steps, and finally by a chromatic scale covering a diminished twelfth (C – F$\sharp$). This rather crude outburst of joy would probably have suited Verdi's early operas, but within the framework of the first *Boccanegra* score, to say nothing of the second, its style seems old-fashioned. Still I believe that the main reason for the piece's removal was a matter of dramatic efficiency. Although in itself the cabaletta may not be unattractive, our awareness of Gabriele's being nearby causes the piece to hamper the necessary continuity of action. Especially the second strophe brings the

---

[8] The original text (contained in the above-mentioned letter to Giulio Ricordi) reads: "Musicalmente si potrebbero conservare la cavatina della donna, il duetto col tenore e l'altro duetto tra padre e figlia, quantunque vi sieno le cabalette!! (Apriti o terra!)".

[9] Letter to Boito, 8 January 1881 (See Appendix III).

dramatic movement practically to a standstill. Needless to say, the short *stretta* replacing the cabaletta in the revised score is much more effective.

An analogous situation occurs after the duet of the lovers. Amelia withdraws and Gabriele has a short dialogue with Andrea (Fiesco), interrupted by the distant sound of trumpets announcing Simone's arrival. In spite of Gabriele's words ("Il Doge vien ... partiam") he strikes up a *giuramento* duet with Fiesco and thus blocks the dramatic continuity. In the 1881 version, Verdi did not simply discard the duet (as he did with Amelia's cabaletta) but postponed the arrival of the Doge by deleting the trumpet signal.[10] Although he nevertheless decided to drop the *Giuramento*, this had nothing to do with dramatic efficiency; he preferred to replace it by a much more tender piece, i.e. Fiesco's blessing of the two lovers. Verdi explains his view in the above-quoted letter to Boito:

"What means most to me is to change the duet between Fiesco and Gabriele: 'Tremble O Doge!' It is too cruel and says nothing. I would rather instead that Fiesco, practically Amelia's father, blessed the future young couple. It could produce a touching moment which would be a ray of light amidst so much gloom. So as to maintain the colour, introduce also a bit of patriotic love. Fiesco can say: Love this angel ... but after God ... your country, etc. All good words for making the ears perk up ..."

Boito provided the new text within a few days, but he significantly changed the order of "God" and "country". The duet ends with the words "L'angiol tuo, la patria, il ciel!", which was probably what Verdi had in mind.

This new duet not only brings "a ray of light", it also elucidates Fiesco's character. The Doge's opponent is not really a ferocious personality. In spite of his adamant attitude he is quite capable of tender feelings. Another important characteristic of the duet is that it has a structural function in the drama, foreshadowing the benediction of the lovers by the dying Simone in the last act.

The fact that in 1881 the *Giuramento* proved to be untenable, certainly does not invalidate its intrinsic qualities. In the first phrase it is already apparent that we are dealing with a remarkable piece of music. The voices are almost continuously accompanied by drum rolls, and the harmonies are exposed horizontally rather than by simultaneous notes. The sixth replacing

---

[10] The second fanfare which occurs after the duet was not only retained but even changed and extended. Cf. Osthoff's remarks on the two versions of the fanfare (*loc. cit.* pp. 76–77). The elaborate passage in the 1881 score foreshadows the scene of Lodovico's arrival in *Otello* (Act III).

the fifth of the tonic triad in the second bar anticipates a device that will appear as a general structural characteristic in *Don Carlos* (ex. 1).

EXAMPLE I

Elsewhere the lowered second step alternating with the tonic on the words "vindice" and "vendico" evokes an even more threatening atmosphere (ex. 2).

EXAMPLE 2

In the middle of the piece a Lisztian juxtaposition of the triads of E minor, C major, A♭ major, E major, C♯ minor and G♯ major supports the homophonic voice parts with an enormous crescendo. The resulting tonal instability is counterbalanced by the E major arpeggio in the last phrase. The structure of the *Giuramento* is more or less determined by strong dynamic contrasts. Apart from the crescendo passages there are only indications for fortissimo and pianissimo. Verdi would probably have loved to write this duet for baritone and bass. As it is, the tenor part has a rather low tessitura, going down to B and not reaching the high G♯ and A until the last four bars.

As is generally known, the main difference between the two versions of the opera is in the first-act finale. In the original score the finale starts with a festal celebration of Simone's silver jubilee as Doge of the Genoese Republic. Here we find the explanation of the seemingly unaccountable period of twenty-five years between the Prologue and the drama proper. In spite of the expunged festal scene, this time gap was retained in the revised libretto and must puzzle everyone who has taken the trouble to make some calculations. In the Prologue Amelia's birth is first mentioned by Fiesco ("l'innocente sventurata"; see VS 39). Subsequently Simone tells him how his little daughter grew up under the care of an old woman, that this woman died, after which the child was seen crying and roaming about for three days and then disappeared; and that in spite of his searches, he had never succeeded in finding her (VS 41–44). On the strength of these data it is safe to assume Amelia to be at least five at the time of the Prologue, which makes her thirty during the rest of the opera. According to both medieval and nineteenth-century standards this is much too old. Of course the anomaly is not at all important, since time in drama does not necessarily obey the rules of time in everyday life. Besides there are flaws in the libretto that are infinitely worse and still acceptable.

The *Coro di populo* ("A festa, a festa, o Liguri") is an attractive piece for male voices and orchestra. The latter is predominant, the voices merely picking up a few notes from the alternating arpeggios or doubling them as far as their tessituras allow (ex. 3).

EXAMPLE 3

Later in the piece the triadic arpeggios are presented in *stretto*, implying a contrary motion between tenors and basses, while toward the end both chorus and orchestra are heard in unison (ex. 4).

EXAMPLE 4

What begins as a rather disorderly situation on the stage is thus steered by the music into straight channels that lead in a natural way to the ceremony proper.

   Next a group of young girls dressed in festive attire arrive in a boat singing an unaccompanied song, the tune of which is a metrical transformation of Fiesco's *romanza* from the Prologue (see ex. 9b below). A mere glance at the following *Inno al Doge* gives the impression of a piece of little distinction. The hymn is first heard in the *banda*, while the Doge makes his entry and takes a seat on the throne; then the first strophe is sung by the men alone, and finally all the Genoese citizens sing the second strophe accompanied by *banda* and full orchestra. The latter setting sounds especially bombastic. One should bear in mind however that the whole festal scene is less a matter of aural drama than visual theatre. Since the hymn plays a rather important structural role in the opera's first version, its tune is given here (ex. 5).

EXAMPLE 5

Vi - va Si - mon!   vi - va   Si - mon!   di   Ge - no - va   a - mor, a - mor e   glo - ria;

Tu sei di guer - ra il   ful - mi - ne, _____ il   sol   del - la vit - to - ria!

The ensuing ballet of the African buccaneers is a much more attractive piece. It consists of two alternating elements: a vigorous dance, full of strong dynamic contrasts and partly accompanied by male chorus, and a lyrical tune supported by the women's voices. The latter melody, played by an oboe solo and violoncellos, is nothing but a second transformation of Fiesco's *romanza*, which in spite of the retained 6/8 notation now assumes the character of a waltz (see ex. 9c below). After a purely instrumental repeat of the buccaneers' dance and a transitional passage, the men's and women's voices join in doubling a repeat of the waltz tune (the "danza del amor" which previously was intended for the female dancers alone). The piece ends with another prolonged variant of the first section. Thus the ballet is built on the scheme of a regular rondo form:

A (E minor) – *B* (G major) – *A'* (E minor) – *B* (E major) – *A"* (E major)

This formal scheme, and particularly the distribution of the two choral divisions, more or less determines the scene's choreographical structure. Toward the end male and female voices are brought together and so are the dancers.

The *festa* is suddenly interrupted by the entry of Gabriele and Fiesco (both crying "Tradimento!") and from here the plot runs more or less parallel to that of the second version. Similarity on the surface does not imply equivalence of dramatic substance however. An evaluation of the original finale should disregard the analogous scene in the revised score, the superiority of which is of course beyond dispute. When judged on its own merits, the 1857 *sestetto* offers particularly effective theatre. The moment of Gabriele's entry is well chosen and so is Amelia's sudden appearance when everyone on the stage thinks she is lost (end of the *scena*, no. 14a). The sextet itself is divided into three main sections: an Andantino in B♭ ("Ella è salva!") with the actors' contrasting reflections on the event (no. 14b), Amelia's relation of her abduction (no. 15a: Allegro moderato), and an impressive final Allegro (C minor – C major) in which the Genoese cry for justice (no. 15b).

The following fragment aptly illustrates the contrasting moods of the principal actors. Amelia and Simone remind us of their duet preceding the finale, while the contour of Gabriele's melody, doubled by violoncellos, seems to foreshadow the King's part in the quartc. of *Don Carlos* (ex. 6).

Although in the second and third acts of the revised score many passages were altered and reorchestrated, only one short piece (no. 23, a *scena* of Fiesco and Paolo) was completely abandoned. Besides Verdi deleted the two repeats of the *Inno al Doge*. At the beginning of the original Act III the hymn functions as a song of victory. The composer uses its 'square' phraseology for a spacial division into alternating sections of two bars each.

EXAMPLE 6

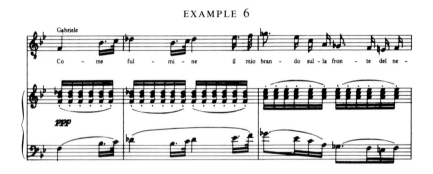

One group (the senate) sings in a room of the ducal palace and is accompanied by the regular orchestra, the other (the people) sings on the *piazza*, supported by an off-stage band. The hymn's third occurrence[11] is at the beginning of the opera's ultimate scene. Here the tune pictures Gabriele's and Amelia's unawareness of the Doge's agony and is heard only in the orchestra. After twelve bars it suddenly breaks off. The dramatic significance of the hymn in the original *Boccanegra* score is far from negligible and will be discussed below.

*   *
*

---

[11] Not counting its *staccato* anticipation in the *Preludio* (no. 1).

Revisions based on first version material

Recitatives and *scene* form the majority of these revisions. In most cases Verdi's reworking resulted in an understatement of the original version. Musical rhetoric is replaced by smooth arioso writing and, instead of mere accompaniment for the voices, the orchestra becomes the bearer of the main musical and dramatical thought. A typical example is found in the first scene of the Prologue. The theme supplanting the rather conventional recitative of 1857 has a remarkably lyrical character. In point of fact no other opera of Verdi opens in such a smooth way and therefore one is hardly astonished to encounter practically the same melody in a Mörike song by Hugo Wolf (ex. 7).

EXAMPLE 7

Wolf may have become acquainted with the melody through the Viennese performances of the opera (1882) or perhaps by Liszt's piano paraphrase (*Réminiscences de Simon Boccanegra*), in which the opening theme plays a predominant part.

A general characteristic of the recitative-like sections in the original Prologue is the declamatory tone. In the 1881 version this was transformed into natural 'speech in music' (called "parlando" by Osthoff). The dialogue preceding the duet no. 4 may illustrate this revisonary procedure. Fiesco's statement of his conditions for peace starts with the word "Ascolta", set on an emphatically descending leap of an octave (B–B). It seems as if he is going to address the audience as well as Simone. In the revised score the leap has become a fifth (F♯ – B), which sounds less theatrical and more natural. The same can be said of Simone's preceding phrase ("Sì, m'uccidi, e almen

sepolta fia con me tant'ira"). In the original version this passage has ascending thirds on "sepolta" and "ira"; in the new score both words picture the
corsair's mood much more convincingly by being set on descending intervals.

In accordance with the 'understated' character of the revised Prologue,
adaptations of original material almost invariably appear on a lower pitch.
Even slightly altered pieces, like the F♯ chorus (no. 2c), are transposed down
a major second.

Revised fragments of otherwise unchanged pieces appear throughout the
score. Osthoff has shown that in several instances Verdi kept the bass, but
changed melody, rhythm or even harmony. Still it is the entirely reworked
arias and duets rather than the fragments which illuminate the most interesting aspects of Verdi's revisionary technique. Most of these are found in the
first act. The original version of Amelia's cavatina is built on a traditional
scheme: two strophes are linked by an intermediate section. The revised
score shows that this scheme was not abandoned; yet the addition of a coda
set on a new text fragment deprives the cavatina of its structural rigidity.
The accompaniment displays another important aspect of the revision.
While melody and bass were left virtually unaltered – only Amelia's *cadenza*
was dropped – the stiff and conventional accompanying formulae of the
1857 version do not appear in the revised score. The orchestra has assumed a
brilliant colour through the use of swift triadic arpeggios played by the high
woodwinds alternating with plucked strings. These instruments clearly
underline the scenery (an early morning view on the sea) which forms a
striking contrast to the darkness of the preceding Prologue.

Mitigation of rigid forms is also characteristic of the revised cabalettas in
Act I. The original G major cabaletta of the lovers (final section of no. 7)
conventionally adheres to the bi-strophic scheme (*A – A'*). In 1881 Verdi
deleted the second strophe but reworked and extended the first. Thus the
piece gained considerably in dramatic force without sacrifice of its intrinsic
qualities (e.g., the surprisingly soft initial bars and the imitative treatment of
the voice parts). Also rejected was the traditional structure of the father-
daughter cabaletta. It seems to me that the composer's main reason for the
revision of this piece was his desire for a closer relationship between melody
and character. In the original version the tune is used in a rather abstract
way. First it is sung by the Doge with the words "Figlia! a tal nome io
palpito" (strophe *A*), then by Amelia on the text "Padre! vedrai la vigile
figlia a te sempre accanto" (*A'*), and finally by both (*A''*). In the revised score
the tune appears only in connection with Simone (ex. 8a); Amelia has been
given a melody of her own, which, however, is rhythmically related to her

father's (ex. 8b). Combined fragments of both themes occur in the last
section. Instead of the discarded interlude between the second and third
strophes the 1881 version has a coda (*Più animato*) written on a new text and
ending with an orchestral recurrence of the Doge's tune.

EXAMPLE 8

Verdi's decision to restrict the melody "Figlia! a tal nome io palpito" to the
Doge's part is quite understandable in terms of dramatic consistency. When
during the second-act slumber scene the tune is heard again in the orchestra,
its reference to Simone's paternal feelings will not escape the audience.

A curious problem concerning this tune should be noted. In the 1857
version, the middle syllables of the words "palpito" (Doge) and "vigile"
(Amelia) are not sung on the subsemitone C♯ (as in ex. 8a above) but on the
chordal note D. On the other hand, the melody's quotation in the *Sogno*
(no. 19a) does have the subsemitone and the same holds for the opera's
Prelude (no. 1). Since from a musical point of view the chordal note seems
less satisfactory than the subsemitone, one is inclined to think of a clerical
error. Still, the fact that D appears in all the sources available to me speaks
against this explanation. It may be that examination of the Venice and
Naples manuscripts will clarify this little problem.

*   *
*

Musical and dramatic relationships

We do not know at exactly what time Verdi began to conceive of each
opera as a whole before starting the actual composition.[12] Musical affinities
between distant passages in the score of *Nabucco* and *I due Foscari* suggest
that he already applied this creative device at a very early stage of his career.
The first tangible evidence, however, is the *Abbozzo del Rigoletto* dating

---

[12] In contrast to Donizetti and Meyerbeer who conceived their operas in a mosaic-like way.

from the winter of 1850–'51.[13] In this sketch practically the whole work was written down on a few staffs. There can be little doubt that Verdi continued making similar sketches for the ensuing operas, including *Simon Boccanegra*, and this procedure must have strongly enhanced the inner unity of the works.

The first *Boccanegra* contains many rhythmic, melodic and harmonic relationships. These are of different kinds, e.g., the reprise of musical material in scenes with explicit dramatic parallels, the reminiscence theme, the repeat of a melody or motif with implicit dramatic meaning, the motif linking two or more characters, and the purely musical affinity contributing to the opera's structural unity. A few of the related items do not re-appear in the second version, since they belonged to pieces and fragments that were expunged altogether. Some new connections were made in the 1881 score however; they prove how clearly the original conception was still in the composer's mind when he started to work on the revision. In the following discussion of the musical and dramatic relationships, the Prelude will be passed over. Its use of various themes and passages taken from the score but lacking specific meaning with regard to the drama proper has already been mentioned. Only the anticipation of three little motifs from Fiesco's "Il lacerato spirito" seems of some interest, since this *romanza* plays an important role in the work's overall structure.

The repeat of the Hymn to the Doge (Act I) at the beginning of Act III (1857 version) is easily explained by the similarity in situations. In the first-act finale Simone is honoured on the occasion of his silver jubilee as Doge of Genoa, in the third act because of his victory gained over the Guelphes. The only meaningful difference between the two versions of the hymn lies in the division of the vocal and instrumental bodies. In the homage chorus only the people sing, first the men alone and then joined by the women. In the victory chorus both singers and players are split into two different groups: the senators, accompanied by the orchestra, and the off-stage people (only men), supported by a band. This points to a political atmosphere which was lacking in the first-act *festa*.

The second recurrence of the hymn at the end of Act III (*scena* no. 25a: twelve bars in the orchestra) is of quite a different order. The orchestral quotation not only accompanies the entrance of Gabriele and Amelia but implicitly expresses their optimism with regard to the future. Thus the shock of seeing the Doge in agony is considerably heightened.

Taking into account the initial bars of the Prelude (no. 1), the hymn

---

[13] Milano 1941 (facsimile edition with a foreword by C. Gatti).

occurs four times in the course of the 1857 score. Not only does the piece underline various dramatic and theatrical situations but it also enhances the opera's structural unity. The device was certainly not new, since it was applied in several of Verdi's previous works, such as *La battaglia di Legnano* (1849) in which the Lombard march has a function similar to that of the hymn in the first *Boccanegra*. However the composer had at his disposal far more subtle means to further the unity of a musical drama and therefore he could very well afford to discard the *Inno al Doge* with its repeats in the 1881 version.

One of Verdi's devices was the reminiscence theme, which he used as early as 1844 (*I due Foscari*). This type of melody generally refers to a particular element of an emotional nature in the drama. In *Boccanegra* it concerns the theme "Figlia! a tal nome io palpito" from the first-act duet of father and daughter (see ex. 8 above). The theme is quoted by woodwinds during the Doge's slumber in Act II (no. 19b) of both versions. The fact that in the revised duet the melody is no longer sung by both Simone and Amelia but only by the father considerably enhances the dramatic efficacy of its quotation. The paternal theme stresses the Doge's half-conscious speech ("O Amelia ... ami un nemico!...") in a particularly poignant way.

Another example of two linked scenes is found in the 1857 *giuramento* duet (Act I). Towards the end of this piece, a rhythmical motif is played pizzicato by violoncellos and double basses. This dotted motif is derived from Fiesco's lament in the Prologue ("Il lacerato spirito"), where it occurs several times, both in the chorus ("Miserere") and the orchestra. The dramatic relationship between the Fiesco's *romanza* and the vengeance duet is too obvious to need further comment. However, this is not the only affinity between the *romanza* and the rest of the work. As mentioned above, the melody which opens the F♯ major section (ex. 9a) reappears twice in the *festa*, first as a barcarole tune (ex. 9b) and then as a 'waltz' written in 6/8 time (ex. 9c). I have been unable to find a dramatic explanation for these affinities. They seem merely to serve the musical unity of the work and may be the result of Verdi's habit of sketching his entire score in outline before filling in the details. Although in the 1881 version both barcarole and ballet were discarded, another, far more meaningful connection was made in the Council Chamber scene (Finale I). In his letter to Boito of 24 January 1881, Verdi strongly insisted on the insertion of the word "pace" in Amelia's text for the *concertato* fragment, and it was this word which he stressed with a melody derived from Fiesco's *romanza*. The musical relationship is somewhat obscured by a rhythmical and metrical change (the former anacrusis being prolongued and moved to a strong beat), but the first five notes are

identical to those of "Il serto a lei de' martiri" and even the key is the same
(ex. 9d).

EXAMPLE 9

EXAMPLE 10

Both the 1857 and 1881 scores include examples of melodic motifs connecting several characters of the cast. Amelia, Gabriele and Simone share a special formula of phrase or subphrase ending. This formula first appears in Amelia's cavatina (Act I; ex. 10a) and then recurs in duets with her lover (ex. 10c) and her father (ex. 10d). It is also found in Gabriele's off-stage *romanza* (ex. 10b), in the terzetto in the second act (ex. 10e), and in the last duet of Fiesco and Simone (ex. 10f).

All these fragments refer to the 'domestic' realm, the personal, non-political relationship between the three persons involved. Conspicuously, during Gabriele's conflict with Amelia and the Doge, the motif does not appear. In his rather conventional aria "Sento avvampar nell' anima" (Act II), Gabriele makes use of a much more common Verdian formula of phrase ending.

Another connection between the three characters is established by this melodic fragment (ex. 11).

EXAMPLE 11

Both ex. 11a and its 'inversion' 11b are taken from the first-act duet of father and daughter, while 11c occurs in the lovers' duet of Act II (Gabriele's plea "Parla, in tuo cor virgineo fede al diletto rendi"). In the latter instance, the music provides an unequivocal answer to Gabriele's suspicions. All three examples occur in both versions.

The melodic characterization of Paolo is quite different, especially in the 1881 score. The chromatic lines, sometimes appearing in the vocal part but more frequently in the orchestral accompaniment, foreshadow the musical physiognomy of Jago. The melodic portrait of Fiesco is less consistent than that of the other characters. This may be due to the fact that, in spite of his unswerving loyalty to his principles, Fiesco's role in the drama remains unclear for a long time. Only towards the end does he take sides with his political opponent and so the work ends with a quartet.

Several musical elements occurring throughout the scores of both versions seem to defy specific dramatic interpretation. The most important of these is the series of parallel sixth chords appearing, for instance, in Amelia's *Racconto* (Finale I), in the fragment preceding the Doge's *Sogno* (Act II), in Simone's 'ritual' in Act III ("M'ardon le tempia . . ."), and in the last Fiesco-Simone duet (the passages accompanying the words "perchè mi splende il ver sì tardi?" and "tu piangi?"). It may be argued that the use of parallel sixth chords was a stylistic trait of Verdi in the 'fifties – they also occur in *Les vêpres siciliennes* – but this does not alter the fact that it is a device which furthers the overall unity of the opera.

Finally a few remarks should be made about the musical and dramatic continuity, especially with regard to the revised score. The Milanese opera-goers who came to applaud Victor Maurel, Anna d'Angeri and others, must have felt frustrated. Most of the arias and duets, including those which end with *strette*, pass without a break into the following item and very little is left of the original sequence of closed numbers. Of course this structural procedure was hardly new in Italian opera (Mozart, for instance, made use of it in the first act of *Idomeneo*). But never before had Verdi carried the precept of continuity to such an extent. Only in the second act a few separate pieces were retained: Gabriele's aria, his duet with Amelia, and the Terzetto. For the rest the applause had to wait for the end of each act. And even there Verdi tried to bridge the gap. The span of 25 years between the Prologue and the drama proper precluded any attempt at continuity but the ending of the first act reverberates at the beginning of the second, where the motifs of Paolo's malediction are heard from bar 17 onward in the same key and with the same orchestration (brass and bass clarinet). The interval between Acts II and III is similarly bridged: the instrumental recurrence of the A♭ "All'armi" chorus suggests that the battle is still raging (the curtain rises only after the cry "Vittoria!" is heard). The case is unique in Verdi's entire operatic output. Even in *Otello* and *Falstaff*, works known for their unbroken thrust, there are no such links between consecutive acts. The endeavour for structural continuity is one of the most important characteristics which mark the second *Boccanegra* as the beginning of Verdi's late style.

*   *
*

The two dramas

The two versions offer a clear example of the essential distinction between plot and drama. These concepts are not antithetical, since a drama generally depends on a plot. They represent, however, two levels of dramaturgical analysis. Plot deals with what happens on the surface, drama, with the interrelation and intergeneration of action and emotion. It is perhaps an oversimplification to say that in opera the plot is contained in the libretto and the drama proper in the score, yet for analytical purposes the distinction may be useful.

An examination of the two *Boccanegra* librettos leads to the conclusion that they are built on the same plot. The replacement of the *festa* by the Council Chamber scene and the change of a few minor details do not really affect the intrigue and the course of events. In both versions the plot deals with a man who is in conflict with the father of his deceased mistress; who on the strength of being the people's hero is elected Doge; who accidently finds his lost daughter; who becomes engaged in a civil war and is murdered by the hand of an opportunist. Other incidents, such as Amelia's abduction and Gabriele's attempt on the Doge's life, also remain unchanged in the second libretto.

On this single plot two different dramas were built however. In the revision several characters underwent a remarkable change. The Doge of 1881 is virtually a new personality; so are Paolo and to a lesser degree Fiesco and Amelia. Moreover both the Genoese senate and people are much more active than they were in the 1857 version.

In only one instance is the change due solely to the person himself. Fiesco's warm feelings, expressed in the 'benediction' duet of Act I, strongly contrast with his ferocious attitude in the original *Giuramento*. The Fiesco of 1881 is still an inflexible personality, but he has gained considerably in humanity and his character has a dimension which was lacking in the first conception.

It is curious to note that the changed image of other protagonists results from the acts and attitudes of the people with whom they are involved rather than from their own doings. Paolo offers a clear example. Up to the last section of the Council Chamber scene he looks like virtually the same person as in the original version, i.e. a man who subordinates every moral consideration to his passion for riches, power and women. His character combines traits of Ezio (*Attila*) and Marcovaldo (*La battaglia di Legnano*) but is nevertheless far less interesting than that of the sinister Wurm (*Luisa Miller*). Then the Doge forces him to curse himself in public and suddenly Paolo turns into a demonic figure. One is aware of Boito's touch in this ceremonial scene as well as in Paolo's bitter soliloquy at the beginning of Act II ("Me stesso ho maledetto!/e l'anatema m'insegue ancor . . ./e l'aura ancor ne trema!"). By showing the act of poisoning on the stage instead of merely recounting it as in the 1857 score, the librettist adds considerably to this new image. Paolo is too strongly motivated and also too impulsive to become a Jago. Yet through the forced self-malediction he carries with him an aura of horror. When lead to the gallows, his words to Fiesco are characteristic in this respect: "Il mio demonio mi cacciò . . ."

The changed image of the Doge is due to the altered attitude of the senate and the people. It is true that the original Simone strikes us as a 'round' character in his dealings with private people, allies as well as opponents. But as soon as he sits on the throne and listens to the hymn addressed to him on the occasion of his jubilee or his victory over the Guelphes, he is no longer present as a human being. He has become a symbol. In spite of its allusion to Simone's past, the dance of African corsairs reinforces this 'act' of de-humanization. Both dance and hymn form an opaque screen separating the Doge not only from his people but from the audience. In the revised score this is radically changed. Here Simone comes into conflict with the senate, which refuses to accept the proposal contained in Petrarca's letter; later he is threatened by the off-stage people and a few moments afterwards cheered. Then follows his very impressive bitter speech addressed to both plebeians and patricians. Still, only one character in the cast is able to understand him. Dominating the *concertato* scene, Amelia makes her plea for peace. She, too, is put in a different light by the revision. In the ensemble of the original score she reflects on Gabriele's safety and joins the others in asking for justice. In the new version she takes sides with her father against the chronic discord between the two civil parties and in favour of a mature ideal: the unity of Italy.

In the second *Boccanegra* Verdi dealt with politics in an adult way, as he had already done in *Don Carlos* fourteen years previously. Simone emerges as a lonely man, as lonely as Montfort, the Spanish King Philippe and Otello. But he is presented with human dimensions that were absent or at least unnoticable in the original version.

In his letter to Boito of 11 December 1880, Verdi wrote: "The act conceived by you in the church of San Siro is stupendous in every respect – for novelty, historical colour, and from the scenico-musical standpoint – but it would involve too much work and I could not undertake it. Having, unfortunately, to renounce this act, we must stick to the scene in the Council Chamber which, written by you, will be effective, I do not doubt. Your criticisms are justified, but you, immersed in more elevated works, and with *Otello* in mind, are aiming at a perfection impossible here. I am lower and, more optimist than you, don't despair. I agree that the table rocks, but adjusting the legs a bit, I believe it will stand up. I agree that here are none of those characters (always very rare!) which make one exclaim: 'How mo-

numental!' Nevertheless it seems to me that there is something in the characters of Fiesco and Simone which could be put to good use."[14]

So Verdi had to curb Boito's drive. To fulfill the latter's wishes would
have meant the creation of an entirely new opera based on a different plot.
This was excluded since like Boito, Verdi had already *Otello* in mind. One of
the consequences of Verdi's temperance is the lack of change in the character
of Gabriele. In both versions he is the same conventionally romantic young
hero, whose emotional overstatements ("Dammi la vita" in his second duet
with Amelia; "Dammi la morte" in the terzetto) form a striking contrast to
Simone's maturity. This youthful impetuosity certainly adds to the dramatic
plausibility of his hot-headed attempt at the Doge's life. But the choice of
Gabriele as Simone's successor at the end of the drama seems anything but a
guarantee for lasting peace.

Gabriele's character was surely a "leg of the rocky table that could not be
adjusted." To rewrite his entire part would hardly have sufficed; what was
needed was a change in the plot. However, in more minor instances Verdi
brilliantly succeeded in adapting 1857 material to his new conception. The
original bridal chorus in Act III (no. 22), for example, was a set piece written
for unaccompanied female voices. In the revision the same chorus is only
heard off-stage, but through the addition of Paolo's bitter comments ("Ah!
orrore! Quel canto nuziale, che mi persegue . . .") it is completely integrated
in the drama.

The revised score surely does not possess the stylistic unity of the original.
Although the heterogeneity may be less disturbing than that of Strawinsky's
Rossignol (written partly before and partly after *L'oiseau de feu*, *Petrushka*
and *Le sacre*), it is easily perceptible. But this holds for the music only. As a
drama the second *Boccanegra* is fairly homogenuous and entirely convincing. Verdi must have felt that its germ was hidden in the 'theatrical' 1857
version and that, although seemingly a tour de force, the re-creation of
Simone as a mature character in a true musical tragedy was possible. He
succeeded because he was able to subordinate theatre to drama.

1973

---

[14] Quoted by Frank Walker (*The Man Verdi*, London 1962, p. 480–81).

CHAPTER 10

RITUAL SCENES

According to a generally accepted theory both ancient and early Christian drama originated from rituals. No wonder then that through the ages ritual scenes have never been completely absent from the Western theatre. In fact these scenes are more suited to musical than verbal drama, since the connection with a supernatural power inherent in the concept of a ritual calls for an atmosphere that can hardly be evoked by the spoken word alone; here music proves a much more effective means of expression.

In modern usage the term "ritual" may adopt various meanings. Like many old concepts, its original signification has been watered down in the course of time. We are accustomed to speak of rituals not only with regard to church and law-court (both preservers of rhetorical language), but in connection with other meeting-places where people are involved in more or less solemn activities governed by rules: parliament, stadium, theatre, concert-hall, and the like. These associations evoke the danger of equating the concept of ritual with the mere survival of customs. In this discussion of rituals in Verdi's operas the term is therefore taken in a narrow sense. A stage scene may be considered a ritual when it answers to these conditions:

(a) It deals with a solemn act which bears a direct or indirect relation to a supernatural element.

(b) It sets an individual against a group which represents or has the illusion of representing a superhuman power.

(c) Structurally the scene is symmetrical and is governed by an arithmetical symbol or formula.

In Italian opera, the act mentioned under (a) is generally either a trial, conjuration, invocation, prophecy or solemn promise. Possible variants are a malediction (not as the result, but instead, of a trial) and the taking of an oath, the *giuramento* (rather than a mere promise). The role of the group referred to in (b) may be an active one; mostly, however (and especially in trials), only a representative stands in opposition to the individual. He is a judge, a priest or an angel, acting as the voice of secular or divine order. The symbol or formula (c) is invariably the number 3 or its multiple.

In addition to true rituals we find in Verdi's works a few semiritualistic scenes and various passages which merely contain some traces of a ritual. It should be pointed out that not every scene in a plot that lends itself to a ritualistic interpretation needs to be treated by the composer as a ritual. On the other hand, I have come across one example of the opposite: a non-ritual scene handled by Verdi as if it were a ritual.

In opera of the *ancien régime* ritual scenes are more frequently encountered than in Italian *melodramma* of the nineteenth century. This is due not only to a different choice of subjects (mythological rather than historical), but also because opera generally had ceremonial character during the age preceding the Revolution. In another context I have discussed the threefold structure of various ritual scenes which occur in operas by Rameau, Gluck, Sacchini and Cherubini.[1] One has only to think of Mozart's *Zauberflöte* to realize that these ritual features were not confined to so-called court operas but penetrated into middle-class genres like the German *Singspiel*. Ritualistic traces are found even in purely instrumental music of the period – for instance, the three initial chords of a symphony (often the tonic played in unison). Although this custom may be of operatic origin, it nevertheless bears witness to the ceremonial character of music in general during the *ancien régime*. Growing interest in individual dramatic characters and psychology may also account for the relative scarcity of ritual structures in early nineteenth-century opera. Had the heroine's conjuration in the second act of *Medea in Corinto* been set by Rameau or Gluck, the scene would almost certainly have been built on a triple formula. Simon Mayr, however, prefers to picture Medea's mental disorder, and therefore in his opera the scene is 'irregular'.

In Verdi's dramatic works too a few situations which seem to call for a ritual structure lack tripartite form with regard to both words and music (e.g. the procession with the prophecy of Bishop Leo in *Attila*). In these scenes dramatic intensity obviously gets the upper hand of ceremonial order. But in many other cases Verdi found a convincing solution to the problem of reconciling these seemingly conflicting conditions. While submitting to the precept of structural triplicity he intensifies the dramatic impact by presenting the three identical sections on stepwise ascending tonalities. Thus, for

---

[1] See Ch. 8, pp. 174–175.

instance, a solemn summons is repeated twice, each time a semitone higher. Other intervals used for the same purpose are the major second, the major third and the minor third. Moreover, Verdi usually divides each section into three subsections, two of which are sung by individuals and one by the group. The first of these actors is the person who conducts the ritual, the second his opponent or a character whose attitude is ambiguous, while the chorus generally adheres rather slavishly to the words and acts of the leader. In this way both the overall structure and its component parts answer to the traditional tripartite formula, while at the same time they stimulate the dramatic tension. A third difference between eighteenth-century and Verdian ritual is that the latter is often embedded in a large ensemble, for instance a finale. In this way the composer avoids a break in the continuity and promotes the integration of the scene in the drama as a whole.

The earliest example of a true ritual in Verdi's operas is found in *Giovanna d'Arco* (Milan, 1845), the libretto of which was written by Temistocle Solera after Schiller's *Jungfrau von Orleans*. During the trial scene in the finale of Act II the interrogator (and accuser) is Giovanna's father Giacomo, who solemnly takes his daughter's hand and asks: "Tell me in the name of God the avenger, have you not committed sacrilege?" After one bar of silence, in which we hear only the murmur in the orchestra, the people comment: "She does not speak! ... she bows her head!" and Carlo implores: "One word, and you shall be believed!" Next the accuser asks his second question: "Speak, by the souls of your parents, have you not committed sacrilege?" The corresponding words of the people ("She does not answer, she does not answer!)" and the King ("Speak, speak!" and aside: "O blind father!") are followed by Giacomo's third and last question: "Speak, by the soul of your mother, have you not committed sacrilege?" At this moment the ritual is suddenly interrupted by thunder and lightning (ex. 1).

In order to understand fully the dramatic function of this ritual one should realize that it is the climax of an extensive scene enacted on the square in front of Rheims cathedral. After the King's coronation Giovanna wants to return home as quickly as possible. Carlo, however, stops her and informs her of his intention to erect a church in her honour. At this moment Giacomo interferes, accusing Giovanna of witchcraft and warning the King against blasphemy. The terrified people ask for a sign from heaven to support Giacomo's accusation and this is the immediate cause of the ritual. The atmosphere is extremely tense, since only the audience knows that Giovanna has betrayed her sacred duty by indulging an earthly love for Carlo and that as a penance she refuses to justify herself. Neither Carlo, Giacomo nor the people have any notion of this self-castigation, and therefore the meaning of

EXAMPLE I

the sign from heaven (the thunder and lightning) is completely misunderstood.

In such a situation a rigid musical framework would lame the dramatic élan and weaken the tension. Verdi's method of avoiding this danger is simple and efficacious. The modulations are carried out in the middle of the sections, and the chromatically ascending bass reflects the structure of the whole scene (ex. 2).

EXAMPLE 2

Another detail adding to the dramatic intensity of the ritual scene is the expressive harmonization of Carlo's words (ex. 3).

EXAMPLE 3

Although Carlo is a weak character and his attitude to the events ambivalent, Verdi does not picture him as a shallow personality. The King's concern for Giovanna is genuine; but in spite of his emotional words he submits strictly to the laws of the ritual. Only a supermundane power is able to destroy its regularity, and this is eactly what happens. The people and Carlo are prevented from speaking for a third time, but the essential (Giacomo's three questions) has been said.

The idea of inserting a ritual in the finale of Act II may have been suggested to Verdi and his librettist by the corresponding scene in the German play (Act IV, scene 11). Although in Schiller there is no question of structural regularity, the poet does use the symbol 'three' in various ways. Johanna's father (Thibault d'Arc) summons his daughter "in the name of the Trinity". His question is followed by urgent appeals to speak, coming from her friends, Agnes Sorel (the King's mistress)[2] and La Hire (an officer of the King and Johanna's brother-in-arms). In all three cases the virgin remains silent. She maintains her silence at the end of the scene, when thunderbolts are heard respectively after a protestation of her innocence by Dunois (the King's bastard), again after a new challenge by Thibault, and finally after the offer of the Cross by the Archbishop of Rheims.

During the productive year 1847 Verdi presented four ritual scenes, two in *Macbeth* and one each in *I masnadieri* and *Jérusalem*. The rituals of *Macbeth* (Acts I and III) are decidedly different from that of *Giovanna d'Arco*. First, they are not trial scenes but statements about the future, one (a prophecy) unsolicited, the other (an oracle) requested by Macbeth. Another difference lies in the dramatic function of the 'group', i.e. the witches, who play a much more active role than the crowd in the scene previously discussed. Actually the witches are the true originators of the first ritual, while in the second they act as invokers of phantoms. Finally, both rituals are preceded as well as

---

[2] In Schiller's play the virgin falls in love not with Charles but with Lionel, an English officer.

followed by scenes containing ritualistic features; in this way the main solemnity is not only foreshadowed but 'reverberates' and keeps the audience's memory alive.

The witches who appear in the 'Introduzione' are not individuals (as in Shakespeare) but consist of three identical groups. In a musical drama this undoubtedly enhances their dramatic power. According to Verdi, the appropriate number for each of the groups was six (eighteen in all), and in this case the multiple of three can hardly be considered fortuitous.[3] The instrumental introduction accompanying the witches' entrance is full of motifs and passages grouped by threes, and the witches themselves sing in symmetrical phrases containing the melodic tritones characteristic of their musical language (ex. 4).

EXAMPLE 4

Macbeth and Banco enter and the former is prophetically hailed in a ritualistic manner (ex. 5).[4]

EXAMPLE 5

[3] Letter of 21 January 1847 to Alessandro Lanari, the impresario of the Florentine Teatro della Pergola. See *I copialettere di Giuseppe Verdi*, ed. G. Cesari and A. Luzio, Milan, 1913, p. 447.

[4] The 'prophecies' contain an oddity which derives from Shakespeare (Act I, scene 3) and his chief source (Holinshed, *Chronicles of Scotland*): only two groups of witches reveal something unknown. Macbeth is surely aware of being Thane of Glamis, and the fact that he is hailed in this quality can only be explained as an artificial means to fill out the tripartite form of the greeting. When immediately afterwards Macbeth is informed by Duncan's messengers of his nomination as Thane of Cawdor, he reflects in an aside on the witches' greetings. In the parallel passage Shakespeare cautiously uses the word "truth" ("Two truths are told/As happy prologues to the swelling act/Of the imperial theme"). In the libretto, however, Macbeth speaks of prophecies ("Due vaticini compiuti or sono/Mi si promette dal terzo un trono"). The word "vaticino" turns the oddity into a misstatement.

Banco solicits a prediction for himself. The witches meet his request, but unlike the hailing of Macbeth their words this time are obscured by inner contradictions. The libretto gives a literal translation of Shakespeare's text, except that the parts of the first and third witches have been exchanged. The English lines read:

FIRST WITCH:	Hail!
SECOND WITH:	Hail!
THIRD WITCH:	Hail!
FIRST WITCH:	Lesser than Macbeth, and greater.
SECOND WITCH:	Not so happy, yet much happier.
THIRD WITCH:	Thou shalt get kings, though thou be none.

EXAMPLE 6

Nor is obscurity the sole difference from the previous prophecy. The ascending interval between the words of each group significantly becomes a minor second instead of a third. The 'linking' semitone invariably symbolizes death, in this opera as well as in other dramas of Verdi. I have been unable to find a single instance of its use in rituals lacking implications of death. It may be argued that Macbeth's predicted future, in spite of being presented in linking thirds, is no less dire than Banco's, but such an objection can be refuted by reference to Schiller's adaptation of the play.[5] This version should not be overlooked in any study of Verdi's *Macbeth*. The composer's lifelong friend, Count Andrea Maffei, who improved Piave's draft of the libretto, was an authority on Schiller and had translated his dramas into Italian. We may assume therefore that Verdi was even more

[5] Schiller adapted *Macbeth* for a performance at the Weimar Court Theatre. See F. R. Noske, *Schiller e la genesi del 'Macbeth' verdiano*, Nuova Rivista Musicale Italiana, vol. 10 (1976), pp. 196–203.

familiar with the Schiller version than with the original. In the German adaptation the first scene is considerably longer than in Shakespeare. The following lines, for example, do not occur in the English text:

ERSTE HEXE:	Aber die Meisterin wird uns schelten,
	Wenn wir mit trüglichem Schicksalswort
	Ins Verderben führen den edlen Helden,
	Ihn verlocken zu Sünd und Mord.
DRITTE HEXE:	Er kann es vollbringen, er kann es lassen;
	Doch er ist glücklich: wir müssen ihn hassen.
ZWEITE HEXE:	Wenn er sein Herz nicht kann bewahren,
	Mag er des Teufels Macht erfahren.
ERSTE HEXE:	Wir streuen in die Brust die böse Saat,
	Aber dem Menschen gehört die That.

FIRST WITCH:	*But the mistress will scold us,*
	if by using deceptive words
	about his destiny we ruin the noble hero,
	and induce him to sin and murder.
THIRD WITCH:	*He may achieve it, he may ignore it;*
	but he is happy, so we must hate him.
SECOND WITCH:	*If he cannot control his heart,*
	may he feel the Devil's power.
FIRST WITCH:	*We sow the seed of Evil in the heart;*
	but the deed belongs to Man.

It is clear that at least in Schiller's version of the play Macbeth is free to act as he wishes. Even if he were to refrain from any violence, then the possibility of his becoming King of Scotland one day is not necessarily excluded. We shall never know. What we do know is that Macbeth takes a mere prediction for an incitement. This is the fatal mistake which implies his own and others' destruction. Shakespeare's text does not really contradict Schiller's. Most Shakespearean scholars interpret the witches' prophecy as a challenge to Macbeth rather than a verdict concerning the lives of Duncan and Banquo. Still, Schiller's words are more explicit in this respect, and the reasonable assumption that the musical drama is based on the German rather than the English text leads to the conclusion that the difference of linking intervals in the tripartite greetings of Macbeth and Banco is perfectly justified. While the latter cannot change his destiny, the former has a free choice of whether to kill or abstain from violence.

In the 1865 Paris version of the opera Verdi added a "Stretta dell' introduzione" which concludes the scene in the word. The witches announce their second meeting with him in due time. Neither in Shakespeare nor in Schiller is there a parallel to this chorus, which Verdi probably inserted to counterbalance the choral introduction and to obtain a macro-tripartite form (Introduction – Predictions and reflections – Conclusion).

After the murder of Duncan and Banco, Macbeth, now King of Scotland, is tortured by his conscience as well as his insecurity about the future. At the beginning of Act III the witches meet in a cave around a cauldron and prepare a ritual (*Incantesimo*). This preparation already contains in itself ritualistic features, the Italian words answering to the triple formula even more strictly than Shakespeare's:

Shakespeare, Act IV, scene 1

FIRST WITCH:	Thrice the brinded cat hath mew'd.
SECOND WITCH:	Thrice and once the hedge-pig whined.
THIRD WITCH:	Harpier cries 'Tis time, 'tis time.

Libretto, Act III, scene 1

THIRD GROUP:	Tre volte miagola la gatta in fregola.
SECOND GROUP:	Tre volte l'upupa lamenta ed ulula.
FIRST GROUP:	Tre volte l'istrice guaisce al vento.

The musical settings of these lines are almost identical and begin successively in E minor, G minor and B minor. The same keys occur in the long solos sung by each group during the wild dance around the cauldron. While ritual phrases generally tend to be short and set in a recitative-like way, here we have three identical periodic melodies of sixteen bars each. The following example shows the E minor solo of the third group (ex. 7).

The rest of the *Incantesimo* also consists of periodic melodies including conspicuous tritone leaps and chromatic middle voices in the orchestra. The obligatory ballet written for the Paris stage is musically attractive but weakens the dramatic tension. The modern practice of passing immediately to the 'Gran scena della apparizione' is therefore entirely justified. Macbeth enters, and at his request the witches conjure up the phantoms. Everything seems to point now to a proper ritual based on the Verdian formula, but the scene which follows is surprisingly irregular in structure. On reflection, however, this design is perfectly logical, since the phantoms' voices are not only unequal (the warrior is a bass, the two children are sopranos) but

EXAMPLE 7

Macbeth himself is far too excited to submit to the rules of the rite. Because his interruptions and misinterpretations of the phantoms' words are dramatically more important than the oracular pronouncements, the scene is dominated by him rather than by the evanescent apparitions.

The following procession of the kings once more illustrates the part played by Schiller's adaptation in the realization of the libretto. While the text of the First Folio clearly indicates the appearance of eight kings (the last with a mirror in his hand) followed by Banquo's ghost, Schiller merely speaks of eight monarchs, the last of whom is Banquo with a mirror. This alteration not only undoes the triple structure of the procession (nine apparitions in Shakespeare, eight in Schiller) but is moreover illogical, since Banquo has never been king. Nevertheless Verdi's Banco answers to Schiller's stage direction, rather than to Shakespeare's: "Otto Re passano uno dopo l'altro (. . .) l'ottavo, Banco, con un specchio in mano".

After the concluding "Coro e ballabile", corresponding more or less with Shakespeare's lines 125–32,[6] we are carried back into an earthly atmos-

---

[6] Far more than the Italian text, the music convincingly expresses the witches' irony found in Shakespeare: "Come sisters, cheer we up his sprites, / and show the best of our delights: / I'll charm the air to give a sound, / While you perform your antic round; / That this great King may kindly say, / Our duties did his welcome pay". These lines are considered spurious however, a fact unknown to Schiller and Verdi.

phere. Macbeth revives from his swoon, Lady Macbeth enters, and it now becomes clear that in spite of his 'spoiling' the regularity of the scene with the three phantoms, Macbeth did experience their pronouncements as a true ritual. His account of what has happened is set in strict conformity to the Verdian rule. He cites the three oracles in a shortened version, the linking interval being no longer a third (as in the first act) but the fatal semitone; and so we hear him unconsciously predicting his own death (ex. 8).[7]

EXAMPLE 8

The "Sogno" in the last act of *I masnadieri*, with only two persons in the room, hardly seems compatible with condition (b) formulated at the beginning of this chapter. Nevertheless, it includes a ritual section which dramatically as well as musically strictly obeys the rules. The title of the scene is misleading, however, since it does not concern an actual dream but the recounting of a dream. The situation is this: Francesco Moor, who has tried to kill his father and to eliminate his brother Carlo, rushes into the room and in a state of agitation tells his servant Arminio about the nightmare from which he has just awakened:

The whole earth seemed ablaze and all human dwellings consumed by the flames. A cry sounded: "O Earth, eject the dead from your womb! Eject the dead from your depths, O Sea!" and the plains became covered with countless bones. Then I was dragged to the top of Mount Sinai, where my eyes were blinded by three splendid figures.

---

[7] *Lady M.:* And what did they say? *Macb.:* Beware of Macduff! ... *Lady M.:* And what else? *Macb.:* No man of woman born will kill you. *Lady M.:* Continue ... *Macb.:* You will be invincible until the forest of Birnam shall move against you.

Neither in Shakespeare nor in Schiller is there a parallel to this scene.

Here Arminio interrupts: "The image is that of the Day of Judgment!"
Francesco continues:

The first figure, armed with a mysterious codex of law, exclaimed: "Woe betide him
who lacks faith!" The second holding a mirror in his hand, spoke: "Here, the lie
dissolves." The third raised a pair of scales high in the air, shouting: "Come hither,
ye sons of Adam!" And from the clouds which covered Sinai like a horrible cloth my
name was the first to be thundered forth.

The ritual section proper consists of the pronouncements by the *splendenti
figure*, presumably three archangels. The entire passage is too long to be
quoted here, but the first section in F major makes it possible to reconstruct
the succeeding two, which according to the rule are in G♭ major and G
major (ex. 9).

EXAMPLE 9

Two features of this ritual are particularly noteworthy. First, because of the absence of any action on the stage, the orchestra is used alone as a means to express the terrible vision. Impetuous scales in the strings and repeated chords in the low wind instruments (especially brass) create the image of doomsday. The second particularity of the ritual is its smooth integration into the whole of the "Sogno". At the beginning of the scene Francesco is very nearly out of his mind.[8] His agitation is pictured by means of an astonishing sequence of chords accompanying the words: "Arminio ... tell me! ... Do the dead rise? ... or is there no truth in dreams? ... Yet, I just had a terrible one ..." (ex. 10).

EXAMPLE 10

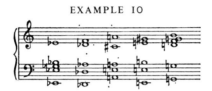

In spite of the extremely emotional atmosphere Verdi happily succeeds in avoiding the danger of excessive contrast between Francesco's unbalanced state of mind and the rigidity of the rite. The harmony in each of the sections of the ritual remains as unstable as in the previous part of the "Sogno" (parallel diminished triads and abrupt transitions from F to G♭ and from G♭ to G). Nor is the rest of the scene unrelated to the ritual passage. Francesco's final verdict ("It was not for you, damned soul, that Man-God has suffered!") is accompanied by three scales in the violins, which remind us of the bars preceding each of the archangelic pronouncements (see above ex. 9).

During the autumn of the same year (1847) Verdi adapted his early opera *I Lombardi alla prima crocciata* for the Paris stage. The French version, called *Jérusalem*, contains several newly-composed fragments, including the entire second part of Act III. This scene is enacted on the square of the Mussulman town of Ramla and deals with the ritual disgrace of Gaston. Previously banished from Toulouse for a crime he did not commit, the French knight is now condemned to death for reasons that remain rather obscure (the libretto is perhaps the most muddled of all the books Verdi set to music during his long career). But in contrast to the rituals of *Macbeth* (Act III) and *I masnadieri* the composer is not faced here with the danger of

---

[8] In Schiller's *Sturm und Drang* play *Die Räuber*, on which the libretto is based, the villain even lies in a swoon for a short time (Act V, scene 1).

psychological incongruity. The whole scene on the square, which includes a
funeral march in E♭ minor and the stripping, piece by piece, of Gaston's
armour, is in the constellation of ceremony. While the accused desperately
protests against the disgrace (considering this part of the sentence far worse
than death), he nevertheless keeps his dignity and complies strictly with the
order of the rites. Thus Gaston marches in his own funeral procession,
which is a 'prelude' to the execution fixed for the next day under the walls of
the Holy City. The death motifs[9] dominating this impressive piece are partly
grouped by threes. After a rather dry recitative, in which the papal legate
pronounces the sentence, and a short aria of Gaston, the malediction proper
is introduced by phrases structurally related to those of the funeral march
(ex. 11):

EXAMPLE 11

Next the herald successively breaks Gaston's helmet, shield and sword,
calling him a traitor. This ritual part of the scene formally resembles the trial

[9] See Ch. 8.

in *Giovanna d'Arco*; there are, however, some important differences. Unlike Giovanna, Gaston does not remain silent; each time he is heard crying: "You lie! you lie!" Moreover the role of the bystanders is much more complex. The French knights comment: "No mercy for a traitor", and a group of females (who seem to appear from nowhere) expresses pity, while a chorus of monks sings Latin texts which can be identified as various parts of Psalm 108.[10] Finally, the ritual is not interrupted as in *Giovanna d'Arco*, but duly completed. This implies that the ascending semitones cover an interval of a minor third, i.e. from C tot E♭ (ex. 12). The scene ends with Gaston's pathetic cabaletta, each strophe of which is followed by an impressive ensemble of everyone on the stage (only the herald, keeping strictly to his ritual role, remains silent).

During the next fifteen years Verdi did not write any scenes that may be called true rituals from a dramatic as well as a musical point of view. His growing interest in domestic drama, with its 'realistic' implications, may account for the absence of these scenes; on the other hand the fact that not only *Luisa Miller*, *Stiffelio* and *La traviata* but *La battaglia di Legnano*, *Il trovatore*, *Les Vêpres siciliennes* and even *Un ballo in maschera* lack the typical Verdian ritual might be explained by his hesitation to re-apply a device that could easily degenerate into mere convention. Paolo's malediction in the first-act finale of *Simon Boccanegra*, for instance, would lend itself very well to a setting similar to that of Gaston's disgrace.[11] All the necessary elements are available: the noble accuser (Simone), the accused (Paolo), the individual bystanders (Amelia, Gabriele, Fiesco, Pietro) and the people. Strictly speaking the scene does not deal with the supernatural or religious, but the Doge's words – "the austere rights of the people", "the honour of the city", "be my witness in the face of heaven", etc. – point to an almost mystical atmosphere, especially for a nineteenth-century Italian audience. Nevertheless Verdi abstains from a true ritual setting of the scene, and prefers instead to create dramatic tension by other means. Since Paolo is not named by the accuser, he is forced to take part in a triple act of damnation and to curse himself:

---

[10] The texts in question are verses 7, 8 (in which the word "episcopatum" is replaced by "heriditatem" and 17 (with various omissions).

[11] In terms of chronology this scene should be discussed later, since it first appears in the revised score of 1881. This fact may account for the Jago-like traits in Paolo's character, which seem much stronger in the second version than in the 1857 original. Verdi started to work on the revision when he was already conceiving *Otello*. See Ch. 9.

EXAMPLE 12

DOGE:	Sia maledetto! (*to Paolo*) e tu repeti il giuro.
PAOLO:	Sia maledetto ... (*aside*) Orrore! orror!
PEOPLE:	Sia maledetto!

An application of the *Jérusalem* formula would almost certainly have weakened the characters, or even reduced them to puppets, and this may be the reason why Verdi constructed the scene differently. Far from being a crude romantic spectacle, *Simon Boccanegra* is a psychological drama in which true human conflicts prevail over theatrically contrived excitements.

Curiously enough, in the same opera a later scene (in Act III), which seems like anything but a ritual, is more or less treated as such by the composer. The scene occurs after the civil war between the patricians and plebeians of the city of Genoa, which ended in the latter's victory. The Doge, anxious for peace, has ordered that the noisy celebration of triumph should be stopped and the lights on the square extinguished in honour of the dead of both parties. A captain accompanied by a trumpet-player announces the order from the balcony of the Doge's room in the palace. His words are preceded by a triple trumpet signal (an anapaestic motif), symbolizing the dignity of the Republic's highest authority; but, as will be seen below, the motif may also express the concept of tragic death.

The Doge enters and speaks three short sentences: "My temples burn ... I feel a dreadful fire creeping through my veins ... Ah, let me breathe the blessed air of the open sky". Each of these phrases is preceded by a series of chromatically ascending and descending parallel sixth-chords in the strings, supported by a trombone pedal-point (successively on E, F and F$\sharp$). The first section runs as follows (ex. 13).[12]

From a purely musical point of view the passage has all the characteristics of a ritual in the Verdian sense, but what about the dramatic explanation? There is neither a leader nor a supporting group on the stage, and Simone's words do not seem to have any connotation of the supernatural, religion or death. He simply soliloquizes about feeling unwell and wanting fresh air, neither of which points to a ritual.

As in many other arresting situations, here too the audience possesses knowledge of an important fact that remains hidden to the protagonist. We know that the Doge has been infected by Paolo with a slow poison, and this enables us to explain the ritualistic features of the scene. What Verdi suggests is that unknowingly Boccanegra has ordered a ceremony concerned with his own death. The relationship between the solemn pronouncement on

---

[12] Parallel sixth-chords frequently occur in this particular work.

EXAMPLE 13

the balcony and the Doge's subsequent soliloquy becomes perfectly clear: the trumpet signal was indeed a death motif and its twofold repetition marks the balcony scene as the introduction to a sort of ritual. Simone's ignorance about his own fate is stressed by the fact that he does not keep to the rules; although his first two unaccompanied sentences are sung on the notes E and F respectively, the last is an outburst starting on high C♯ (ex. 14).

EXAMPLE 14

Any remaining doubt about the interpretation of the scene is removed if we look at Verdi's stage direction a few pages later in the score: "The lights on the square gradually weaken till at the Doge's death they are fully extinguished".[13] The meaning of this stage direction is moreover reinforced by *ostinato* death motifs in the orchestra (bassoons, trombones, tuba and timpani).[14]

[13] See p. 259 of the most recent Ricordi edition (1968; plate number 131142).

[14] The passage quoted above first appears in the revised score. In the original the phrase starts on F♯ with different words. Besides, the Doge is not soliloquizing but addressing Pietro. The essential difference between the two versions, however, lies in the exchanged order of

If the above fragment of *Simon Boccanegra* turned out to possess certain
implications which explain Verdi's ritualistic setting, the same is not at all
the case with the third-act dialogue of Renato and Amelia in *Un ballo in
maschera*. Although the situation is far from trivial – accused of adultery,
Amelia is told by her husband that she will have to die – it nevertheless
concerns a domestic scene enacted in Renato's study and lacking any ritual
features. Yet Verdi makes use of his well-known device, the only licence
being a prolongation of both Amelia's last sentence and Renato's rejoinder
(ex. 15).

EXAMPLE 15

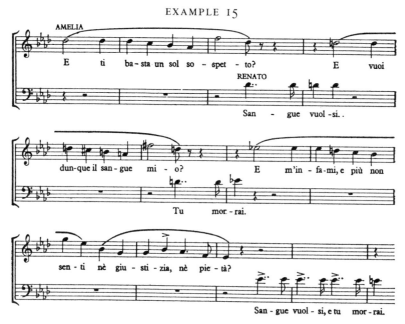

The passage forms an integral part of a rather complicated harmonic construction which starts in F minor and passes through Ab major, Db major,
D major, Eb major, E major, Ab minor, Fb major (= E major) before
reaching Eb minor, the key of Amelia's aria "Morrò, ma prima in grazia".
The only dramatic feature reminding us of scenes previously discussed is the
death connotation of the semitone which links the keys of Db, D, Eb and E;
this, however, does not at all give sufficient cause to speak of a ritual. One
cannot but conclude therefore that the musical 'rite' should not be isolated

events. The balcony passage is lacking in the first version, and Simone's order (to Pietro)
concerning the extinguishing of the lights is given after the 'ritual' complaint instead of before.
This procedure is dramatically less effective than the one in the revised score.

from the remainder, and that in this instance Verdi made use of his formula for other purposes, i.e. to express Renato's and Amelia's agitation, and to enhance the dramatic tension in general.

A negative example from the same opera confirms the composer's independent attitude towards his own device. Ulrica's incantation in the second part of the first act possesses all the characteristics of a potential rite. The cauldron (*cf.* the witches' scene in the third act of *Macbeth*) is among her requisites, and her words refer to the magic number three:

> Omai tre volte l'upupa
> dall'alto sospirò;
> la salamandra ignivora
> tre volte sibilò,
> e delle tombe il gemito
> tre volte a me parlò!

> *Three times now the owl*
> *on high has sighed;*
> *three times the fire-eating*
> *salamander has hissed,*
> *and from the graves a groan*
> *three times to me has spoken!*

The gypsy's first consultant, the sailor Silvano, also refers to the number:

> Tre lustri son corsi
> del vivere amaro,
> tre lustri che nulla s'è fatto per me.

> *Three lustrums of bitter*
> *existence have gone by,*
> *three lustrums that have done nothing for me.*

Still, apart from a few triple motifs in the orchestral introduction, nothing in the score reminds us of Verdi's device. It may be that he wanted to sustain the atmosphere of spontaneity, incompatible with the strictness of a rite. Another possible consideration for not letting the people partake in the act of incantation could be Ulrica's isolated position. Since she does not represent any group, she alone is able to perform the solemnity. Whatever his reasons may have been, Verdi must have consciously abstained from applying his ritual formula in this scene.

A true ritual is held in the second finale of *La forza del destino* (1862). Haunted by feelings of guilt with regard to her father's death and pursued by her vindictive brother, Leonora di Vargas has obtained a promise of refuge from Padre Guardiano, the prior of a Franciscan monastery. Only he is acquainted with her identity and previous history; his monks are under the illusion that she is a (male) pilgrim. In order to prevent their prying into Leonora's secret, Guardiano assembles the monks and solemnly makes them promise obedience (ex. 16).[15]

EXAMPLE 16

This ritual differs essentially from all previous examples. Guardiano does not address an antagonist but the group (Leonora remains silent during the rite). Moreover the matter is not really essential in the drama, and unlike any other Verdian ritual it lacks implications of violence, treason, tragic death, etc. Probably for this reason the linking interval is not the usual semitone but a major second. Furthermore the modulations from C minor to D minor and from D minor to E minor are carried out neither by crude juxtaposition of keys nor by diminished-seventh chords. Verdi simply uses

[15] A translation of the complete text reads as follows. *P. Guard.:* The holy cave shall be opened for him. Do you know the location? *Monks:* We do. *P. Guard.:* Let no one violate this sacred refuge. *Monks:* We shall obey. *P. Guard.:* The low encircling wall separating us from the cave shall never be crossed. *Monks:* We shall not overstep it.

the dominant of the preceding key as a linking harmony. The most remarkable feature of the scene is its ambiguity, however. I believe that, in spite of the solemn and devout atmosphere, even a nineteenth-century audience could not help but smile at these good monks dutifully answering their prior's questions with impressive octave leaps. Among the brothers is Fra Melitone, a *buffo* character who only shortly before was involved in a comic dialogue with his superior (Act II, scene 8). But the humorous aspect of the scene should not be exaggerated. When a few moments later the monks repeat the punishment waiting for anyone who breaks the promise, Verdi relates their cry to the basic musical motif of the drama (ex. 17).

EXAMPLE 17

This ambiguity is characteristic of *La forza del destino*, an opera in which comic and tragic scenes not only alternate but are fused in a manner that would have been unacceptable to an audience of the 1840's.

Considering Verdi's attitude toward rituals during the preceding 20 years, one might wonder why in the Paris version of *Don Carlos* (1867) he returned to the formula of *Giovanna d'Arco* and *Jérusalem*. The last finale of this *grand opéra* contains a ritual which is almost a replica of the trial scenes written during the 1840's, the only difference being that instead of a single accuser there are two (Philippe and the Grand Inquisiteur). They offer their victim to each other:

PHILIPPE: À vous l'indigne fils que de moi Dieu fit naître!
                 Un détestable amour le brûle, à vous ce traitre!
CARLOS, ÉLIS.:   Dieu me/le jugera!
MOINES: Dieu l'a dit,
                 Que le traitre soit maudit!
G. INQ.:   À vous ce contempteur de la foi catholique,
                 Cet ami de Posa, ce parjure hérétique!
CARLOS, ÉLIS.:   Dieu me/le jugera!
MOINES: Dieu l'a dit,
                 L'hérétique soit maudit!

PHILIPPE:	À vous ce corrupteur de mon peuple fidèle,
	Cet ennemi des rois et de Dieu, ce rebelle!
CARLOS, ÉLIS.:	Dieu me/le jugera!
MOINES:	Dieu l'a dit,
	Le rebelle soit maudit!

PH.:	*I give you the ungrateful son whom God gave me!*
	He is consumed by a vile passion! I give you this traitor!
CARLOS/ELIS.:	*God will be my/his judge!*
MONKS:	*God has spoken,*
	may the traitor be accursed!
GR. INQ.:	*I give you this despiser of the catholic faith,*
	this friend of Posa, this heretic perjurer!
CARLOS/ELIS.:	*God will be my/his judge!*
MONKS:	*God has spoken,*
	may the heretic be accursed!
PH.:	*I give you this corrupter of my faithful people,*
	this enemy of kings and God, this rebel!
CARLOS/ELIS.:	*God will be my/his judge!*
MONKS:	*God has spoken,*
	may the rebel be accursed!

The three sections start in D♭, D and E♭, each of them modulating in the middle, up a semitone (the tonic becomes the leading note of the next key). All three keys are minor; only the final chord (E) has a major third and marks (together with a change of tempo – *poco più mosso* instead of *largo*) the end of the rite. In the 1884 version Verdi deleted the entire ritual and reduced this finale to less than one half (41 against 95 bars). A comparison of the two versions is particularly interesting with regard to Verdi's treatment of crisis in musical tragedy. Both are extremely effective, but not in the same way. The Paris version has a sort of *scène à faire*, the roots of which lie in the Scribe-Meyerbeer tradition. In contrast to this the Scala score presents the action in accelerated dramatic rhythm. The Paris finale offers great theatre, the Milan finale great drama.

In *Aida*, too, Verdi reverted to the old device, but here the ritual scene exactly fits the character of the drama as a whole. Compared to previous scores, this opera may seem 'old-fashioned', since it shows no traces of the psychological subtleties found in *Simon Boccanegra* and *Don Carlos*; nor does it express the domestic realism of *Luisa Miller*, *Stiffelio* and *La traviata*. Its classical libretto is of a kind that flourished some 40 years earlier and of which Felice Romani was the indisputable master (*Norma* dates from 1831).

As we know, the simple justification of the composer's choice was the result: Verdi provided irrefutable proof that in 1871 the drama *Aida* was as viable as it would have been in 1831. The same principle applies as well to a separate scene: the trial of Radamès is dramatically as effective as the corresponding rituals in *Giovanna d'Arco* and *Jérusalem*; musically it is more elaborated and of a higher quality. The old formula surely possessed hidden possibilities which only now surfaced.

The *dramatis personae* are Ramfis (the high priest who acts as the accuser), Radamès (the accused), Amneris (whose role somewhat resembles Carlo's in the trial of *Giovanna d'Arco*) and the priests. The ritual scene is preceded by a triple unaccompanied invocation of Heaven, indicating that justice will be administered in the name of the Gods (ex. 18).[16]

EXAMPLE 18

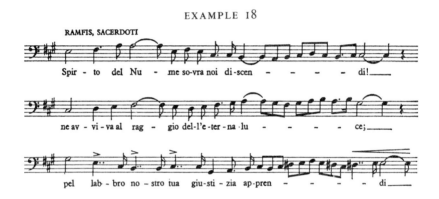

The ritual proper starts with the summoning of Radamès, the anapaestic scansion of whose name suggests his imminent death.[17] The same motif, played in unison by trumpets and trombones, inaugurates the second subsection, in which Ramfis briefly formulates the accusation ("You have delivered your country's secrets to a foreigner") and Radamès is invited to exonerate himself. When instead of an answer only a soft drum roll is heard, the priests cry: "Traitor!" The last subsection is Amneris's desperate entreaty: "Mercy! he is innocent . . . Mercy, O Gods!" Then the entire section is repeated twice, each time a semitone higher (ex. 19).

---

[16] "Spirit of God, descend upon us! . . . May a ray of eternal light inspire us; . . . Do justice through our lips . . ."

[17] See Chapter 8, p. 209.

EXAMPLE 19

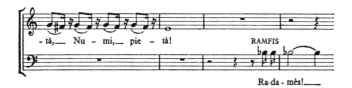

The scheme shown below clearly reveals the complex structure of the scene. Not only is the ritual divided into three sections, but each of these in turn consists of three subsections, the first of which is again subdivided into three identical motifs (the summons of Radamès):

Aida (Act IV): "Scena del Giudizio"
Scheme of Ritual

R

a(I)   a(II)   a(III)

b(1) c(2) d(3)   b(4) c(5) d(6)   b(7) c(8) d(9)

e(1) e(1) e(1)   e(4) e(4) e(4)   e(7) e(7) e(7)

R = Ritual.
a = Section of Ritual (complex rite).
b = First subsection (rite of Ramfis).
c = Second subsection (rite of Ramfis and the priests).
d = Third subsection (complaint of Amneris).
e = Summons (by Ramfis) of the defendant.
(I)   = Intonation on the note A; modulation; phrase in E minor.
(II) = Intonation on the note B♭; modulation; phrase in F minor.
(III) = Intonation on the note B; modulation; phrase in F♯ minor.
(1), (4), (7) = Intonations on the notes A, B♭ and B respectively.
(2), (5), (8) = Modulations.
(3), (6), (9), = Phrases in E minor, F minor and F♯ minor respectively.

The steady growth of tension in the consecutive sections by means of ascending semitones is known from the previous discussion of rituals in earlier operas. The subsections further present a progression realized through the accumulation of musical parameters: the first is a naked intonation lacking variety of pitch and harmonic support, the second a 'melody', also unaccompanied and tonally rather indeterminate; only the last section possesses tonal stability (Amneris's fully harmonized phrases are in E, F, and F♯ respectively).

Threefold structure is not restricted to the proper ritual. I have referred to the preceding triple invocations by the priests with their melismatic endings. In addition, Amneris's expression of self-reproach also foreshadows the solemnity through its tripartite form (ex. 20).[18]

---

[18] "I myself delivered him!"

EXAMPLE 20

After the ritual another triple exclamation of the priests ("Traitor!") functions as a reverberation.[19] Furthermore the initial notes of the three sections (A, B♭ and B) are summarized in this passage (ex. 21).

EXAMPLE 21

The regular, almost mathematical construction of the "Scena del giudizio" does not weaken its dramatic intensity. On the contrary, this regularity strongly enhances our consciousness of the tragic situation. The characters are involved in deeply human conflicts, but all three of them, the despairing Amneris no less than the accusing Ramfis and the silent Radamès, submit to the divine order which rules the stage. And so does the audience.

Just as tragedy climaxes in the ritual of *Aida*, comedy dominates in that of *Falstaff*. In the second part of Act III Sir John is outwitted and exposed by those whom he intended to become his victims. The question remains however: is Falstaff's 'trial' in Windsor Park really a ritual? On the surface the situation has the characteristics of a Verdian ritual scene. And yet, because of the complete lack of solemn atmosphere, the scene around Herne's Oak seems like the opposite of all rituals encountered in earlier operas. Its tempo (*prestissimo*) is so fast that the events are a matter of seconds rather than minutes. The role of the accuser is assigned not to a single person, but a group of actors operating in various combinations: Alice, Meg, Mrs. Quickly, Dr. Cajus, Ford, Pistola and Bardolfo. Only the latter has a very

---

[19] It occurs at the moment when the priests leave the underground prison, and once again when they withdraw from the stage.

short solo ("Reform your life!", upon which Falstaff surprisingly rejoins: "You smell of brandy!"). The 'people' (Spirits, Follies and Devils) are not only vocally active but also make use of their hands, continuously pinching their victim, flogging him with nettles and forcing him to kneel. All these circumstances contribute to create an atmosphere of disorder rather than ceremony.

The scene contains two ritual fragments, one rather freely treated, the other strictly answering the Verdian formula. The first is a threefold bidding by Sir John's adversaries: "Say that you repent". The last word ('penti') is stressed by rapid scales in the woodwind and violins, starting *pianissimo* and leading to a *forte* of the full orchestra. Exactly at this moment Falstaff receives his first *bastonata* from Bardolfo (the second time he is beaten by Pistola, the third by Bardolfo again).[20] Each one of the commands is in Db major but the knight's three answers show a gradually ascending motion, their highest notes being Db, Ebb and Fb respectively (ex. 22).

EXAMPLE 22

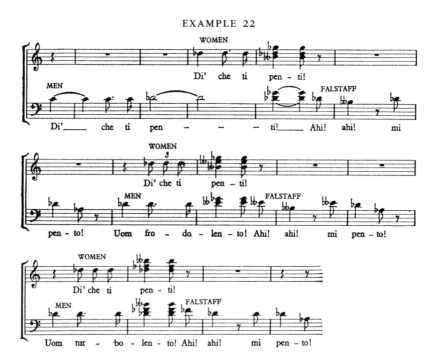

---

[20] In his autograph Verdi noted the exact moments at which the beatings should be given – *cf.* the indications for Otello's kisses in the fourth-act bedchamber scene; unlike these, the signs for the triple beating of Falstaff do not appear in the printed orchestral score (Ricordi, 1967, plate number P.R. 154, pp. 406–8).

Next a delightful antiphonal intermezzo of the women and Falstaff happily provides a relaxation in the general turbulence:

WOMEN:	Lord, chasten him.
FALST.:	But save his abdomen.
WOMEN:	Lord, ruin him.
FALST.:	But save his abdomen.
WOMEN:	Lord, punish him.
FALST.:	But save his abdomen.
WOMEN:	Lord, make him repent.
FALST.:	But save his abdomen.

Each pair of lines is set to the same melody, but differently harmonized. Dramatic continuity is assured by repeated interruptions coming from the four men and the Spirits, Follies and Devils; these interruptions, however, do not cover the expressive *alternatim* singing.

Since Falstaff has failed to give a satisfactory answer to Bardolfo's words ("Reform your life"), the men renew their pressure on him. This time Verdi applies his device strictly by setting the three questions and answers successively in the keys of D, E♭ and E. Scales of woodwind and strings on the word "rispondi" relate this fragment to the D♭ passage discussed above (ex. 23):

EXAMPLE 23

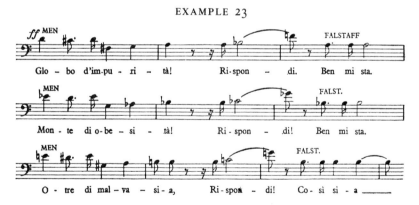

Thus the entire ritual has a tripartite form, both the first and last sections being divided into three subsections:

'Free' rite – Antiphonal intermezzo – Strict rite
(3 × D♭)   (D, E♭, E)

The scene is clearly a piece of self-mockery on the part of the composer, who carries his own device *ad absurdum*. What should be a solemnity is presented in a breath-taking tempo; premature punishment is administered before and during the trial; the accusers are omniscient, the defendant is under a false illusion, and the supernatural is a fabrication.

Nevertheless the scene is ambiguous. An audience generally tends to identify itself with a hero on the stage, and this occurs in the case of Sir John, in spite of, as well as because of, his shortcomings. And so we, too, undergo to a certain extent the influence of the supernatural atmosphere, though it does not frighten us as it does Falstaff. Characteristically neither Fenton nor Nannetta take any part in the mock trial. But it is they who from the beginning set the atmosphere of the Windsor Park scene and ratiate a spell that makes us forget the masquerade. Fenton and Nannetta are in fact the true fairies, not only in the final act but in the entire drama. While lightly expressing the eternal poetry of love, they mix with the other characters in the everyday world. They make it clear that the opera is neither a domestic comedy nor a dramatized fairytale, but a mirror of the human universe with its interchangeable dreams and realities. In this sense *Falstaff* is Verdi's most realistic drama.

1973

CHAPTER II

THE NOTORIOUS CABALETTA

Operas of the *Risorgimento* period were applauded enthusiastically by audiences all over Europe, but the genre also had its foes, even in Italy itself. One of the principal targets of attack was the section concluding a complex aria, duet or ensemble: the cabaletta. All the invectives addressed to Italian opera in general seem to fit this particular 'piece': crudity, vulgar taste, hollow virtuosity and lack of dramatic sense. Hanslick spoke of "a musical box on the ear" (*eine musikalische Ohrfeige*) and although he can hardly be considered an impartial judge in this matter, many contemporaries expressed themselves in equally abusive terms.

Today judgment tends to resort less frequently to generalizations and emotionalism; nevertheless, Joseph Kerman has called the cabaletta "one of the worst conventions of early nineteenth-century opera". His description is worthy of quotation in its entirety:

"This cabaletta was a fast vehement aria or duet of extremely crude form and sentiment; it always came after a slower, quieter piece for the same singer or singers, and served to provide a rousing curtain. The form was strophic, and of the simplest pattern (*aaba* or *abb*); the accompaniment consisted of a mechanically repeated polonaise or fast march rhythm. Between the slower aria and its cabaletta a passage of recitative or *parlante* served to present some sort of excuse for the singer to change his mind. The whole complex indeed is a simplification and stereotyping of the older composite aria of Mozart and Beethoven. Instead of the rather subtle interrelation of one sentiment and the next, and a sense of flux between them, there was now a formalized break into two crude self-contained pieces. Though Rossini still employed composite arias for the most part, Donizetti arranged for half a dozen cabalettas in every opera".[1]

The emotional attitude of former generations is still discernable in these lines. The quoted passage denounces not only the cabaletta itself but also the aria or duet section that precedes it. Such an assertion practically condemns

[1] J. Kerman, *Opera as Drama*, New York 1956, p. 146.

Italian opera as a whole and therefore seems hardly tenable. But the chief objection to Kerman's description is that it does not apply to "early nineteenth-century opera" but to a particular type of cabaletta occurring mainly in works dating from the fourth and fifth decades. More than a century before Kerman, Pietro Lichtenthal, an Italian scholar of Austrian descent, had attacked the cabaletta on quite different grounds:

> "... dopo un picciolo Andante od Andantino la *Regina Cabaletta* apre la ridente bocca, e canticchiando una specie di Walzer con un ritmo e prosodia stravolta, modula co' graziosi a languenti *si* e *no* nella favorita Terza o Sesta minore, e vola sulle ali d'un dolce Eco tutta giubilante e gorgheggiante a tuono".[2]

Obviously this *boutade* refers to the 'lyrical' cabaletta as found in many operas of Rossini, Bellini and Donizetti. Even today, specialists continue to disagree about the meaning of the term. Two distinguished researchers of Italian opera, for example, use the word in entirely different ways. In Julian Budden's monograph on Verdi, only the final strophic section of an aria or cavatina is called cabaletta, the corresponding fragment of a duet being indicated as *stretta*.[3] Friedrich Lippmann, on the other hand, assigns the name cabaletta to all final *tempi*, regardless of form or number of voices.[4] The question therefore remains: what exactly *is* a cabaletta?

To answer this is far from easy. The term cabaletta was an unofficial one, appearing during the nineteenth century in letters or newspaper reviews, but rarely in dictionaries and almost never in manuscript or printed scores. Up to the present musical encyclopedias have provided us with contradictory definitions and even the origin of the word is unclear, since two possible derivations are both disputed. The term may be a corruption of *cobla* (a strophe in Provençal poetry) or it may have arisen from *cavatinella* (little cavatina). The first supposition is supported by the fact that nearly all pieces referred to as cabalettas are in strophic form, the second by evidence found in operas written for the Paris stage (an unequivocal cabaletta like Procida's "Dans l'ombre et le silence", which appears in the second act of *Les vêpres*

---

[2] P. Lichtenthal, *Dizionario e bibliografia della musica*, vol. I, Milano 2/1836 (pp. 106–107): entry *Cabaletta*. Translation: "... after a little Andante or Andantino *Queen Cabaletta* opens her laughing mouth and, warbling a kind of waltz with distorted rhythm and prosody, moves with gracious and languishing exclamations of *si* and *no* to the favourite minor third and sixth, and all exulting and trilling, flies in an appropriate fashion on the wings of a sweet echo".

[3] J. Budden, *The Operas of Verdi*, vol. I, London 1973. The author's use of the term is not always consistent however. In some cases a strophic ending of a complex duet is called cabaletta (in conformity with Verdi's own usage).

[4] Fr. Lippmann, *Vincenzo Bellini und die Italienische Oper seiner Zeit*, Analecta Musicologica, vol. IV (1969), pp. 66–67.

siciliennes, is indicated as "Cavatine" in the libretto[5]). Still another interpretation, offered by Berlioz, speaks for the author's wit rather than his etymological knowledge:

"L'art de la claque reágit même sur l'art de la composition musicale. Ce sont les nombreuses variétés de claqueurs italiens, amateurs ou artistes, qui ont conduit les compositeurs à finir chacun de leurs morceaux par cette période, redondante, triviale, ridicule et toujours la même, nommée *cabaletta*, petite cabale, qui provoque les applaudissements".[6]

In spite of the lack of clear description and the confusing usages of the term, it is possible to arrive empirically at a definition of the cabaletta, based on its formal properties. This may be achieved by eliminating the variables, and retaining only the constant attributes. My investigation of nearly two hundred operatic scores written by Mayr, Paer, Rossini, Bellini, Donizetti, Pacini, the brothers Ricci, Mercadante and Verdi reveals that only two properties remain unchanged:

I)   The cabaletta forms part of an aria or duet, a complex or composite piece of which it invariably functions as a conclusion. Although in the course of time a process of evolution conferred on the cabaletta a more rounded form, no composer would indicate it as a self-contained 'number'.

II) The cabaletta is always in strophic form, of which roughly three types may be distinguished:[7]
     (a) Type S-S: two strophes, the second of which is a complete restatement of the first with regard to both text and music. Between the strophes occurs an episode which may consist of a short orchestral transition or a more extended vocal fragment usually involving one or more other actors (*pertichini*) and even the chorus. This scheme is applied to all solo cabalettas as well as to homophonic duets, terzettos and quartets.
     (b) Type S-S' (only duets): Different words for each of the strophes, the first of which is sung by one of the actors, the second by his antagonist. The second strophe usually contains interruptions or short phrases

---

[5] See *Les vêpres siciliennes / I vespri siciliani*, ed. M. Mila, Torino 1973, p. 24.

[6] H. Berlioz, *Les soirées de l'orchestre*, ed. L. Guichard, Paris 1968, p. 118 (*7e soirée: La claque*). The boutade is taken seriously by Antonio Fernandini, however (*Enciclopedia dello spectacolo*, vol. II, Roma 1954, entry *Cabaletta*).

[7] In the present chapter the terms "strophe" and "strophic" refer to a *musical* entity (a stanza set to music) which is repeated at least once, regardless of whether the second time the words are different or the same. In the latter case, however, also the term "restatement" is used.

sung by the first actor on his own words. The episode is either very short or lacking altogether. Composers often use this type in conflict situations.[8]

(c) Type S-S'-S" (only duets): Each of the actors sings a strophe; their words may be identical but need not be so. Strophe III is sung by both, either homophonically or with the melody exchanged between the two voices. In the latter case only the final phrase will have a homophonic setting. The episode always occurs between the second and third strophes.

It is hardly astonishing to find that in the course of the first half of the century the rigidity of these patterns was not always strictly maintained. Some duet cabalettas include elements of both types (b) and (c), e.g. "Per guarir di tal pazzia" in the first act of Donizetti's *L'Elisir d'amore*. In pieces structured according to scheme (a) the vocal line of the restatement is sometimes slightly varied (e.g. Bianca's "Di tua fede" in the first act of Mercadante's *Il giuramento*, and the aria finale of Donizetti's *Anna Bolena*). Strophes could be set in different keys, if only to suit the tessituras of 'unequal' voices, such as the combinations tenor-bass or soprano-bass. Rossini's *Maometto II°* contains a cabaletta in which the first strophe sung by Anna (soprano) modulates from C to G, and the second sung by Maometto (bass) returns from G to C.[9]

Since these deviations and extensions leave the main patterns virtually intact, we might claim to have given a precise definition of the cabaletta, enabling us to proceed with a study of its historical development. However, such a pretention would be nothing but self-deception. According to the above-established rules, "O terra addio" (*Aida*, final scene) would be called a cabaletta, whereas "Cadran, cadranno i perfidi" (*Nabucco*, Act IV) would not. Such a classification is, of course, quite unacceptable. History does not allow itself to be captured in formulas. A cabaletta is more than a formal scheme clad in music; it possesses a character which cannot be disregarded in spite of inconsistencies apparent during successive generations. Uncompromising descriptive criteria must therefore be avoided, and the limits of our rules occasionally extended.

*   *
*

[8] Philip Gossett kindly informs me that before 1830 type (b) is practically always a truncated version of the type (c).

[9] Instead of concluding the cabaletta with a final strophe, each character repeats its own solo strophe and it is only in the extensive coda that the voices are joined (scheme S-S'-S-S'-Coda).

There can be no question here of drawing a complete historical picture of the pre-Verdian cabaletta. Such a project would require much more extensive investigation than I have accomplished. But a few points may be touched upon in order to convey an understanding of Verdi's handling of the convention.

Among the works of Mayr and Paer written during the century's first decade I have not found a single regular cabaletta.[10] Nevertheless, these composers paved the way for its appearance by extending the final sections of their composite arias or duets and repeating parts of them. In the light of this practice Mayr's severe criticism of Rossini for his use of strophic aria endings was not quite justified. As a matter of fact, in the early operas of Rossini it is only the application of this strophic scheme which constitutes an innovation; for the rest his arias and duets are still composite rather than complex pieces.[11] An example is found in the first act of *Tancredi* (1813): the duet of Amenaide and Tancredi ends with two short strophes, homophonically set and written in the elegant lyrical style reminiscent of eighteenth-century opera seria. The solo cabalettas are less fluent and require more vocal virtuosity; still their melodies do not show the discontinuity of the arias proper. According to Lippmann, Rossini's cabaletta is generally governed by a clear periodicity of corresponding phrases, in contrast to his first *tempo* which usually has a paratactic juxtaposition of florid motifs.[12]

Many of the cabalettas written by Bellini and Donizetti are built on fluent lyrical melodies or dance-like tunes, starting with a syllabic setting of the words and leading to a florid conclusion. Characteristic examples are found in Bellini's *Il pirata*, Act II (Gualtiero's "Ma non fia sempre odiata la memoria") and *Beatrice di Tenda*, Act I (Beatrice's "Ah! la pena in lor piombò"), as well as in Donizetti's *Lucia* (delirium scene: "Spargo amaro pianto", and the heroine's first-act duet with Edgardo: "Ah! verranno a te").

Obligatory vehemence is not the only myth connected with the notion of a cabaletta. Another fictive trait is its invariable fast movement. In actual fact the majority must be sung in a moderate tempo, sometimes even slower than the preceding sections. For example, Percy's cavatina "Da quel dì" in

---

[10] In view of the restricted number of scores available to me no conclusions can be drawn from this observation. Prof. Gossett writes me that regular pre-Rossinian cabalettas do indeed exist.

[11] The words "composite" and "complex" used in this chapter represent different degrees of disintegration, the former term implying a closer relationship between the components than the latter.

[12] See Lippmann, *op. cit.* p. 164 ff.

Donizetti's *Anna Bolena* consists of two Allegro fragments followed by a strophic Moderato. Occasionally the first *tempo* lasted for only a brief span – the slow section of Smeton's cavatina in the same opera covers only eleven bars – and therefore more and more variety was required of the ensuing cabaletta. March-like pieces and polonaise rhythms are found next to slow 'waltzes' and patterns of repeated chords. The principle of variety was even applied within the strophes. Donizetti's *Lucrezia Borgia* contains a duet cabaletta (Lucrezia and Gennaro), in which each strophe is divided into two contrasting subsections, one lyrical (moderato), the other lively (poco più moto). The score of *Il pirata* provides an overview of the variety of sentiments expressed by cabalettas. They picture the exultant mood of the victorious warrior (Ernesto), noble resignation (Gualtiero, Act II), grief (Imogene, Act I), vehemence and conflict (Imogene-Ernesto), and delirium (Imogene, aria finale).

If these characteristics speak for the cabaletta's evolution during the third and fourth decades of the century, other traits remind us of its structural dependency. Ernesto's strophes in *Il pirata*, for example, are set on the same words as the preceding Andante ("Sì, vincemmo"). Many cabalettas still function as a means of reinforcing the sentiments expressed in the foregoing section. Instances of cabalettas resulting from a drastic change in the dramatic situation are found mostly in pieces in which the chorus interposes between the two *tempi*.

The lesser composers of this period strongly influenced the cabaletta's development, though not always in a positive way. Even during his lifetime Pacini's nickname, *il maestro delle cabalette*, may have been intended as an expression of criticism rather than praise. Pacini applied the cabaletta scheme whether suitable or not, rarely missing an opportunity to provoke applause. Italian opera being what it is, the 'artificial' arousal of audience enthusiasm must be considered a composer's legitimate resource. Pacini's abuse, however, resulted from his frequent disregard of dramatic situations and the characters involved. Readers of Sir Walter Scott know Rebecca as an artless, innocent girl and so she is in the libretto of Pacini's *Ivanhoe* (1832). But the music of her cabaletta in the second act radically contradicts this image by adding a wealth of coloratura to the words "Oh cielo, imploro il tuo favor" (ex. 1).

Catarina in *La regina di Cipro* (1846) is a less ingenuous person; in the two strophes of her cabaletta, "Alfin pietoso il cielo", a similar vocal part is much more in accord with character and situation.

A striking example of the cabaletta's maltreatment occurs in the second act of Federico Ricci's *Estella di Murcia* (1846). Although it may express

EXAMPLE I

any mood or sentiment, a cabaletta is entirely unsuited to a situation in which a character is performing an act. Still this is exactly what Diego does in his strophes. In terms of linguistic pragmatics his text, "Se della notte al sorgere me qui non rivedrete" etc., is a performative speech act: he gives an explicit order to the Moorish warriors who, functioning as a choral *per-tichino*, dutifully acknowledge the words of their leader. The situation compellingly calls for a recitative or *scena*, but having sung the first section of his aria Diego must conclude with a cabaletta at any price. The result is disastrous: in the obligatory repeat of the strophe the act of giving an order is stripped of its dramatic force. In musical drama actions, unlike sentiments, do not lend themselves to restatement.

In other instances Pacini and Federico Ricci must have felt the laming effect of the rigid bi-strophic form; they tried to remedy this by shortening the restatement. Thus Pacini omits the second quatrain[13] in Gusmano's "Da tanti anni ch'io non sento" (*I cavalieri di Valenza*, 1828) and Margarita's "Ma nè un guardo, nè un detto" (*Il duca d'Alba*, 1842), while Ricci in the terzetto cabaletta of *Estella* (Act III) sacrifices the first four lines.

Another effective means of softening the rigidity of the scheme and thereby enhancing dramatic effectiveness lies in free treatment of the final strophe in duets of type (c). In the first act of Mercadante's *I Normanni a*

[13] A cabaletta strophe usually consists of two quatrains.

Parigi (1832) the final strophe of a duet cabaletta (Berta and Odone) is considerably extended by imitative treatment of material taken from the preceding strophes. The same opera contains a duet for two sopranos (Osvino, Berta) in which not only the final but also the second strophe differs melodically from the first, though it is written on the same bass.

Among secondary composers, Mercadante was certainly the most strongly profiled figure. His melodic inventiveness was restricted, but he often succeeded in compensating for this defect by a gripping sense of the dramatic. In the cabalettas, however, this quality is rarely encountered. The operas written during the 1820's contain numerous strophic *tempi* written in the style of Rossini. They clearly show Mercadante, in his role as an imitator of Rossini, to be Pacini's inferior, lacking the latter's dexterity and elegance. After 1830 the number of cabalettas varies greatly from one opera to another. While in the first act of *I Normanni* five arias and duets are concluded by strophic sections, the entire score of *Ismalia* (1832) contains only a single regular cabaletta.

Although in his reform operas of the years 1837–39 (*Il giuramento, Elena da Feltre* and *Il bravo*) Mercadante banned the "cabalette triviale" almost entirely from the stage,[14] they frequently reappear in his later works, simpler but also less inventive than before. However, the relation between text and music is closer than in Pacini, and even in a rather indifferent work like *Medea* (1851) the composer shows his concern for the dramatic situation (in her first-act cabaletta, "Per te divenne, o barbaro, nome d'orror Medea", the heroine's ambivalent feelings are pictured by strong dynamic contrasts).

Among the devices used by Mercadante is a slight rhythmic variant of the popular polonaise pattern (ex. 2).

EXAMPLE 2

Occasional subsections found in Mercadante's strophes are contrasted not only by tempo (as in the duet from Donizetti's *Lucrezia Borgia*, mentioned above), but also by tonality. Creusa's cavatina in *Medea* concludes with an expressive Andante in the key of G♭, followed by a brilliant Allegro in E♭ (both repeated). Another idiosyncrasy is the extended coda. In the second-act duet cabaletta of Decio and Amelia from *La Vestale* (1840) this

---

[14] See his often-quoted letter to Francesco Florimo written on New Year's day 1838 (Lippmann, *op. cit.*, p. 332). *Il giuramento* has three cabalettas, *Elena da Feltre* and *Il bravo* each one.

coda takes the form of an additional strophe, homophonically set on new musical material.

A final word should be said about the influence of celebrated singers on the cabaletta's style. In many instances the melody was constructed to suit the vocal capacities of the *diva* rather than the dramatic situation. Composers of the 1830's were still subservient to singers and although some of them, like Giuditta Pasta and Malibran, combined exceptional voices with genuine dramatic talent, others probably contributed to the cabaletta's notoriety. Pieces written for famous singers could give us clues as to their special aptitudes. The roles of Amelia and Ermano in Mercadante's *I briganti* (Paris 1832), for example, were composed for Giuditta Grisi and Giovanni Rubini respectively and it would be worthwhile to study their arias and duets in this work. The music intended for the great singers of the period in question often conveys the impression that the style of the vocalist lagged behind that of the composer, forcing the latter to fall back on a Rossini-like idiom. This hypothesis, however, still needs documentation.

*   *

*

In his first two operas Verdi paid ample tribute to the fashion of the day. *Oberto* has no less than nine cabalettas[15] and *Un giorno di regno* eight. None of these pieces are in themselves outstanding and their effect depends entirely on the situations in which they are sung. Thus, in spite of its conventional construction, Oberto's "Ma tu, superbo giovane" (Act II) is dramatically quite satisfactory and so is the Marchesa's "Se dee cader la vedova" (*Un giorno di regno* I). But in other instances convention clashes with dramatic exigency. In the last-named opera, Eduardo's rather tedious cabaletta ("Deh! lasciate a un alma amante") weakens an already far from interesting character, and the élan of Cuniza's "Più che i vezzi a lo splendore" (*Oberto* II) is diluted by an excess of florid vocal writing. Verdi probably felt more at ease with the 'vigorous' cabaletta type, as shown in the initial duet of *Un giorno di regno* (Eduardo and Belfiore). Still, the best strophes found in this opera are those of the ingenuous Giulietta ("Non vo' quel vecchio"); this is the more remarkable since in her cavatina there is not the slightest dramatic need for a cabaletta. The melody and waltz

---

[15] In *Oberto* there are even ten cabalettas, if one counts Cuniza's "Ma ne' primi anni un angelo", contained in the cavatina which Verdi added to the score for the Milan performances of 1840.

rhythm are derived from the female chorus "Sì festevole mattina", in the initial part of the scene. By relating Giulietta to the *contadine* and *cameriere* Verdi not only stresses her innocence and modesty but unifies the scene musically if not dramatically.

It should be noted that both operas contain a terzetto cabaletta and that even the quartet of *Oberto* has a strophic ending. The terzetto "Noi siamo amanti" in *Un giorno di regno* is one of the few unison cabalettas written by Verdi (type S-S). The opera's autograph also contains a second, more elaborate setting of the words, one which has an undeniably higher musical quality. Nevertheless, in view of the parallel interests of the three characters involved (Marchese, Giulietta, Eduardo), the rather crude unison version is dramatically more arresting and therefore Verdi's choice seems entirely justified.

Although the formal and stylistic treatment of the cabaletta in *Oberto* and *Un giorno di regno* does not differ essentially from that seen in Verdi's predecessors, some traditional characteristics are given more emphasis. March rhythms with polonaise patterns predominate and the tempo ranging from moderato to allegro vivo tends to be faster. Syncopation of the vocal melody, already found in Donizetti, Pacini and Mercadante, is used in a much cruder way. Oberto's cabaletta, mentioned above, may be considered the model of a type which will often recur in Verdi's operas of the 1840's. The musical setting of the two quatrains contained in a single strophe is based on the Bellinian pattern a–a′–b–a″, each section of which comprises two lines. The varied repeat of the initial phrase (a″) is effectively doubled by wind instruments and followed by an extension climaxing on the singer's highest note. The formula is perfectly suited to the expression of strongly emotional feelings by baritones or dramatic sopranos, and, if appropriate to the situation, its crude efficacy will silence all aesthetic objections.

The fact that *Nabucco* contains but five cabalettas is in itself of little significance, since the restricted number of arias and duets in this opera did not offer the opportunity for more. What is remarkable however is that only two of these pieces follow the orthodox pattern, and that none of them show any traces of unimaginative writing. Little needs to be said about Abigaille's "Salgo già del trono aurato". Although all the known conventions seem to be applied to this cabaletta, still it is one of the best in Verdi's output. The extensive duet of Abigaille and Nabucco in Act III ends with strophes of proportionate length ("Deh, perdona"). In each of them the baritone sings two quatrains and the soprano one. The restatement is varied: while Nabucco repeats his former text, Abigaille has new words. The repetition of her 'mocking' theme from the first *tempo* has been criticized more than once, lately by Budden, who calls it "the one doubtful feature of the duet".[16] I do not share his objection; although admittedly lacking subtlety, the repetition stresses Abigaille's ruthless character and moreover functions satisfactorily as a unifying element in the complex piece.

Zaccharia's "Come notte a sol fulgente" is Verdi's earliest cabaletta for bass. The strophes unite two central 'themes' of the drama: religion and patriotism. The latter is expressed by the vocal melody which is closely related to that of the chorus "Va pensiero"; Jehova's 'voice' is heard through the demisemiquaver motifs in the accompaniment, which otherwise is dominated by the conventional polonaise pattern. Despite its integration into the opera's basic idea, the piece remains completely regular with respect to both form and style. Elsewhere, however, Verdi did not hesitate to overstep the 'rules' in order to strengthen the impact. In Nabucco's fourth-act cabaletta "Cadran, cadranno" the traditional bi-strophic form is abandoned in favour of a five-part scheme:

Scheme:	A	–	B	–	A′	–	B′	–	A″
Performers:	Orchestra		Chorus		Nabucco		Nabucco		Nabucco/Chorus
Key:	A♭		D♭		A♭		D♭		A♭
Text:	–		"Cadran..."		"O prodi..."		"Di questo..."		"Per te..."

The deviation from the strophic form originates in the initial section (A), which is not just an orchestral prelude but an integral part of the cabaletta. After the first choral stanza Nabucco's return to the main key with the four-note motif "O prodi miei" produces an unique and consequently unrepeatable effect. This must be the reason why in the final section (A″) the motif is first given to the chorus.

Although Nabucco has but a single aria in the opera, another fragment of his needs to be mentioned in the present context. Verdi's handling of the scene following the *concertato* in the second-act finale (the King's mental breakdown) has always been praised as a highly original touch. Instead of concluding the finale with the usual *stretta*, he gave Nabucco an extended solo piece with alternating allegro and adagio sections. In view of the dramatic situation the idea of a cabaletta would seem anything but obvious. Still its formal scheme is clearly discernible:

[16] See Budden, *op. cit.*, p. 106.

Strophes:	I		II	
Subsections:	A	B	A′	B (extended)
Tempi:	Allegro	Adagio	Allegro	Adagio
Keys:	F minor	A♭ major	F minor	A♭ major
Lines:	4	2	4	2

In the first subsection (A) the terrified King wonders what really happened
to him ("Who lifted the crown from my head?"). The orchestra answers
unequivocally by playing the Jehova motifs. This is followed by Nabucco's
appeal to Fenena (B). The second fast subsection, a free variant of the first,
is set to different words; a repetition of the question and the orchestral reply
would certainly have weakened the impact. Instead the King exclaims that
the blood-red sky fell on his head, a thought promptly pictured by the
rapidly descending strings. In the final Adagio Nabucco pathetically asks
why a tear is dropping from his eye. Here again the new text enhances the
dramatic effect.

The question of whether this finale fragment may be called a cabaletta
must be left unanswered. The slow endings of the two 'strophes' and the lack
of an intermediate episode are certainly most unusual traits. But in the fast
subsections one recognizes quite a few traditional features: the marchlike
rhythms, the emphatic syncopation and the polonaise pattern (moreover the
combination of the latter with the Jehova motifs is reminiscent of
Zaccharia's first-act cabaletta). Regardless of how the piece should be classified, it shows that even at an early stage of his career Verdi brilliantly
succeeded in using traditional elements for genuine dramatic purposes. In
Nabucco the cabalettas are made subservient to the opera's essential substance.

Although it would certainly be incorrect to say that after 1842 Verdi
relapsed into the conventional style of his first two operas, none of the works
written during the remainder of the decade shows the careful handling of the
cabaletta found in *Nabucco*. The quality is generally uneven. Next to splendidly effective pieces like Elvira's "Tutto sprezzo" (*Ernani* I), the third-act
duet of father and daughter in *Giovanna d'Arco* ("Or del padre benedetta"),
and Miller's "Ah fu giusto il mio sospetto" (*Luisa Miller* I), one comes
across curiously trite strophes, such as Oronte's *cabaletta nuova* from *I
Lombardi* II ("Come poteva un angelo"), Jacopo's "Odio solo" (*I due
Foscari* I) and Corrado's "Sì, de'corsari il fulmine" (*Il corsaro* I). In a highly
'theatrical' work like *Attila* the unbridled energy displayed in the final
sections of arias and duets strongly enhances the dramatic impact. In *Alzira*,

on the other hand, several attractive pieces are spoilt by the ensuing strophes (e.g. Zamora's second-act aria). Extremes of quality are even encountered within a single work. Lady Macbeth has two cabalettas, the first of which, "Or tutti sorgete" (Act I), is an undisputable masterpiece, whereas the second, "Trionfai securi alfine" (Act II), seems to contain the worst of which Verdi was capable at that period. Small wonder that in the 1865 revision the latter piece was replaced by "La luce langue" (a composite aria without a cabaletta).

Nearly all Verdian cabalettas are dramatically justified by a change of mood or situation occurring between the initial and final sections of the scene in question. The composer repeatedly insisted on this point[17] and consequently his librettists were forced to invent 'incidents', some of which may strike us as rather artificial. At the beginning of Act III of *Stiffelio*, for example, Stankar (who wishes to challenge Raffaele to a duel) is reading a letter from which it appears that his daughter's seducer has fled. Feeling dishonoured, he then decides to kill himself (aria: "Lina pensai che un angelo"). Suddenly Jorg enters, informing him that Raffaele has returned, whereupon Stankar bursts out in his exuberant strophes, "O gioia inesprimibile". One wonders about the reason for Raffaele's flight and subsequent return – could it have been to enable the composer to write an Andante and a cabaletta?

The 'vigorous' cabaletta mentioned above is Verdi's most personal contribution to the tradition. Some of these pieces are musically related to foregoing sections. Lady Macbeth's "Or tutti sorgete, ministri infernali" provides an excellent example of the device. The consecutive appoggiaturas at the beginning of this cabaletta correspond with those of the cavatina proper. On the other hand, their ascending line illustrating the text ("sorgete") forms a contrast with the descending movement in the Andantino (ex. 3).

EXAMPLE 3

[17] See for example his letters to Piave, dated 22 May, 1844 (*Copialettere* p. 426) and to Ghislanzoni, dated 28 September 1870 (*ibid.*, p. 645).

Occasionally Verdi turned to other modes of expression. The first version of Oronte's cabaletta in *I Lombardi* (II) has a strong Bellinian touch that may be said to fit the young man's character. The concluding strophes of Medora and Corrado in the first act of *Il corsaro*, on the other hand, remind us of the famous farewell scene in *Lucia di Lammermoor*, not only because of the analogous situation, but also by their musical setting: a very lyrical melody is supported by steadily repeated chords. Still, the composer manages the form with more flexibility than Donizetti, in whose cabaletta the episode between the strophes and coda stands more or less apart; in Verdi's score these fragments are integrated into the musical material of the strophes.

Alzira's cavatina (Act I) introduces a salon-like type ("Nell'astro che più fulgido"). Budden aptly speaks of a 'prancing' cabaletta in referring to its rhythm.[18] Although at first hearing the short-winded coloraturas may seem Rossinian, they actually mark an aspect of Verdi's personal style, contrasting both with his slow expressive and fast energetic melodies. Gulnara's cavatina "Ah! conforto à sol la speme" (*Il corsaro* II) ends with strophes in the same vein, and the style is also encountered in arias proper, such as Amalia's "Lo sguardo avea degli angeli" (*I masnadieri* I), which significantly lacks a cabaletta. *Luisa Miller* contains several 'prancing' pieces; these, however, are fully integrated into highly dramatic scenes and no longer show traces of drawing-room music.

The history of the Verdian cabaletta is in fact the history of its formal disintegration, and therefore the arias and duets in which the composer transgresses the 'rules' are most worthy of attention. Cavatinas written in a single tempo and lacking a cabaletta or even a free *stretta* occur in various works. Besides Amalia's cavatina in *I masnadieri* (mentioned above), examples are found in three other operas. Both Giselda's "Salve Maria" (*I Lombardi* I) and Giovanna's "Sempre all'alba" (*Giovanna d'Arco*, Prologue) are slow one-movement pieces. In these cases the deviation from the rule is easily explained by the fact that they consist of a prayer, the effect of which would have been spoiled by an ensuing lively cabaletta. (Giovanna even falls asleep at the end of her cavatina). The slow entrance aria of Arrigo in *La battaglia di Legnano* I ("La pia materna mano") also lacks a cabaletta; considering the opera's terse conception, there may have been reasons of economy for the omission in this instance of the traditional strophes.

The opposite device, treatment of the cabaletta as if it were a self-contained piece, constitutes a more radical innovation. It is applied in situations

---

[18] See Budden, *op. cit.*, p. 235.

which are not suitable for the insertion of a preceding slow *tempo* for the same character. From a purely dramatic point of view the effect of Lady Macbeth's "Trionfai securi alfine" would have been weakened by a foregoing aria, and therefore the piece, in spite of its low quality, stands at the right place in the 1847 score. In contrast to this, the independence of Lucrezia's third-act cabaletta in *I due Foscari* ("Più non vive!") is only seeming; these strophes actually form a part of a complex scene opened by the sad monologue of Francesco Foscari ("Egli ora parte"). Two interruptions provide the required change of situation. First the Doge receives the happy tidings of Jacopo's innocence; then, in the middle of an outburst of joy, Lucrezia suddenly appears on the stage, telling him that his son has died of grief. Although the soprano starts to sing her cabaletta almost immediately after her entrance, she nevertheless *concludes* a scene which is constructed more or less in accordance with the traditional scheme. Its one unusual feature is that the slow and fast sections are assigned to two different characters.

Less than two years before, Verdi had already made use of a similar design in the final act of *I Lombardi*. The soprano aria "Non fu sogno" is nothing but an orthodox cabaletta written in the composer's most brilliant style. In the printed score the piece stands apart as a separate number, but in fact it is closely related to the preceding *Visione*, in which the sleeping Giselda is led by a celestal chorus to the spirit of Oronte. Although the latter's solo ("In cielo benedetto") forms the climax of the vision, it is Giselda who dominates the stage. Therefore the chorus as well as the soprano's arioso and the tenor's aria must be considered slow sections of a complex scene which is regularly completed by the cabaletta.

Like his predecessors Verdi sometimes tried to mitigate the rigid symmetry by shortening the final strophe. Macbeth's third-act cabaletta ("Vada in fiamme") consists of two stanzas, in A minor and A major respectively, a formal pattern characteristic of many a *rondò finale* and usually written for a female voice. In this case the restatement is abridged and contains only the second quatrain. The shortening is counterbalanced, however, by the episode between the strophes, which is a fragment sung in the minor mode by the baritone. Although dramatically effective, the piece is musically poor – hence its expunction from the score in the 1865 revision. Equally unorthodox is the treatment of a cabaletta in *Giovanna d'Arco* (finale of the Prologue). It starts as a regular duet with double quatrains for Giovanna and Carlo. Then Giacomo, though unseen by the others, joins them in an *a cappella* fragment. The piece ends with a terzetto strophe containing only the latter half of the melody. With its coarse abuse of syncopation the music represents Verdi at his worst; nevertheless the piece constitutes a remarkable innovation. While at the beginning Carlo merely wonders about the virgin and her prophetic words ("Qual prodigio!"), at the end he decides to actually follow her ("Sì, ti seguo"). So here we have a cabaletta serving the progress of action. Admittedly this is effected by the text rather than by the music; had Verdi written different melodies for each of the three strophes, he would have obliterated the cabaletta form. Nor does the music do justice to the synchronic aspect of the situation. The final strophe, mainly sung in unison, completely ignores the different moods of the characters involved.

In *Alzira* Verdi found a rather simple solution to the problem of reconciling dramatic needs with traditional form. It occurs in the second-act duet cabaletta of Alzira and Gusman, which combines the expression of the latter's joy with the former's remorse (Alzira has forcibly consented to marry the governor in order to save her lover's life). The first strophe for the baritone ("Colma di gioia") is followed by a second for the soprano, with a different, even contrasting melody ("Dove mi tragge ahi misera"). The final strophe restates Gusman's first quatrain and Alzira's second. Thus the cabaletta is built on this scheme:

Strophes:	A	B	$\frac{1}{2}$A–$\frac{1}{2}$B
Stanzas:	α–β	γ–δ	α–δ
Musical phrases:	a-a′-b-a″	c-c′-d-e	a-a′-d-e

While serving the expression of contrasting sentiments, the tight design preserves the formal rigidity inherent in the cabaletta. Although in this case, too, the musical quality of the piece is quite undistinguished, the scheme bears witness to Verdi's efforts to find an acceptable synthesis of tradition and innovation.

To write a cabaletta in *da capo* form is but one step further. This occurs in the final section of the Gulnara-Seïd duet (*Il corsaro* III), which starts with the Pasha's savage outburst, "Sia l'istante maledetto". The strophe is followed by an *a parte* stanza of his (formerly) favourite slave, set to a different melody. Contrary to tradition, the voices are not combined in the final strophe; instead Seïd restates his text and music. Gulnara nevertheless manages to have the last word, exclaiming after Seïd's exit "Guai, tiranno!" on high B♭, challenging not only her master but also the orchestra whose tremolo is marked *fff*.

The usual episode is lacking in this piece; it has obviously become superfluous because of the contrasting middle section. The omission of the episode in the duet of Federica and Rodolfo (*Luisa Miller* I), on the other hand, is less easily explained. The different keys of the first two strophes (resulting from the unequal tessituras) seem to ask for an intermediate fragment modulating back to the tonic. Nevertheless the final strophe starts almost immediately after the conclusion of the second and Federica's rather artificial counterpoint to the restatement of Rodolfo's melody cannot dispel the impression of staleness.

The third-act cabaletta of Rolando in *La battaglia di Legnano* lacks an episode for the simple reason that it consists of but a single strophe. As in the case of Arrigo's cavatina from the same opera, the shortening may be explained by reasons of dramatic efficacy.

The operas written between *Nabucco* and *Rigoletto* reveal a tendency more or less to stretch the standard cabaletta form to its breaking point. Verdi knew unerringly where he had to disregard convention for the sake of dramatic truth. In view of his growing artistic independence, he could afford to proceed in this direction and so everything seemed to point to a gradual disintegration of the cabaletta and its final disappearance from his scores. This process was retarded, however, by an opposing tendency: the strict retention of the traditional design combined with a change of the piece's *character*. Thus the cabalettas written during the next two decades can be roughly divided into three categories: (1) the orthodox type based on one of the customary schemes and emphatically expressing feelings of joy, remorse, pugnacity, vengeance, etc.; (2) structurally irregular pieces of the same character; (3) formally strict cabalettas, but reflecting more subtle feelings, such as tenderness, concern, sadness, etc.

During the 1850's the first category predominates with respect to quantity. *Il trovatore* contains no less than four orthodox cabalettas, *La traviata* three, *Rigoletto*, *Les vêpres siciliennes*, *Simon Boccanegra* and *Un ballo in maschera* each two. As in the previous decade they are of unequal value. The style of the Duke's cabaletta in *Rigoletto* II ("Possente amor") and that of Amelia's in *Boccanegra* I ("Il palpito deh frena") does not differ essentially from many a mediocre piece written before 1850. The same holds for the Count's strophes in *Il trovatore* II ("Per me ora fatale"), although the melody's persistent doubling by solo trumpet and woodwinds admittedly adds to their dramatic effectiveness. On the other hand, pieces like Violetta's "Sempre libera" (*La traviata* I) and Manrico's "Di quella pira" (*Il trovatore* III) convincingly prove that the form's artistic possibilities were far from exhausted. Manrico's C major cabaletta consists of a series of two-bar motifs, perfectly modelled on the nine-syllable lines. Ever since *Luisa Miller* the vocal rhythmic pattern was a favourite of Verdi (see in the latter opera the father's cabaletta "Ah fu giusto il mio sospetto"; other examples include Germont's duet with Violetta and his own strophes in Act II of *La traviata*). But the most remarkable feature of "Di quella pira" is its 'modal' flexibility. The lowered sixth in the accompaniment of the first phrase and the inflexion to the key of G minor in the third effectively counterbalance the rigidity of the motivic design.

Violetta's cabaletta is distinguished by the expert use of coloratura to express her 'frivolous' attitude. However, since she faces a dilemma, the opposite feelings have to be pictured too. The use of Alfredo's off-stage voice for this purpose is a particularly happy stroke. By means of this device the episode is completely integrated into the scene's dramatic substance; moreover its different tempo imparts a particular lustre to the ensuing obligatory restatement. Naturally Alfredo's amorous melody is heard again in the coda and so the first act ends with an arrestingly dramatic question mark.

Not unjustly these two cabalettas are among the most famous in Verdi's oeuvre. Another masterpiece is the duet cabaletta, "Oh qual soave brivido", in the second act of *Un ballo in maschera*. In all three strophes the first quatrain is set on one of those rhythmically uniform melodies that are so characteristic of the opera as a whole. Since in a tri-strophic form this kind of melodic writing invokes the danger of monotony, Verdi harks back to previous material in the episode (the fragment in 6/8 in which Amelia confesses her love for Riccardo: "Sì . . . io t'amo"). As in Violetta's piece, the contrivance is a happy one, from a dramatic as well as a musical point of view. Actually Amelia's confession was the only justification for concluding the scene with a cabaletta and therefore its varied repeat is quite appropriate. As for the music, the change of tempo and metre in this little intermezzo completely redeems the strophe's final resumption in which in accordance with tradition the two voices are combined.

The father-daughter cabaletta concluding Act II of *Rigoletto* also ranks high with most Verdians; nevertheless I believe the piece to be overestimated. On 20 January 1851 the composer wrote to Piave that he had a cabaletta *sfarzosa* in mind (a "splendidly effective cabaletta").[19] In this intention he succeeded beyond any doubt, but the melody of the strophes fits Rigoletto's vindictive mood rather than Gilda's concern. Although quite capable of strong feelings, Gilda remains throughout the drama an ingenuous young girl who has no affinity with the violent contradictions in her

[19] See Francesco Abbiati, *Verdi*, Milano 1959, vol II, pp. 98–99.

father's nature. The cabaletta is therefore fundamentally inconsistent with her character.

After 1859 Verdi no longer wrote strictly orthodox cabalettas; instead his scores contain pieces of the second and third categories. An early example of the former is Hélène's "Courage! ... du courage!" in the first act of *Les vêpres siciliennes*. After having sung her first strophe, which has the standard form of a double quatrain set on the pattern a-a′-b-a′, the soprano addresses the people around her in an extensive solo (eight lines). The chorus and the *pertichini* answer with another stanza of eight lines and only then Hélène resumes her initial strophe on a slightly different text. The fragment between the two strophes has neither the character nor the restricted proportions of an episode and the coda, too, is of considerable length. Like Procida's cabaletta in the second act of the same opera, the piece is called "Cavatine" in the libretto.

The deviations in two cabalettas of *La forza del destino* (the last section of the Leonore-Alvaro duet in Act I and Carlo's exit solo in Act III) are altogether more drastic. In the former piece the final strophe does not develop but merges into a short coda. The obvious reason is that the lovers are in a hurry; they hear noises in the house and are afraid that their elopement will be thwarted. During the 1840's such a situation could hardly have afforded a valid excuse for omitting the final strophe, but since that time taste has changed and this kind of realism in *La forza del destino* has become acceptable to the audience. Carlo's cabaletta starts with a single strophe set on three quatrains instead of the usual two. Its design (a-b-a) is strictly symmetrical, each subsection covering eight bars. This seems to point to a *da capo* form, but the cabaletta continues with an additional free section which is even longer than the foregoing strophe. The disintegration of its melody into a series of short motifs is another felicitous stroke of realism: Carlo is much too excited to maintain the initial periodical structure of the piece.

The F major cabaletta of the lovers in the third act of *Aida* resembles the above-mentioned duet of *La forza del destino*. In both cases the decision to escape is expressed by regular solos for each of the two characters (A-A). But in contrast to the latter opera in which the final resumption of the strophic melody is interrupted by an external cause, in *Aida* a closing section (B) is duly completed. Set on a single quatrain its melody written in triplets differs from the square gavotte rhythm of the preceding strophes. As in the Leonore-Alvaro duet the piece uninterruptedly passes into a recitative starting in a key a major second below the former tonic. Thus the cabaletta no longer answers its former 'theatrical' purpose of inciting the audience's applause.

Examples of the third category, the formally regular cabaletta expressing more or less delicate feelings, span a period of some twenty years (from *Rigoletto* to *Aida*). Although far from numerous, almost all of them are of high musical and dramatic quality. The customary characteristics (march rhythms, the polonaise pattern, continuous triplets or crude syncopation) have completely vanished, although in some instances Verdi reverts to an accompaniment of steadily repeated chords. On a superficial level this is reminiscent of Donizetti's "Ah! verranno a te" and similar pieces of that period; in point of fact the device is fundamentally renewed by a most refined harmonic idiom. The last duet of Alfredo and Violetta ends with particularly moving strophes written in this style: "Gran Dio! morir si giovane". Its harmonic design curiously resembles that of another cabaletta written in the same key but expressing diametrically opposite feelings: the Amelia-Riccardo duet of *Un ballo in maschera* II ("O qual soave brivida").

The father-daughter cabaletta in the first version of *Simon Boccanegra* (Act I: "Figlia! a tal nome io palpito") is more conventional. Yet in the 1884 revision Verdi kept the Doge's initial phrase; as for the remaining part of the strophe, despite alterations in both melody and harmony, the chordal accompaniment was left virtually unchanged.

Another father-daughter duet should be mentioned in this context: the cabaletta in the first act of *Rigoletto* ("Ah! veglia o donna"). The piece is exceptional as a cabaletta, because Rigoletto does not address Gilda but a third person, the silent duenna Giovanna. But it is the daughter who answers her father with tender words of concern (second strophe in the subdominant key). Rigoletto starts to repeat his stanza but after four bars suddenly breaks off in the middle of the word "confidai". He has heard a noise outside and rushes into the street to investigate. Meanwhile the Duke disguised as a student enters the garden, throws a purse to Giovanna to keep her silent, and hides behind a tree. All this happens in the episode, which in this way adopts an important dramatic function. Returning to the garden Rigoletto once more resumes his instruction of the duenna and this time his melody is joined by Gilda's counterpoint. As we know, the device had already been applied in the Federica-Rodolfo duet of *Luisa Miller* but in this instance it is handled with considerably more skill. The one doubtful aspect of this highly original piece is its noisy ending, a concession to theatrical convention that contradicts the soft "addio" of father and daughter in the coda. The time when Verdi could afford to write a pianissimo conclusion for a scene of this kind was still far ahead.

Anyone listening to the strophes of the dying Posa in Act IV of *Don Carlos* seeks in vain for stylistic affinities with the traditional Verdian cabaletta. The melody has a curiously lyrical colour reminiscent of Bizet's *Pêcheurs de perles*. Between the stanzas the well-known friendship theme is appropriately quoted and the coda contains the Marquis' last words: "Ah! sauve la Flandre . . .". In the various revisions of the opera undertaken after the Paris première of 1867 this piece was left unaltered; however in the Milan version of 1884 it passes without interruption into the next scene (the finale).

The last cabaletta of this category and not the least remarkable is the final duet section of *Aida*: "O terra addio". Formally the piece is completely regular. Each of the lovers sings a strophe based on a single quatrain (melodic pattern: a-a-b-a with an extension of the last phrase). In the episode, the third strophe, and the coda, both the remorseful Amneris and the impassive chorus function as *pertichini;* finally during the slow curtain the principal melody is heard again, played by four violins *con sordino* in the upper register. The cabaletta's tempo (andantino) and the whispering ending are truly unique in Verdi's oeuvre.

Can a piece like "O terra addio" still be termed a cabaletta? The answer depends on whether one applies the standard of form or of content. Verdi's own labels are not very helpful in solving this problem. In his correspondence he sometimes speaks of a *stretta* referring to an unequivocal cabaletta; elsewhere his use of the term cabaletta clearly indicates a final section of a complex aria, duet or ensemble lacking any trace of a strophic design. Regardless of whether he applies wide or narrow criteria, the investigator will inevitably encounter borderline cases. And with respect to pieces written after 1850 the old question of "what exactly is a cabaletta" becomes an academic one.

A more fruitful field of research is the study of the genre's paradoxical development. While it is certainly true that in general the cabaletta as a formal design submitted to a process of disintegration, yet the remarkable opposite tendency to maintain its strict form while giving it a wider scope of expression cannot possibly be ignored. Despite the restricted number of examples, this trend is anything but an isolated phenomenon. The operas written between 1850 and 1870 contain many strophic airs belonging to other genres, such as the Duke's "Canzona" in *Rigoletto;* Violetta's and Germont's arias in *La traviata* I and II; Hélène's "Romance" and so-called "Sicilienne" in *Les vêpres;* Amelia's cavatina in *Simon Boccanegra;* Riccardo's and Oscar's "Canzone" and the latter's "Ballata" in *Un ballo in maschera;* Preziosilla's "Strofe" in *La forza del destino;* Posa's "Ballade", Eboli's "Chanson du voile" and Elisabeth's "Romance" in *Don Carlos*. As for *Il trovatore*, this work exceeds all the others in the number of song-like pieces. Virtually the entire first act consists of strophic airs, several of which have a narrative content resulting from the opera's complicated *antefatto*.

All this points to a highly individual attitude concerning the controversy that divided musical Europe during the second half of the century: continuity *vs* closed forms. Actually Verdi managed to achieve a synthesis of both trends, as witnessed by *Otello*, a 'continuous' opera full of 'separate' scenes. It is anything but fortuitous that this work dating from 1887 still includes a cabaletta, the tenor-baritone duet based on the scheme S–S′–S″ at the end of Act II ("Si, pel ciel marmoreo giuro!"). Although Otello's and Jago's personalities are clearly recognizable in their respective strophes, the traditional design is maintained. Nor can the use of the cabaletta form for writing a *giuramento* be considered a novelty; it already occurs in a work as early as *I masnadieri* (the strophes "Nell'agrila maledetta" sung by Carlo and the chorus in Act I).

Verdi never rejected the cabaletta. On the contrary, during his whole life he retained a weakness for this much-criticized but nevertheless characteristic attribute of Italian opera, a weakness which became an object of self-mockery at the time that the form was extinct.[20] *Verismo* – whatever that term may signify – no longer had use for it. But in 1951, exactly one hundred years after the Venetian première of *Rigoletto*, the audience attending the first performance of *The Rake's Progress* in the same Teatro La Fenice had the opportunity to hear a splendid cabaletta written in a modern idiom: Anne Truelove's Allegro following her invocation of the Night in Act I, sc. 3. Being a great admirer of Verdi's genius and craftmanship, Strawinsky fittingly paid this tribute to Italian opera of the *ottocento*.

A last word must be said about today's performance practice. It is particularly distressing to record that renewed scholarly interest in *Risorgimento* opera has as yet failed to rectify the barbarous treatment accorded the cabaletta in theatres all over the world, including the most renowned. Many complex arias and duets are constantly being sacrificed to the compelling convention of 'cutting' and of course it is the cabaletta section that invariably becomes a victim of this practice. The underlying *faux raisonnement* is that since action does not develop in a cabaletta, its omission cannot harm understanding of the drama. The fact that amputations of this kind completely upset the structural balance of the piece in question and even that of the entire drama is conveniently overlooked or ignored. A few examples may suffice to show this. The expunction of Alfredo's "Oh mio rimorso!" in *La traviata* II deprives the young man of his only opportunity to express

---

[20] See his letter to Giulio Ricordi on the revision of *Boccanegra*, quoted in Ch. 9, p. 222.

truly moral feelings and to become a three-dimensional personality. The equally customary omission of Germont's strophes in the same act creates an awkward ending to the country house scene. As for the cutting of the first-act cabaletta of father and daughter in *Rigoletto*, this cannot even be argued by (mistaken) aesthetic considerations; it is simply dramatic sacrilege.

Another wide-spread custom, omission of the first strophe in solo cabalettas, also results in an unbalanced structure. The mere 'restatement' does not justify the ensuing coda, the proportion of which is essentially dependent on two strophes rather than one. Moreover the sacrifice of the episode may be detrimental in other respects, since this fragment often adopts a dramatic function, especially in operas written after 1850.

Cabalettas are anything but superfluous appendices; they are milestones in the dramatic process, establishing or confirming relevant moods and situations. Their history is still marked by many unresolved questions, and consequently the definitions and classifications given in this chapter may be liable to criticism. The fact remains, however, that today's performers must learn to accept the cabaletta as an integral feature of nineteenth-century Italian opera, just as it was accepted by Verdi himself.

1974–5

CHAPTER 12

'DON CARLOS': THE SIGNIFIER AND THE SIGNIFIED

The uncertainty as to whether *Le Roi s'amuse* will be prohibited [by the Censor] causes me serious embarrassment. – Piave had assured me there would be no obstacles with regard to this subject and trusting my librettist, I have begun to study it, to think thoroughly about it, and the general idea as well as the musical *tinta* are already present in my mind.

In this passage, quoted from Verdi's letter of 24 August 1850 to Marzari, the President of La Fenice, the word *tinta* has intentionally been left untranslated.[1] Although dictionaries inform us that *tinta* means "colour", such a translation would be misleading in this context. Musically speaking, "colour" generally refers to "timbre", or more specifically "orchestral timbre", and surely this was not what Verdi had in mind. Here and elsewhere he invariably uses the term to indicate the individual character of the score in question, setting it apart from other works written during the same period.[2] Thus *I due Foscari* differs essentially from *Ernani*, not only because of its subject but also with regard to its musical realization. The same holds for *Don Carlos* and *Aida* as well as for the three 'popular' operas written in the early fifties, *Rigoletto*, *Il trovatore* and *La traviata*. Each of these works possesses its special *tinta musicale*.

The term admittedly designates a rather vague concept. Although two early biographers of Verdi, Abramo Basevi and Filippo Filippi, use the word *tinta* as well as its synonyms *colore* and *colorito* in an almost technical sense,

---

[1] See *I Copialettere di Giuseppe Verdi*, ed. G. Cesari and A. Luzio, Milano 1913, p. 106.

[2] My friend and colleague Jan Kamerbeek, Professor of Comparative Literature at the University of Amsterdam, has kindly provided me with an extensive list of quotations from writings of the late eighteenth to the middle of the nineteenth century. In these passages, dealing not only with literature, visual arts and music but also with religion, politics and social customs, the words "coloris", "ton" and "teinte" are invariably used to indicate something particular or individual. Among the authors are Herder, Pixerécourt, Berchet, Nodier, B. Constant, Balzac, Ch. Kingsley, Hawthorne and Berlioz. Thus it appears that Verdi's use of the term is anything but exceptional.

the reader is none the wiser as a result.[3] Still it must be possible to give a
more concrete meaning to the *tinta* of a Verdian opera and to describe it in
musical terms. A few years ago I took up this challenge in a study of three
Don Carlos versions (Paris 1867, Naples 1872 and Milan 1884) and came to
the conclusion that the opera's *tinta* lies in a special treatment of the dominant or rather the fifth degree of the tonal scale. Soon after I came across
two papers written by Jack Buckley and Péter Pál Várnai that deal with
more or less the same subject, and consequently I abstained from developing
a barely conceived article.[4] On further reflection, however, I feel justified in
resuming the study, since in my opinion both Buckley's and Várnai's arguments appear questionable from a methodological point of view.

The starting point of Buckley's paper, *Drama through Tonality*, is the
weakened tonic-dominant relation in *Don Carlos* as compared to earlier
works like *Rigoletto* and *La traviata*. Although this hypothesis corresponds
in part with my own, it is supported by invalid arguments, as for example the
incorrect harmonic analysis of the initial horn 'quartet' in Act II (ex. 1).

EXAMPLE I

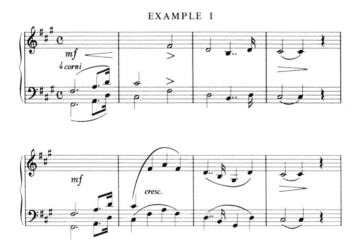

According to Buckley "à rising D major chord falls onto the leading note of
D."[5] What we hear is quite different, and our aural impression is confirmed

[3] Abramo Basevi, *Studio sulle opere di Giuseppe Verdi*, Firenze 1859, pp. 114–115; Filippo
Filippi, *Il passato, il presente, l'avvenire: Rossini, Verdi, Wagner* in *Almanacco pel 1864*, Milano
1864.
[4] J. Buckley, *Drama through Tonality* in *Atti del 2° congresso internazionale di studi verdiani
1969*, Parma 1971, pp. 302–310; P. P. Várnai, *Unità musicale e drammaturgica nel "Don Carlo"*,
ibid., pp. 402–411.
[5] Buckley, *loc. cit.*, pp. 302–303.

by a glance at the corresponding bar 6; here the C♯ is easily identified as the
fifth of an arpeggioed tonic chord (F♯) instead of the third of a dominant (A).
As a matter of fact the first eight bars are entirely in the key of F♯ minor.

Equally misinterpreted is the initial unaccompanied phrase of the
Elisabeth-Carlos duet in the same act (ex. 2).

EXAMPLE 2

Buckley conveniently isolates from their context the second bar's three last
notes and speaks of a "fall onto what might be considered a tonic of C♭
major".[6] Nothing could be farther from the truth. The three notes cannot be
separated from the ensuing B♭, with which they form a descending tetrachord firmly embedded in the key of E♭ minor. Needless to say, this rather
common formula exactly corresponds with the rhythmic pattern of the text
(the four-syllable word "solliciter").

Analytical mistakes of this kind hardly serve the cogency of the author's
conclusion: "I have tried to show that Verdi has a contribution to make in
the history of tonality quite as important, though certainly not so startling,
as Debussy and Schoenberg".[7]

Although Várnai's study, *Unità musicale e drammaturgica nel "Don
Carlo"*, does not suffer from this kind of amateurism, his argument is
questionable both in essence and details. Among the latter, the first example
on p. 404, which is supposed to show a sequence of first and sixth degrees of
C major, would only make sense if sung and played in retrograde motion,
which can hardly have been the composer's intention. On the same page
another example (the final bars of the Fontainebleau act) is described as a
succession of C major and E minor, whereas it is in fact an alternation of the
first and sixth degrees in C. Lastly, an example on p. 403 (the theme of the
monks' chorus) is printed with the wrong words. Instead of "Charles-Quint,
l'auguste Empereur" the text should consist of the ensuing line, "N'est que
cendre et que poussière". As will be seen below, this turns the argument
against itself.[8]

---

[6] *Ibid.*, p. 307.

[7] *Ibid.*, p. 310.

[8] The author may have been misled by a printing error on p. 51 of Ricordi's edition of the
vocal score (five-act version; plate number 40666). Here the fourth bar has D instead of

Despite these flaws Várnai's paper might open interesting perspectives, were it not based on an extremely doubtful method. The essay starts with a sharp statement about the general dramatic idea of *Don Carlos* and then attempts to demonstrate how this idea was rendered in music. In other words, the author proceeds from the 'signified' to the 'signifier'. Verdi of course followed this path, first finding the *idea* (in and through the fable) and then the *tinta musicale*. The researcher, however, should move in the opposite direction. The 'signifier', which by definition is material and perceptible, must be determined first and may then lead to the 'signified', which is conceptual and intelligible. To start from the latter is a most dangerous procedure.

Várnai claims that the drama's fundamental idea is the conflict between "power" and "the individual", or "the political factor" and "[human] sentiments". On the one hand the component of power is realized as an impersonal conception, on the other it is embodied in two characters, King Philippe and his father Charles V. The concept of power is further specified as "tyrannical power of the state".

With this narrow statement the author places himself in a position with extremely limited prospects. And the outlook becomes even more restricted when he identifies a certain basic nucleus as the musical expression of the state's tyrannical power. This nucleus is presented in both melodic and harmonic form, with the characteristic feature of alternation of the key's first and sixth degrees.[9]

As might be expected most of the musical examples quoted in support of this thesis either bely the stated limitations of the 'signified' or those of the 'signifier', or even both. When sung with the right text the fragment of the monks' chorus mentioned above does not deal with tyrannical power; on the contrary, the Emperor who according to Várnai embodies this power has become "nothing but ashes and dust". In view of Posa's liberal philosophy his words addressed to Carlos in the dungeon can hardly refer to tyranny (Várnai, p. 408: "Tu devais régner"). The same holds for Elisabeth who reminding Don Carlos of her matrimonial state says: "Le devoir, saint flambeau, devant mes yeux a lui" (p. 405). The expression of loyalty to her husband has of course nothing to do with tyrannical power of the state. Nor

---

C♯. In the original score published by Escudier in 1867 (plate number 2765) the passage reads C♯ in accordance with the autograph manuscript (Paris, Bibliothèque Nationale). It should be observed that in spite of the fact that its title page refers to the Paris première, the Ricordi edition presents the Naples version of 1872. This, however, does not affect the passage in question.

[9] Várnai, *loc. cit.*, pp. 403–404.

do the Emperor's words at the end of the opera, "Mon fils, les douleurs de la terre", refer to this idea (p. 408).

Many stitches are dropped on the musical side too. Only a few examples answer the condition of alternation; the others simply show the harmonic succession of the key's first and sixth degrees (without repetition of either of them) or a melodic line proceeding from the tonic to the fifth by way of the sixth. One case where there is even no question of the sixth is the second example on p. 407, taken from the auto-da-fé scene in which Don Carlos challenges his father to disarm him: "J'attends celui qui l'osera! A me venger ma main est prête!" The author obviously has been misled by the similarity of this motif with another occurring in the garden terzetto (". . . il est en délire . . . Ne croyez pas cet insensé") as well as in Eboli's aria ("Je te maudis").

The second component is as narrowly described as the first: "Opposite to the political element, the power, stand the individual predestined to his fall and the sentiment condemned to a tragic fate. Their personifications are Elisabeth and Don Carlos".[10] This idea is said to be characterized "homogeneously" in the music by two constructive elements: "On the one hand an almost "monomaniacally" repeated ternary rhythm, above all the formula

$$\underset{3}{\overset{}{\rule{0pt}{0pt}}}\;\text{♩}\;\overset{3}{\text{♫♩}}\;\overset{3}{\text{♫♩}}\;,$$ on the other a characteristic melodic formula moving

within the compass of a third, or maximally a fourth, and 'turning around' a key-note or sometimes varying or combining this direction of movement".[11]

Ten fragments are quoted in support of his argument. Although these are not unconvincing in themselves, the occurrence of the "tyrannical" nucleus in the third example on p. 410 is unintentionally ironic in the context (it concerns a passage from Elisabeth's monologue in the last act: ". . . porte en pleurant mes pleurs aux pieds de l'Eternel"). The lapse is an exception in the otherwise strict application of the author's method, which consists of making a careful choice of examples corroborating his theory, while ignoring all contradictory evidence. Even a superficial examination of the score shows that melodies rotating around a key-note do not occur only in the parts of Elisabeth and Don Carlos, but also in those of King Philippe and Eboli. As for the so-called musical nucleus, we have already seen that it is found in

[10] Ibid., pp. 408–409. The Italian text reads: "Di fronte all'elemento politico, al potere, stanno l'individuo predestinato alla caduta e il sentimento condannato a una sorte tragica. Le loro personificazioni sono Elisabetta e Don Carlo".

[11] The wording is far from clear. One wonders how a (single) "direction of movement" can be "combined". I have given a literal translation of the Várnai's text which reads: ". . . o che talvolta varia e combina questa direzione di movimento".

various situations having no connection whatever with the idea of political power, let alone tyranny.

Várnai bases his study on the four-act Milan score of 1884, calling it the "definitive version". Although few Verdi scholars would agree with this assertion, the restriction might be considered acceptable in view of the difficulty of gaining access to other versions. The author adds however: "... only in case of necessity shall I examine the discarded Fontainebleau act". One is inclined to ask: necessity for what? Obviously for the sake of presenting corroborating evidence. But it is precisely this Fontainebleau Act which provides several other examples disproving Várnai's thesis; these are conveniently ignored. On the basis of such inconsistent procedures the author's conclusions must unfortunately be considered invalid. This is the more regrettable since several of Várnai's observations do touch the opera's *tinta* and may consequently be related to the work's general dramatic idea.

*   *
*

My own investigation of the various *Don Carlos* versions has resulted in the identification of two distinctive elements dominating the score: (a) a motif ascending from the tonic to the sixth (either directly or by way of the third) and then descending to the fifth (in solmisation symbols: *do-(mi)-la-sol* or *la-(do)-fa-mi*), and (b) non-ornamental, chromatic rotation around the fifth. It should be observed that these two formulae are but rarely encountered in other Verdian operas of the period, *Un ballo in maschera* (1859), *La forza del destino* (1862 and '69), the newly composed fragments of *Macbeth* (1865), and *Aida* (1871 and '72). In *Don Carlos*, on the other hand, they recur with remarkable frequency and therefore may be considered to constitute the opera's specific character, in other words its *tinta musicale*.

The two elements differ from those of Várnai in being essentially melodic; despite their dependence on a tonal center they may be harmonized in various ways. Another device mentioned by Várnai, the alternation of the first (or fifth) and sixth degrees of the scale, cannot be taken as an essential characteristic of the score, because of its relative infrequency. As for the *diatonic* rotation around the dominant involving a compass of a minor or major third, this trait lacks specificity, since it is a feature of Verdi's melodic idiom that is encountered quite often among his other works.

In the following lists, examples of the two basic musical elements described above are arranged according to the individuals in whose parts they occur, with special categories for purely orchestral fragments, ensembles and choruses. Capital letters refer to the opera's different versions (P., N., M. = Paris, Naples and Milan), Roman numerals to the acts.

Element (a)

Orchestra: P.N. II, M. I, initial bars (see ex. I above); P.N. III, M. II, Finale, "Marche du cortège", bars 20 and 32. – *Chorus:* P.N. III, M. II, Finale, "Choeur du peuple", principal theme ("Ce jour heureux"). – *Don Carlos:* P.N. I, Cavatine (Romanza), final phrase ("Dieu bénit nos chastes amours"); P.N. I, Duet with Elisabeth, bars 22–23 ("La victoire ou l'amour"), see ex. 3 below; P.N. III, M. II, Duet with Eboli, section "più ritenuto" (text: "Oublions l'univers, la vie et le ciel même! / Qu'importe le passé, qu'importe l'avenir?"), different words in M.; P.N. V, M. IV, Duet with Elisabeth, C minor section (C♯ minor in M), ostinato motif played by double-basses, violoncellos and solo bassoon (text: "Lorsque tout est fini"). – *Elisabeth:* P.N. II, M. I, Duet with Don Carlos ("Le devoir, saint flambeau, devant mes yeux a lui"); P.M. II, M. I, coda of Romance ("Porte lui mes adieux"), see ex. 4 below; P.N. V, M. IV, Duet with Don Carlos ("Les fleurs du Paradis réjouront son ombre"); P.M. V, ibid., section in B♭ major ("Cet éternel absent"), also M. IV, in B major with different words. – *Philippe:* P. II, Duet with Posa, section in E♭ major ("J'ai de ce prix sanglant payé la paix du monde"),see ex. 5 below; N. II, ibid., section in D♭ (". . . mi renda la pace"); P.N. IV, M. III, Scène et Air, a descending variant in D minor (F–D–B♭–A) played by a violoncello solo, bars 11–12, 26–27 and 39–40 (text: "Je la revois encor regardant en silence / Mes cheveux blancs, le jour qu'elle arriva de France"); P.N. IV, Scène et Finale, orchestral quotation of the motif occurring in the E♭ section of the duet with Posa (only in P. II, see above). – *Eboli:* P.N. III, M. II, Terzetto, second Allegro agitato section, E minor ("Malheur sur toi, fils adultère"); P.N. IV, M. III, Aria ("Je te maudis"). – *Posa:* P.N. III, M. II, Terzetto, initial bars (". . . il est en délire . . . Ne croyez pas cet insensé . . ."); P.N. IV, M. III, Aria, section Moderato, in N. and M. "Lo stesso movimento" (text: "Oui, tu devais régner"). – *Ensembles* (motifs shared by two or more characters, or occurring in the orchestra): P.N. I, Duet Elisabeth – Don Carlos, Allegro giusto section, D♭, bars 3–4, 6–7 etc., quoted in M. I (first scene, bar 93) and in P.N. V, M. IV (aria of Elisabeth); P.N. II, M. I, Scène et Ballade (Terzettino dialogato), passim (orchestra); P.N. III, M. II, Terzetto, E minor section, bars 23–24 and 27–28 (each part with its own text).

EXAMPLE 3

EXAMPLE 4

EXAMPLE 5

(Philippe)

J'ai de ce prix san - glant pay - é la paix du mon - de,

Element (b)

Orchestra: P.N. V, M. IV, Prelude to Elisabeth's aria, the last three bars of the Largo section (strings without double-basses). – *Chorus:* P.N. I, "Choeur des femmes", initial bars (orchestra); P.N. III, M. II, Finale, "Choeur des moines", E minor, *passim* (orchestra). – *Don Carlos:* P.N. II, M. I, Duet with Elisabeth, second "meno mosso" section, bars 1–3 and 5–6 ("Par quelle douce voix mon âme est ranimé?"); P.N. III, M. II, Terzetto, second Allegro agitato section, E minor, bars 17–18 ("Douleur, douleur dont je me sens mourir"), see ex. 6 below; P.N. III, M. II, Finale, Allegro section, A♭, bars 1–4 ("Sire, il est temps que je vive"); P. V, M. IV, Duet with Elisabeth, Allegro marziale section, bars 17–18 and 20–21 ("Oui! c'est par votre voix que le peuple m'appelle. / Et si je meurs pour lui, que ma mort sera belle"); P. V, ibid., section "Un peu plus animé", bar 2 ("N'aurait pu séparer"). – *Elisabeth:* P.N. II, M. I, Scène et Ballade (Terzettino dialogato), bars 6–7 after Posa's first strophe ("O destinée amère . . . le revoir . . . je frémis . . ."), see ex. 7 below; P.N. II, M. I, Romance, bars 20 and 42 ("Tu vas la revoir"); P.N. IV, M. III, Scène preceding the quartet, bars 20–21 ("Je suis dans votre cour indignement traitée"); P.N. IV, M. III, ibid., bar 42 ("Justice, justice je réclame de votre majesté!"); P.N. V, M. IV, Aria, second Allegro agitato section, bars 19–21 ("C'est la paix dans la mort!"). – *Philippe:* P.N. II, M. I, Duet with Posa, bars 7–9, strings ("Auprès de ma personne, pourquoi jamais demandé d'être admis?"); M. I, ibid., second Allegro section, bars 53–55 ("Vous changerez d'avis, quand vous saurez le coeur de l'homme à l'égal de Philippe"); M. I, ibid., "Poco più mosso" section, bars 9ff, orchestral accompaniment (viola), text: "La reine . . . un soupçon me tourmente . . . mon fils! . . ."; P.N. III, M. II, Finale, Andante assai mosso, bars 26 and 28 (violoncelli), text: "A Dieu vous êtes infidèles, / infidèles à votre Roi"; P.N. IV, M. III, Scène et Air, bar 37 (violoncelli), text: "Elle ne m'a jamais aimé!"; P.N. IV, M. III, ibid., bars 52 and 56–57 ("Hélas! le sommeil salutaire, / le doux sommeil a fui pour jamais ma paupière!"), see ex. 8 below. – *Eboli:* P.N. III, M. II, Terzetto, Andante sostenuto, bars 4–6 ("Ah! la lionne au coeur est blessée! / Craignez, craignez une femme offensée!"), see ex. 9 below; P.N. III, M. II, ibid., bar 10 ("Redoutez tout de ma furie") and bar 18 ("La lionne est blessée"); P.N. IV, M. III, Aria, Allegro bars 9–11 (O don fatal et détesté, / Présent du ciel en sa colère!"). – *Ensembles* (motifs shared by two or more characters, or occurring in the orchestra): P.N. I, Duet Elisabeth-Don Carlos, Allegro agitato non presto, and Finale, *passim* ("L'heure fatale est sonnée"); P.N. III, M. II, Finale, Andante assai mosso, bar 35 ("Sire, prenez pitié d'un peuple infortuné").

EXAMPLE 6

EXAMPLE 7

EXAMPLE 8

EXAMPLE 9

Along with the two melodic elements described, the rhythmic motif mentioned by Várnai (a minim or crotchet tied to a number of triplets) should not be overlooked. Though occasionally found in other Verdian scores, the formula is predominant in *Don Carlos* and must therefore be considered to belong to the opera's *tinta*. As this particular rhythmic element (c) is easy to locate, there is no need to list examples here.

So much for the 'signifier'. The question now arises: to what dramatic concept do these characteristics refer? Elsewhere in this book I have tried to determine the relationships between specific musical and dramatic elements with regard to special events, situations or personalities. In this case, however, we are dealing with the score as a whole and therefore the 'signifier' should correspond to an equally *general* dramatic conception. According to Várnai this conception revolves around the antithesis of political power and human sentiments, in other words the tyranny wielded by King Philippe over Elisabeth and Don Carlos. With this interpretation I must disagree, since the drama is not concerned with a tyrant and his victims, but deals with *frustration* in various manifestations. With the exception of the Grand

Inquisiteur all the leading characters (including the King) are to some extent hampered in their development as human beings or in the realization of their practical aims. The fundamental cause of this general frustration is the established System, the sociopolitical framework within whose bounds the individual is forced to live. The idea is a familiar one in this age. In the course of the twentieth century we have become increasingly aware of the fact that almost everywhere in the world certain groups (e.g. racial minorities or the female sex) are labouring under the yoke of social rather than personal oppression. The enemy is not a human tyrant but the subtle tyranny of the System. Modern dramatists have dealt amply with this theme, the earliest treatment of which is found in Büchner's *Woyzeck* dating from 1836. The dialectic of 'social' dramas of this kind does not allow the application of Aristotelian principles; it concerns tragedies without awe, guilt, catharsis or even a final crisis.

In *Don Carlos*, the reigning System is that of the Spanish court, a disguised extension of the Church whose universal power is threatened elsewhere in Europe by the Reformation. The term 'establishment', which has become so fashionable during the last decade, fits the situation at this court very well: the firmly established status quo is based on the Rule of the Church. There is no question of balance between ecclesiastical and secular power; the impersonal Church subjugates the King as well as everyone else. A particular feature of its anonymous oppression is immobility. Change is considered fundamentally nefarious and so the individual is doomed to an existence of mental vegetation. Hence his frustration.

The libretto frequently alludes to this atmosphere. Examples include Don Carlos' words in the second-act duet with Elisabeth: "L'air d'Espagne me tue, il me pèse, il m'opprime / comme le lourd penser d'un crime", and his outburst in the middle of the third-act finale: "Sire, il est temps que je vive!" As for Elisabeth, she has a foreboding in the Fontainebleau act. Even at the moment that she believes herself Carlos' fiancée she exclaims: "Ah, de l'inconnu j'ai peur malgré moi-même! / Cet hymen, c'est l'exil . . ." While in the second act Eboli comments on the "âme oppressée" of her mistress, the Queen clearly characterizes her own situation in the fourth-act quartet: "Je suis sur la terre étrangère". The text of Philippe's monologue speaks for itself and so does his encounter with the Grand Inquisiteur. Each of the three members of this royal family expresses the wish for death as the ultimate solution of an unbearable existence.

Now that we have identified the general dramatic idea with the concept of frustration we must try to demonstrate the relationship between 'signifier' and 'signified'. The most obvious method, which consists of checking each occurrence of the signifying elements with the corresponding dramatic situation, produces poor results. Although a majority of the items may be considered to refer explicitly or implicitly to frustrated feelings, too many seem to be used for the expression of other emotions or situations. Another possibility is to seek a *direct* relation between 'signifier' and 'signified'. Its existence would imply that the *tinta* being causally affected by its referential object must be regarded as a composite *index* (one of the three sign categories established by Charles Sanders Peirce). It is tempting indeed to assume this kind of relation by taking the 'signifier' for a symptom of the 'signified', in other words to connect the two coercive 'dominant' devices, (a) 'detour' and (b) 'rotation', with a kind of compulsion neurosis caused by frustration. On second thought, however, this interpretation is too far-fetched to be plausible. Moreover it leaves out of consideration the third signifying element (c) which is neither positively nor negatively conditioned by the centripetal force of the dominant. As for the two remaining categories of the Peircian trichotomy, the *icon* and the *symbol*, when taken in their strict sense neither fits the sign vehicles in question. A symbol indirectly refers to its object by means of a rule or convention. In music this implies the use of one or more traditional and semantically interpretable formulae (*topoi*, see Ch. 8). None of the three signifying elements answers this condition. The icon calls for a certain degree of identity of sign vehicle and referential object. In our case this would involve musical word painting, a device which in view of the designatum's abstract character (frustration) is simply unrealizable.

Thus far we have not succeeded in producing a shred of evidence to indicate a meaningful relationship between *tinta musicale* and *idea generale*. Before succumbing to the temptation of postulating such an affinity by mere conjecture, which of course would be invalid from a scholarly point of view, let us test our hypothesis with another analytic procedure still at our disposal: the checking of 'signifier' on the various *dramatis personae*. To be valid such a method should include examination of each of the six leading characters with regard to antecedents, situations and personality.

We may safely assume that the cause of Don Carlos' frustration goes back to his infancy. An education in the austere climate of the Castilian court, the failure to establish a human relationship with his father, the consequent oppressive loneliness, the cultivation of ideals detached from reality – all these factors have resulted in producing a thoroughly neurotic personality, everlastingly preoccupied with his own problems (and as such probably unique in nineteenth-century opera). Elsewhere in this book I have pointed out that, rather than a hero fighting for the freedom of the oppressed, Carlos must be considered an immature young man in search of a substitute father (Posa, Charles V) and mother (Elisabeth).[12]

In contrast to the Infant, Elisabeth has enjoyed a happy youth as a princess growing up in the liberal atmosphere of Fontainebleau. Her deep concern for people suffering under the hardships of war is clearly revealed in the Woodcutters scene that Verdi discarded for non-artistic reasons before the opera's first performance in 1867.[13] It is this scene which gives us the clue to her self-sacrifice (the marriage with the King of Spain marking the end of the war). Immediately at the opening of the drama Elisabeth is presented as a character who makes the most of her human faculties. Once arrived in Madrid she loses her *raison d'être* as an individual. Since the Spanish court has no use for truly human qualities, Elisabeth is expected to act exclusively as a Queen, that is, a symbol representing the System. The resulting frustration renders her existence meaningless. Hence her words in the last-act aria: "... mon jour est fini".

Philippe's frustration stems from his mental contradictions. While willingly acting his role of a Spanish monarch, he feels disinclined to accept its main implication: the necessity of bowing to the Church's supremacy behind the secular décor. The bitter remark with which he concludes the scene with the Grand Inquisiteur clearly testifies to this: "L'orgueil du Roi fléchit devant l'orgueil du prêtre". Equally ambivalent is his attitude toward the domestic atmosphere, where he would like Elisabeth to be his loving wife as well as a Queen of Spain. Unaware of the incompatibility of these wishes he sulks in the scene preceding his aria: "Elle ne m'aime pas ... Non, son coeur m'est fermé".

In the Marquis of Posa he then finds the human qualities which he could not recognize in Elisabeth. Here at last is a man! But Philippe does not realize that a Spanish King may not establish a personal relationship with a subject, however independent the latter's mind may be. The Inquisitor voices the System's cold logic, when to the King's words, "Un homme, un ami sûr, je l'ai trouvé!", he replies: "Pourquoi un homme? Et de quel droit vous nommez vous le Roi, si vous avez des égaux?" And so Philippe becomes the destroyer of the one character in the drama who had shown him a path to humanity. Not Posa but Philippe is the true victim of the System. At the summit of his power the King muses about his death:

---

[12] See Ch. 8, p. 208.

[13] See Ursula Günther, *Le livret français de 'Don Carlos': le premier acte et sa révision par Verdi* in *Atti del 2° congresso internazionale di studi verdiani 1969*, Parma 1971.

Je dormirai dans mon manteau royal,
Quand sonnera pour moi l'heure dernière,
Je dormirai sous les voûtes de pierre
Des caveaux de l'Escurial!

When my final hour sounds
I will sleep in my royal cloak;
I will sleep under the stone canopy
of the burial chambers of Escurial!

Eboli is less clearly designed. As we are unacquainted with her antecedents, her character has to be judged solely on the basis of her actions and
sentiments expressed in the drama. The princess' attitude to the reigning
System differs from that of the other principals. She chooses the course of
adaptation and indulges in court life with its petty intrigues. Her attributes
are masks and veils, instruments of dissimulation. The 'Chanson du voile' is
not just a decorative set piece, but characterizes the behaviour of the woman
who is singing. When at the beginning of Act III (Paris and Naples versions)
we see Eboli masked and disguised in the Queen's attire, a quotation from
this Saracen song aptly illustrates her words:

Pour une nuit me voilà Reine
Et dans ce jardin enchanté
Je suis maîtresse et souveraine,
Je suis comme la beauté
De la légende du voile,
Qui va luire à son coté
Le doux reflet d'une étoile!
Je vais régner jusqu'au jour
Sous les doux voiles de l'ombre ...

I am here as Queen for one night,
and am mistress and sovereign
in this enchanted garden;
I am like the beautiful woman
in the legend of the veil,
who sees shine by her side
the sweet reflection of a star!
I will reign until daybreak,
under the sweet veil of night.

Dressed in this misleading garment the princess meets Don Carlos, but at the moment when she takes off her mask she faces reality: not she but the Queen is the object of the Infant's love. And suddenly we see Eboli in her true colours: a ruthlessly passionate woman.

The dénouement of the subplot after the fourth-act quartet has an ironic touch. Eboli is condemned to wear the veil for the rest of her days:

> Dans un couvent
> Et sous la bure
> Je m'ensevelis pour toujours!
>
> *In a convent,*
> *under sackcloth,*
> *I will shroud myself for ever!*

In the last section of her aria it appears that Eboli's love for Don Carlos, which we may have taken for mere ambition, is genuine indeed. Although she has lost the Infant forever she decides to save him, and when during the rebellion scene she reappears on the stage calling out to him to fly she is again wearing a mask (another ironic touch).[14]

If in the atmosphere of the court Eboli seems less frustrated than the other principals, then this may be explained by her being the most Spanish character in the cast. The occasional *couleur locale* in her music points to this. Still between her personality and behaviour there is a striking contradiction which ultimately leads to her defeat. The princess is too passionate a character to be able to maintain the attitude of dissimulation. And so the mask, attribute of court life, becomes a symbol of frustration.

As a warrior Posa has passed most of his life outside the court and even during his sojourns in Madrid he has strictly avoided asking royal favours. Only his love for Carlos and his concern for the oppressed Flemish induce him to face a spiritual atmosphere completely alien to his character. In contrast to the Infant, Posa is a *practical* idealist, a man who knows and accepts the price for the realization of his ideals. If he is hampered in his endeavours, it is solely by external causes. The suffocating climate of the court does not affect his personality. While the King, his wife and his son are longing for the end of their day, Posa deliberately chooses death not for his own sake but for that of others. During the drama we have rarely heard him speaking about himself and even while dying his words express concern for his fellow creatures: "Ah! sauve la Flandre . . .".

---

[14] Only in the Milan version.

Lastly the Grand Inquisiteur, who does not merely represent the Church as an institution of power, but has identified himself with the System in all its aspects. As a result the high priest appears to us as an almost dehumanized figure strictly serving an Idea at the expense of truly Christian principles. In another context his age – over ninety – and his state of blindness might have symbolized the qualities of wisdom and perspicacity. In the present drama, however, these features must be interpreted negatively: they clearly point to the petrifaction of his mind. Needless to say, a man subjected to this kind of spiritual atrophy is virtually incapable of feeling frustrated.

The six characters have been discussed in a deliberately chosen order ranging from the neurotic Infant to the almost impassive Inquisitor and showing a gradually lessening degree of frustration. Now if we turn to the 'signifier' it appears that the occurrence of the three musical elements in these roles is almost exactly proportionate. The elements are most frequently found in the parts of Don Carlos, Elisabeth and King Philippe, less in Eboli's and still less in Posa's, while in the part of the Grand Inquisiteur they are totally absent. Nor do they occur in minor roles like those of Thibaut, the Count of Lerma, the Monk and the Herald. As for the choruses, only the women's plea for peace in the Fontainebleau act and the contrasting words of people and monks in the auto-da-fé scene ("Ce jour heureux" – "... un jour de colère") involve one or more of the three formulae (a), (b) and (c).

From the above observations we must conclude that the relationship between 'signifier' and 'signified' or *tinta musicale* and *idea generale* is to be found in the characters rather than in certain dramatic situations. On reflection this seems a logical procedure for the composer to have followed. The broad variety of situations and emotions inherent in the drama precludes a connection with an overall *tinta*. The characters, on the other hand, are constant elements (despite their possible development in the course of the action) and therefore well-suited to the musical expression of a general idea. With his strong dramatic instinct Verdi unerringly knew how to handle his signifying devices in the most efficacious way.

1975

APPENDICES

I

SEMIOTIC DEVICES IN MUSICAL DRAMA

Note – The text printed below is a revised version of a paper read at the First International Congress of Semiotic Studies (Milan, 1974) and the International Colloquium on 'The Function of Tragedy' (Ghent University, 1975). It summarizes various matters discussed in this book, as seen from the viewpoint of semiotics. The paper's main section dealing with the subject proper is preceded by an introduction which describes several semiotic concepts. This introduction – read in Ghent only – is highly selective and focused on the ensuing discussion of operatic sign properties and categories.

* *
*

Semiotics is the study of signs, derived from the Greek word for sign, σημείον. Since in our world communication takes place almost exclusively by means of signs, semiotics may be considered a fundament of social sciences and humanities. Beyond that, semiotics is a self-contained discipline as well as an instrument for scientific research. As the former, it deals with signs as a system and consequently as object-language, while in its latter capacity it studies signs as a meta-language describing an object-language. As musicologist I am occupied with the object-language *music*, more specifically music expressing dramatic thought, and therefore I study signs as a meta-language.

Semiotics has a long history ranging from the Ancients through the Roman Stoa, Saint Augustine, medieval scholasticism, seventeenth-century Rationalism, to the fathers of modern semiotics, the American logician

Charles Sanders Peirce and the Swiss linguist Ferdinand de Saussure. Still it is curious to note that in Western history the discipline had never been used as a helpful instrument for the various social and human sciences until some twenty years ago. This might be explained by the fact that semiotics can only function as an underlying discipline if two essential conditions are fulfilled: first there must be a general need for systematics and methodology, secondly a strong interest in social questions. Looking back through the ages, it appears that in no period did these trends occur simultaneously. For example, as we know, the seventeenth century was the age of methodology and systematic reasoning. The interest in social matters was scanty however, except perhaps during the years around 1700 in England. In the eighteenth century, the situation was diametrically opposite: social problems were studied on a large scale but nearly always inductively and empirically, not deductively and systematically. Only in our time, actually since the 1950's is there a general interest both in methodological and social questions. During the last years semiotics has even become a fashion, veering off toward a pseudo-science.

Whatever its purpose may be, the study of semiotics should start from the basic question: what exactly *is* a sign? The most common definition is: "Something which stands for something else and which refers to it". I consider this description acceptable only when the referential function is recognized as such. This results in the following definition: *A sign is an entity which stands for and refers to another entity, and whose referential function is recognized by the perceiving subject.* The addition changes the character of a sign from that of an object into that of a process.

In my experience the most useful model for the analysis of a sign process is that of Charles William Morris who in his pre-war writings has remoulded the semiotic doctrines of Peirce.[1] Although certain aspects of Morris' thoughts have been criticized, his model has the great advantage of not being dependent on linguistics and also of being applicable to all kinds of communication. Its principles are the following:

The sign process which is called *semiosis* involves four elements.

First, the *sign vehicle*. Almost everything conceivable may serve as a sign vehicle. Typical examples are: a traffic light, a facial expression, a word taken as a sound or a composition of written or printed letters, a dark cloud, etc.

---

[1] See Ch. W. Morris, *Foundation of the Theory of Signs*, Chicago, 1938; *Esthetics and the Theory of Signs*, The Journal of Unified Science, vol. viii (1939–'40), pp. 131–150. Both essays are reprinted in the author's *Writings on the General Theory of Signs*, The Hague-Paris 1971. As for Ch. S. Peirce see his *Collected Papers*, Cambridge, Mass. 1931–'35.

Secondly, the *interpreter*. He or she is always a living organism, practically speaking a man, a woman or an animal. A glass of milk, a thought or a typewriter cannot interpret.

Third, the *interpretant*. This difficult concept in Peirce's writings has been simplified by Morris to "the disposition to interpret or the act of interpreting". Morris has been criticized on this point, but I consider the description useful.

Finally, the *designatum*, sometimes called *denotatum*. The difference between the two terms is that a designatum represents a class and a denotatum an element taken from a class. When in the second act of the opera *Don Carlos* King Philip II declares "La mort, entre mes mains, peut devenir féconde", he does not refer to a special death, nor to a certain number of people who may die, but to the concept of death as a class. So in this case the word "mort" is a designatum. But when in the fourth act of the same opera, Posa alludes to his own death with the sentence "La mort a des charmes, o mon Carlos, à qui meurt pour toi", then "la mort" is a denotatum. Although a denotatum always depends on a designatum, the opposite is not true: a designatum may exist without a denotatum. In that case the designatum represents a so-called zero-class, that is, a class without elements. I may assume that in our time the following references will be interpreted as designata with a zero-class: the god Neptune, a unicorn, a football referee whose decisions are always met with complete agreement by both parties, or an absolutely just intonation of the musical interval of a third.

The importance of the distinction between designatum and denotatum became particularly clear to me when I undertook a study of the function of the witches in three versions of *Macbeth*, namely, that of Shakespeare dating from 1607, that of Schiller from 1800, and that of Verdi from 1847. Shakespeare's audience undoubtedly considered the three boys who impersonated the witches on the stage as sign vehicles of the strange creatures encountered by the historical Macbeth six hundred years before in Scotland. The actors *denoted* special witches, a fact explained by the audience's firm belief in the physical existence of witches. This belief certainly had an influence on the interpretation of the tragedy as a whole: Shakespeare's contemporaries will have considered Macbeth *possessed* by evil powers and therefore only partly responsable for his misdeeds. If we take a look in Weimar Court Theatre of the year 1800, here, too, we see witches on the stage, this time perhaps impersonated by women, although that makes no difference. What *is* different is the belief of the 18th-century spectator. For that person the witches referred to an idea, i.e. the challenge of man's moral force or weakness:

Wir streuen in die Brust die böse Saat,
Aber dem Menschen gehört die That.

We sow the seed of Evil in the heart
But the deed belongs to Man.

These lines do not occur in Shakespeare; they were added by Schiller. But even without the additional text, we can be sure that in the mind of the enlightened audience in Weimar the witches did not denote anything; they *designated* a zero-class.

With Verdi things are more complicated. Several years ago I discovered that the opera *Macbeth* is based on Schiller's adaptation, rather than Shakespeare's original version. However interesting this may be, it is irrelevant in the present context. We may safely assume that audiences in the opera houses of Florence and Bologna took the witches for the embodiment of an idea. However, with regard to theatre-goers in Naples and the smaller towns of the Italian *mezzo giorno* I am not so sure. It is quite possible that many of them still believed in the physical existence of witches and consequently interpreted the singers as *denoting* sign vehicles.

So it is the interpreter who decides on the character of the reference: designatum or denotatum. This relation between sign vehicle and interpreter is called by Morris the *pragmatic dimension* of semiosis. The relation between sign vehicle and other sign vehicles is called the *syntactic dimension*, and the relation between sign vehicle and reference, the *semantic dimension* (see Diagram I). By using the term "dimension" instead of "level", Morris stresses the equivalence of the three relationships. On this particular point I totally disagree. As we have seen in the case of the *Macbeth* versions, the pragmatic dimension may determine the character of the two others. The supremacy of the pragmatic aspect of semiosis is an extremely important feature that must not be overlooked, whether the study involves musical drama or any other form of human communication. In discussing semiosis I have intentionally ignored the *sign giver* and his relation to the sign vehicle, since in my opinion the sign giver does not take any part in the sign process which only starts after the sign has been given. Besides, in many cases the sign giver is unknown or perhaps non-existent. Who, for instance, is the originator of a dark cloud denoting bad weather? I must admit however that my omission of the sign giver has shocked not only several of my colleagues in the field of musicology but also semioticians with whom I have discussed this problem. In point of fact this elimination may lead to the denial of immanent or intrinsic qualities in the work of art.

DIAGRAM I

Semiosis (sign process)

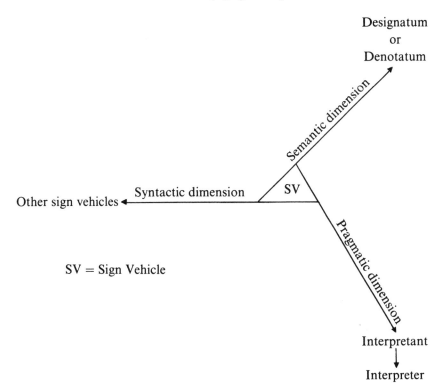

SV = Sign Vehicle

Finally a few words about the character of the sign vehicle with regard to its relation to designatum and denotatum, that is, the semantic dimension. Peirce distinguished between *index* signs, *symbolic* signs and *iconic* signs (see Diagram II). The index sign has a dynamic or causal relation to its denotatum. All symptoms are indexes, as for example a steamed window glass or a smile. Symbols are sign vehicles which designate or denote indirectly, that is, by means of an intervening rule or convention. All words are symbols, also punctuation marks, the 6/8 time signature of an opera chorus (which denotes people of a low social class), or a young man wearing long hair. The last-named example again shows the influence of the pragmatic factor on the semantic dimension. Some ten years ago long hair and a beard designated progressive ideas and challenge of the social Establishment. Nowadays these sign vehicles simply mean adherance to fashion.

DIAGRAM II

Semantic Dimension

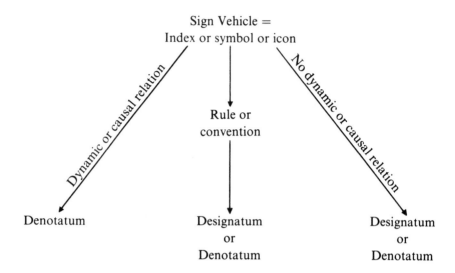

Sign Vehicle =
Index or symbol or icon

Rule or
convention

Denotatum

Designatum
or
Denotatum

Designatum
or
Denotatum

Dynamic or causal relation

No dynamic or causal relation

The icon is the most problematic of the three types. Peirce's description is difficult to understand and moreover inconsistently applied. Morris is as always very clear but also completely beside the mark. According to his definition an icon is a sign vehicle which has properties in common with its denotatum or designatum. This implies unintentionally that *every* sign vehicle may be called an icon, because it will always be possible to find a common property. For instance, sign vehicle and referential object may have in common that they are both perceived and interpreted in the twentieth century. Or let us say that both are able to stand up against a thunderstorm raging over the city of Ghent. However absurd these examples may be, they nevertheless refute Morris' description of the iconic sign. Elsewhere Morris states that sign vehicle and denotatum or designatum need to have *specific* properties in common; but it remains unclear what kind of properties he has in mind.

I propose another description which, although not pretending to clarify the essence of the matter, at least seems less easy to undermine: "An icon is a sign vehicle which directly refers to its designatum or denotatum, despite the fact that it has no dynamic or causal relation to its referential object." A map of a country is an icon, and so is a chemical formula (but not its separate letters and figures; these are symbols). According to many semioticians works of art, like a symphony, a drama or a sculpture are icons; however, this question, which involves the delicate problem of semantics of art, is still disputed. The essential differences between the components of the triad may be clarified by the presentation of a certain concept viewed from three different angles, for instance the concept "weathercock". The *position* of a weathercock is an index, the *word* weathercock is a symbol, and the *picture* of a weathercock is an icon.

*   *
*

I now pass on to the principal part of this paper which deals not only with tragedy but also with comedy. Personally I have no scruples about this deviation from the theme of our colloquium [The Function of Tragedy], since I can hardly conceive anything more tragic than high comedy. However I need to make another preliminary remark regarding the title of my paper, which might suggest a discussion of the nineteenth-century concept of *Das Musikdrama*; but this is certainly not the case. The Wagnerian spell has long been broken, and today we can no longer accept the artificial dichotomy of opera and drama. Although the distinction made by Wagner undoubtedly served his own artistic interests, this distinction must be considered incorrect both in a phenomenological and in a historical sense. One may differentiate, of course, between 'continuous' and 'non-continuous' opera, but this does not alter the fact that both forms are dramas realized through music. The concepts of opera and musical drama must be considered synonymous.

One of the implications of this view is that not only 'continuous' but also 'non-continuous' opera must necessarily possess an overall musico-dramatic structure, which can be disclosed through analysis. Curiously enough, musicologists have paid little attention to the structural analysis of works belonging to the latter category. Although form and style of separate recitatives, arias and ensembles have been the objects of extensive research, the study of structural features pertaining to the musical drama as a whole has been badly neglected. This is the reason why in the past several years I have concentrated on this aspect of the so-called non-continuous opera, focusing my interest particularly on the works of two composers who match Wagner in dramatic power and musical quality: Mozart and Verdi. My research has led me imperceptibly into the field of musical semiotics and the present paper summarizes some of my observations on the musico-dramatic sign.

The order in which these observations are presented should not be considered as a classification; my remarks are only intended as discussion material on the phenomenology of musical drama and its structure.

In order to avoid terminological misunderstanding it may be useful to start with a few working definitions of various dramatic concepts:

(a) *Libretto* – A number of coherent events, presented in written dialogue form, with stage directions.

(b) *Plot* – The story abstracted from the libretto.

(c) *Drama* (in a specific sense) – The intergeneration of action and emotion, based on the libretto, presented on the stage, and expressed through music.

(d) *Musico-dramatic sign* (henceforth called *sign*) – A musical unit which stresses, clarifies, invalidates, contradicts or supplies an element of the libretto. The sign is semantically interpretable and discloses dramatic truth.

For the sake of clarity I have divided my observations into two series, the first of which deals with the properties of the musico-dramatic sign. It should be understood that the term "property" is taken in a broad sense and includes the sign's function.

*   *
*

1. First I would like to mention an important condition: in order to make itself communicable the sign must *recur*. A sign, invented by the composer, which appears only once in the opera, will not lead to semiosis and will therefore miss its mark. The condition, however, does not necessarily imply recurrence within the drama, since the sign may appeal to the audience's previous knowledge. An example of this is found in Bartolo's aria in *Le nozze di Figaro*, the text of which includes both his own name and that of Figaro:

> Tutta Siviglia connosce Bartolo;
> Il birbo Figaro vinto sarà!
>
> *The whole of Seville knows me, Bartolo;*
> *That scoundrel Figaro shall be defeated!*

Mozart scans both names in the normal way: a dotted note on the first syllable and a short note on the second. However, Bartolo's name is set in a rhythm twice as slow as Figaro's (see Ch. 2, ex. 8). No one in the audience will have any difficulty in explaining this, since we all have previous knowledge of the fact that a pompous attitude is associated with slow and anger with fast speech movement. Therefore the sign's first occurrence in the drama is in fact a recurrence in our minds. In addition, an eighteenth-century audience would certainly have gone beyond this explanation: it would have interpreted Bartolo's pompousness and anger as an expression of the doctor's professional disdain for the barber. Today barbers do not practice medicine anymore, and therefore this semantic aspect of the sign may easily escape us.

2. The sign's function in the musical drama may be *prospective*, *retrospective* or *both*. An example of the last-named case (in which the sign is ambivalent) is found in Verdi's *Macbeth*. In the second act Banco speaks to his son:

> Come dal ciel precipita
> L'ombra più sempre oscura!
> In notte ugual trafissero
> Duncano, il mio signor.

> *See how the shades of night descend,*
> *The shadows grow deeper and darker.*
> *Just such a night as this brought death*
> *To Duncan, my sovereign lord.*

These lines are accompanied by an orchestral motif which unequivocally designates the concept of tragic death and to which I shall return below. The musical formula is explicitly retrospective, confirming Banco's allusion to the previous murder of King Duncan. In addition, however, the motif has an implicit prospective meaning, since shortly afterwards Banco himself will be murdered by Macbeth's bravos.

It should be observed that the predictive or retrodictive character of a sign is highly dependent on the pragmatic dimension of semiosis. The interpreter's acquaintance with the drama prior to its performance may affect this function.

3. The *referential force* of a sign is proportionate to its degree of perceptibility. This may seem a truism; still, one should keep in mind that not all musical parameters are equally perceptible or, rather, will be perceived with equal facility. For example, pitch and tone duration generally lend themselves more easily to communication than dynamics and tone colour. This does not mean that a musical dramatist will abstain from using these relatively weak sign vehicles. In *Così fan tutte* the farewell terzetto in the first

act contains a particularly subtle example of the use of a weak sign. After Ferrando and Guglielmo have embarked, Don Alfonso and the two sisters pray for favourable weather. They ask the wind and the waves to comply with their wishes ("risponda ai nostri desir"). Nothing could be more harmless. Yet on the strong syllable of the word "desir" we suddenly hear the flute being added to the orchestral sound (see Ch. 6, ex. 5). It should be observed that in Mozart the flute nearly always functions as a disturber of equilibrium; the instrument serves the intrigue and in addition often has an erotic connotation. So the word "desir" sung by the two girls adopts an ambiguous meaning quite in accordance with the irony characteristic of the whole opera.

4. A weak sign may be reinforced by its *formal*, that is non-semantic, *properties*. In the last-mentioned example this is done with the aid of a special chord. The second syllable of the word "desir" is not sung on the tonic chord, as one would expect, but on a strongly dissonant harmony (a diminished seventh chord on the augmented subdominant based on a dominant pedal: B – A♯ – C♯ – E – G). Another example of a reinforced sign vehicle is found in Verdi's *Otello*. Jago's destruction of the Moorish general, Otello, takes three full acts. In the first scene of Act I we hear Jago singing an aside to Roderigo in which he refers to Otello's ship:

> L'alvo frenetico del mar
> sia la sua tomba.

> *May the frantic belly*
> *of the sea be her tomb.*

At the end of Act III, Otello lies in a swoon and now Jago uses practically the same melody for the following words:

> Chi può vietar che questa fronte
> Premar con il mio talone?

> *Who can now prevent me pressing*
> *this forehead beneath my heel?*

The sign clearly marks the beginning and end of Jago's path, but the great span of time between the melody's first occurence and its repeat weakens the referential force. Therefore a formal property of the sign vehicle, the key of A♭ minor, functions as a strengthening factor. Although in itself uninterpretable, this key stresses the relationship of Jago's two phrases (see Ch. 7, ex. 9).

5. Finally a distinction should be made between *extra-dramatic* and *intro-dramatic signs*. The latter type designates an entity which is contained within the musical drama, while the former refers to matters lying outside the drama. The intro-dramatic sign always functions as a structural element, since every drama (and for that matter every work of art and literature), notwithstanding its possible allusions to the so-called real world, presents itself within the framework of a closed system, the elements of which are essentially interdependent. Generally the extra-dramatic sign has no such structural function, although one may come across borderline cases.

* *
*

A second series of observations deals with special sign categories.

1. The *corroborative sign* stressing and enrichting an element contained in the libretto may be easily overlooked, paradoxically because of its frequent occurence. Its value as a semio-dramatic tool for operatic composers is beyond any doubt, especially since in a musical drama the textual message is not always transmitted with the same clarity as in a verbal drama, covered as it may be by the orchestral sound.

2. A more specific category is that of the *ironic sign*, which I shall define as a sign contradicting or invalidating an element contained in the libretto. Although signs of this kind are encountered frequently in high comedy, they are almost as often used in tragedy. I choose again an example from Verdi's *Macbeth*. In the first act the solemn entrance of King Duncan into the castle of Macbeth at Inverness is musically illustrated by a gay march which closes with a four-note motif abstracted from the piece's thematic material. During the following night Duncan is slain by Macbeth. In the third act we see Macbeth, now King of Scotland, lying in a swoon, overcome by his emotions on seeing the show of eight Kings followed by Banco's ghost. The text of the ensuing danced chorus of the witches expresses their wish to cheer up the senseless King. But the piece ends with exactly the same motif as that of the first-act march. And so the orchestra contradicting the words subtly announces the fact that Macbeth's destiny will be the same as Duncan's: death by violence.

3. The *parodical sign* generally refers to an object lying outside the scope of the drama. Naturally, its interpretant depends on the audience's acquaintance with this object. For example, in *Così fan tutte* Fiordiligi's aria, "Come scoglio", appeals to our familiarity with *opera seria* style and the

Metastasian metaphor. However, other parodical signs in the same work
may have been overlooked even by eighteenth-century audiences. I refer to
four 'quotations' from *Don Giovanni*. Hidden in the score of *Così fan tutte*
they seem to have been inserted for the sole pleasure of the composer. The
most hilarious of them is a march-like distortion of a tender phrase from
"Là ci darem la mano", which at the beginning of the sextet announces the
first attack of the burlesque lovers on the sisters' virtue (see Ch. 5, ex. 8). So
far as I am aware the quotations have not been noticed hitherto in the
literature on Mozart, a fact that may speak for the usefulness of semiotic
analysis of opera.

4. The *physiognomic sign* shapes and strengthens individual characters in
the drama. Susanna is characterized by large descending intervals, Jago by
chromaticism and melodies in triple time, Aida by a special recurrent theme.
The device may be applied in a negative way, that is, by conspicuous absense
of a musical design. This happens with Don Giovanni and Don Alfonso.
The libertine lacks a clear musical physiognomy, because of his astonishing
adaptability to various persons and situations; Don Alfonso, on the other
hand, hides his true self under the cover of his shallow philosophy.

5. The category of *signs designating concepts* which pertain to the essential
nature of the drama is structurally the most important. It goes without
saying that this type of sign needs frequent recurrence. A characteristic
example is found in both versions of *Simon Boccanegra*, where an unusual
kind of phrase ending (a descending third returning to the initial pitch)
marks the domestic realm of the drama in opposition to the political realm
(see Ch. 9, ex. 10). Another striking example of a motif functioning in this
way occurs in *Don Giovanni*. In that opera through persistent connotation a
completely neutral and common formula increasingly adopts the meaning
of 'treason' (see Ch. 3, ex. 28). The motif occurs no less than ten times in
the score, not counting its frequent repeats within each number or finale-
section. The sign is conditioned by a formal property, the key of B♭ major.
Serving the unity of the drama, the treason motif stresses in addition the
conflicting attitudes of the characters.

6. In conclusion I will refer to the *topos*. A topos is a traditional formula
transmitted from one generation to the next. The chromatically descending
tetrachord which designates a *lamento* is one of the best-known examples.
Another topos, which occurs mainly in French and Italian opera, is the musical figure of death: two, three or four short notes, followed by a long one, all
of them on the same pitch (see Ch. 8). I have traced its history from the
tragédie lyrique of Lully to the late works of Verdi. Out of hundreds of
examples I choose one occurring in Rossini's last opera, *Guillaume Tell*.

During the first act we hear Tell speaking of "le bonheur d'être père", a phrase which is accompanied by the musical figure of death in the orchestra. The motif prospectively refers to the famous archer-scene in the third act, when Tell is forced to shoot at the apple on his son's head. The example shows that my sign categories may overlap; in this case the topos is an ironic sign.

I am aware of the fact that my distinction of sign properties and sign categories is a question of point of view rather than intrinsic qualities. It seems doubtful whether the observations presented in this paper will inductively lead to a classification, let alone to a theory of the musico-dramatic sign. Nevertheless I hope that in other respects they may contribute to the phenomenology of musical drama.

II

THE INSTRUMENTATION OF SEPARATE ITEMS
IN MOZART'S OPERAS (1781–1791)

It is a curious fact that, in spite of the vast amount of literature on Mozart's dramatic works, exact information about the orchestral scoring of separate arias, ensembles and choruses (discussed in chapter 6) is rather difficult to obtain. Köchel's Catalogue (6th edition) is not only incomplete in this respect but even misleading: in some cases the orchestration given for a *buffo* or *Singspiel* finale applies only to its initial section, in others to the number of instruments that appears in the entire finale. To gather the information from the full score is a tiresome process, quite apart from the fact that relatively few people will have these volumes at hand. It is for this reason that the scoring of separate items is described below. As a complete list would have exceeded the scope of this book, only the original versions of the mature operas have been included. The 'normal' wind instrument are indicated by two groups of numbers (1202 220 = 1 flute, 2 oboes, no clarinets, 2 bassoons, and 2 horns, 2 trumpets, no trombones), the other instruments by their customary abbreviations.

IDOMENEO (1781)

Ouverture: 2222 220 timp., str.

Atto I°

Sc. I.   Recitativo: str.
No. 1.   Aria (Ilia): 0202 200 str.
No. 2.   Aria (Idam.): 0222 200 str.
No. 3.   Coro: 0202 200 str.
Sc. IV.   Recitativo: str.
No. 4.   Aria (Elett.): 2202 400 str.
No. 5.   Coro: 2202 400 str.
Sc. VIII. Pantomima-recitativo: 2202 200 str.
Sc. IX.   Recitativo: str.
No. 6.   Aria (Idom.): 2222 200 str.
Sc. X.   Recitativo: 2202 200 str.
No. 7.   Aria (Idam.): 1101 200 str.

Intermezzo

No. 8.   Marcia: 2202 220 timp., str.
No. 9.   Ciacona (Coro): 2202 220 timp., str.

Atto II°

No. 10.   Aria (Arbace): 0200 200 str.
No. 11.   Aria (Ilia): 1101 100 str.
Sc. III.   Recitativo: str.
No. 12.   Aria (Idom.): 2202 220 timp., str.
Sc. IV.   Recitativo: str.
No. 13.   Aria (Elett.): str.
No. 14.   Marcia: 2222 220 timp., str.
No. 15.   Coro: 2020 200 str.
No. 16.   Terzetto (Elett., Idam., Idom.,): 0200 200 str.
              (Più Allegro: 2202 400 str.)
No. 17.   Coro: 2202 400 picc., str.
Sc. VI.   Recitativo: 2202 220 timp., str.
No. 18.   Coro: 2202 420 timp., str.

Atto III°

Sc. I.   Recitativo: str.
No. 19.   Aria (Ilia): 2022 200 str.
Sc. II.   Recitativo: str.
No. 20.   Duetto (Ilia, Idam.): 0202 200 str.
Sc. III.   Recitativo: str.
No. 21.   Quartetto (Ilia, Elett., Idam., Idom.): 2022 200 str.
Sc. V.   Recitativo: str.
No. 22.   Aria (Arbace): str.
No. 23.   Recitativo: 2202 420 timp., str.
No. 24.   Coro: 2202 220 timp., str.
No. 25.   Marcia: 0200 000 str.
No. 26.   Cavatina con coro (Idom., Sacerdoti): 2222 200 str.
          (Allegro vivace: 0000 020 timp.)
No. 27.   Recitativo: str.
No. 28.   Adagio (La Voce): 0000 203
No. 29.   Recitativo: 2202 220 timp., str.
No. 30.   Recitativo: 0020 200 str.
No. 31.   Coro: 2202 220 timp., str.
No. 32.   *Ballet*
          Chaconne: 2202 220 timp., str.
          Larghetto: 0202 200 str.
          Chaconne: 2202 220 timp., str.
          Pas seul: 2200 220 timp., str.
          Pour le ballet: 2200 220 timp., str.

DIE ENTFUHRUNG AUS DEM SERAIL (1782)

Ouverture: 1222 220 picc., timp., triangle, cymbals, gran cassa, str.

I. Akt

No. 1.   Arie (Belmonte): 0022 200 str.
No. 2.   Lied und Duett: (Belm., Osmin): 1202 200 str.
No. 3.   Arie (Osmin): 0202 220 picc., cymbals, gr. cassa, str.
No. 4.   Arie (Belmonte): 1101 200 str.
No. 5.   Chor: 0222 220 picc., timp., triangle, cymbals, gr. cassa, str.
No. 6.   Arie (Constanze): 0222 200 str.

No. 7.   Terzett (Belm., Pedr., Osmin): 0222 220 timp., str.

II. Akt

No. 8.   Arie (Blonde): str.
No. 9.   Duett (Blonde, Osmin): 0202 200 str.
No. 10a. Rezitativ (Constanze): str.
No. 10b. Arie (Constanze): 2202 200 corni di bassetto (2), str.
No. 11.   Arie (Constanze): 0022 220 timp., fl. solo, ob. solo, vl. solo, vc. solo, str.
No. 12.   Arie (Blonde): 2002 200 str.
No. 13.   Arie (Pedrillo): 2000 220 timp., str.
No. 14.   Duett (Pedrillo, Osmin): 2222 020 picc., triangle, cymbals, gran cassa, str.
No. 15.   Arie (Belmonte): 0222 200 str.
No. 16.   Quartett (Const., Bl., Belm., Pedr.): 2202 220 timp., str.

III. Akt

No. 17.   Arie (Belmonte): 2022 200 str.
No. 18.   Romanze (Pedrillo): str.
No. 19.   Arie (Osmin): 0222 200 picc., str.
No. 20a. Rezitativ (Const., Belm.): str.
No. 20b. Duett (Const., Belm.): 2022 200 str.
No. 21.   *Vaudeville*
          Andante (Const., Bl., Belm., Pedr., Osm.): 2202 200 str.
          Allegro assai (Osm.): 0202 220 picc., triangle, cymbals, gr. cassa, str.
          Andante (Const., Bl., Belm., Pedr.): 2202 200 str.
          Chor: 0202 220 picc., timp., triangle, cymbals, gr. cassa, str.

DER SCHAUSPIELDIREKTOR (1786)

Ouverture: 2222 220 timp., str.

No. 1.   Arietta (Madame Herz): 0202 200 str.
No. 2.   Rondo (Mademoiselle Silberklang): 0022 200 str.
No. 3.   Terzett (Mme Herz, Mlle Silb., M. Vogelsang): 0222 200 str.
No. 4.   Schlussgesang (Mme Herz, Mlle Silb., M. Vog., Buff.): 0222 220 timp., str.

Le Nozze di Figaro (1786)

Sinfonia: 2222 220 timp., str.

Atto I°

No. 1.   Duettino (Susanna, Figaro): 2202 200 str.
No. 2.   Duettino (Sus., Fig.): 2202 200 str.
No. 3.   Cavatina (Figaro): 0202 200 str.
No. 4.   Aria (Bartolo): 2202 220 timp., str.
No. 5.   Duettino (Susanna, Marcellina): 2202 200 str.
No. 6.   Aria (Cherubino): 0022 200 str.
No. 7.   Terzetto (Sus., Basilio, Conte): 0222 200 str.
No. 8.   Coro: 2002 200 str.
No. 9.   Aria (Figaro): 2202 220 timp., str.

Atto II°

No. 10. Cavatina (Contessa): 0022 200 str.
No. 11. Arietta [Canzona] (Cherub.): 1111 200 str.
No. 12. Aria (Susanna): 2202 200 str.
No. 13. Terzetto (Sus., Contessa, Conte): 0202 200 str.
No. 14. Duettino (Sus., Cher.): str.
No. 15. *Finale*
         Sc. VI, Allegro (Contessa, Conte): 0222 200 str.
         Sc. VII, Molto andante (Sus., Contessa, Conte): 0222 200 str.
         Sc. VIII, Allegro (Sus., Contessa, Conte): 2222 200 str.
         Sc. IX, Allegro-Andante (Sus., Contessa, Conte, Fig.): 2202 200 str.
         Sc. X, Allegro molto-Andante (Sus., Contessa, Conte, Antonio, Fig.): 2222 200 str.
         Sc. XI, Allegro assai – Più allegro – Prestissimo (Sus., Contessa, Marc., Bas., Conte, Bart., Fig.): 2222 220 timp., str.

Atto III°

No. 16. Duettino (Sus., Conte): 2002 200 str.
Sc. IV. Recitativo: 0202 200 str.
No. 17. Aria (Conte): 2202 220 timp., str.

No. 18. Sestetto (Sus., Marc., Don Curzio, Conte, Bart., Fig.): 2202 200
, str.

Sc. VIII. Recitativo: str.

No. 19. Aria (Contessa): 0202 200 str.

No. 20. Duettino (Sus., Contessa): 0101 000 str.

No. 21. Coro: 1201 200 str.

No. 22. *Finale*
Marcia (Sus., Contessa, Conte, Fig.): 2222 220 timp., str.
Allegretto (Due Donne, coro): 2202 220 timp., str.
Andante (Conte, Fig.): 1101 200 str.
Recitativo (Conte): 2202 200 str.
Allegretto (coro): 2202 220 timp., str.

Atto IV°

No. 23. Cavatina (Barbarina): str.

No. 24. Aria (Marcellina): str.

No. 25. Aria (Basilio): 1022 200 str.

Sc. VIII. Recitativo: str.

No. 26. Aria (Figaro): 0022 200 str.

Sc. X. Recitativo: str.

No. 27. Aria (Susanna): 1101 000 str.

No. 28. *Finale*
Andante (Sus., Contessa, Cher., Conte, Fig.): 0202 200 str.
Con un poco più di moto (Sus., Contessa, Conte, Fig.): 2202 200
str.
Larghetto-Allegro di molto (Sus., Fig.): 2022 200 str.
Andante (Sus., Conte, Fig.): 2222 200 str.
Allegro assai – Andante (Sus., Contessa, Barb., Cher., Marc., Bas.,
Conte, Ant., Fig.): 2202 200 str.
Allegro assai (Sus., Contessa, Barb., Cher., Marc., Bas., Conte,
Ant., Fig.): 2222 220 timp., str.

Don Giovanni (1787)

Ouverture: 2222 220 timp., str.

Atto I°

No. 1. *Introduzione*
Molto allegro, F major (Leporello): 0202 200 str.

Molto allegro, B♭ major (Donna Anna, Don Giovanni, Lep.): 2202 200 str.

Molto allegro (D. Giov., Commendatore, Lep.): 2202 200 str.

Andante (D. Giov., Comm., Lep.): 2202 200 str.

Sc. III.   Recitativo: 2202 200 str.

No. 2.   Duetto (D. Anna, Don Ottavio): 2202 200 str.

No. 3.   Aria (D. Elvira, D. Giov., Lep.): 0022 200 str.

No. 4.   Aria (Leporello): 2202 200 str.

No. 5.   Coro: (Zerlina, Masetto, contadini): 2202 200 str.

No. 6.   Aria (Masetto): 2002 200 str.

No. 7.   Duettino (Zerlina, Don Giov.): 1202 200 str.

No. 8.   Aria (D. Elvira): str.

No. 9.   Quartetto (D. Anna, D. Elv., D. Ott., D. Giov.): 1022 200 str.

Sc. XIII. Recitativo: 2202 220 str.

No. 10.   Aria (D. Anna): 0202 200 str.

No. 11.   Aria (D. Giov.): 2222 200 str.

No. 12.   Aria (Zerlina): 1101 200 vcl. obbligato, str.

No. 13.   *Finale*

Allegro assai (Zerl., Mass.): 2222 220 str.

Sc. XVII, (D. Giov., 4 servi): 2222 220 timp., str.

Andante-Allegretto (Zerl., D. Giov., Mass.): 2202 200 str., orchestra I sopra il teatro (2 ob., 2 cor., str.)

Sc. XIX, [Allegretto] (D. Anna, D. Elv., D. Ott.): 2202 200 str.

Menuetto (D. Anna, D. Elv., D. Ott., Lep.): orchestra I sopra il teatro (2 ob., 2 cor., str.).

Adagio (D. Anna, D. Elv., D. Ott.): 2222 200 (str. only the two initial bars).

Allegro (Zerl. D. Giov., Lep., Mas.): 2022 200 str.

Maestoso (D. Anna, D. Elv., D. Ott., D. Giov., Lep.): 2222 020 timp., str.

Menuetto (D. Anna, D. Elv., Zerl., D. Ott., D. Giov., Lep., Mas.): orchestra I sopra il teatro (2 ob., 2 cor., str.); orch. II sopra il treatro (vl., basso); orch. III sopra il teatro (vl., basso).

Allegro assai (D. Anna, D. Elv., Zerl., D. Ott., Mas.): 2222 200 str.

Andante maestoso (D. Anna, D. Elv., Zerl., D. Ott., D. Giov., Lep., Mas.): 2222 200 str.

Allegro – Più stretto (D. Anna, D. Elv., Zerl., D. Ott., D. Giov., Lep., Mas.): 2222 220 timp., str.

Atto II°

No. 14. Duetto (D. Giov., Lep.): 0200 200 str.
No. 15. Terzetto (D. Elv., D. Giov., Lep.): 2022 200 str.
No. 16. Canzonetta (D. Giov.): mandolino, str.
No. 17. Aria (D. Giov.): 2202 200 str.
No. 18. Aria (Zerlina): 2022 200 str.
No. 19. Sestetto (D. Anna, D. Elv., Zerl., D. Ott., Lep., Mas.): 2222 220 timp. str.
No. 20. Aria (Leporello): 2002 200 str.
No. 21. Aria (D. Ottavio): 0022 200 str.
Sc. XI. Adagio (Commendatore): 0222 003 vcl., cb.
No. 22. Duetto (D. Giov., Comm., Lep.): 2002 200 str.
Sc. XII. Recitativo: str.
No. 23. Rondo (Donna Anna): 1022 200 str.
No. 24. *Finale*
    Allegro vivace (D. Giov., Lep.): 2222 220 timp., str.
    [Allegro vivace] D major, 6/8 (D. Giov., Lep.): 0222 200 str.
    [Allegro vivace] F major, 3/4 (D. Giov., Lep.): 0222 200 str.
    [Allegro vivace] B♭ major (D. Giov., Lep.): 0222 200 vcl., cb.
    Allegro assai (D. Elv., D. Giov., Lep.): 2222 200 str.
    Molto allegro (D. Giov., Lep.): 2222 200 str.
    Andante (D. Giov., Comm., Lep.): 2222 223 timp., str.
    Allegro (D. Giov., Lep., Coro): 2222 223 timp., str.
    Allegro assai (D. Anna, D. Elv., Zerl., D. Ott., Lep., Mas.): 2202 200 str.
    Larghetto (D. Anna, D. Ott.): 2202 200 str.
    [Larghetto] (D. Elv., Zerl., Lep., Mas.): 2222 200 str.
    Presto (D. Anna, D. Elv., Zerl., D. Ott., Lep., Mas.): 2222 220 timp., str.

Così FAN TUTTE (1790)

Ouverture: 2222 220 timp., str.

Atto I°

No. 1. Terzetto (Ferrando, Don Alfonso, Guglielmo): 0202 200 str.
No. 2. Terzetto (Ferr., D. Alf., Gugl.): 1001 000 str.

No. 3.   Terzetto (Ferr., D. Alf., Gugl.): 0202 020 timp., str.

No. 4.   Duetto (Fiordiligi, Dorabella): 0022 200 str.

No. 5.   Aria (D. Alfonso): str.

No. 6.   Quintetto (Fior., Dor., Ferr., D. Alf., Gugl.): 0022 200 str.

No. 7.   Duettino (Ferr., Gugl.): 0022 200 str.

No. 8.   Coro: 2202 020 timp., str.

No. 9a. Quintetto (Fior., Dor., Ferr., D. Alf., Gugl.): 0022 000 str.

No. 9b. Coro: 2202 020 timp., str.

No. 10. Terzettino (Fior., Dor., D. Alf.): 2022 200 str.

Sc. VII. Recitativo: str.

Sc. IX. Recitativo: str.

No. 11. Aria (Dorabella): 2022 200 str.

No. 12. Aria (Despina): 1101 000 str.

No. 13. Sestetto (Fior., Dor., Desp., Ferr., D. Alf., Gugl.): 0222 020 timp., str.

Sc. XI. Recitativo: str.

No. 14. Aria (Fiordiligi): 0222 020 str.

No. 15. Aria (Guglielmo): 1001 000 str.

No. 16. Terzetto (Ferr., D. Alf., Gugl.): 2202 200 str.

No. 17. Aria (Ferrando): 0022 200 str.

No. 18. *Finale*

Andante (Fior., Dor.): 2002 200 str.

Allegro, G [minor] (Fior., Dor., Ferr., D. Alf., Gugl.): 2202 020 str.

[Allegro], E♭ major (Fior., Dor., Desp., Ferr., D. Alf., Gugl.): 0022 200 str.

[Allegro], C minor (Fior., Dor., Ferr., Gugl.): 0022 200 str.

Allegro, G major (Fior., Dor., Desp., Ferr., D. Alf., Gugl.): 2202 200 str.

Andante, B♭ major (Fior., Dor., Desp., Ferr., D. Alf., Gugl.): 0022 020 str.

Allegro-Presto, D major (Fior., Dor., Desp., Ferr., D. Alf., Gugl.): 2222 220 timp., str.

Atto II°

No. 19. Aria (Despina): 1001 200 str.

No. 20. Duetto (Fior., Dor.): 0202 200 str.

No. 21. Duetto con coro (Ferr., Gugl.): 2022 200 str.

No. 22. Quartetto (Desp., Ferr., D. Alf., Gugl.): 2002 020 str.

No. 23. Duetto (Dor., Gugl.): 0022 200 str.

Sc. VI.   Recitativo: str.

No. 24.   Aria (Ferrando): 0021 020 str.

Sc. VII. Recitativo: str.

No. 25.   Rondo (Fiordiligi): 2022 200 str.

Sc. VIII. Recitativo: str.

No. 26.   Aria (Guglielmo): 2202 220 timp., str.

Sc. IX.   Recitativo: str.

No. 27.   Cavatina (Ferrando): 0222 200 str.

No. 28.   Aria (Dorabella): 1222 200 str.

No. 29.   Duetto (Fior., Ferr.): 0202 200 str.

No. 30.   Andante (Ferr., D. Alf., Gugl.): str.

No. 31.   *Finale*

Allegro assai (Desp., D. Alf., coro): 0202 020 timp., str.

Andante (Fior., Dor., Ferr., Gugl., coro): 0222 220 timp., str.

Larghetto (Fior., Dor., Ferr., Gugl.): 0022 200 str.

Allegro (Fior., Dor., Desp., Ferr., D. Alf., Gugl.): 2202 020 str.

Maestoso (Fior., Dor., Desp., Ferr., D. Alf., Gugl.): 2202 020 timp., str.

Allegro (Fior., Dor., Desp., Ferr., D. Alf., Gugl.): 2022 200 str.

Andante (Fior., Dor., Desp., Ferr., D. Alf., Gugl.): 0022 200 str.

Allegro (Ferr., Gugl.): 0222 020 timp., str.

Andante (Fior., Dor., Ferr., D. Alf., Gugl.): 0022 200 str.

Allegretto-Andante-Allegretto (Fior., Dor., Desp., Ferr., D. Alf., Gugl.): 2202 000 str.

Andante con moto (Fior., Dor., Desp., Ferr., D. Alf., Gugl.): 2202 200 str.

Allegro molto (Fior., Dor., Desp., Ferr., D. Alf., Gugl.): 2222 220 timp., str.

LA CLEMENZA DI TITO (1791)

Sinfonia: 2222 220 timp., str.

Atto I°

No. 1.   Duetto (Vitellia, Sesto): 1202 200 str.

No. 2.   Aria (Vitellia): 2002 200 str.

No. 3.   Duettino (Sesto, Annio): 0022 200 str.

No. 4.   Marcia: 2222 220 timp., str.

No. 5. Coro: 2022 200 str.
No. 6. Aria (Tito): 2002 200 str.
No. 7. Duetto (Servilia, Annio): 1202 000 str.
No. 8. Aria (Tito): 0202 200 str.
No. 9. Aria (Sesto): 0202 200 clarinetto solo, str.
No. 10. Terzetto (Vitellia, Annio, Publio): 2202 200 str.
No. 11. Recitativo (Sesto): 0202 200 str.
No. 12. Quintetto con coro (Vit., Serv., Sesto, Annio, Publio): 2222 220 timp., str.

Atto II°

No. 13. Aria (Annio): str.
No. 14. Terzetto (Vitellia, Sesto, Publio): 0202 200 str.
No. 15. Coro (Tito, patrizi etc.): 2022 200 str.
No. 16. Aria (Publio): 0200 200 str.
No. 17. Aria (Annio): 0202 200 str.
Sc. VIII. Recitativo: str.
No. 18. Terzetto (Sesto, Tito, Publio): 2022 200 str.
No. 19. Rondo (Sesto): 1202 200 str.
No. 20. Aria (Tito): 2202 200 str.
No. 21. Arietta (Servilia): 1101 200 str.
No. 22. Recitativo (Vitellia): str.
No. 23. Rondo (Vitellia): 1202 200 corno di bassetto, str.
Sc. XV. Andante maestoso: 2202 220 timp., str.
No. 24. Coro: 2202 220 timp., str.
No. 25. Recitativo (Tito): str.
No. 26. Sestetto con coro (Vit., Serv., Annio, Sesto, Tito, Publio): 2222 220 timp., str.

Die Zauberflöte (1791)

Ouverture: 2222 223 timp., str.

I. Akt

No. 1.   *Introduction*
         Allegro (1., 2. und 3. Dame, Tamino): 2222 220 timp., str.
         Allegretto (1., 2. und 3. Dame): 2202 000 str.

Allegro (1., 2. und 3. Dame): 0202 220 timp., str.
No. 2.   Arie (Papageno): 0202 200 str., [panpipe]
No. 3.   Arie (Tamino): 0022 200 str.
No. 4.   Rezitativ und Arie (Königin der Nacht)
         Rez.: 0202 200 str.
         Arie: 0202 200 str.
No. 5.   Quintett (1., 2. und 3. Dame, Tamino, Papageno)
         Allegro: 0202 200 str.
         Andante: 0222 200 str.
No. 6.   Terzett (Pamina, Monostatos, Papageno): 1202 200 str.
No. 7.   Duett (Pamina, Papageno): 0022 200 str.
No. 8.   *Finale*
         Larghetto (1., 2. und 3. Knabe, Tamino): 2022 023 timp., str.
         Recitativo (Tam., Eine Stimme, Ein Priester, Chor): 2222 003 str.
         Andante (Tamino): 0202 000 fl. solo, panpipe
         Andante (Pamina, Papageno): 2202 200 str., [panpipe]
         Allegro (Pamina, Monostatos, Papageno, Chor): 2202 200 str.,
         Glockenspiel (strumento d'acciaio)
         Allegro maestoso (Pamina, Papageno, Chor): 0202 020 timp., str.
         Larghetto (Pamina, Sarastro): 2202 000 corni di bassetto (2), str.
         Allegro (Pamina, Tamino, Monostatos, Sarastro, Chor): 2202 000
         corni di bassetto (2), str.
         Presto (Chor): 2202 223 timp., corni di bassetto (2), str.

II. Akt

No. 9.   Marsch: 1002 203 corni di bassetto (2), str.
Sc. I.   Adagio: 2202 223 corni di bassetto (2)
No. 10.   Arie mit Chor (Sarastro): 0002 003 corni di bassetto (2), str.
No. 11.   Duett (Zweiter Priester, Sprecher): 2222 223 timp., str.
No. 12.   Quintett (1., 2. und 3. Dame, Tam., Papageno): 2202 223 timp., str.
No. 13.   Arie (Monostatos): 1022 000 picc., str.
No. 14.   Arie (Königin der Nacht): 2202 220 timp., str.
No. 15.   Arie (Sarastro): 2002 200 str.
No. 16.   Terzett (1., 2. und 3. Knabe): 2002 000 str.
No. 17.   Arie (Pamina): 1101 000 str.
No. 18.   Chor der Priester: 2202 223 str.
No. 19.   Terzett (Pamina, Tamino, Sarastro): 0202 000 str.
No. 20.   Arie (Papagenò): 1202 200 Glockenspiel (strumento d'acciaio), str.

No. 21. *Finale*

Andante (1., 2. und 3. Knabe): 2022 200 str.

[Andante]-Allegro (Pamina, 1., 2. und 3. Knabe): 2022 200 str.

Adagio (Pamina, Tamino, 1. und 2. geharnischter Mann): 2202 003 str.

Allegretto (Tam., 1. und 2. geharnischter Mann): 2022 000 str.

Andante (Pamina, Tamino, 1. und 2. geharnischter Mann): 2202 200 str.

Marsch (Pam., Tam., Chor): 2202 223 fl. solo, timp., str.

Allegro-Andante (Papageno): 1202 200 str., [panpipe]

Allegretto (1., 2. und 3. Knabe, Papageno): 1202 200 str.

Allegro (1., 2. und 3. Knabe, Papageno): 1101 200 Glockenspiel (strumento d'acciaio), str.

[Allegro] (Papagena, Papageno): 2202 200 str.

Più moderato (Köningin d. N., 1., 2. u. 3. Dame, Monostatos): 2222 223 timp., str.

Recitativo (Sar.): 2222 223 timp., str.

Andante-Allegro (Chor): 2222 223 timp., str.

THE 'BOCCANEGRA' REVISION:
CORRESPONDENCE BETWEEN VERDI AND BOITO

Note – I am indebted to Harold Lindberg of Saskatoon, Saskatchewan, Canada, for kind permission to publish his translation of Verdi's and Boito's letters on *Boccanegra*. I also wish to thank David Rosen and Flynn Warmington (Brandeis University, Waltham, Mass.) for their help in solving several problems with regard to the chronology.

The correspondence between Verdi and Boito concerning the revision of *Simon Boccanegra* that was undertaken during the winter of 1880–1881 gives us a most interesting glimpse into the workshops of composer and librettist. While some of the letters have already been published elsewhere either in the original or in English translation, others, including two telegrams, appear here in print for the first time. The task of establishing the correct chronological order offered many obstacles. Several letters of both correspondents are either undated or merely provided with the day of the week (e.g. *Sabato* or *Lunedì*), while in one case a letter proved to be preserved in an envelope belonging to another letter. However, careful examination of the texts and a reconstruction of the calendars for December 1880 and January/February 1881 enabled me to resolve nearly all problems. It should be noted that both Verdi and Boito sometimes write Fieschi for Fiesco; they also occasionally count the Prologue as Act I, resulting in a renumbering of the other acts. Boito's letters are preserved in the Library of the Villa Verdi at Sant'Agata; those of Verdi have recently been donated to the *Istituto di Studi Verdiani* in Parma by Boito's heirs, the Albertini family.

1. Genova, 2.XII.1880 – Verdi a Boito

Genova 2 Dic. 1880

Car. Boito

Ben trovato il Finale Terzo! Lo svenimento d'Otello mi piace più in questo Finale che nel posto ov'era prima. Solo non trovo, nè sento il *Pezzo* d'insieme! Ma di questo si potrà anche farne senza. Ne parleremo più tardi, ché ora, come le avrà detto Giulio, bisogna pensare ad altro. – Credevo in questo Boccanegra vi fosse molto a fare, ed ho visto che se possiamo trovare un *Bel Principio* di Finale, che darà varietà, molta varietà, al troppo di uniforme che vi è nel Dramma, il resto a farsi si riduce solo a qualche verso quà e là, per cambiare alcune frasi musicali et. . . .

Ci pensi dunque un po' e me ne scriva appena abbia trovato qualche cosa. Una buona stretta di mano in fretta dal Suo aff.

G. Verdi

2. Milano, 8.XII.1880 – Boito a Verdi

Mercoledì

Caro Maestro. Da idea nasce idea e bastano due idee sole per generare il dubbio che è il nemico naturale dell'azione. Ecco perché mi rivolgo a Lei affinché Ella mi ajuti ad escire da questa titubanza e mi indichi la via da seguire. Veramente la via era molto nettamente segnata nelle lettere ch' Ella scrisse a Giulio e sarebbe bastato ch'io mi fossi messo al lavoro senza chiedere altro, ma l'uomo non è sempre padrone del proprio cervello.

For the earlier correspondence between Verdi and Giulio Ricordi concerning the revision of *Simon Boccanegra*, the reader is referred to Franco Abbiati's monograph (*Verdi*, Milano 1959, vol. IV, pp. 130–137) and *I copialettere*, ed. G. Cesari and A. Luzio (Milano 1913, pp. 558–560). Verdi's first letter on this subject to Boito deals with *Otello* as well as with *Boccanegra*.

1. Genoa, 2.XII.1880 – Verdi to Boito

Genoa, 2 Dec. 1880

Dear Boito,

Well contrived, the Third Finale! I like Otello's fainting more in this Finale than where it was before. Only I can neither find nor feel the ensemble *Piece!* But we can even do without this. We'll discuss it later, since now, as Giulio must have told you, it is necessary to consider other things. – I believed there would be a lot to do in this *Boccanegra*, but I see now that if we can find a *Good Beginning* for the Finale, which will give variety, a lot of variety, to the monotonous uniformity which exists in the Drama, the remainder to be done is reduced to only some lines here and there, changing a couple of musical phrases, etc. ...

Therefore think about it a bit and write me as soon as you have come up with something.

A warm, if hasty, handshake from your affectionate

G. Verdi

Boito's letter, containing not only the outline of the Senate scene but also the alternative San Siro project, was for a long time considered lost, but has been rediscovered recently at Sant'Agata. The original text has been published by Gabriella Carrara Verdi in *Biblioteca 70*, *Busseto*, Anno 4 (Parma 1975), pp. 173–178; the translation is by Mr. Roger Parker.

2. Milan, 8.XII.1880 – Boito to Verdi

Wednesday

Dear Maestro,

One idea stimulates another, and two ideas are all that are needed to generate uncertainty – the natural enemy of any activity. That is why I am applying to you to help me out of my indecision and show me the path to follow. Certainly the path was very precisely indicated in the letter you wrote to Giulio, and had I set to work without looking for others, things

Ecco dunque come svilupperei la scena del Senato: l'indicazione più esatta dal punto di vista storico sarebbe la seguente:

Sala del consiglio nel Palazzo degli Abati.

Il Doge. Il Podestà. I consiglieri nobili. I consiglieri popolari. I consoli del mare. Conestabili.

Un usciere annuncia una donna la quale implora di parlare al Doge. Il Doge ordina che si dia ricetto a quella Donna ma la vedrà soltanto dopo che si sieno librati i destini della patria.

Il Doge annuncia al Consiglio che Toris il Re di Tartaria invia un ambasciatore richiedente pace ai Genovesi. (Veda Annali della Repubblica di Genova del Giustiniani T.II, L.IV).

Tutto il Consiglio ad una voce accorda la pace. Allora il Doge invoca che si cessi la guerra alla Repubblica di Venezia. Ripulse del Consiglio, tumulto.

Il Doge esclama: Coi barbari, cogli infedeli acconsentite alla pace e volete la guerra coi fratelli. E non vi bastano i vostri trionfi? e il sangue sparso sulle acque del Bosforo non *ha ancora estinta la vostra ferocia? Voi avete portato il vostro vessillo vittorioso sulle onde del Tirreno, dell'Adriatico, dell'Eusino, dell'Ionio, dell'Egeo,* e qui possiamo servirci dei più bei brani della lettera V del XIV Libro, *epistolario di Petrarca.* Specialmente là dove dice: *bello è superare l'avversario alla prova del brando; bellissimo è vincerlo per magnanimità di cuore* e dove parla così liricamente degli splendori della riviera (purché questa ultima digressione non prolunghi troppo la scena) ma è così bello là dove dice: *ed ammirato il nocchiero alla novità dello spettacolo lasciavasi cadere il remo dalle mani e fermava per meraviglia la barca a mezzo il corso.* Pure la perorazione del Doge deve terminar fieramente e interrotta quà e là da qualche grido della moltitudine; i popolari stanno per la pace, i nobili per la guerra. Antagonismo assai vigoroso fra nobili e plebei. Tumulto alla porta della sala, è annunciato l'arresto d'un nobile il quale col ferro in pugno voleva penetrar nel consiglio. Nobili e popolari, veementemente, vogliono che questo nobile s'avanzi. Entra Gabriello Adorno il quale accusa il Doge d'aver fatto rapire Amelia Grimaldi. Sorpresa e sdegno dei nobili; il Doge rimane come fulminato e ordina che si faccia comparire la donna che poco prima chiedeva aiuto e asilo nel palazzo. È Amelia che si getta ai piedi del Doge e che annuncia d'essersi salvata. Qui troverebbero posto alcuni versi coi quali il Doge ringrazia il Cielo per aver salvata Amelia e l'atto terminerebbe come nell'opera già esistente.

Passiamo all'esposizione dell'altra idea:

È basata su questo concetto: fondere in un atto solo i pezzi principali dei due atti intermedi, saltando a piè pari le scene X. XI. XII colle quali si

would have been satisfactory – but a man is not always master of his own mind.

Here then is how I would develop the Senate scene. The most precise plan, historically speaking, would be this:

Council chamber in the *Palazzo degli Abati*.

The Doge. The Podestà. The noble councillors. The popular councillors. The maritime consuls. Constables.

An usher announces a woman who begs to speak to the Doge. The Doge gives orders that he will receive the woman, but only after the affairs of state have been discussed.

The Doge announces to the Council that Toris, King of the Tartars, is sending an ambassador to ask for peace with the Genoese. (See *Annals of the Genoese Republic* by Giustiniani, Vol. II Bk. IV). With one voice the whole Council agrees to peace. The Doge then asks for an end to the war with the Venetian Republic. This is rejected by the Council amid uproar.

The Doge exclaims: With barbarians, with unbelievers you agree to peace, but you want war with your brothers. Are you not satisfied with your triumphs? Has not the blood shed on the Bosporus *dissolved your fierce anger? You have carried your victorious standard on the waters of the Tyrrhenian, the Adriatic, the Black Sea, the Ionian and the Aegean*, and here we can use some of the most beautiful passages from Letter V, Book XIV of *Petrarch's Letters*. Especially where he says: *It is a fine thing to overcome your adversary by force of arms; it is even finer to conquer him through the magnanimity of your heart* ... and also where he speaks so lyrically about the splendours of the seashore (provided that the digression doesn't prolong the scene too much), because these lines are so beautiful: ... *and, suprised by the freshness of the scene, the boatman let the oars fall from his hands and marvelling, stopped the boat in midcourse.* However, the Doge's peroration must finish strongly, and be interrupted from time to time by cries from the crowd – the people want peace, the nobles war. Sharp antagonism between the nobles and the plebeians. A disturbance at the door of the chamber, a nobleman is arrested trying to break into the council, sword in hand. Both the nobles and the people vehemently desire that this noble be allowed in. Gabriello Adorno enters, and accuses the Doge of having caused Amelia Grimaldi's abduction. Surprise and indignation from the nobles; the Doge seems thunderstruck and orders that the woman who a short time before had been asking for help and asylum in the palace be brought forward. It is Amelia Grimaldi, who throws herself at the Doge's feet, announcing that she has been saved. Here there would be room for some lines in which the Doge gives thanks to Heaven for having saved Amelia, and the act would finish as it does in the original version.

conchiude ora il II° atto (ossia il I°, computando il prologo) e finire tutto quest'atto (rifuso) col *terzetto* col quale termina l'attuale penultim' atto. Fatto questo, aggiungere un atto intiero, nuovo, non lungo e collocarlo al posto del penultim' atto.

Parliamo prima di tutto del modo di raggiungere la fusione dei due atti intermedj. Anzi tutto conviene semplificare gli avvenimenti. Rinunziare al rapimento d'Amelia. Vediamo.

Atto I°
Giardino de' Grimaldi

Scena Iª – Amelia sola
Scena IIª – Amelia e Gabriele
Scena IIIª, IV, VI, VII come stanno

Si farebbe senza la scena Vª per poter far seguire alla IV la VI senza interruzione e senza mutamento di luogo e quindi il duetto fra il Doge e Amelia. Dopo il duetto Amelia s'allontana lentamente mentre segue rapidissima la scena VIII fra il Doge e Paolo [;] in questa scena bisogna aggiungere una minaccia di Paolo, egli è l'anima della fazione popolare e muoverà una rivolta se il Doge non gli cede Amelia. Il Doge irremovibile accetta la disfida e ricusa a Paolo di dargli Amelia. Paolo esce. Amelia non è ancora molto lontana nel giardino, il Doge la chiama per dirle addio e abbracciarla in quell'ora di periglio. Sull'abbraccio del padre e della figlia entra Gabriele, impugna la spada per avventarsi sul Doge. Amelia difende il padre. Segue il terzetto, l'atto si chiude come sta ora colle grida d' *all'armi*.

Atto II° (penultimo)

L'interno della Chiesa di S. Siro, attigua alle case dei Boccanegra (antico chiostro dei Benedettini). La chiesa è piena d'armati, sulle loggie i balestrieri, dal rosone centrale della facciata si sta caricando una catapulta. Al di fuori grida e tumulto d'assalitori, trombe, nell'interno dall'altare un sacerdote benedice i combattenti, Gabriele è sulla loggia centrale accanto alla catapulta in osservazione, Boccanegra dà dei comandi, entrano degli esploratori; i Fieschi, i D'Oria, i Grimaldi si sono uniti a quella parte dei faziosi popolari che assaltano la Chiesa. Al Boccanegra sono rimasti fedeli i consoli

Let us go on to an outline of the other idea:

It is based on this concept: to fuse into a single act the principal numbers of the two middle acts, omitting completely scenes X, XI and XII, which now finish Act II (or Act I if you count the Prologue), and to close this new, fused act with the *terzetto* which now finishes the existing penultimate act. Having done this, we would add an entirely new act – not a long one – and put it in place of the original penultimate act.

Let us discuss first of all a means of fusing the two middle acts. It would be better to simplify the plot, to give up the abduction of Amelia. Let's see.

Act I
The Garden of the Grimaldis

Scene I – Amelia, alone
Scene II – Amelia and Gabriele
Scenes III, IV, VI, VII as they are now

We would do without Scene V, thus allowing Scenes IV and VI to follow without interruption and without a change of location, and follow all this with the duet between the Doge and Amelia. After the duet Amelia moves slowly away and Scene VIII, between the Doge and Paolo, follows as quickly as possible. In this last scene we need to add a threat from Paolo, who is the guiding spirit of the popular faction and will instigate a revolt if the Doge does not give him Amelia. The immovable Doge accepts the challenge and refuses to give Amelia to Paolo. Paolo leaves. Amelia is still quite near at hand in the garden and the Doge calls her to say goodbye and to embrace her in this hour of danger. As father and daughter embrace Gabriele enters, drawing his sword to attack the Doge. Amelia protects her father. The *terzetto* follows and the act closes as it does now, with shouts of *"To arms."*

Act II (penultimate)

Inside the chuch of S. Siro, adjacent to Boccanegra's dwelling (the ancient cloister of the Benedictines). The church is full of armed men, on the balconies are crossbowmen, by the central rose at the front stands a loaded catapult. Outside, cries and uproar from the attackers, trumpets; inside at the altar a priest blesses the soldiers, Gabriele is on lookout, on the central balcony, near the catapult, Boccanegra is giving orders, some scouts enter; the Fieschi, the D'Oria and the Grimaldi have joined forces with that part of the popular faction now attacking the church. Remaining loyal to Bocca-

del mare con tutto l'esercito di marina e i balestrieri e la maggior parte del popolo. Ad ogni tratto Gabriele chiede se si deve lanciare la catapulta (gli antichi Genovesi chiamavano le catapulte *trabocchi*) ma il Doge s'oppone. Intanto sono colpite fragorosamente le porte della chiesa, la *grossa campana* suona a stormo. Arriva un annuncio d'un esploratore che racconta come gli assalitori sieno accerchiati da una forte schiera di balestrieri sbucati da una casa dei Boccanegra (gli esploratori entrano ed escono da una porta che comunica alla casa di Simone).

La porta della chiesa minaccia ruina, Boccanegra con un gruppo di balestrieri si mette di fronte alla porta, la porta crolla, entra Fiesco a capo d'un turbine di nobili e popolani e ferisce alla mano il Boccanegra, ma d'un tratto vedendo la chiesa piena d'armati pronti ad irrompere gli assalitori s'arrestano intimoriti. Boccanegra, ferito, mostra a Fiesco la catapulta minacciosa sulla testa degli assalitori e giura che non la scaglierà e che nessuna offesa verrà fatta ai rivoltosi se questi in quel sacro asilo ove sono promettono solennemente la pace.

Momento di silenzio. Intanto Paolo che è il capo della rivolta chiede sommessamente a Pietro che è fra i sostenitori di Boccanegra (per tradirlo) se non vi sia speranza pei rivoltosi. Pietro risponde che sono accerchiati dai balestrieri e che Boccanegra li ha colti nei suoi lacci. Allora Paolo strappa la fascia della sua spada e dopo aver messo su quella fascia alcune goccie d'un'ampolla di veleno che estrae dal suo giustacuore getta la spada ai piedi di Boccanegra e inginocchiandosi davanti ad esso gli chiede di fasciargli la ferito della mano sanguinosa. Allora tutti gli assalitori mettono le loro armi nelle guaìne. Boccanegra si lascia bendare la mano e dice a Paolo d'alzarsi e gli perdona. Intanto giunge Amelia dalla porta da dove escirono gli esploratori. Gabriele è sceso dalla loggia. Boccanegra solennemente fa giurar la pace e dà le formule del giuramento e vuole che questa pace fra nobili e plebei sia consacrata dalle nozze dell'Adorno con Amelia sua figlia. – *Giuramento* che avrà le proporzioni volute da un ampio e forte pezzo musicale. Così finirebbe l'atto. – Vediamo ora i vantaggi di questo secondo progetto: Assistere all'avvelenamento del Doge e perciò assistere ad un fatto che lega colla catastrofe finale e quindi la rende più evidente, più tragica. Secondo vantaggio: rappresentare un fatto (registrato negli annali del Giustiniani Libro IV anno 1356) che diffonde un poco di colore storico e locale sul dramma. (Quelle chiese d'un tratto trasformate in trinciere, in fortezze si riscontrano nella storia genovese). Mostrare al pubblico il Boccanegra mentre compie un grande atto di forza e di magniminità e colpito dal tradimento di Paolo appunto mentre compie una azione ge-

negra are the maritime consuls, the navy, the crossbowmen, and most of the common people. Gabriele repeatedly asks permission to fire the catapult (the old Genoese called their catapults *trabocchi*), but the Doge forbids it. As the doors of the church receive resounding blows, *the great bell* rings the alarm. A scout arrives with a message recounting how the attackers have been surrounded by a strong group of crossbowmen who came from one of the Boccanegra houses (the scouts enter and leave by a door which leads to Simone's house).

The door of the church is on the verge of collapse; Boccanegra stands in front of the door, with a group of crossbowmen, the door gives way, Fiesco enters at the head of a swirling mass of nobles and common people and wounds Boccanegra in the hand, but as the attackers suddenly see that the church is full of armed men ready to burst upon them they become frightened and hesitate. The wounded Boccanegra shows Fiesco the catapult, which stands threateningly over the heads of the attackers, and swears that he will not fire it, nor will any assault be made against the insurgents if they, in the sacred place where they are standing, will solemnly promise peace.

A moment of silence. Paolo, who is leading the revolt, quietly asks Pietro, who is among Boccanegra's supporters in order to betray the Doge, whether there is any hope for the insurgents. Pietro replies that they are surrounded by crossbowmen and completely in Boccanegra's power. Paolo then tears off the sash which holds his sword, and after putting on this sash some drops from a phial of poison he pulls from his jerkin, throws the sword at Boccanegra's feet. He kneels before Boccanegra and asks permission to dress the Doge's bloody hand. At this all the attackers sheath their swords. Boccanegra allows Paolo to bandage his hand, then tells him to get up, and finally pardons him. Meanwhile, Amelia enters through the door used by the scouts. Gabriele has come down from the balcony. Boccanegra solemnly swears peace, gives the form of the oath, and asks that the concord between nobles and common people be consecrated by the marriage of Adorno to his daughter Amelia. – A *Giuramento* which will be grand enough to sustain a broad, powerful musical number. The act would end here. – Let's now look at the advantages of this second project: the audience will see the poisoning of the Doge, and thus be present at an occasion which ties up with the final catastrophe, making the latter more obvious, more tragic. Second advantage: it depicts an occasion (registered in the annals of Giustiniani, Bk. IV, for the year 1356) which will add a little local and historical colour to the drama. (In Genoese history one meets these churches which are suddenly transformed into front-line fortresses). The public will see Boccanegra in the

nerosa e grande. Altro vantaggio: far derivare le nozze logicamente dal fatto che le precede.

Ma il tenore non avrà una scena ove far mostra della sua virtuosità? Questa scena potrebbe aver luogo in principio dell'ultim' atto.

————————

Ecco. Le ho detto tutto ciò che m'è passato per la mente in questi giorni mentre mi tuffavo nella lettura delle storie Genovesi. Indovino le critiche ch'Ella farà alla prima come alla seconda idea.

La scena del Senato può parer fredda a meno che il concetto patriottico e politico che la anima sia reso con tale calore di forma da renderlo drammatico, ma allora se questo concetto arriva a toccare l'emozione del dramma e a interessare l'uditorio un altro inciampo ci attende, l'arrivo di Gabriele (e poi d'Amelia) viene a interrompere questo concetto prima del suo esaurimento e la quistione di Venezia che ci ha tanto impressionati in sul principio non trova il suo scioglimento per causa del nuovo incidente. E allora sarà questo incidente nuovo che ci scapiterà e la fine dell'atto con esso.

La critica del secondo progetto non è molto recondita, quella guerra in chiesa può parer forse abbastanza nuova ma l'effetto teatrale può parere assai problematico. Abbiamo già un'azione cupa per sè stessa e l'atto che si aggiungerebbe non ne correggerebbe la tinta generale. Quella chiesa armata non è certo nè serena, nè gaja.

Il nostro compito, Maestro mio, è arduo. Il dramma che ci occupa è storto, pare un tavolo che tentenna, non si sa da che gamba, e, per quanto ci si provi a rincalzarlo, tentenna sempre. Non trovo in questo dramma nessun carattere di quelli che ci fanno esclamare: *è scolpito!* Nessun fatto che sia realmente *fatale* cioè indispensabile e potente, generato dalla ineluttabilità tragica.

Faccio una eccezione pel prologo, quello è veramente bello e nella sua cupa interezza è forte, solido tenebroso come un pezzo di basalte. Ma il prologo (sempre parlando della tragedia, da molti e molti anni non ho più avuto occasione di riudire la musica del Boccanegra) il prologo è la gamba diritta del tavolo, la sola che poggi solidamente, le altre tre, Ella lo sa meglio di me, zoppicano tutte. V'è molto intrigo e non molto costrutto.

Tutto in quel dramma è superficiale, tutti quei fatti sembrano ideati lì per lì, al momento, per occupare la scena materialmente, non hanno radici profonde nè vigorosi legami, non sono il risultato di caratteri, sono *apparenze di fatti*. Per correggere un simile dramma bisogna mutarlo.

act of demonstrating his force and magnanimity, and being struck down in the middle of a great and generous gesture. Another advantage: it makes the marriage derive logically from the action which precedes it. But the tenor will not have a scene in which he can display his virtuosity? This could take place at the beginning of the last act.

There it is then. I have told you everything that has passed through my mind while looking at books on Genoese history. I can guess the criticisms you will make, both of the first and the second idea.

The Senate scene could turn out to be lifeless unless the patriotic and political theme which inspires it is furnished with a lively dramatic form. But if this theme *does* succeed in touching the emotional core of the drama and in interesting the listener, another obstacle awaits us – the arrival of Gabriele (and later, Amelia) interrupts the theme before it has worked itself out fully, and because of this incident the question of Venice, which struck us so forcefully at the beginning, is never resolved. And so this new incident will be damaged and with it, the end of the act.

A criticism of the second project is fairly obvious – battles in church might perhaps seem rather novel, but the theatrical effect would present some difficulties. We have a plot which is naturally sombre already, and the additional act would do nothing to alter this. A church full of armed men certainly is neither peaceful nor joyful.

Our task, Maestro, is a hard one. The work we are dealing with is mis-shapen – like a wobbly table; but we don't know which leg is wrong, and however much we try to prop it up, it's still rickety. I do not find any character in the drama who makes me shout: *What a sharp profile!* No incident which is really *fatale*, that is to say indispensable and powerful, generated by the inevitability of the tragedy.

I'll make an exception of the Prologue, which is really beautiful and draws strength from its unrelieved grimness – solid and gloomy like a piece of basalt. But the Prologue (speaking always of the libretto – I have not had the chance to listen to the music of *Boccanegra* for many, many years), the Prologue is the secure leg of the table – the only one that rests on a solid base; you know better than I that the other three are all shaky. There's a great deal of incident, and not much construction.

Everything in the drama is superficial – all the episodes seem planned on the spur of the moment, literally to fill up the stage; they have neither deep roots nor strong connecting links, they are only *the semblance of real events*. To correct such a drama we will have to change it.

S'Ella, Maestro mio, potesse leggere nel mio pensiero (e perchè usar reticenze o mentire?) vi leggerebbe una grande ripugnanza a ripigliar questo dramma per rappresentarlo, questo dramma esente così di virtù profonde come di pregi leggieri, questo dramma, (a parte il prologo) mancante di potenza tragica come di *teatralità*.

Pure io metto il mio desiderio nel suo ed ora che le ho aperto l'animo mio, le dichiaro che farò ciò ch'Ella crede di dover fare visto che il supremo arbitro in una tale quistione è Lei, non io.

Attendo dunque la sua decisione per fare o il Senato o la Chiesa di S. Siro o per far nulla di tutto ciò.

———

Lei non *sente* il nesso d'assieme del 3° atto dell'Otello, per verità non lo sento neppur io, ne faremo senza, tanto meglio, l'importante è che la fine dell'atto ci sembri felicemente raggiunta.

Avrò in quella fine qualche verso da mutare.

———

Non voglio terminare questo *fascicolo* senza dirle il riconoscente affetto ch' Ella ha destato nell'animo mio per una certa frase detta da Lei l'inverno scorso a Parigi al Barone Blaze de Bury, frase che mi onora altamente e che lessi con emozione in une delle ultime rassegne musicali della *Revue des deux mondes*. Ho tenuti in freno questi ringraziamenti per più di un mese, per non tediarla, ma ora che mi si è offerto il modo di scriverle, li lascio andare a briglia sciolta verso di Lei.

Tanti e tanti saluti alla sua Signora.

suo aff.mo
Arrigo Boito

If, Maestro, you could read my thoughts (and why be reticent, or lie?), you would see a strong aversion to reviving this drama in performance. It portrays profound virtues as though they had little value and (apart from the prologue) is lacking in tragic power and *theatricality*.

However I put my wishes entirely at your disposal and now that I have opened up my mind, let me say that I will do whatever you think necessary. You of course are the supreme arbiter in these matters, not I.

I await then your decision on whether to do either the Senate or the Church of S. Siro, or nothing at all.

———

You don't *feel* the connecting link in Act III of *Otello* – to be honest: neither do I. We'll do it without, all the better; the important thing is to reach the end of the act successfully.

I shall have to change a few lines in this ending.

———

I don't want to end this lengthy letter without telling you of the grateful affection you awoke in my heart by making a certain remark to Baron Blaze de Bury in Paris last winter – a remark which does me high honour, and which I read with emotion in one of the latest music chronicles in the *Revue des deux mondes*. Not wishing to bore you, I have held back these thanks for more than a month, but now that the opportunity to write them presents itself, I am giving my gratitude full rein.

Many kind regards to your wife.

Your affectionate
Arrigo Boito.

3. Genova, 11.XII.1880 – Verdi a Boito

Gen. 11 Dic. 1880

Car. Boito,

O il senato . . . o la Chiesa di S. Siro . . . o far nulla . . .

Far nulla sarebbe la cosa migliore, ma ragioni, non d'interesse, ma, dirò così, di professione m'impediscono di abbandonare l'idea di aggiustare questo Boccanegra, almeno senza aver tentato prima di farne qualche cosa. Fra parentesi, è interesse di tutti che la *Scala* viva! . . . Il cartellone di quest'anno, ahimè, è deplorabile! Benissimo l'opera di Ponchielli, ma il resto? Eterni Dei!!!! Vi sarebbe l'opera che sveglierebbe un grand' interesse nel pubblico, e non capisco perchè Autore, ed Editore si ostinino a rifiutarla! Parlo del Mefistofele. Il momento sarebbe propizio, ed Ella renderebbe servizio all'Arte ed a tutti.

L'atto da Lei ideato nella Chiesa di S. Siro è stupendo sotto ogni rapporto. Bello per novità – bello per colore storico – bello dal lato scenico-musicale; ma mi impegnerebbe troppo, e non potrei sobbarcarmi a tanto lavoro.

Rinunciando disgraziatamente a quest'Atto, bisogna attenersi alla Scena del Senato, che fatta da Lei, non dubito possa riescir fredda. Le sue critiche son giuste, ma Ella ingolfata in lavori più elevati, ed avendo in mente Otello, mira ad una perfezione che qui sarebbe impossibile raggiungere. Io guardo più in basso, e, più ottimista di Lei, non dispero. Convengo che il tavolo è zoppo, ma, aggiustando qualche gamba, credo, potrà reggersi. Convengo ancora, che non vi sono di quei caratteri (ben rari sempre!) che vi fanno esclamare "è scolpito"; nonostante a me pare che vi sia nei personaggi di *Fiesco* e *Simone* qualche cosa da trarne buon partito.

Infine tentiamo, e facciamo questo Finale col respettivo Ambasciatore Tartaro, colle lettere di Petrarca et . . . et . . . et . . . Tentiamo, ripeto: Noi non siamo poi tanto inesperti da non capire anche prima cosa sarà per

The opera of Ponchielli referred to by Verdi in his next letter is *Il figliuol prodigo*. Other operas performed during the same Scala season were *Ruy Blas* (Marchetti), *Ernani*, *Der Freischütz*, *Don Giovanni*, *La Sonnambula*, *Semiramide*, *Il Guarany* (Gomes) and finally also *Mefistofele*.

3. Genoa, 11.XII.1880 – Verdi to Boito

Gen. 11 Dec. 1880

Dear Boito

Either the Senate . . . or the Church of S. Siro . . . or do nothing at all . . .

To do nothing at all would be the best thing, but reasons, not financial but let us rather say professional, prevent me from abandoning the idea of revising this *Boccanegra* without at least having tried first to make something of it. Parenthetically, it is in the interest of us all that *La Scala should survive!* . . . The repertoire for this year, alas, is deplorable! Fine and good the opera by Ponchielli, but the rest? Good God!!!! There is one opera which would arouse great interest from the public and I don't understand why Author and Publisher persist in refusing it! I'm talking about *Mefistofele*. The moment would be right and you would render a service to Art and to all of us.

––––––

The act you envisioned in the Church of S. Siro is stupendous from every angle. Beautiful in its novelty – beautiful for its historical colour – beautiful from the point of view of musical theatre; but it would demand too much of me and I could not undertake so much work.

Unfortunately having to give up this idea, it is necessary to stick to the Scene of the Senate, which as written by you will prove anything but theatrically cold. Your criticisms are correct but you, enveloped in more elevated labours and having Otello in mind, are aiming at a perfection which here would be impossible to attain. My scope is more limited, and, more optimistic than you, I don't give up. I agree that the table is wobbly, but after some of the legs are fixed I believe it will be able to stand upright. I agree also that there are none of those characters (always very rare!) which cause you to exclaim "what a sharp profile" but nevertheless it seems to me that there is something in the figures of *Fiesco* and *Simone* which could be put to good use.

At least let's try, and let's write this Finale with the Tartar ambassador,

succedere sul Teatro. – Se a Lei non pesa, e se ha tempo, si metta immediatamente al lavoro. Io intanto guarderò di raddrizzare quà e là le molte gambe storte delle mie note, e . . . vedremo!

Con affetto mi dico

Aff.
G. Verdi

4. Genova, 28.XII.1880 – Verdi a Boito

Genova 28 Dic. 1880

Car. Boito,

Bellissima questa Scena del Senato, piena di movimento, di color locale, con versi elegantissimi e potentissimi come al solito Lei fà. Stà bene per i versi da cambiare nel principio del Terz'Atto, e benissimo l'avvelenamento del Doge in quel modo. Ma per disgrazia mia, il pezzo è vasto assai, difficile a musicare, e non so se, ora che non sono più *dans le mouvement*, avrò il tempo per rimettermi in sella per far questo, ed accomodare tutto il resto.

Mi permetta adesso alcune osservazioni per semplice mio schiarimento.

1°. Crede Ella necessario far presentire nel principio che Amelia è salva, ed *invoca giustizia?*

2°. Crede Ella che sia bastante l'affare solo di Tartaria per unire il Senato? Non si potrebbe aggiungervi altro affare di Stato per es: una presa di Corsari; e magari la guerra di Venezia maledetta dal Poeta? Tutto, s'intende, alla sfuggita, in pochissimi versi?

3°. Se Adorno dice "*Ho ucciso Lorenzino perchè mi rapia la sposa*" ed Amelia "*Salva lo sposo mio*" si viene a distruggere la Scena dell'Atto Terzo fra il Doge ed Amelia. Scena poco importante per se stessa, ma che prepara assai bene il sonno del Doge ed il Terzetto. A me pare che l'azione non perderebbe nulla, se quando il Doge dice "*Perchè impugni l'acciar?*" Gabriele rispondesse "*Tu facesti rapire Amelia Grimaldi . . . Vile Corsaro coronato muori*".

with the letters of Petrarch, etc ... etc ... etc ... Let's try, I repeat: after all we are not so inexpert as not to realize, even beforehand, what will succeed in the Theatre. – If it is not a burden for you, and if you have time, go right to work. Meanwhile I'll seek to straighten out here and there the many crooked legs of my notes, and ... we'll see!

With affection I sign myself

G. Verdi

Verdi's letter of 28 December is obviously the reply to a lost letter by Boito. For "Third Act" one should read "Second Act".

4. Genoa, 28.XII.1880 – Verdi to Boito

Genoa 28 Dec. 1880

Dear Boito

This Scene in the Senate is wonderful, full of movement, of local colour, with the very elegant and powerful lines which you usually write. I agree about the lines to be changed at the beginning of the Third Act, and I consider very effective the poisoning of the Doge in that way. But to my misfortune, the piece is very long, difficult to set to music, and I don't know, now that I'm no longer *dans le mouvement*, if I'll have the time to get back into the saddle to write this scene and to arrange all the rest.

Allow me now several observations simply for my own clarification.

1° Do you think it necessary to have it foreseen from the beginning that Amelia is safe, and *invokes justice?*

2° Do you think that the matter of Tartary alone is sufficient to unite the Senate? Couldn't some other affair of State be added, for example an attack of Corsairs; and even the war with Venice cursed by the Poet? Everything, it is understood, almost in passing, in very few lines?

3° If Adorno says "*I killed Lorenzino because he abducted my fiancée*" and Amelia "*Save my beloved*" this will destroy the scene in the Third Act between the Doge and Amelia. Not a very important scene in itself, but one which leads very well to the Doge's slumber scene and the Terzetto. It seems to me that the action would lose nothing if, when the Doge says "*Why have you drawn your sword*", Gabriele replied "*You had Amelia Grimaldi abducted ... Vile enthroned Pirate, die!*"

D[OGE]   Ferisci . . .
G[ABRIELE]   Amelia
T[UTTI]   Amelia
DOGE   *Adorno: tu la vergin difendi: t'ammiro, e t'assolvo . . .*
         Amelia, dì come tu fosti rapita et. et.

Il resto benissimo. Stupendo dal "*Plebe, Patrizi, Popolo*" sino alla fine che chiuderemo col "*Sia maledetto*".
Mi risponda al più presto.
Auguri sincerissimi.

G. Verdi

5. Genova, 8.I.1881 – Verdi a Boito

Genova 8 del 1881

Car. Boito
Non abbia rimorso d'avermi rubato il tempo. Non mi sono affatto occupato finora di musica. Ora però ci penso, anzi ho pensato tutt'oggi a questo Boccanegra, ed ecco cosa mi pare si potrebbe fare,
Passo il Prologo di cui cambierò forse il primo Rec: e qualche battuta quà e là in orchestra.
Nel primo Atto toglierei nel primo pezzo la Cabaletta, non perchè sia una Cabaletta, ma perchè è brutta assai. Cambierei il Preludio, a cui unirei il *Cantabile* della Donna cambiando l'orchestrazione e ne farei un *pezzo unito*. Ripiglierei alla fine un movimento d'orchestra del Preludio su cui Amelia direbbe . . . *Spuntò il giorno* . . . *Ei non vien!* . . . o qualche cosa di simile. Mi aggiusti dunque un pajo di versi piccoli a frasi spezzate . . . Non amerei quelle parole di gelosia d'Amelia!
La Romanza interna del Tenore resterebbe tal e quale.

D[OGE]   *Strike . . .*
G[ABRIELE]   *Amelia*
T[UTTI]   *Amelia*
DOGE   *Adorno: You defended the girl: I admire you, and I forgive you . . .*
         Amelia, explain how you were abducted etc. etc.

The rest very good, Stupendous from "*Plebeians, Patricians, People*" up
to the end, which we shall close with "*May he be cursed*".
Answer me as quickly as possible. Very best wishes.

G. Verdi

We must leave unanswered the question of whether the first line of Verdi's letter of 8 January
refers to a lost letter by Boito. It is possible that the composer merely anticipated Boito's
feelings. In this letter the "first act" should be taken literally; it does not refer to the Prologue.
The final passage is of great importance, since it proves that Verdi set his librettos in a
'chronological' order, in contrast to his predecessors who conceived of their works in a mosaic-
like way.

5. Genoa, 8.I.1881 – Verdi to Boito

Genoa, 8th of 1881

Dear Boito,

Don't feel remorse for having wasted time. I haven't up to now done
anything at all about the music. However, now I am thinking about it, or
rather I spent the whole day considering *Boccanegra*, and here is what it
seems to me could be done.

I leave the Prologue, of which I shall perhaps change the opening
Recitative and some bars here and there in the orchestration.

In the first act, I would cut the Cabaletta to the first piece, not because it is
a Cabaletta, but because it is very ugly. I would change the Prelude, which I
would link to the *Cantabile* for the soprano, changing its orchestration, and
I would make a *unified piece* of it. At the end I would repeat a part of the
orchestral Prelude on which Amelia would say . . . *The day has dawned . . .*
He has not come! . . . or something similar. Therefore add for me a couple
of short lines in broken phrases . . . I would not like those words of jealousy
from Amelia!

Nel Duetto seguente cambierei la forma della Cabaletta ed Ella non avrebbe nulla a fare . . .

––––––

Nella Scena V tra Fieschi e Gabriele amerei qualche parola di più nel Rec: dopo il verso "*A nostre nozze assenti* [?]" Se il Pubblico perde la parola "*Umil*" non capisce più nulla. Se dicesse per es: "*Ascolta . . . alto segreto*" et. et. Queste son sempre parole che fanno drizzare le orecchie al pubblico. E però, se crede, aggiunga un pajo di versi, oppure nò, come vuole. Quello che a me preme si è di cambiare il Duetto tra Fieschi e Gab: "*Paventa o Doge*". È troppo fiero, e non dice nulla. Io amerei invece che Fieschi, quasi padre d'Amelia, benedisse i futuri giovani sposi. Potrebbe sortirne un momento patetico che sarebbe un raggio di luce fra tanto scuro. Per mantenere il colore introduca pure un po' di *cittadini affetti*. Fieschi può dire . . . *ama quell'angelo . . . Ma dopo Dio . . . la Patria* et . . . Tutte parole buone per far drizzare le orecchie . . . Infine otto bei versi a Fieschi ed altrettanti a Gabriele, affettuosi, patetici, semplici per farvi sù un po' di melodia, o qualche cosa che ne abbia almeno l'apparenza. Ah se si potesse far ritornare in scena Amelia e fare un Terzettino a voci sole! che bella cosa scrivere a tre voci! . . . Amelia e Gabriele inginocchiati, Fiesco in mezzo, alto, che li benedice! . . . Ma capisco che oltre la difficoltà di far ritornare in scena Amelia avressimo [*sic*] la scena Finale dell'ultimo atto quasi simile . . .

Mi sono spiegato? – Non ne sono ben sicuro. Procuri d'indovinare quello che non ho saputo dire, e mi mandi intanto questi pochi versi al più presto possibile, che domani o dopo gli dirò del resto. Io intanto comincierei a lavorare al Primo pezzo di questo primo Atto, se non altro per mettermi *dans le mouvement* prima di arrivare al Finale. Io vorrei fare tutto in seguito come se si trattasse d'un' opera nuova.

Aspetto, e mi creda suo

G. Verdi

The off-stage Romanza for the Tenor would remain as it is.

In the following Duet I would change the form of the Cabaletta and you would have nothing to do . . .

In Scene V between Fieschi and Gabriele I would like a few extra words in the Recitative after the line "*Do you consent to our marriage*". If the audience loses the word *humble* it would understand nothing that follows. If he said for example: "*Listen . . . a deep secret*" etc. etc. . . . These are words which always catch the ears of the public. And therefore, if you think best, add a couple of lines, or don't, as you wish. What means most to me is to change the Duet between Fieschi and Gab., "*Tremble o Doge*". It's too cruel and says nothing. I would rather instead that Fieschi, practically Amelia's father, bless the future young couple. It could produce a touching moment which would be a ray of light amidst so much gloom. So as to maintain the colour, introduce also a bit of *patriotic love*. Fieschi can say . . . *Love that Angel . . . But after God . . . your Country* etc. . . . All good words for making the ears perk up . . . Eight beautiful lines then for Fieschi and an equal number for Gabriele, affectionate, moving, simple, something on which to write a bit of melody, or something which at least has the appearance of such. If it could only be arranged to have Amelia come back on stage and to write a little Terzetto for solo voices! What a lovely thing to write for three voices! . . . Amelia and Gabriele kneeling, Fiesco standing in between, blessing them! . . . But I see that apart from the difficulty of bringing Amelia back on stage we would have a scene almost identical to the final scene of the last act . . .

Have I explained myself? – I'm not quite sure. Try to guess what I haven't been able to say and meanwhile send me these few lines as soon as possible, as tomorrow or the day after I'll tell you the rest. Meanwhile I shall begin to work on the first piece of this first act, if for no other reason than to put myself *dans le mouvement* before coming to the Finale. I would like to do everything in sequence, just as if a new opera were concerned.

I am waiting – believe me yours.

G. Verdi

6. Milano, 9[?].I.1881 – Boito a Verdi

Caro Maestro,
   Veda gli effetti della miopia congiunti a quelli della distrazione: trovo sul
tavolo questo foglio che va unito alle varianti del prim'atto. Poco male. Spero
che lo riceverà col resto.
   Saluti affettuosi

                                                           Arrigo Boito

VARIANTI PER L'ATTO I.

SCENA I.

(*Prima della romanza del tenore*).

.   .   .   .
S'inalba in ciel, ma l'amoroso canto
Non s'ode ancora.
Ei mi terge ogni di, come l'aurora
La rugiada dei fior, del ciglio il pianto.

AGGIUNTA AL DIALOGO FRA GABRIELLO E FIESCO

SCENA V.

.   .   .   .
GABRIELLO   A nostre nozze assenti?
ANDREA   Alto mistero
                   Sulla vergine incombe.
GABRIELLO   E qual?
ANDREA   Se parlo

Luzio (*Carteggi verdiani* II, p. 80) presumes that the following letter (actually two installments of one letter) dates from December 1880. Obviously the editor was not aware of the fact that between 11 and 28 December Boito had already replied to no. 3 (see the commentary to no. 4, above). The present letter was probably written on 9 January, since it was answered by no. 8, dated 10 January. Note that for the role of the tenor Boito uses the name Gabriello instead of Gabriele.

6. Milan, 9[?].I.1881 – Boito to Verdi

Dear Maestro,
Here you see the effects of short-sightedness combined with absent-mindedness: I find on my desk this sheet which should go together with the variants for the first act. Little harm. I hope you will receive it with the rest.
Affectionate greetings

Arrigo Boito

VARIANTS FOR ACT I

SCENE I

(*Before the romanza for the tenor*)

. . . .
The sky grows bright, but the amourous song
Is not yet heard,
Each day, as the dawn
Dries the dew on the flower, it dries my tears.

ADDITIONS TO THE DIALOGUE BETWEEN GABRIELLO AND FIESCO

SCENE V

. . . .

GABRIELLO	Do you consent to our marriage?
ANDREA	A dark secret
	Enshrouds the girl.
GABRIELLO	What is it?
ANDREA	If I speak

Forse tu più non l'amerai.

GABRIELLO   Non teme
Ombra d'arcani l'amor mio! T'ascolto.

ANDREA   Amelia tua d'umile stirpe nacque ...

GABRIELLO   La figlia dei Grimaldi?!

ANDREA   No. La figlia
Dei Grimaldi morì fra consacrate
Vergini in Pisa ecc. ecc. ecc.

ATTO I.

´(*Chiusa della Scena V dopo i versi sciolti*).

. . . .

ANDREA   Pio guerrier, del tempo antico
L'alta fede in te rampolla;
No, la spada tua non crolla
Per nemico odio crudel (*abbracciandolo*).
Vieni a me, ti benedico
Nell'amore e nella guerra,
Sii fedele alla tua terra,
L'angiol tuo ti sia fedel.

GABRIELLO   Del tuo labbro il sacro detto
Come balsamo raccolsi,
Saldi son pel brando i polsi,
M'empie il petto un vasto ardor.
Se da te fui benedetto
L'alma mia più in me non langue,
Freme e m'agita nel sangue
Odio immenso e immenso amor.

VARIANTE PER LA SCENA DEL SENATO

SIMONE   Messeri il re di Tartaria vi porge
Pegni di pace e ricchi doni e annunzia
Schiuso l'Eusin alle liguri prore.
Acconsentite?

TUTTI   Sì.

Perhaps you will no longer love her.

GABRIELLO   My love does
Not fear the shadow of mystery! I am listening.

ANDREA   Your Amelia was born of common blood ...

GABRIELLO   The daughter of the Grimaldi?!

ANDREA   No. The daughter
Of the Grimaldi died in a convent
In Pisa etc. etc. etc.

ACT I

(End of Scene V after the recitative)

. . . .

ANDREA   Pious warrior, the great faith
Of ancient times finds support in you;
No, your sword falls not in front of
The cruel hate of the enemy (*embracing him*)
Come to me, I bless you
In love and in war.
Be faithful to your country,
May your angel be faithful to you.

GABRIELLO   From your lips the holy word
I received like balsam,
My hand is ready for the sword,
My heart is filled with an immense ardour.
If by you I've been blessed,
My spirit no longer fails me,
My blood boils and is agitated
By an immense hatred and an immense love.

CHANGES FOR THE SCENE IN THE SENATE

SIMONE   My lords, the king of Tartary sends you
Tokens of peace and rich gifts, and declares
The Eusin open to Ligurian ships.
Do you agree?

ALL   Yes.

SIMONE (*dopo una pausa*)	Ma d'altro voto Più generoso io vi richiedo.
ALCUNI	Parla.
SIMONE	La stessa voce che tuonò su Rienzi Vaticinio di gloria e poi di morte Or su Genova tuona. Ecco un messaggio Del romito di Sorga, ei per Venezia Supplica pace...
	(*s'incomincia a udire un tumulto lontano*)
PAOLO	Attenda alla sue rime Il cantor della bionda Avignonese.
SIMONE (*con forza*)	Messeri!... (*il tumulto s'avvicina*)
PIETRO	Qual clamor?
ALCUNI	D'onde tai grida? ecc. ecc. ecc. ecc.

ALTRA VARIANTE ALLA SCENA DEL SENATO
PRIMA DELL'ENTRATA D'AMELIA

. . . .

SIMONE (*a Gabriello*)	Perché impugni l'acciar?
GABRIELLO	Ho trucidato Lorenzino.
POPOLO	Assassin.
FIESCHI	Ei la Grimaldi Avea rapita.
SIMONE	(Orror!)
POPOLO	Menti!
GABRIELLO	Quel vile Pria di morir disse che un uom possente Al crimine l'ha spinto.
PIETRO (*a Paolo*)	(Ah! sei scoperto).
SIMONE (*con agitazione*)	E il nome suo?
GABRIELLO (*fissando il Doge con tremenda ironia*)	T'acqueta! Il reo si spense Pria di svelarlo.

SIMONE (*after a moment of silence*)	But for other agreement More magnanimous, I ask you.
SOME SENATORS	Speak.
SIMONE	The same voice which thundered over Rienzi Prophecies of glory and then of death Now thunders over Genoa. Here is a message From the hermit of Sorga, he pleads for peace On behalf of Venice . . . (*A distant uproar begins to be heard*)
PAOLO	Let the poet of the fair Avignonaise attend to his rhymes.
SIMONE (*forcefully*)	My Lords! . . . (*the noise draws nearer*)
PIETRO	What is this noise?
SOME	From where this screaming? etc. etc. etc. etc.

FURTHER CHANGE TO THE SCENE IN THE SENATE PRIOR TO THE ENTRANCE OF AMELIA

. . . .

SIMONE (*to Gabriello*)	Why have you drawn your sword?
GABRIELLO	I have killed Lorenzino.
PEOPLE	Assassin.
FIESCHI	He had abducted The Grimaldi girl.
SIMONE	(Horrors!)
PEOPLE	You are lying!
GABRIELLO	Before dying The fiend said that a man of authority Had driven him to the crime.
PIETRO (*to Paolo*)	(Ah! you're discovered).
SIMONE (*agitated*)	And his name?
GABRIELLO (*glaring at the Doge with great sarcasm*)	Stay calm! The villain died Before revealing it.

SIMONE	Che vuoi dir?
GABRIELLO	Pel cielo!!
(*terribilmente*)	Uom possente tu se'!
SIMONE (*a Gabriello*)	Ribaldo!
GABRIELLO (*al Doge slanciandosi*)	Audace Rapitor di fanciulle!
ALCUNI	Si disarmi!
GABRIELLO (*divincolandosi e correndo con Fiesco per ferire il Doge*)	Empio corsaro incoronato! Muori!
AMELIA (*entrando e interponendosi fra i due assalitori e il Doge*)	Ferisci
SIMONE, FIESCO, GABRIELLO	Amelia!
TUTTI	Amelia!...
AMELIA	O Doge! (o padre!) Salva l'Adorno tu.
SIMONE (*alle guardie che si sono impossessate di Gabriello per disarmarlo*)	Nessun l'offenda!! Cade l'orgoglio e al suon del suo dolore Tutta l'anima mia parla d'amore. Amelia di' come tu fosti rapita E come ecc. ecc. ecc. ecc.

. . . .

Piccolissima variante per mio uso e consumo e pace della mia timorata coscienza.

FINALE ATTO I.

(*Stanza del Coro*):	Il suo commosso accento Sa l'ira in noi calmar; Vol di soave vento Che rasserena il mar.

SIMONE	What do you mean?
GABRIELLO	By Heaven!
(*forcefully*)	Are you not a man of authority!
SIMONE (*to Gabriello*)	Traitor!
GABRIELLO (*rushing	Audacious
at the Doge*)	Abductor of girls!
SOME SENATORS	Disarm him!
GABRIELLO (*freeing	You vile enthroned pirate! Die!
himself and rush-	
ing with Fiesco to	
stab the Doge*)	
AMELIA (*entering	Strike
and throwing herself	
between the two	
assailants and	
the Doge*)	
SIMONE, GABRIELLO,	Amelia!
FIESCO	
ALL	Amelia! ...
AMELIA	O Doge! (o father!)
	Please do save Adorno.
SIMONE (*to the	Let no one touch him!!
guards who have	My pride succumbs and at the sound of her grief,
seized Gabriello	My whole being speaks of love.
to disarm him*)	Amelia, explain how you were abducted,
	And how *etc. etc. etc. etc.*

. . . .

A tiny change for my use and consumption and the peace of my scrupulous conscience.

FINALE ACT I

(*Stanza for the	His voice so moved knows
Chorus*)	How to calm our anger,
	A breeze of gentle wind
	Which smooths the sea.

(Nel primo manoscritto non mi andavano quelle due immagini accatastate dell'*altare* e del *mare*, si elidevano l'una coll'altra. Questa variante non è balla, no, ma ha un poco più di senso comune).

VARIANTI PER L'ATTO II

VARIANTE ALLA I E II SCENA DELL'ATTO II

SCENA I.

(*Palazzo degli Abati – Camera del Doge, ecc. – Seggiolone, Tavola, un'alcova. Sul tavolo un'anfora e una tazza*)

PAOLO e PIETRO

PAOLO Quei due vedesti?

PIETRO Si

PAOLO Li traggi tosto
Dal carcer loro per l'andito ascoso
Che questa chiave schiuderà.

PIETRO T'intesi (*esce*).

SCENA II.

PAOLO (*solo*).

Me stesso ho maledetto!!...
E l'anatema
M'insegue ancor ... e l'aura ancor ne trema!
Vilipeso ... rejetto
Dal Senato e da Genova, qui vibro
L'ultimo stral pria di fuggir, qui libro
La sorte tua, Doge, in quest'ansia estrema.
Tu che m'offendi e che mi devi il trono
Qui t'abbandono
Al tuo destino
In quest'ora fatale.
(*Estrae un'ampolla, ne versa il contenuto nella tazza*).

(In the first manuscript I didn't like these two piled up images of '*altare*' [altar] and '*mare*' [sea], as the one ran together with the other. Nor is this change beautiful, certainly not, but it has a bit more common sense).

CHANGES FOR ACT II

CHANGES IN SCENES I AND II OF ACT II

SCENE I

(*The palace of the Abati – Chamber of the Doge, etc. – a large chair, a table, an alcove. On the table a carafe and a cup*).

PAOLO and PIETRO

PAOLO	You saw them both?
PIETRO	Yes.
PAOLO	Have them brought at once From their cells by the secret passage, Which this key will open.
PIETRO	I understand. (*he leaves*)

SCENE II

PAOLO (*alone*)

I have cursed myself!! ...
And the anathema
Still follows me ... and the air still
                            resounds with it!
Vilified ... rejected
By the Senate and all Genoa, here I free
The last dart before my flight, here I seal
Your fate, O Doge, in this last desire,
You who insult me and yet owe your throne to me.
Here I leave you
To your destiny
In this fatal hour.
        (*He produces a flask, and pours its contents
        into the cup*)

Qui ti stillo una lenta atra agonia,
Là t'armo un assassino.
Scelga Morte sua via
Fra il tosco ed il pugnale.

ATTO II.

SCENA III (breve variante).

(DETTO, ANDREA, GABRIELLE *dalla destra condotti da* PIETRO).

FIESCHI	Prigioniero in qual loco m'adduci?
PAOLO	Nelle stanze del Doge, e favella A te Paolo.
FIESCHI	I tuoi sguardi son truci!
PAOLO	Io so l'odio che celasi in te. Tu m'ascolta.
FIESCHI	Che brami?
PAOLO	Al cimento Preparasti de' Guelfi la schiera ecc. ecc. ecc. ecc.

VARIANTE ALLA SCENA VIII DELL'ATTO II

(DOGE *e* GABRIELE *nascosto* – *Il* DOGE *entra meditabondo, siede*).

DOGE	Doge! Ancor proveran la tua clemenza I due ribelli? – Di paura segno Fora il castigo – M'ardono le fauci...

                          (*Versa dall'anfora nella tazza e beve*)

Perfin l'onda del fonte è amara al labbro
Dell'uom che regna ... ho l'alma oppressa ...
                                   infrante
Dal duol le membra ... già ...
                   mi vince il sonno (*s'addormenta*).
Oh Amelia ... ami ... un nemico.
        ecc. ecc. ecc. ecc.

Here I prepare for you another, slow agony,
There I arm your assassin.
Let Death choose its path
Between the poison and the knife.

ACT II

SCENE III (a small variant)

(THE SAME. ANDREA, GABRIELE *led on from the left by* PIETRO)

FIESCHI	Where do you take me, as a prisoner?
PAOLO	You are in the chambers of the Doge, And Paolo speaks to you.
FIESCHI	Your glance is cruel!
PAOLO	I am aware of the hatred which you hide within you. Listen.
FIESCHI	What do you wish?
PAOLO	Are you preparing A riot of the forces of the Guelphes? etc. etc. etc. etc.

CHANGE IN SCENE VIII IN ACT II

(THE DOGE, *and* GABRIELE *hidden* –
THE DOGE *enters, lost in thought, and sits down*)

DOGE — Doge! do the two rebels test once again
The extent of your clemency? – Punishment will be
A sign of fear – My throat is burning ...
         (*He pours from the carafe and drinks*)
Even the water of the fountain is bitter to the lips
Of him who rules ... My spirit sinks ... broken
By grief my body ... already ... sleep overcomes me
... (*he falls asleep*)
Oh Amelia ... you love ... an enemy.
        etc. etc. etc. etc.

Caro Maestro,

Avrò indovinato? Non so. Attendo le sue istruzioni e mi limito per oggi a salutare cordialmente Lei e la sua Signora.

suo Arrigo Boito

7. Genova, 9.I.1881 – Verdi a Boito

Genova 9 del 1881

Car. Boito

Continuo la lettera dell'altro giorno . . .

Non so se Le dissi di non farmi dei versi troppo lunghi nel Duettino tra *Gab:* e *Fiesco*.

Nella scena VI in vece delle Trombe che annunciano il Doge preferirei un Coro lontano di Cacciatori. Che ne dice?

Col nuovo Finale sono inutili i due primi versi del Doge "Il nuovo dì . . ." et. Aggiusti l'altro che vien dopo e lasciamo tal quale il Duetto tra Padre e figlia. Solo alla fine amerei che Amelia invece dei quattro versi

"*Non di regale orgoglio*
L'effimero splendor
Mi cingerà d'aureolo
Il raggio dell'amor"

dicesse in altro [sic] quattro versi eguali "*Vivrò nel mistero perchè tu non sia bersaglio all'odio dei nemici*". In questo modo darei maggior sviluppo alla così detta Cabaletta, e non la ripeterei.

Più la pregherei di cambiarmi il verso o i versi del Padre per evitare la parola *aureola*. Io non sono difficile per le parole ma in un Cantabile quell'*Au . . . eo . . .* danno un suono nasale, gutturale, antipatico.

Ben poco, anzi quasi nulla, vi sarà a fare negli altri atti.

Io mi sono messo al lavoro seriamente. – Procuri di mandarmi al più presto quanto le domandai jeri, e le domando oggi.

Di fretta

suo
G. Verdi

Dear Maestro,

Have I grasped your ideas correctly? I don't know. I await your instructions and limit myself to greeting warmly both you and your wife.

Your Arrigo Boito

Verdi's letter of 9 January (hitherto unpublished) crossed no. 6.

7. Genoa, 9.I.1881 – Verdi to Boito

Genoa, 9th of 1881

Dear Boito

I continue the letter of the other day ...

I don't know if I told you not to make the lines too long in the little Duet between *Gabriele* and *Fiesco*.

In Scene VI, I would prefer a distant Chorus of Huntsmen instead of the Trumpets which announce the Doge. What do you say?

In the new Finale the first two lines of the Doge *"The new day"* ... etc. are useless. Fix up the rest which comes afterwards and we will leave the Duet between Father and Daughter as it is. At the end however I would like for Amelia, to replace the four lines:

"Instead of the ephemeral
Splendour of royal pride
I will be encircled
By the golden rays of love"

another four lines of equal length in which she would say *"I'll live in mystery so that you are not the target of your enemies' hatred"*. In this way I would give greater development to the so-called Cabaletta, which I won't repeat.

Moreover I would ask you to change for me the line or lines of the Father so as to avoid the word *aureola*. I am not difficult about words, but in a Cantabile those *Au ... eo ...* give a nasal, gutteral, unpleasant sound.

In the other acts there will be very little to do, indeed almost nothing.

I have set myself seriously to work. – Try to send me as quickly as possible what I asked of you yesterday, and what I ask you for today.

In haste

Yours
G. Verdi

8. Genova, 10.I.1881 – Verdi a Boito

Gen. 10 del 1881

Car. Boito

Le due lettere raccomandate colle varianti m'arrivano a puntino. Coi quattro versi "*S'inalba il Ciel* ..." ec. finirò il primo pezzo che si può dire anzi finito.

Bene i pochi versi aggiunti nella Scena seguente fra *Andrea* e *Gab:* – Il Duettino temo riesca lungo e troppo forte. Io desidererei proprio in questo momento qualche cosa di calmo, di solenne, di religioso. Si tratta di un matrimonio. È un padre che benedice i suoi figli adottivi. Io non amo molto il ritmo *8rio* causa quelle maledette due note in levare

ma io le eviterò, e per non perdere tempo mi metto a far subito questo Duetto sui quattro versi di Andrea

Vieni a me, ti benedico

.   .   .   .

.   .   .   .

.   .   .   .

Io impasticcierò intanto altre quattro parole [*sic*] per *Gab:* onde andar avanti nel lavoro, finché arrivino i suoi versi. – Bastano quattro versi per ciascuno. – Per spiegarmi meglio vorrei che *Gab:* potesse dire la sua strofa in ginocchio; quindi qualche cosa di religioso. Oltre che questo, parmi, non guasti nulla; questa calma, e quella delle Scene seguenti, gioverebbe a far saltar fuori meglio il trambusto del Finale. Ella mi dice che il *Duettino* attaccherebbe *dopo i versi sciolti* ... Tutti? A me pare che il Duettino dovrebbe attaccare dopo "*In terra e in ciel* ..." oppure dopo:

"Ma non rallenti amor
La foga in te de cittadini affetti"

"The two registered letters" mentioned in no. 8 are of course the two installments of no. 6.

8. Genoa, 10.I.1881 – Verdi to Boito

Genoa, 10th of 1881

Dear Boito,

The two registered letters with the changes reach me at just the right moment. With the four lines "*The sky grows bright ...*" etc. I'll finish the first piece which can in fact be called already finished.

Fine the few lines added in the following Scene between *Andrea* and *Gabriele.* – The little Duet, I fear, comes out long and too strong. I would like exactly at this moment something calm, solemn, religious. A marriage is involved. He is a father who is blessing his adopted children. I am not very fond of the quaver rhythm because of those damned two notes moving up

but I shall avoid them, and so as not to lose time I'll set to work right away on this Duet on the four lines of Andrea

      Come to me, I'll bless you

      ·   ·   ·   ·   ·   ·   ·   ·
      ·   ·   ·   ·   ·   ·   ·   ·
      ·   ·   ·   ·   ·   ·   ·   ·

I'll throw together meanwhile another four words [*sic*] for *Gabriele*, so as to proceed with the work, until your lines arrive. – Four lines for each are sufficient. – So as to explain myself better I'd like *Gabriele* to be able to sing his stanza on his knees, therefore something religious. Apart from this, it seems to me nothing is spoiled; this calm, and that of the Scenes following will benefit by making the confusion of the Finale stand out better. You say that you would insert the *little Duet after the unrhymed lines* ... All of them? It seems to me that the Duettino should begin after "*On earth and in heaven ...*" or else after

      "But don't allow love of Amelia
      To reduce your patriotic enthusiasm"

aggiustando, s'intende, le rime ed i versi come crederà ... S'Ella poi crede, potremo far dire

>"*Il doge vien. Partiam*
>
>. . . . .
>
>*Fiesco in Andrea*"

dopo il Duettino durante lo squillo delle Trombe, o il Coro de' Cacciatori ...

Tutte le altre varianti benissimo, e bellissimo il Rec: del *veleno*. – Forse ci troveremo un po' imbarazzati, come posizione scenica, alle parole d'Amelia

>"O Doge (o padre)
>*Salva l'Adorno tu* ..."

Come dirà queste parole? ... sotto voce al Doge? ... non sarebbe troppo bello ... Ma queste sono inezie, che si aggiustano con un movimento di scena, o con una parola.

Coraggio dunque mio caro Boito, mi faccia questi quattro versi ottonarj per Gabriele. Non più di quattro versi ciascuno. Bastano. Li mandi al più presto. Io intanto lavoro ...

I saluti anche per mia moglie

G. Verdi

9. Genova, 11.(?)I.1881 – Verdi a Boito (telegramma)

Non faccia coro cacciatori + Scrivo + Verdi

adjusting, of course, the rhyme and the lines as you think best. . . . Then if you think it right, we could put in

> "*The Doge is coming. Let us leave*
>
> . . . .
>
> *Fiesco in Andrea*"

after the Duettino during the fanfare of the Trumpets, or the Chorus of Huntsmen . . .

All the other changes very fine, and very beautiful the Recitative of the *poison*. – Perhaps we'll find ourselves a bit embarrassed, in terms of staging, at the words of Amelia

> "O Doge (o father)
> *Save Gabriele Adorno . . .*"

How will she sing these words? . . . sotto voce to the Doge? . . . it wouldn't work very well . . . But these are trifles which will settle themselves by a movement onstage, or by a word.

Courage therefore my dear Boito, write me these four 8-syllable lines for Gabriele. Not more than four lines each. They are sufficient. Send them as soon as possible. I meanwhile am working . . .

Greetings also from my wife.

G. Verdi

The text of the unpublished telegram, no 9, is preserved in the notebook of Boito's biographer Nardi (*Istituto di Studi Verdiani*, Parma). Its date 12/1 is puzzling, since in no. 10 (11 January) Verdi speaks of a "telegram sent this morning" (see below). Whether the conflicting dates are due to a slip by Nardi or to the fact that the telegram was only delivered the following day must be left undecided. An argument for the latter hypothesis is the incorrect address in the telegram ("Via Principe Umberto" instead of "Via Principe Amadeo"). The text of the telegram refers to a suggestion made in no. 7.

9. Genoa 11.(?)I.1881 – Verdi to Boito (telegram)

Do not prepare huntsmen chorus + Will write + Verdi

10. Genova, 11.I.1881 – Verdi a Boito

Martedì 11

Car. Boito

Credo inutile, come dissi nel telegramma inviatogli questa mattina, di fare il Coro dei Cacciatori. Sarebbe un'altro pezzo di musica, ed in quest'atto (calcolando anche Preludio – Aria Sopr: – Romanza Tenore come un solo pezzo) avressimo sempre sei pezzi uno dei quali, il Finale, lunghissimo. Una *strillacciata* di Trombe di *12* o *16* battute, per l'entrata del Doge, basterà.

Ieri sera ho fatto il Duetto fra Andrea, e Gabriele. Le aggiunte m'hanno obbligato a rifare in parte il Recitativo, e mi sono fermato alle parole, "*In terra e in Ciel*". Posso però aggiungere anche:

> .   .   .   Ma non rallenti amore
> La foga in te de' cittadini affetti.

Aggiusti Ella, come crede, la fine di questo Rec:
Pel cantabile mi sono servito dei quattro versi d'Andrea

> "*Vieni a me ti benedico*   .   .   .
> .   .   .   .
> .   .   .   .
> .   .   .   .

e mi sono aggiustato un'altra strofa per Gabriele tanto per finire. Non ho bisogno che di 4 versi per Andrea (e possono servire i quattro citati sopra) ed altri quattro versi per Gabriele da farsi. Il pezzo ha un carattere calmo, solenne, un po' religioso, un po' antico … La prego dunque di questa strofa: io intanto vado avanti per arrivare al Finale. Finito il Duetto *Andrea-Gab:* attaccheranno le Trombe internamente ed intanto, se è necessario, si potranno dire i versi

> *Il Doge vien … Partiam* ec.

Mi dica ove devo fermarmi … Di fretta la saluto

G. Verdi

The following unpublished letter is the one announced in the telegram.

10. Genoa, 11.I.1881 – Verdi to Boito

Tuesday 11

Dear Boito

I think it useless, as I said in the telegram sent this morning, to prepare the Chorus of Huntsmen. It would mean another piece of music and in this act (counting Prelude – Aria for Sopr. – Romanza for Tenor as a single piece) we would still have six numbers, one of which, the Finale, is very long. A *blast* of Trumpets for *12* or *16* bars will be enough for the entrance of the Doge.

Last evening I wrote the Duet between Andrea and Gabriele. The additions have forced me to rewrite in part the Recitative and I have stopped at the words "*On earth and in Heaven*". I can however also add:

> *But do not let your love*
> *Reduce your patriotic enthusiasm*

Adjust the end of this Recitative, as you think best.

For the cantabile I have used the four lines for Andrea

> *Come to me, I'll bless you* . . .
> . . . .
> . . . .
> . . . .

and I scribbled down another stanza for Gabriele just so as to finish. I only need 4 lines for Andrea (and the four mentioned above can serve) and another four lines for Gabriele yet to be written. The piece has a character which is calm, solemn, a bit religious, a bit in the old style ... I would ask you therefore for this stanza; meanwhile I am going ahead so as to get to the Finale. The duet *Andrea-Gabriele* finished, the Trumpets will begin offstage and meanwhile, if necessary, they can sing the lines:

> *The Doge is coming ... Let us leave* etc.

Tell me where I must stop ... Greetings in haste,

G. Verdi

11. Milano, 14.I.1881 – Boito a Verdi

14. I, Via Principe Amedeo 1

Maestro mio.

Ho atteso la lettera ch'Ella m'annunciava col suo dispaccio prima di rimettermi al tavolo per le nuove varianti. Ebbi la lettera ieri ed ecco il risultato d'una attenta lettura di tutto ciò ch'Ella mi scrisse in questi giorni. Mi pare che il recitativo, della scena Andrea e Gabriele, dovrebbe arrivare sino alle parole *In terra e in ciel*, completando il verso, come dirò, e attaccando subito la parte lirica: p. e.:

ANDREA	Di lei sei degno!
GABRIELE	A me fia dunque unita!
ANDREA	In terra e in ciel.
GABRIELE (*con effusione*)	Ah! mi ridai la vita!
ANDREA	Vieni a me, ti benedico
	Nella pace di quest'ora;
	Lieto vivi e fido adora
	L'angiol tuo, la patria, il ciel.

(Veda un *oppure* a tergo di questo foglietto).

GABRIELE	Eco pia del tempo antico
	La tua voce è un casto incanto;
	Serberà ricordo santo
	Di quest'ora il cor fedel (*Squilli di trombe*).
	Ecco il Doge – Partiam – Ch'ei non ti scorga.
ANDREA	Ah! presto il dì della vendetta sorga.

Le pare che basti? a me pare che basti; della congiura dei Guelfi è meglio,

Boito's letter of 14 January contains the reply to nos. 7, 8 and 10. The original text has been published in *Carteggi verdiani* II, pp. 85-87.

11. Milan, 14.I.1881 – Boito to Verdi

14.I, Via Principe Amadeo 1

My dear Maestro,

I awaited the letter which you announced in your telegram, before sitting down at my desk to make the new changes. I received the letter yesterday and here is the result of an attentive reading of all that you have written me in these days. It seems to me that the Recitative, in the scene for Andrea and Gabriele, should come right up to the words *On earth and in heaven*, completing the line, as I'll explain, and beginning the cantabile section at once; for example:

ANDREA	You are worthy of her!
GABRIELE	Let her therefore be united with me!
ANDREA	On earth and in heaven.
GABRIELE	You have given me back my
(*with emotion*)	reason for living
ANDREA	Come to me, I will bless you
	In the peace of this moment;
	Live happily and love faithfully
	Your angel, your country, and Heaven.

(See an *instead* on the back of this page)

GABRIELE	Holy echo of ancient times,
	Your voice is a chaste inchantment;
	My heart ever faithful will
	Retain the memory of this saintly hour.
	(*A fanfare of trumpets*)
	The Doge is coming – We must leave – Don't let him see you.
ANDREA	Ah! may the day of vengeance soon appear.

Do you think it is enough? It seems so to me; I think it best not to discuss the

credo, non parlare; confonderebbe forse le idee, sempre un po' pigre, del pubblico e nuocerebbe alla chiarezza del finale.

Se però Ella crede si debba parlarne, niente le impedisce di conservare tal quale i sei versi del libretto primitivo che vengono subito dopo lo squillo.

Una osservazione. Sarebbe desiderabile che si potesse evitare, giunti a questo punto, il cambiamento di scena. Tre scene in un atto mi paiono troppe, distruggono quell'impressione d'unità così necessaria alla vita bene organizzata dell'atto.

Pensi che di tutto il dramma questo giardino è la sola scena ridente. Tutte le altre sono gravi, solenni o cupe. Vi abbondano troppo gli *interni:* Sala del Consiglio, Camera del Doge, aula Ducale. Poichè in questo principio del prim'atto siamo all'aria aperta restiamoci più che possiamo. Da un lato, nel fondo del giardino, ci possono stare un paio di quinte, rappresentanti l'ingresso del palazzo Grimaldi. Amelia verrebbe incontro al Doge sulla soglia del palazzo e la scena che segue troverebbe nel giardino il suo posto abbastanza naturale. Del resto non ci sarebbe ragione, se la scena mutasse, di allontanare Fiesco e Gabriele da un luogo dove il Doge, ch'essi fuggono, non dovrebbe mettere il piede. Ma non perdiamo tempo.

SCENA VI.

DOGE, PAOLO, ecc. ecc.

DOGE	Paolo	
PAOLO		Signor.
DOGE		Ci spronano gli eventi.

Di qua partir convien ecc. ecc.
con quel che segue.

Così sarebbe raffazzonato *alla bell'e meglio* il verso del *dì festivo.*

SCENA VII.

Passo all'au . . . eo . . .

Mettiamo *gloria* invece d'*aureola.*

Di mia corona il raggio
La gloria tua sarà?

plot of the Guelphes; it would perhaps confuse the always slightly lazy minds of the audience and would damage the clarity of the finale.

If however you think it must be included, nothing prevents you from retaining as they are the six lines which appear in the original libretto immediately after the fanfare.

One observation. It would be desirable to avoid, if possible, a change of scene at this point. Three scenes in one act are, in my opinion, too many; they destroy the feeling of unity so necessary to the carefully organized 'life' of the act.

Consider that in the whole drama this garden scene is the only bright one. All the others are heavy, solemn or dark, There are too many *interiors:* Council Chamber, Chambers of the Doge, Ducal Hall. Since at this opening of the first act we are in the open air let us stay there as long as we can. On one side, in the back of the garden, there can be a pair of columns, representing the entrance to the Grimaldi palace. Amelia would come to meet the Doge on the threshold of the palace, and the scene which follows would seem natural enough in the surroundings of the garden. Moreover, there would be no reason, if the scene were changed, to remove Fiesco and Gabriele from a place where the Doge, whom they are fleeing, should not set foot. But let's not waste time.

SCENE VI

DOGE, PAOLO, etc. etc.

DOGE	Paolo	
PAOLO		My lord
DOGE		Events are pressing.

It is necessary to leave etc. etc.

with that which follows.

Thus the line about the *festive day* would be mended *for the good, and even better.*

SCENE VII

I move on to the *au . . . eo . . .*

Let's put *gloria* instead of *aureola*

The splendour of my crown
Will be your glory?

E poi vediamo se, trascrivendoli, i quattro versi nuovi si intonano coi vecchi là dove Amelia risponde al padre:

AMELIA   Padre, vedrai la vigile
                Figlia tua sempre accanto;
                Nell'ore melanconiche
                Asciugherò il tuo pianto ...
                Avrem gioie romite
                Note soltanto al ciel:
                Io la colomba mite
                Sarò del regio ostel.

E per oggi mi sembra di aver finito il mio compito; pronto a ricominciarlo in tutto ciò che non le garba.

La accerto, caro Maestro, che Giovedì partirò da Milano per recarmi a Padova.

Mi fermerò una settimana in quella città per aiutare la cottura del *Mefistofele* e per servirlo caldo ai miei concittadini. Fino a Mercoledì sera potrò ricevere le sue lettere a Milano, indi a *Padova, Albergo della Croce d'Oro*. Ma pel 29 sarò tornato a casa.

Giulio Ricordi stette a letto, malato, molti giorni; non s'alza ancora ma sta meglio.

Tanti tanti saluti

suo Arrigo Boito

Oppure:
                La tua voce un'eco, un canto
                Quasi par del tempo antico,
                Serberà ricordo santo
                De' tuoi detti il cor fedel.

Questi maledetti ottonari, Lei ha ragione, sono la più noiosa tiritera della nostra metrica. Li ho scelti per disperazione. Non volevo i settenari perchè quasi tutto il libretto è nella sua parte lirica in settenari; non volevo i quinari perchè già in quel punto il vecchio testo è scritto in quinari e pensavo che forse lei sarebbe tornato di mala voglia al vecchio ritmo.

And then let's see if, in rewriting them, the four new lines fit in with the old ones at the place where Amelia replies to her father:

AMELIA　　　　　Father, you'll see your vigilant
　　　　　　　　Daughter always at your side;
　　　　　　　　In your hours of melancholy
　　　　　　　　I'll dry your tears . . .
　　　　　　　　We'll have our secret joys
　　　　　　　　Known only to Heaven:
　　　　　　　　I'll be the mild dove
　　　　　　　　Of the royal dwelling.

And for today I seem to have finished my homework; ready to begin it again in whatever you don't like.

I should advise you, dear Maestro, that Thursday I leave Milan to go to Padua.

I'll stay for a week in that city to help in the cooking of *Mefistofele* and to serve it hot to my fellow citizens. Up to Wednesday evening I'll be able to receive your letters at Milan, afterwards at *Padua, Albergo della Croce d'Oro*. But by the 29th I'll be back home.

Giulio Ricordi was ill in bed for many days; he is still not up but he's feeling better.

Many many greetings

　　　　　　　　　　　　　　　　　　　　　　　　　　your Arrigo Boito

Instead:

　　　　　　　　Your voice seems almost an echo,
　　　　　　　　A song of ancient times;
　　　　　　　　My faithful heart will
　　　　　　　　Retain a saintly memory of your words.

These damned 8-syllable lines, you're right, are the most annoying rig-marole of our poetic metre. I chose them out of desperation. I did not want 7-syllable lines because almost the whole libretto, at least in the cantabile sections, is in 7-syllable lines; I avoided 5-syllable lines because just here the old text was written in 5-syllable lines and I thought that perhaps you would be carried back unwillingly to the old rhythm.

12. Genova, 15.I.1881 – Verdi a Boito

Gen. 15. 1881

C. Boito

Và tutto bene, e sono due volte felice di non cambiare la scena prima del second' Atto.

Ella, caro Boito, s'immaginerà d'aver finito? Tutto'altro! Avremo finito dopo la prova generale, se pure arriveremo fin là. Intanto nel Duetto tra Padre e figlia vi è cosa cui bisognerebbe dare maggior rilievo. Se il pubblico perde quel povero verso *"Ai non fratelli miei"* non capisce più nulla.

Vorrei che dicessero per es:

D. *Paolo!*

A. *Quel vil nomasti! . . . Ma a te buono*
   generoso, devo dire il vero

[Cancellato: D. *Che!*]

A. *I Grimaldi non sono i miei fratelli*

D. *Ma e tu?*

A. *Non sono una Grimaldi*

D. *E chi sei dunque?*

Così l'attenzione si ferma, e si capisce qualche cosa . . . Se crede mi faccia tre o quattro versi sciolti, chiari e netti. Ella farà sempre dei bei versi, ma qui non m'importerebbe fossero anche brutti. Perdoni l'eresia; io credo che in teatro, come nei Maestri è lodevole talvolta il talento di non far musica, e di saper *s'effacer;* così nei poeti è meglio qualche volta più del bel verso, la parola evidente e scenica. Dico questo solo per conto mio.

Un'altra osservazione sul Finale. Fra i 2000 spettatori della prima sera, forse ve ne saranno venti appena che conoscono le due lettere del Petrarca. A meno di non mettere qualche nota, riesciranno pel pubblico oscuri i versi di Simone. Io vorrei che, quasi a comento [*sic*], dopo il verso

Il cantor della bionda Avignonese

Verdi answered no. 11 on the following day.

12. Genoa, 15.I.1881 – Verdi to Boito

Gen. 15. 1881

Dear Boito,

Everything works well, and I am doubly happy at not having to change the first scene of the second act.

Do you, dear Boito, imagine that you have finished? Far from it! We'll have finished after the dress rehearsal, if indeed we get that far. Meanwhile in the Duet between Father and Daughter there is something which should be given greater emphasis. If the audience loses that little line *"To brothers not my own"* it will not understand anything which follows.

I would like them to say for example:

D. *Paolo!*

A. *You've named the fiend! But to you, so kind, so generous,*
   I must tell the truth

[Cancelled:] D. *What!*

A. *The Grimaldi are not my brothers*

D. *But what about you?*

A. *I am not a Grimaldi*

D. *And who are you then?*

Thus the attention is halted, and something is understood ... If you think well of it, write me three or four unrhymed lines clear and straight-forward; you would write beautiful lines in any case, but here I wouldn't mind even if they were ugly. Forgive my heresy; I believe that in the theatre, as the talent for not writing true music and for knowing how to deny one's own personality is sometimes praiseworthy in composers, so for poets, instead of a lovely line, a plain and theatrical word is sometimes better. I say this only for my own account.

Another observation about the Finale. Among the 2000 spectators on the first evening there may be perhaps at most twenty who know about the two letters of Petrarch. Unless we give a footnote, the lines of Simon will prove obscure for the audience. I would prefer that, almost as a comment, after the line

The poet of the fair Avignonaise

Tutti dicessero
      Guerra a Venezia!
DOGE   È guerra fratricida. Venezia e Genova hanno una patria comune:
      Italia
TUTTI   Nostra patria è Genova
      Tumulto interno et.
[*Cancellato:* Del resto faccia come crede]
   Mi risponda prima di partire. Auguro intanto buon viaggio e buona
fortuna ...

                                   Aff.
                                 G. Verdi

P.S. Mi spiace di Giulio. Credevo cosa più leggiera [*sic*]. Son ben lieto sentire
che stia meglio.

13. Milano, 16.I.1881 – Boito a Verdi

                                  Domenica

   Mi accordo con Lei, caro Maestro, pienamente, intorno alla teoria del
sacrificare, quando occorra, l'eufonia del verso e della musica alla efficacia
dell'accento drammatico e della verità scenica. Lei desiderava tre o quattro
versi sciolti magari brutti, ma chiari invece di quel verso:
                  dei non fratelli miei
che non è bello davvero.
   Ho fatto i quattro versi (non ho saputo farne tre) ma non ho creduto di
farli sciolti giacchè temevo che fra i settenari rimati che li precedono, e gli
ottonari rimati che li seguono, quell'abbandono della rima, per quattro sole
righe, riescisse fiacco alla lettura:

everyone said:

> War against Venice!

DOGE   It is a war of fratricide. Venice and Genoa
> have a common home: Italy

ALL   Our home is Genoa
> *Confusion within etc.*

[*Cancelled:*] However do as you think best

   Send me a reply before leaving. Meanwhile I wish you a good trip and good luck . . .

> Aff.
> G. Verdi

P.S. I am sorry about Giulio. I thought it was less serious. I am very glad that he's improving.

The following letter was misdated by Luzio (*Carteggi verdiani* II, pp. 89–91). January 17th was a Monday.

13.   Milan, 16.I.1881 – Boito to Verdi

> Sunday

   I entirely agree with you, dear Maestro, concerning the idea of sacrificing, when necessary, the euphony of poetry and music to the effectiveness of dramatic emphasis and scenic truth. You wanted three of four unrhymed, even ugly, but straightforward lines, instead of that line:

> to brothers not my own

which isn't beautiful anyway.

   I wrote the four lines (I wasn't able to write only three) but I did not think it wise to make them unrhymed, since I feared that between the 7-syllable rhymed lines which precede them and the 8-syllable rhymed lines which follow, the sacrifice of rhyme for only four lines would seem lame to the reader:

. . . .

DOGE	Paolo!
AMELIA	Quel vil nomasti. – E poiché tanta
	Pietà ti move dei destini miei
	Vo' svelarti il segreto che mi ammanta

(*Dopo breve pausa*)	Non sono una Grimaldi.
DOGE	O ciel! Chi sei?

. . . .

Passiamo nella sala del Consiglio:

PAOLO (*ridendo*)	. . . Attenda alle sue rime
	Il cantor della bionda Avignonese.
TUTTI I CONSIGLIERI (*poi* PAOLO *ferocemente*)	Guerra a Venezia!
DOGE	E con quest'urlo atroce
	Fra' due liti d'Italia erge Caino
	La sua clava cruenta! Adria e Liguria
	Hanno patria comune.
TUTTI	È nostra patria
	Genova!
PIERO	Qual clamor?
ALCUNI	D'onde tai grida?
	ecc. ecc.

. . . .

Ho evitato la parola: guerra *fratricida* indicata dalla sua lettera, perchè non tolga effetto alla esclamazione: *Fratricidi!* che scoppia prima dei versi del Doge:

Plebe, patrizi! . . . ecc.

Certo non ci saranno in teatro più di venti persone abbastanza colte per riconoscere l'allusione che fa il Doge alle due lettere che il Petrarca diresse al Principe di Roma, ma il cielo ci tenga lontani dalla tentazione delle note e dei commenti.

. . . .

DOGE   Paolo!

AMELIA   You've named the fiend. – And since so much

Pity for my destiny moves you
I want to reveal to you the secret which
                            surrounds me.

(*After a short pause*)   I am not a Grimaldi.

DOGE   Heaven! Who are you then?

. . . .

Let's move into the Council chamber:

PAOLO (*laughing*)   Let the poet of the fair
Avignonaise attend to his rhymes.

ALL COUNCILLORS   War against Venice!
(*then Paolo fierce-*
ly)

DOGE   And with this horrible cry

Between two factions of Italy, Cain
Raises his bloody club! The Adriatic and Ligurian
                              shores
Share a common home.

ALL   Our home is
Genoa!

PIETRO   What is this noise?

SEVERAL   From where these screams?

etc. etc.

. . . .

I have avoided the word: *fratricidal* war, indicated in your letter, so as not to lose the effect of the exclamation: *Fratricides!* which bursts out before the lines of the Doge:

Plebians, patricians . . . etc.

Certainly there will not be more than twenty people sufficiently well read to be able to pick up the Doge's allusion to the two letters which Petrarch wrote to the Prince of Rome, but heaven preserve us from the temptation to insert notes and comments.

Pure se si vuole che le 20 persone diventino duecento e più, basta mutare l'allusione e invece delle lettere (note oggi a pochi, mentre ai contemporanei del Petrarca erano notissime) alludere alla canzone che tutti imparano a scuola e modificare così:

> La stessa voce che inneggiò su Roma,
> Pria che recasse tutta alle sue mani
> Rienzi protervo la civil possanza,
> Or su Genova tuona . . .

Ma il periodo riesce prolisso troppo e troppo contorto per gli schietti e veloci bisogni dell'accento musicale.

D'altra parte la prima versione non è esatta storicamente; invece di

> Vaticino di gloria e poi di morte

sarebbe più vero il dire:

> Vaticinio di gloria e poscia d'onta.

Ma così il verso riesce brutto, pure di ciò nè a Lei nè a me importa. La lascio arbitro della scelta.

Il publico del resto è un animale che beve grosso e di questi scrupoli se ne infischia e in ciò non ha torto.

Se le occorre qualche altra goccia d'inchiostro della mia penna io potrei ricevere prima della mia partenza, fissata sempre a Giovedì, un'altra lettera sua.

Tanti e cordiali saluti

suo Arrigo Boito

Giulio ieri stava peggio, oggi meno male, ha un ingorgo al polmone, gli si dovettero applicare dei vescicanti al petto, è un affare che ci tiene un poco allarmati, non tanto per ora come per l'avvenire.

Still, if you want the 20 people to become two hundred or more, it suffices to change the allusion and instead of the letters (known today to few, while to the contemporaries of Petrarch they were well known) to refer to the song which everyone learns at school and to change it thus:

> The same voice which exalted Rome,
> Before the insolent Rienzi in his own hands
> Assumed all civic power,
> Now thunders over Genoa . . .

But the sentence turns out too wordy and too contorted for the need of clarity and speed with regard to the musical expression.

On the other hand the first version is not historically exact; instead of

> Prophecies of glory and then of death

it would be more correct to say:

> Prophecies of glory and then of shame.

But in this way the line is ugly; however this makes no difference either to you or to me. I leave you arbiter in the choice.

The audience moreover is an animal which swallows everything and doesn't really give a damn about these scruples, and in this is not wrong.

If you need some further drops of ink from my pen I could receive another letter from you before my departure, still set for Thursday.

All my warmest greetings

yours
Arrigo Boito

P.S. Yesterday Giulio was worse, today a little better, he has an accumulation of fluid in the lungs, they had to apply vesicatories to his breast; it's a matter which keeps us rather uneasy, not so much for today as for the future.

14. Genova, 17.I.1881 – Verdi a Boito

Lunedì

C. Boito
Una parola sola per dirle che ho ricevuto stamattina i suoi versi e che
vanno benissimo.
Per ora basta . . .
In seguito poi non so . . .
Affettuosi saluti

. . . [illeggibile]
G. Verdi

15. Genova, 24.I.1881 – Verdi a Boito

Lunedì

Car. Boito
Ho bisogno ancora d'un'altra goccia del suo inchiostro. Dico *altra* . . .
non dico *ultima*!
Senza volerlo ho fatto un pezzo *Concertato* nel Finale nuovo. S'intende
che Simone canta prima *a solo* tutti i suoi sedici versi

Plebe! Patrizi! Popolo!

. . . .

Dopo viene questo *Concertato* che è poco concertato, ma pur sempre
concertato. Io non amo in generale gli *a parte* perchè obbligano l'artista
all'immobilità; e vorrei che almeno Amelia si volgesse a Fieschi rac-
comandando "*Pace . . . perdono . . . oblìo . . . Sono fratelli nostri! . . .*" Mi
riescirebbe così più calda la piccola frase fatta per Amelia. Non dimentichi
in questa nuova strofetta la parola *pace* . . . che mi gioca assai bene.

Verdi's unpublished letter acknowledging receipt of no. 13 is only dated "Monday". There can be no doubt that it was written on 17 January.

14. Genoa, 17.I.1881 – Verdi to Boito

Monday

Dear Boito
Just a word to let you know that I received your lines this morning and that they work very well.
Enough for now . . .
Later however I don't know . . .
Affectionate greetings

. . . [illegible]
G. Verdi

Like its predecessor the following unpublished letter is simply dated "Monday". As it was answered by Boito on 31 January with an apology for the delay, it must have been written on 24 January.

15. Genoa, 24.I.1881 – Verdi a Boito

Monday

Dear Boito
Again I need another drop of your ink. I say *another* . . . I don't say *the last!*
Without wanting to I've written an Ensemble piece in the new Finale. Obviously Simone sings first *alone* all his sixteen lines

Plebians! Patricians! People!

. . . .

Afterwards comes this *Ensemble* which is hardly ensemble, but nevertheless ensemble. In general I'm not fond of *asides* as they force the artist into immobility; and I would prefer that at least Amelia turned to Fieschi urging "*Peace . . . pardon . . . oblivion . . . They are our brothers! . . .*" In this way the little line written for Amelia would prove warmer. In this new little stanza don't forget the word *peace* . . . which for me goes very well.

Nel racconto più indietro d'Amelia, non ho mai potuto nè posso, nè potrò far declamare bene quel verso "*Non egli è di tanto misfatto il più reo* ed è così vero che nel vecchio spartito, io feci (sbagliando verso e rima)

Di tanto misfatto, il più reo non è

Per evitare tanto sconcio guardi se mi può aggiustare il verso facendo posa tanto al primo che al secondo *senario*.

Ho finito . . . per ora! La saluto di cuore

Aff.
G. Verdi

16. Milano, 31.I.1881 – Boito a Verdi

31 gennaio 1881 – Milano

Caro Maestro mio. Ebbi la sua lettera a Padova, ma non ho potuto eseguire che oggi, a Milano, la variante ch'Ella aspettava da me. Mi acquetavo pensando che Ella intanto stava lavorando a qualche altra parte dell'opera.

Dalle parole ch'Ella mi scrisse compresi che in questo pezzo d'insieme la parte d'Amelia, dopo quella del Doge, è riescita musicalmente la più importante e dedussi da ciò che quattro soli versi forse non sarebbero bastati e ne scrissi otto. Veda se vanno bene:

AMELIA   Pace! l'altero sangue
 (*to Fiesco*)   Doma e l'orgoglio piega!
                Pace! la patria langue
                Per l'ira tua crudel.
                Col labro mio ti prega
                L'alma fra gli astri assunta
                Della gentil defunta
                Che ti contempla in ciel.

In Amelia's narrative earlier, I have never been able to, nor can I, nor shall I be able to have declaimed properly that line "*He is not the most guilty in such a crime* and it is very true that in the old score I wrote (damaging line and rhyme):

> *In this crime, the most guilty he's not*

So as to avoid such a poetic obscenity see if you couldn't fix up the line for me placing an accent on the first as well as on the second *6-syllable line*.

I've finished . . . for now! I greet you from the heart,

Affectionately
G. Verdi

Boito's reply to no. 15 (*Carteggi verdiani* II, pp. 91–92) was delayed because of his visit to Padua (see no. 11 above).

16. Milan, 31.I.1881 – Boito to Verdi

31 January 1881 – Milan

My dear Maestro. I received your letter at Padua, but I was not able until today, in Milan, to complete the version that you were expecting from me. I calmed myself thinking that you were meanwhile working on some other part of the opera.

From what you wrote me I understood that in the ensemble number the role of Amelia, after that of the Doge, has become musically the most important, and I deducted from this that only four lines would perhaps not be enough and so I wrote eight. See if they are suitable:

AMELIA (*to Fiesco*) Peace! the noble blood
Rules and the pride bows!
Peace! the country fails
Through your cruel anger.
Through my mouth pleads with you
The soul of the gentle departed,
Now risen among the stars,
Who watches over you from Heaven.

Avrei voluto dare un po' di moto alla parte di Gabriele ma non m'è riescito e la ragione è chiara: Se il Doge parla a tutti e se Amelia va implorando il Fiesco, Gabriele non ha più con chi parlare, visto che anche Pietro e Paolo parlano insieme, ed è necessariamente condannato all'immobilità.

Ed ora provi, caro Maestro, a collocare al posto del verso reo del vecchio libretto il verso seguente:

AMELIA   V'è un uom più nefando
                Che illeso ancor sta.

M'accorsi che qui Ella ha bisogno d'un tronco e dovuto cercare parecchi versi più in sù una finale tronca per condurre una rima qualsiasi.

Ora ho ripreso a Milano la mia vita consueta e sono a sua disposizione per tutto ciò che le farà bisogno.

Saluti cordiali

del suo Arrigo Boito

17. Genova, 2.II.1881 – Verdi a Boito

2 Feb. 1881

Car. Boito,

E prima di tutto le mie sincere congratulazioni per l'esito del Mefistofele a Padova.

Otto versi son troppi per Amelia. Il pezzo non è altro che un *Gran Solo* del Doge coll'aggiunta delle altre parti infine. Amelia sola ha una piccola frase. Per me vanno benissimo i primi quattro, ma, Ella forse vorrà cambiare il secondo per la rima.

Andrà bene il verso del racconto.

Ed ora veniamo all'ultimo atto. – Il primo Coro di quest'atto non ha più ragione d'essere, ed io, a sipario calato, ripeterei all'orchestra la musica

I would have liked to give the role of Gabriele a bit more movement but it didn't work out and the reason is clear: if the Doge addresses everyone and if Amelia is imploring Fiesco, Gabriele has no one left to whom he can speak, seeing that Pietro and Paolo are also talking together, and so he is necessarily condemned to immobility.

And now try, dear Maestro, to put in the place of the ugly line in the old libretto the following:

AMELIA   There is a man more wicked
                  Who is still beyond justice.

I was aware that here you needed a *tronco* line and I had to search through several previous lines to find some *tronco* ending with which I could make any sort of rhyme.

Now I have resumed my usual life in Milan and am at your disposal for everything which will prove necessary for you.

Warmest greetings

from your
Arrigo Boito

The following item is a reply to no. 16.

17. Genoa, 2.II.1881 – Verdi to Boito

2 Feb. 1881

Dear Boito,

And first of all my sincere congratulations on the success of *Mefistofele* at Padua.

Eight lines are too many for Amelia. The piece is after all no more than a *Grand Solo* for the Doge with the addition of the other parts. Only Amelia has a short phrase. For me the first four are fine, but you will perhaps want to change the second four for the rhyme.

The line for the narrative will work well.

And now we come to the last act. – The first Chorus of this act no longer has its raison d'être, and I, with the curtain closed, would simply repeat in

della *rivolta* colla quale si chiude l'atto precedente, colle grida interne = *Vittoria, Vittoria!* Alzato il sipario il Doge comincierebbe

Brando guerrier et. et.

La scena che segue tra Pietro, Paolo, e Paolo-Fieschi resta? – Se avessimo finito! La saluto di cuore

Suo
G. Verdi

18. Milano, 5.II.1881 – Boito a Verdi

Sabato – Milano.

Caro Maestro,

Ricorro al mio vecchio paragone del tavolo, ora è la quarta gamba che tentenna. Conviene saldarla e usare in questa operazione molta avvedutezza per impedire che, rinfrancata questa, non tornino a zoppicare le altre.

Da due giorni penso e ripenso al quart'atto.

L'idea dell'introduzione d'orchestra a sipario calato colle grida interne mi piace assai, è utilissima, lega mirabilmente la fine del terz'atto col principio del quarto, raduna gli avvenimenti dei due ultimi atti in una unità di tempo rapida, stringata, drammaticissima. Ma quest'idea non basta. La scena fra Fiesco e Paolo non può più rimanere quale è.

Converrà mutare qualche condizione della scena fra il Doge e Fieschi (Fieschi e il Doge si sono già trovati a fronte in un moto violento, due atti prima cioè nel pezzo d'insieme). Fin dalle prime parole del Doge nel quart'atto bisogna far presentire la catastrofe. Nel libretto vecchio, Simone, quando dice: *brando guerrier* ha una salute troppo soddisfacente. Insomma le invierò domani un tentativo di ristauro, versificato, ed Ella giudicherà.

La ringrazio, caro Maestro mio, per le cortesi parole colle quali Ella incomincia la sua lettera.

A domani. Un saluto di cuore

suo Arrigo Boito

the orchestra the music of the *revolt* with which the preceding act ends, with offstage cries: *Victory! Victory!* The curtain up, the Doge would begin

Sword of war etc. etc.

Does the scene which follows between Pietro-Paolo, and Paolo-Fieschi remain? –

If only we had finished! I greet you from the heart,

yours
G. Verdi

Although only dated "Saturday" there can be no doubt that no. 18 was written on 5 February. It contains the reply to no. 17. The "fourth act" should be read as "third act" and the "third" as the "second". The letter has been published in *Carteggi verdiani* II, 92.

18. Milan, 5.II.1881 – Boito to Verdi

Saturday – Milano

Dear Maestro,

I return to my old metaphor of the table – now it is the fourth leg which wobbles. We must secure it and in this operation we must use great care so as to assure that once this leg is set straight, the others don't start wobbling again.

I have been thinking and rethinking about the fourth act for two days. I like very much the idea of the orchestral introduction with a closed curtain and shouts offstage; it is most useful, as it links the end of the third act well with the beginning of the fourth, it gathers the events of the last two acts in a unity of time, rapid, compressed, very dramatic. But this idea is not enough. The scene between Fiesco and Paolo can no longer remain as it is.

It will be necessary to change some aspects of the scene between the Doge and Fieschi (Fieschi and the Doge have already been seen in a violent movement two acts previously, that is, in the ensemble). Right from the first words of the Doge in the fourth act we must foreshadow the catastrophe. In the old libretto, Simon, when he says: *sword of war*, looks much too healthy. In short, I shall send you tomorrow an attempted remedy, set in verse, and you can judge.

Thank you, my dear Maestro, for the kind words with which you begin your letter.

Till tomorrow. A heart-felt greeting

Yours
Arrigo Boito

19. Genova, 5.II.1881 – Verdi a Boito

Genova, 5 Feb. 1881

Car. Boito

Non abbiamo finito!!!! Nella scena prima dell'atto primo dopo le strofe interne di Gabriele, bisognerebbe fare alcune battute d'orchestra, per lasciar il tempo d'entrare: io preferirei una frase agitata e corta d'Amelia. Anzi io mi sono fabbricato quattro versi tronchi di quinarj tronchi [*sic*]

> *È desso! O ciel!*
> *Mi manca il Cor*
>
> .   .   .   .   .   .
>
> .   .   .   .   .   .

ed ho fatta la frase. La prego di questi quattro versi. Se saranno sei, sarà meglio, ma non più di sei.

Nel Finale nuovo alla scena della *rivolta* ho procurato malgrado un movimento agitato di orchestra, di far sentir bene tutte le parole: l'orchestra rugge, ma rugge piano. È necessario però, che alla fine anche l'orchestra faccia sentire la sua formidabile voce, e vorrei fare un gran forte dopo le parole del Doge "*Ecco le plebi* . . ." Qui si scatenerebbe in tutta la sua forza l'orchestra a cui si aggiungerebbero, appena entrati, *Popolo, Patrizi, Donne* et. et. . . . Avrei quindi bisogno di due versi, per far gridare tutto il mondo. Che in questi versi non manchi la parola "*Vendetta!*" Stò facendo per *Paolo* quel bel Rec: ch'Ella ha aggiunto nel principio del Second'Atto. Peccato! Quei versi così potenti, in bocca ad un mascalzone qualunque! Ho dato però disposizioni, perchè questo Paolo sia un mascalzone dei meno mascalzoni.

Ed ora mi dica.

Sarebbe peccato inassolubile se nel Coro Finale del Second'Atto "*All'armi, all'armi Liguri*" aggiungessi le donne? . . .

Sarebbe altro peccato se nella Scena Ultima, la morte del Doge, Maria divenuta sposa di Gab: entrasse in scena seguita da alcune Damigelle? *Alcune* vorrebbe dire tutto il *Coro delle Donne* . . .

Dopo questo forse avremo finito.

Mi creda sempre

Suo
G. Verdi

Verdi's letter of 5 February crossed Boito's of the same date.

19. Genoa, 5.II.1881 – Verdi to Boito

Genoa, 5 Feb. 1881

Dear Boito,

We haven't finished!!!! In the first scene of the first act, after the offstage stanzas for Gabriele, it is necessary to insert several bars of orchestra, so as to have time for him to come on: I would prefer a short and agitated line for Amelia. Indeed I have thrown together four 5-syllable *tronco* lines:

> It is he! Oh Heaven!
> My strength fails me
>
> . . . . .
> . . . . .

and I wrote the musical phrase. I would therefore ask you for these four lines. If they become six, better yet, but no more than six.

For the scene of the revolt in the new Finale I have tried, in spite of an agitated movement in the orchestra, to have all the words clearly audible: the orchestra roars, but roars softly. It is necessary, however, that at the end even the orchestra make its formidable voice heard, and I would like to place a great forte after the Doge's words "*Such are the plebeians* . . ." Here the orchestra would break forth in all its force; to it would be added, as soon as they enter, *People, Patricians, Women* etc. etc. . . . Therefore I would need two new lines, so as to have the whole world shouting. Don't let the word "*Vengeance!*" be missing from these lines. I am composing for *Paolo* that beautiful Recitative that you added at the beginning of the Second Act. What a pity! Those lines so powerful, in the mouth of an ordinary villain. I have arranged however, so that this Paolo becomes a villain of the less villainous.

And now tell me.

Would it be an unforgivable sin if the Final Chorus of the Second Act "*To arms, to arms, Ligurians*" I added the women? . . .

Would it be another sin if, in the Final Scene, that is, the death of the Doge, Maria, now the wife of Gabriele, came onstage followed by several female attendants? *Several* would mean the whole *Women's Chorus* . . .

After this perhaps we shall have finished.

Believe me always

Yours
G. Verdi

20. Genova, 6.II.1881 – Verdi a Boito

Domenica

Car. Boito

Aggiustiamo pure anche la quarta gamba ... ma Ella mi spaventa dicendo che bisogna modificare la scena tra *Fieschi* ed il *Doge!* Se si tratta di poca cosa, stà bene: ma se bisogna rifare, vi è un impossibile, il tempo. Basta: aspetto con impazienza la lettera di domani.

E mi dica: non si potrebbe evitare tutta la prima scena? Così non si vedrebbe in quest'Atto che una sola volta il Doge quando entra avvelenato ... *M'ardon le tempia* et. L'Atto comincierebbe col preludio d'orchestra e la grida interne *Vittoria* ... All'alzare del sipario si sentirebbe interno il *Coro di nozze* ed i due SS. Pietro e Paolo potrebbero dire che il Doge ha vinto, e Gabriele sposa Amelia. –

Ora aspetto quei quattro o sei versi di quinarj tronchi di cui la pregai jeri. Li mandi al più presto.

Di fretta.

Suo
G. Verdi

P.S. Non mi ha scritto nulla sulla strofa d'Amelia nel Finale nuovo –

The following unpublished letter, dated "Sunday", contains the reply to no. 18 and therefore must have been written on 6 February.

20. Genoa, 6.II.1881 – Verdi to Boito

Sunday

Dear Boito,

Let us adjust the fourth leg as well ... but you frighten me by saying that it is necessary to change the scene between *Fieschi* and the *Doge!* If something minor is concerned, that's fine, but if it is necessary to rewrite, then lack of time would make it impossible. Enough – I await with impatience tomorrow's letter.

And tell me: couldn't the whole first scene be avoided? Thus the Doge would be seen only once in this act when he enters after having been poisoned ... *My throat is burning* etc. The act would begin with the orchestral prelude and the offstage cry of *Victory* ... At the rise of the curtain the *Wedding chorus* would be heard and the two Saints Pietro and Paolo could comment that the Doge has won, and Gabriele is marrying Amelia –.

Now I await these four or five *tronco* lines of five syllables for which I asked you yesterday. Send them as soon as possible.

In haste,

Yours
G. Verdi

P.S. You've written me nothing about the stanza for Amelia in the new Finale –

21. Milano, 7 [?].II.1881 – Boito a Verdi

Caro Maestro,

Questa volta sono io quello che dice che non abbiamo ancora finito. Tengo le sue tre ultime lettere sul tavolo e le consulto ad ogni tratto, ma per ciò che risguarda le prime scene dell'ultimo atto ho le idee ancora avviluppate. Varii tentativi riescirono male. Pure Ella mi suggerisce oggi un pensiero che mi pare molto pratico: Aprire l'atto col canto nuziale lontano (bel contrasto dopo la vivacità guerresca del preludio) mentre si svolge in scena il dialogo rapidissimo ma indispensabile di *Fiesco* e *Paolo* (l'altro apostolo Pietro lo possiamo dimenticare, nessuno se ne accorgerà) e questo dialogo deve assumere un carattere diverso di quello che apparisce nel vecchio libretto.

Paolo deve aver preso parte attiva al tumulto dei Guelfi per rovesciare il Doge ed è stato colto e imprigionato e condannato dal Doge stesso a morte. Sta bene che finalmente il Doge condanni qualcuno e poichè abbiamo per le mani un furfante il quale ha tradito il partito popolare per unirsi ai Guelfi ed ha commesse ogni sorta di ribalderie condanniamolo alla forca e non se ne parli più.

Viceversa il Fiesco nello stesso momento che Paolo passa fra le guardie per andare al supplizio, il Fiesco, dico, è per ordine del Doge liberato ed è giusto che lo sia, egli non ha preso parte al tumulto, sfido io, era in prigione; così il condannato e il liberato s'incontrano mentre l'inno delle nozze continua e nel loro dialogo Paolo svela l'affare del veleno e dalle parole dei due si dilucidano i fatti che devono essere dilucidati. Una quindicina di versi, non lirici, basterà.

Veniamo alla scena fra il Doge e Fiesco. Non s'allarmi, caro Maestro, capisco l'importanza di quella scena che fra le altre cose è la più bella del dramma. Dissi che conveniva mutare alcune condizioni di quel dialogo, alcune è dir troppo, basta una, quella che si condensa nelle parole *risorgon dalle tombe i morti*. Ma capisco anche la grande importanza di queste parole, non le toglierò ma aggiungerò forse un verso o due per condurle nel dialogo in un modo più logico, visto che noi ora abbiamo nel prim'atto

Boito's letter starting with the words "This time it is I who say that we haven't yet finished" was misdated by Luzio (C.V. II, pp. 87–89), since he had found it in an envelope bearing the postmark of 16 January (obviously belonging to no. 13). The letter however clearly answers several points contained in Verdi's letters of early February. One passage suggests that Boito wrote it on the day he received no. 20 ("Yet today you gave me an idea"). If, as I presume, no. 20 was delivered the day after it was sent, then no. 21 should be dated 7 February.

21. 7 [?]II.1881 – Boito to Verdi

Dear Maestro,

This time it is I who say that we haven't yet finished. I keep your last three letters on my desk and I consult them at each step, but concerning the first scene of the last act my ideas are still far from clear. Various attempts have come out badly. Yet today you gave me an idea which seems to me very practicable: To open the act with the wedding song offstage (a fine contrast after the warlike vivacity of the prelude), while onstage the very rapid but indispensable dialogue would take place between *Fiesco* and *Paolo* (the other apostle Pietro we can forget, no one will ever notice) and this dialogue must assume a character different from the one which appears in the old libretto.

It must be discovered that Paolo has taken an active part in the uprising of the Guelphes to overthrow the Doge and that he has been taken and imprisoned, and condemned to death by the Doge himself. It is good that the Doge should finally condemn someone and, since we have in our hands a scoundrel who has betrayed the side of the people to join with the Guelphes and has committed every sort of villainy, let's condemn him to the gallows and let nothing more be said about him.

Quite the opposite for Fiesco who, at the same moment that Paolo passes with guards on his way to be executed, is freed by order of the Doge, and it is right that he should be, since he has not taken part in the uprising – quite obviously, as he was in prison; thus the condemned man and the freed man meet while the wedding hymn continues and in their dialogue Paolo reveals the business of the poison, and from the words of the two are clarified the facts which must be clarified. Some fifteen lines, in prose, will be sufficient.

We come now to the scene between the Doge and Fiesco. Don't be alarmed, dear Maestro, I understand the importance of that scene which among other things is the most effective in the drama. I said that it is necessary to change some elements of that dialogue. "Some" is in fact too many, one is enough, that which is summarized in the words *the dead rise from their tombs*. But I do understand the great importance of these words;

creato dei fatti e degli attriti che prima nella vecchia versione non esistevano. Ecco in che consiste la condizione da mutarsi.

Ma a proposito di Fiesco, prima che mi dimentichi, le devo proporre due minuscolissime modificazioni alla scena fra Fiesco e Paolo nel penultimo atto e ciò per amor di chiarezza. Invece di quella parola che dice Paolo: *Stolido, va* che è assai rozza e che può parer ridevole per la sua volgarità (diciamo pure *verismo*) al pubblico direi:

FIESCO   Osi a Fiesco proporre un misfatto?

PAOLO   Tu ricusi? (*dopo una pausa*) Al tuo carcer ten va.

In questo modo si chiarisce questo fatto: *Fieschi piuttosto che acconsentire ad un tradimento ritorna in carcere.*

Questo fatto ci è indispensabile per un mondo di ragioni.

Il vecchio testo diceva a quel punto: *Fieschi parte dalla destra.* E partendo dalla destra dove andava? In prigione? non pare. Dunque accettava non già il patto codardo di Paolo, ma la libertà che era, sembra, il premio di quel patto. E ciò non era da Fiesco. È utile per noi che Fiesco non prenda parte attiva alle sommossa dei Guelfi per non gravarlo d'un'offesa di più verso il Doge e ripeto il miglior modo per impedir ciò è di tenerlo sotto chiave.

Eccole intanto le scheggie di poesia che Lei mi chiede:

ATTO I.

SCENA I.

(Quinari tronchi dopo il canto interno di Gabriele).

AMELIA   Ei vien! . . . l'amor
                M'avvampa in seno (sen)
                E spezza il freno
                L'ansante cor.

Scommetto che quelli che ha scritto Lei sono assai migliori, ma questi quinari tronchi sono nemici della penna.

so I won't remove them but will perhaps add a line or two to introduce them into the dialogue in a more logical manner, seeing that we now have in the first act created some facts and some problems which in the old version didn't exist. This is the way in which the element is to be changed.

But in connection with Fiesco, before I forget, I must suggest to you two very tiny modifications in the scene between Fiesco and Paolo in the penultimate act and this for the love of clarity. Instead of that word which Paolo says: *Get off, you fool*, which is very rough and which may seem ridiculous to the audience for its vulgarity (let's say even *verismo*), I would say:

FIESCO   Do you dare to propose to Fiesco a crime?

PAOLO   You refuse? (*after a moment of silence*) Get back to your
                                                                                            cell.

In this way this fact is made clear: *Fieschi rather than agree to a betrayal returns to prison.*

This fact is indispensable for a world of reasons.

The old text said at this point: *Fieschi exit to the right.* And when he leaves to the right, where exactly is he going? To prison? It wouldn't appear so. So he did not accept the cowardly pact with Paolo, but only the freedom which was, it seems, the reward for that pact. And this is not in the character of Fiesco. It is useful for us that Fiesco does not take an active part in the revolt of the Guelphes so as not to make him guilty of yet another offence against the Doge, and I repeat the best way of preventing this is to keep him under lock and key.

Meanwhile here are the scraps of poetry which you requested:

ACT I

SCENE I

(Five-syllable *tronco* lines after the offstage song of Gabriele)

AMELIA   He's coming . . . love
                         Fills my breast
                         And the throbbing heart
                         Bursts its confines.

I'll wager that those which you wrote are much better, but these five-syllable *tronco* lines are enemies of the pen.

VARIANTE ALL'INGRESSO DEL CORO
NELLA SCENA DEL SENATO

DOGE	Ecco le plebi!
LA FOLLA	Vendetta! Vendetta!
	Spargasi il sangue del fiero uccisor! ...
DOGE	Questa è dunque del popolo la voce?
(*ironicamente*)	Da lungi tuono d'uragan, da presso
	Gridìo di donne e di fanciulli ...

. . . .

Ella scorge che può ripetere *Vendetta* fin che vuole non solo ma anche l'endecasillabo seguente. Lo scoppio istrumentale e corale può così avere la sua manifestazione e se le note stridenti delle donne nel registro alto trovano il loro posto in quello scoppio il voto del suo poeta è esaudito ed è spiegata la frase sarcastica del Doge. Quella frase la ho posta per affrontare con coraggio la prima difficoltà che ci preoccupava: quella cioè di far comparire le donne in un Senato. Se noi faremo rimarcare al pubblico che le donne ci sono e ciò coraggiosamente, nessuno si sognerà di farci il più piccolo appunto. Del resto è un fatto noto che le donne hanno una parte principale nei tumulti popolari, pensi alla *Comune* di Parigi. Ma dove diavolo sono capitato? Torniamo al libretto. Eccole i quattro versi d'Amelia per la fine del frammento lirico dello stesso atto:

AMELIA	Pace! lo sdegno immenso
(*a Fiesco*)	Raffrena per pietà!
	Pace! t'ispiri un senso
	Di patria carità.

Ed ora rispondo a due sue domande semiserie:
L'osservazione fatta prima le dimostra che io non credo essere censurabile l'aggiungere delle voci di donne al Coro guerresco

All'armi! All'armi o liguri.

Altre due righe e poi ho finito per oggi.
Amelia nell'ultim'atto può essere seguita dalle sue damigelle e come no? Essa ritorna dalla chiesa, dalle nozze, col suo corteo di donne e anche se vuole di paggi.
Saluti cordialissimi. Non credo d'illudermi se le prometto un altro colloquio per domani

suo aff.mo Arrigo Boito

CHANGE FOR THE ENTRANCE OF THE CHORUS
IN THE SENATE SCENE

DOGE	Such are the plebeians!
THE CROWD	Vengeance! vengeance!
	Let the blood of the cruel murderer be spilled! ...
DOGE	This is then the voice of the people?
(*sarcastically*)	From afar thunder of a hurricane, from
	Nearby screams of women and children

. . . .

You notice that you can repeat not only *Vengeance* as much as you want, but also the eleven-syllable line which follows. Thus there will be room for the instrumental and choral outburst, and if the strident notes in the high register of the women find their place in that outburst, the wish of your poet is carried out and the sarcastic line of the Doge is explained. I have placed that line so as to face with courage the first difficulty which worried us: that of having the women appear in a Senate meeting. If in all frankness we make it clear to the audience that women *are* present, no one would dream of raising the slightest objection. Moreover it is a known fact that women play a principal role in a popular uprising, consider the *Commune* in Paris. But where the devil am I going? Let's get back to the libretto. Here are the four lines for Amelia for the end of the cantabile fragment of the same act:

AMELIA	Peace! control your immense
(*to Fiesco*)	Loathing for pity's sake!
	Peace! let a feeling of patriotic
	Love inspire you.

And now I answer two semiserious questions of yours.

The observation made earlier shows you that I don't believe it wrong to add the women's voices to the war chorus:

To arms! To arms, o Ligurians!

Another two lines and then I've finished for today.

Amelia in the last act could be followed by her attendants and why not? She is returning from the church, from her wedding, with her train of women and also if you like of pages.

Warmest greetings. I don't think I'm wrong if I promise you another discussion for tomorrow.

your most affectionate
Arrigo Boito

22. Genova, 8.II.1881 – Verdi a Boito – Telegramma

Benissimo + Ma badi strettezza temp + Tornaghi le parlerà

23. Genova, 15.II.1881 – Verdi a Boito

Genova 15 Feb. 1881

Car. Boito

Non abbiamo ancor finito! Il bello bellissimo Finale ch'Egli m'ha fatto, ha pregiudicato un po' la scena dell'ultimo Atto tra Fieschi e il Doge. Nel vecchio libretto, dopo il Prologo non s'erano più incontrati. Ecco passati 25 anni perchè Boccanegra fù eletto Doge nel 1339, ed è morto nel 1364. – Ora il Doge conosce troppo Fieschi, e questi non può più *apparirgli come un Fantasima*. Parmi però non sia difficile aggiustare tutto evitando

1° di dire "*accanto ad esso combatte il Fiesco*"

2.do Fieschi dovrebbe star nascosto più che può sotto le spoglie *d'Andrea* e non dire *Ei la Grimaldi avea rapita* nè avventarsi contro il Doge et.

3. Nella scena 8.ª del second'Atto sarebbe bene evitare *i Due ribelli*, e dire *i traditor* in generale.

4. Nella Scena nuova dell'ultimo atto non direi *Libero il Doge ti proclama!*, ma ... Il Doge perdona a tutti: *Tu sei libero!*

Ed altre ed altre piccole cose!

From a passage at the end of no. 21 it appears that Boito intended to send "another discussion for to-morrow". No trace of this letter has been found. If it was ever written, then it probably included the verses promised in no. 18. The fact that Verdi quotes from these lines in no. 23 proves that by 15 February they were in his possession. Another explanation may be that Boito personally handed the verses to Verdi during the latter's visit to Milan. The following unpublished telegram refers to the composer's intention to attend a performance of *Ernani* at La Scala. He wanted to 'test' the same singers who were scheduled to appear in the first performance of *Boccanegra:* Victor Maurel (Doge), Maria d'Angeri (Amelia), Francesco Tamagno (Gabriele) and Edouard de Reszke (Fiesco) – (see the fragments of Verdi's letters to Tito Ricordi and the conductor Franco Faccio, published in Abbiati, IV, pp. 145–147). Eugenio Tornaghi was an agent for Ricordi.

22. Genoa, 8.II.1881 – Verdi to Boito (telegram)

Excellent + But time is pressing + Tornaghi will discuss it with you.

Verdi must have written the following unpublished letter early in the morning of 15 February, since it was delivered the same day in Milan.

23. Genoa, 15.II.1881 – Verdi to Boito

Genoa, 15 Feb. 1881

Dear Boito,

We haven't yet finished! The beautiful, indeed very beautiful Finale which you have written for me has injured a bit the scene in the last act between Fieschi and the Doge. In the old libretto, after the Prologue they had not met again. Twenty-five years have passed since Boccanegra was elected Doge in 1339 and he died in 1364. – But now [in the new libretto] the Doge knows Fieschi too well, and therefore he cannot *appear to him like a Spectre* anymore. It doesn't seem to me too difficult however to fix everything by avoiding

1. saying "*at his side fights Fiesco*"

2. Fieschi should stay hidden as long as possible in the disguise of *Andrea* and must not say *He has abducted the Grimaldi girl*, nor rush against the Doge etc.

3. In the 8th scene of the second act it would be well to avoid the words *the two rebels*, and instead refer to *the traitors* in general.

Ci pensi un po' ed Ella troverà qualche cosa di meglio. Mi scriva subito. Nel caso saremo sempre in tempo di parlarne a voce.

Mi creda suo aff.

G. Verdi

24. Milano, 15.II.1881 – Boito a Verdi

Martedì, 15

Caro Maestro,

Non abbiamo finito! Gli stessi scrupoli che tormentavano Lei, tormentavano me. Accetto ed approvo tutti gli espedienti che Lei mi suggerisce. Diremo: *Accanto ad esso combatte un Guelfo* (1). Oppure: *Accanto ad esso pugna un vegliardo.* Oppure: *Accanto ad esso pugna un patrizio.* Scelga.

Le parole: *Ei la Grimaldi avea rapita* (2) le faremo dire dall'*Adorno* o da una parte del Coro. Invece dei *due ribelli* diremo: *I traditori* (3), oppure: *i rivoltosi*, come più le garba.

Non diremo più: *libero il Doge ti proclama*, ma bensì: *Libero sei; ecco la spada.* Oppure: *Libero sei; quest'è il tuo brando* . . . e l'uffiziale consegna al Fiesco la spada.

Credo che questi piccoli ritocchi basteranno ad aggiustarci le ova nel paniere.

Quand'io in una della mie ultime lettere parlavo, a proposito della scena fra Fiesco e il Doge, di condizioni mutate, alludevo precisamente ai punti rilevati da Lei; io spingevo anzi l'allarme sino a credere di dover mutare qualche tratto della scena in quistione, ma capivo d'altra parte che questa risoluzione poteva riescire dannosa all'ultimo atto. Ho creduto di salvare capra e cavoli facendo sclamare a Fieschi quel suo verso (pur sempre utilissimo):

Alfine
E giunta l'ora di trovarci a fronte!

4. In the new scene of the last act I wouldn't say *The Doge proclaims you free*, but ... the Doge pardons everyone – *You are free!*

And a hundred and one other little things!

Think about it a bit and you'll find something better. Write me at once. Should the need arise we still have time to discuss it in person.

Believe me your aff.

G. Verdi

Boito complied with Verdi's request to answer "at once" (*Carteggi verdiani* II, pp. 92–93). His reply was written late in the afternoon or during the evening of 15 February. From the last sentence it appears that Verdi was expected in Milan soon, which explains the lack of further correspondence on the revision.

24. Milan, 15.II.1881 – Boito to Verdi

Tuesday, 15

Dear Maestro,

We haven't finished! The same scruples which bothered you, also bothered me. I accept and approve all expedients which you suggest. We'll say: *At his side fights a Guelph* (1). Or better: *At his side fights an old man.* Or else: *At his side fights a Patrician.* You choose.

The words: *He has abducted the Grimaldi girl* (2) we'll have said by *Adorno* or by a part of the Chorus. Instead of saying *the two rebels* we'll say *the traitors* (3), or else *the rioters*, whichever you like best. We'll no longer say: *the Doge proclaims you free*, but instead: You are *free; here is your sword.* Or rather: *You are free; this is your sword* ... and the official hands the sword to Fiesco.

I think that these little touches will suffice to settle the eggs in the basket.

When I spoke, in one of my last letters, of changed details in connection with the scene between Fiesco and the Doge, I was referring to precisely those points you mention; I even pushed the alarm as far as thinking it wise to change some aspects of the scene in question, but I understand on the other hand that this solution could prove damaging to the last act. I thought it best to save baby and bath-water by having Fiesco exclaim that line of his (still very useful):

At last
The hour has come for us to meet!

Intendevo spiegare con questo verso che s'anco si fossero intravisti in una folla tumultuosa nella scena del *Palazzo degli Abati* pure dopo gli anni trascorsi dalla scena del Prologo, i due antagonisti non si erano mai trovati *a fronte*, cioè al *tu per tu*, soli, padroni dei loro atti e delle loro parole, isolati e liberi da influenze estranee, da estranei episodi; o per usare una frase che il nostro Schakespeare [*sic*] predilige, non si erano mai trovati *barba contro barba*. E questo è vero e la frase del *fantasima* a stretto rigore poteva reggere *quand même*. Pure le brevi sostituzioni di parole che abbiamo stabilito oggi giovano assai a chiarire i nostri affari.

Dunque, caro Maestro, a rivederci presto a Milano.

Un saluto di cuore

del suo aff.mo Arrigo Boito

I intended to explain with this line that even had they met in a tumultuous crowd in the scene in the *Palazzo degli Abati*, still after the many years which have passed since the Prologue scene, the two antagonists had never found themselves *in confrontation*, that is, *face to face*, masters of their own actions and words, alone and free from external influence, from external events, or to use an expression which our Schakespeare [*sic*] prefers, they had never found themselves *beard to beard*. And this is very true, and the line about the *spectre* in complete honesty could stand up *quand même*. Still the brief changes of words which we have set down today work very well in clarifying our affairs.

Therefore, dear Maestro, *a rivederci* soon in Milan.

A heart-felt greeting

from your most affectionate
Arrigo Boito

INDEX